All Things New

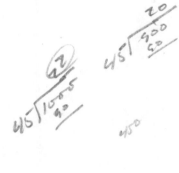

All Things New

The Significance of Newness for Biblical Theology

Carl B. Hoch, Jr.

Baker Books

A Division of Baker Book House Co
Grand Rapids, Michigan 49516

Published by Baker Books
a division of Baker Book House Company
PO Box 6287, Grand Rapids, Michigan 49516-6287

Printed in the United States of America

Library of Congress Cataloging–in–Publication Data

Hoch, Carl B.
    All things new : the significance of newness for biblical theology / Carl B. Hoch, Jr.
      p.   cm.
    Includes bibliographical references and index.
    ISBN 0-8010-2048-4 (pbk.)
    1. New and old—Biblical teaching. 2. Bible. N.T.—Theology.
  I. Title.
BS2545.N48H63   1995
230—dc20   95-21479

Contents

Preface

*T*his book represents the fruit of my thinking over the last twenty years of teaching. It reflects on a part of biblical theology that I have come to recognize as a very significant theme in the New Testament, newness. The importance of newness surfaced as I was working through the biblical passages listed under the words *kainós* (Gk. καινός, "new") and *néos* (Gk. νέος, "new") and *palaiós* (Gk. παλαιός, "old") in Moulton and Geden's *Concordance to the Greek New Testament*. The number of passages where these words occurred greatly impressed me, as did the significance that newness seemed to have for New Testament biblical theology.

I was not prepared, however, for the discovery I made when I began to look for scholarly works on the subject of newness and other topics covered in this book. I found that only one substantial work had been devoted to newness, the volume by Roy Harrisville published by Augsburg Publishing House in 1960. It was distressing to find commentaries and other theological literature not developing the *theological* significance of such basic concepts as *new teaching, new covenant, new commandment, new creation, new man, new Jerusalem, new heaven and new earth, and "all things new."* A plethora of literature on the church as a *new Israel* (hardly a biblical expression) was available, but otherwise discussion was limited to historical and literary concerns. The recent appearance of Ulrich Mell's German work on the new creation marked a significant break in the pattern[1]. At last, a full length monograph that dealt with this theme in depth was available. Recent writing on the new covenant has helped to expand the discussion on that theme. But much work remains to be done on that topic along with the other topics addressed in this book.

1. Ulrich Mell, *Neue Schöpfung*, ed. Erich Grasser, Beiheft zur Zeitschrift für die neutestamentliche Wissenschaft und die Kunde der alteren Kirche, vol. 56 (Berlin: Walter de Gruyter & Co., 1989).

The purpose of this book is to show that newness is a topic of biblical theology that needs exploration and exposition. It is not intended to be a comprehensive investigation of each of the topics designated new. Rather, it should serve as a catalyst to more creative thinking on newness and for more work on biblical theology in evangelical circles. I would be pleased to see many monographs and books appear on each of the topics addressed in this book. I expect many readers to object to some aspect of what I have written. However, my goal in writing is not agreement, but interaction. The church of Jesus Christ can only move forward theologically when her members interact with one another. The death knell of theological development is the attitude that "the old is good enough." If the church is to experience the dynamic newness her Lord inaugurated, she cannot stifle the Spirit who guides her into all theological truth by tenaciously embracing theological systems as absolute.

During the period of revising the manuscript of this book for publication I suffered a second heart attack, requiring a double-bypass operation. While recuperating, I read a book by Mike Bryan, *Chapter and Verse*. Bryan, a skeptic, made this comment:

> In the final analysis, for some of the faithful, the purpose of Christianity is to deal with death. The question came up early and often at Criswell, and I told people that concern for my fate at death has never been an issue. I've always assumed it will be at that moment just as it was before I was born: nothingness. Not a knowledge of nothingness (a pretty good hell, that), but pure nothingness.[2]

I had faced the possibility of death during my operation. As a Christian I believe that our Lord offers us *newness*, not *nothingness*. I trust that all who read this book will not only be stimulated to reflect more deeply on newness, but encouraged to give thanks to God who will ultimately make "all things new" (Rev. 21:5).

Soli Deo gloria.

Look at Elwell
"NEWNESS"

---

2. Mike Bryan, *Chapter and Verse: A Skeptic Revisits Christianity* (New York: Random House, 1991), 243.

Acknowledgments

I would like to express my appreciation to the staff of the Cornerstone College and Grand Rapids Baptist Seminary library for providing invaluable help in obtaining research materials. Rich Langton, Dave Slusher, and Gail Atwood found titles and acquired materials through interlibrary loan that otherwise would have been inaccessible to me.

I appreciate the help of Conrad Bult of the Calvin College library, who provided assistance in accessing materials that I needed but was having difficulty locating in the large holdings of the library.

I am indebted to Brian Vander Ark for his hard work in producing a laser printer copy of the first draft of my manuscript submitted to Baker Book House for consideration.

I want to thank Allan Fisher, Jim Weaver, and Gary Knapp of Baker Book House for the gentle prodding they have given me over the years to stimulate me to write and the patience they displayed in waiting for the final revision of the manuscript.

I am grateful to the students in my classes in New Testament Studies II who over the years endured my reading a long manuscript before them, encouraged me to seek publication, and provided many helpful suggestions for improvement.

Mrs. Joan A. Kelly took almost stenographic notes of my class lectures on "newness" before I had actually prepared a manuscript. Her notes served as a base upon which I could build. Without that base, this book would have been much more difficult to write and the time required writing it greatly extended. Thank you, Joan!

Last, but not least, I want to thank my wife Jane for her encouragement. She and my son, Carl III, spent countless hours helping me with all the mechanics of using a computer in the production of this book. I could not have finished without their help.

Introduction

Newness is a central theme for New Testament theology. Jesus inaugurated a new age which brought redemptive history one step closer to culmination. He enabled Christians to become heirs to the promises made to the patriarchs and to God's people, Israel. The New Testament is a book of fulfillment. Jesus begins that fulfillment during his lifetime as recorded in the Gospels and continues that fulfillment after his ascension to heaven and the birth of the church. He will culminate that fulfillment when he returns to establish his reign over the earth and when he submits all things to the Father in the creation of the new heaven and the new earth.

Jesus' lifetime was transitional—a phasing out of the old era of redemptive history and an inauguration of the new era. His earthly ministry was conducted under the old covenant economy and moved within the structures of that covenant. Yet his intention was to establish the new covenant. His death on the cross and resurrection were the prerequisites to the institution of this covenant with the attendant new economy, teaching, creation, covenantal stipulations, and reconstituted people.

Jesus also inaugurated the age of the Spirit. The amount of revelation about the Holy Spirit in the New Testament is immense compared to revelation about the Spirit in the Old Testament. In the Old Testament, the Spirit had a selective and sometimes temporary ministry to selected charismatic leaders in Israel. In the new economy, the Holy Spirit "comes" for the first time to a whole people, the church. The new covenant ministry of the Spirit is corporate and pervasive: *all* Christians possess the Spirit and are recipients of the Spirit's power. The Spirit is the sine qua non of this new age. Jesus declared that it was necessary that he leave this earth so that the Spirit, as Paraclete, could come and lead Jesus' people into the truth about his person and work (John 16:7–15). The Spirit is *the gift* of the resurrected Christ to his people. The Greek noun πνεῦμα occurs 379 times in the New Testament and refers to the Holy Spirit in the majority of cases. Of these occurrences, 106 instances (nearly one-third) of πνεῦμα appear in the writings of Luke. He is therefore correctly understood as *the* theologian of the Holy Spirit.

Luke regards his writings as a two-volume work. He refers to his Gospel as the *former* treatise. Therefore, Acts is a sequel to the Gospel of Luke. It is unfortunate that the Gospel of John intervenes between Luke and Acts in the present canonical arrangement. This order tends to disrupt the vital connection between the Gospel of Luke and Acts. The present infinitives of ποιέω, "do," and διδάσκω, "teach," in Acts 1:1 seem to imply that the work of Jesus did not end with his ascension. The church continues his work on the earth while Jesus orchestrates it from heaven.

Luke demonstrates that Jesus' coming to earth was not unplanned or without purpose. All that Jesus did was an anticipation of his ultimate purpose: to save his people from their sins (Matt. 1:21; Luke 19:10; cf. John 1:29). Since Jesus' work on earth was preparatory and inaugural, at his departure he would not leave his people who remained on earth without a Helper.

A critical task before Jesus ascended to heaven was to enlighten his followers concerning the relationship of his work on the earth to the establishment of the church and the kingdom of God. Jesus spent forty days giving his followers a "crash course" in kingdom theology. The close links between the Spirit and the kingdom in Acts 1 show that the Spirit was indispensable to the establishment of this kingdom. Luke 24 shows that Jesus had to open the disciples' minds so that they could understand the Old Testament Scriptures. One can conclude that Jesus provided a hermeneutic that would allow the disciples to interpret the Old Testament in the light of his death, resurrection, pouring forth of the Spirit, and advance of the kingdom. This is exactly what occurs in the early chapters of Acts where Peter uses the Old Testament extensively in his preaching to the people of Israel. But the disciples could no longer read the Old Testament as a non-Christian Jew read it. They now had to read it christologically as seen through the lens of Jesus' redemptive work as the Messiah of Israel.

Jesus charged his followers to remain in Jerusalem and await the fulfillment of the promise of the Spirit. Since the time of David, Jerusalem had been regarded as the physical center of God's redemptive program. It was called the city of God because this was the place where Yahweh dwelt with and met with his people. Although Walter Kaiser has forced the "promise theme" on too many Old Testament texts, his contention about the fundamental importance of the *promise* (ἐπαγγελία) is certainly correct. The two testaments are linked together in a promise-fulfillment continuum.

The coming of the Holy Spirit is a constant expectation in all four Gospels (Matt. 3:11; Mark 1:7; Luke 3:16; 24:49; John 1:22). This "baptism" is starkly contrasted with John's baptism. It would appear, therefore, that the day of Pentecost marks a significant break between "before" and "after" in the development of God's kingdom program. The coming of the Spirit will be a decisive deed of the risen Christ that will result in a dynamic provision for his people. Since the Book of Acts is the record of that outpouring of the Spirit, it is necessary for us to begin our discussion of newness in terms of the commencement of newness as this theme relates to Acts as Lucan salvation history and to the distinctive nature of Pentecost.

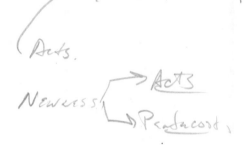

Abbreviations

AB	The Anchor Bible
EB	Etudes Bibliques
Gk.	Greek
HNTC	Harper's New Testament Commentaries
ICC	International Critical Commentary
IB	Interpreter's Bible
IDB	Interpreter's Dictionary of the Bible
lit.	literally
MNTC	Moffatt New Testament Commentary
MT	Masoretic text
NASB	New American Standard Bible
NCB	New Century Bible
NICNT	New International Commentary on the New Testament
NIGTC	New International Greek Testament Commentary
NIV	New International Version
NTC	New Testament Commentary
OTL	Old Testament Library
RSV	Revised Standard Version
SP	Sacra pagina
TNTC	Tyndale New Testament Commentary
WBC	Word Biblical Commentary

Part 1

The Commencement of Newness

1

Luke-Acts as
Lucan Salvation History

*E*ven a cursory reading of Luke-Acts shows that Luke had a major purpose in writing. According to Squires, a distinctly Lucan theme is the plan of God, a theme which undergirds the whole of Luke-Acts.[1] This plan emphasizes the sovereignty of God over every event of history.[2] According to Marshall, the key concept in the theology of Luke is "salvation."[3] Universal in scope, this salvation includes not only Israel, but also the Gentiles. [4] The continuity between the Gospel and Acts shows that Jesus' preaching, traveling, betrayal, suffering, death, resurrection, return, and judgment are necessary elements in the plan of God.[5] These salvific acts of Jesus are the necessary prerequisites for the establishment of the church. The pouring out of the Spirit ended the mission of Jesus on earth and began his ongoing mission through the church as the ascended Christ orchestrated that mission from heaven.[6] In Stott's words, "In one sense, for example, the Day of Pentecost was unique and is unrepeatable, because the outpouring of the Spirit on that day was the final act of Jesus

1. John T. Squires, *The Plan of God in Luke-Acts* (Cambridge: Cambridge University Press, 1993), 1.
2. Ibid., 25.
3. I. Howard Marshall, *Luke: Historian and Theologian* (Grand Rapids: Zondervan, 1971), 9.
4. Robert Tannehill, *The Narrative Unity of Luke-Acts*, Volume 1: The Gospel According to Luke; Volume 2: The Acts of the Apostles (Minneapolis: Fortress, 1986 and 1990), 1:3.
5. Squires, 173.
6. Marshall, 87 n. 2; see also 157.

following those equally unique and unrepeatable events, his death, resurrection, and ascension."[7] Neither Luke nor Acts suggests that God's purpose for his people as announced in the Jewish Scriptures has been supplanted. Luke represents Jesus as declaring that what has been God's announced plan throughout the history of Israel has now to come to fruition through the worldwide mission of the church.[8]

It is important to consider how the Old Testament hope permeates the Lucan birth narrative and celebrates the fulfillment of God's purposes.[9] The "all people" of Luke 2:31 is explicitly defined in 2:32 as the Gentiles and Israel. Both entities, Israel and the Gentiles, must see and share God's salvation in order to fulfill the prophecy of Isaiah 40:5 (LXX), "All flesh will see the salvation of God." Anything less is a tragic restriction of God's saving purpose.[10]

The realization of this saving purpose is not without obstacles. The theme of human opposition does not stop the mission but contributes to its spread. The overruling of opposition is an important theme in Luke-Acts and contributes to its picture of the overruling God (Luke 4:16–37; Acts 8:1–8; 11:19–21; 13:44–48; 18:6; 28:25–28).[11]

The transition from Jerusalem to the last part of the earth (Acts 1:8) was not easy. Since David's time in the tenth century B.C., Jerusalem had been the center of Israel's cultus and had served as the gathering place for all of God's people. The central sanctuary was in Jerusalem, and it was mandatory for every Israelite to visit the temple at least three times per year. The temple served as a visible sign of God's presence among his people. The priesthood officiated and sacrifices were offered there. Until the time of the Exile, the temple served as the locus for all the worship of the Lord. The Exile produced a crisis because the Jews suddenly had to continue their relationship with God without temple, priest, or ephod, all of which were central to the theocracy. During this interim of drastic changes, several notable developments occurred. First, the new institution of the synagogue arose in Israel. Second, the scribe almost replaced the priest as the most important religious figure in Israel.[12]

For those who returned to Jerusalem from the Exile, the primary item on the agenda was rebuilding the temple. Although they successfully rebuilt

---

7. John Stott, *The Spirit, the Church, and the World* (Downers Grove, Ill.: InterVarsity, 1990), 7.

8. Howard Clark Kee, *Good News to the Ends of the Earth: The Theology of Acts* (Philadelphia: Trinity Press International, 1990), 7.

9. Tannehill, *Narrative Unity of Luke-Acts*, 1:19.

10. Ibid., 1:42.

11. Ibid., 30.

12. James D. Newsome, *Greeks, Romans, Jews* (Philadelphia: Trinity Press International, 1992), chap. 4.

from Jerusalem to Rome
Acts 1:8

the temple, not until Herod the Great enlarged the postexilic temple did the new building approximate the former glory of the Solomonic temple. The work under Herod began in 20 B.C. and continued through A.D. 63.[13] In A.D. 70 the temple fell once more, this time to another foreign power, Rome. The remark of the disciples when they and Jesus were passing before the temple showed the great splendor that the Herodian temple possessed: "Look, Teacher! What massive stones! What magnificent buildings!" (Mark 13:1)

One of the tasks of Luke is to show how this center of Israelite worship for ten centuries gradually faded from this role and yielded to as many cities as there were churches established in them. The word of the Lord went forth from Jerusalem, but it did not stop there. Luke's omission of the phrase, "for all nations" in the quote from Isaiah 56:7 in Luke 19:46 is probably intentional because of the temple's eventual disappearance.[14] As the geographical center of the church shifted from Jerusalem to Antioch, Asia Minor, Greece, and Rome, the temple faded into the background. Bruce considers the movement of the church from Jerusalem to Rome as a major purpose in Luke's writing of Acts.[15] The first chapter of Acts links with the last chapter through the key verse, 1:8. The church began in Jerusalem but it ended, as far as Acts is concerned, with the "ends of the earth," that is, Rome. The movement away from Jerusalem is not intended to displace Jerusalem as one of the cities, but to decentralize it as the *only* city. The declaration of God's independence of the Jerusalem temple is also a declaration of God's availability to all people—with or without the temple. The temple was a special provision for the Jewish people in fulfillment of God's promise, but it was not needed to worship God, for God's presence spans heaven and earth, and all creation bears God's fingerprints.[16]

Luke demonstrates that God's *place* (Gk. τόπος) is his presence. This theme is seen most clearly in Stephen's exposition of the Old Testament in Acts 7. Stephen functions as a transitional figure as the church moves out of Jerusalem into Samaria and out of a very limited conception of the change in salvation history that Christ brought into a fuller, more developed understanding. Of course, this greater understanding did not come without a price. Part of that price was the death of Stephen, the first Christian martyr. But Stephen's death was not in vain: a young man named Saul heard Stephen's defense before his accusers. Even though Saul consented to

---

13. Everett Ferguson, *Backgrounds of Early Christianity*, 2d ed. (Grand Rapids: Eerdmans, 1993), 527.

14. Frederick W. Danker, *Jesus and the New Age*, rev. ed. (Philadelphia: Fortress, 1988), 315.

15. F. F. Bruce, "The Church of Jerusalem in the Acts of the Apostles," *Bulletin of The John Rylands Library*, 67 (1985): 661.

16. Tannehill, 2:93.

his execution, Stephen planted seeds in Saul's mind that would sprout into a theology of the church as the pinnacle of redemptive history (Eph. 3:10), as articulated by the apostle Paul.

Stephen is a pivotal figure, a man ahead of his time, who saw the implications of Christ's death and the inauguration of the new covenant.[17] Occupying fifty-two verses, Stephen's speech is the longest recorded speech of all that appear in Acts. Luke must have had a good reason for allotting this much space to such a lengthy speech, and the probable reason is that the speech had such tremendous theological implications!

Drawing many typological allusions from a survey of Old Testament history, Stephen proceeded to develop three fundamental points:

1. God's place (τόπος) is his presence.
2. God's people are a pilgrim people.
3. Physical descent from Abraham does not guarantee or provide a basis for salvation.

Stephen began with Abraham, a person all Jews considered as their father. He quickly showed that Abraham was on the move his entire life. God had appeared to Abraham in Mesopotamia. In response to God's call Abraham moved to Haran. After Terah's death, Abraham moved again to Canaan. Even though Canaan was the land of promise, Abraham never received a foot of it! His descendant, Joseph, fared no better: he ended up in Egypt. A famine in Palestine required Jacob and his other sons to abandon the land of promise and travel to Egypt. Just as Israel was settling down in Egypt after a 400-year residence, God moved them out again. First, Moses fled to the land of Midian. While Moses was returning to Egypt, God appeared to him in the wilderness of Sinai and called that desolate place holy ground! Moses was told that Israel would vacate Egypt and head back to Canaan. When David attempted to build a temple for God, God refused and allowed Solomon to undertake the task. But even Solomon's temple was inadequate for such a God who had followed his servants throughout the Middle East. The Most High does not dwell in houses made with human hands. Even Solomon conceded that when he dedicated the temple: "But will God really dwell on earth? The heavens, even the highest heaven, cannot contain you. How much less this temple I have built!" (1 Kings 8:27). The point stung: Even a temple such as the magnificent Herodian temple would have to give way to a greater building. Although it would take Paul to name that

---

17. For relevant literature, see John Kilgallen, *The Stephen Speech* (Rome: Biblical Institute Press, 1976); Martin H. Scharlemann, *Stephen: A Singular Saint* (Rome: Biblical Institute Press, 1968); and Marcel Simon, *St. Stephen and the Hellenists in the Primitive Church* (New York: Longmans, Green and Co., 1950).

building, the church, the groundwork had been laid and the raw material had already been prepared theologically by Stephen.

A careful reading of the text shows that Stephen used three Greek words to establish the pilgrim character of God's people: κατοικέω, "settle down," in 7:2, 4, 48; μετοικίζω, "resettle," in 7:4, 43; and πάροικος, "stranger," in 7:6, 29. By using these three words, contrasting the first with the other two, Stephen implied that the true people of God in the Old Testament were always on the move. They were out of the land as much as they were in it. He refuted the charge that God's people must be in some specific place in order to approach him. God was with his people wherever they were on the face of the earth (7:2, 4, 9, 33, 46). According to Kee, "The subtle but cumulatively powerful thrust of his address is that God is not and never has been localized as the ground of his relationship to his people."[18]

For Luke, then, God was no longer restricted to a single city. No longer would God's people need to look to Jerusalem or Israel as *the* place. Anyone, anywhere by faith could enter into God's presence. The time had come when worship would indeed be in Spirit and truth. Place no longer mattered (see John 4:21). Therefore, the city, the building, and the worship-system associated with that building were to be superseded. As the gospel message spread, the scope of God's people and his presence with them enlarged. Bruce detects a progression of people in Acts: the Jews of Jerusalem, Hellenist Jews, Samaritans, and Gentiles.[19] The inclusion of the Gentiles was a watershed in redemptive history and caused some of the greatest debates in the early church concerning the status of Gentiles vis-à-vis Israel. Paul would become the apostle to these Gentiles and would devote two major letters, Galatians and Romans, to the question of Gentile circumcision, and one letter, Ephesians, to the equality between Jew and Gentile in Christ.

This centrifugal geographical and ethnic movement from Jerusalem to Rome involved intermediate steps. It took time to move from a restricted, isolated, unique city and nation with its geographical, ethnic, and, for the most part, agrarian socioeconomic barriers to a world comprised of many cities and a breadth of ethnic backgrounds. Since the new covenant no longer included these barriers, people living anywhere in the world, regardless of ethnic background or socioeconomic class, could become a part of God's people simply by faith in Jesus Christ. This removal of former distinctions brought a tremendous amount of conflict in the church. The chapters in the Book of Acts alternate between progress and hindrance, showing progress as less than smooth during the transition. Rejection and resistance are major factors in the unfolding story. The strong experience of resistance and rejection results in a necessary tempering of the mission.[20]

18. Kee, 44.
19. Bruce, 659.
20. Tannehill, 2:2–3.

Initial progress was tremendous as 3000, then 2000 responded to Peter's preaching after the Pentecostal outpouring of the Holy Spirit. But soon a Jewish court heard about the spread of this new sect. They immediately repressed Peter and John from teaching and preaching. The opposition was unsuccessful as the apostles praised God that they were counted worthy of suffering for Christ. The witness continued.

The external threat, however, was then matched by internal threats.[21] Ananias and Sapphira acted deceitfully about their contribution to the church's benevolent fund, which resulted in their instantaneous deaths as the Lord intervened in judgment to keep the church pure. Further problems developed internally as the Hellenistic widows were the objects of discrimination. The crisis was resolved through the appointment of deacons, a new order within the church. The preaching of Stephen brought violent opposition to the Christian message, resulting in his martyrdom. The resulting persecution scattered everyone except the apostles from Jerusalem to Judea and Samaria. Through the preaching of Philip, the Samaritans heard the gospel and believed. Thus, the scattering of the Jerusalem church resulted not in the disruption and weakening of the mission but in the spread of the word of God to new areas.[22]

A North African eunuch returning to his home from Jerusalem learned through Philip's help that the prophet Isaiah was speaking about Jesus as the Suffering Servant and was baptized. The black clouds gathered once again as Saul received letters from the Jewish authorities authorizing him to travel to Damascus in Syria in order to arrest Christians. Saul was stopped abruptly as the risen Christ appeared to him on the road to Damascus. Saul would become the proponent instead of the opponent of Christ and his community. The risen Christ commissioned him to be his witness to kings, the Gentiles, and the people of Israel. The story of Paul is necessary to complete the story begun in Luke 1–2, for with Paul the crucial prophecy of light for the Gentiles, as well as for Israel, began to be fulfilled as the gospel moved through the Mediterranean world.[23]

Another major development transpired when the Lord appeared to Peter and commanded him to go to the house of Cornelius, a Gentile. A lifetime of separation from Gentiles was now on the line. The Gentile obstacle was uncleanness.[24] Would Peter really do something that his entire background told him was unthinkable? Despite his better judgment, Peter went to Cornelius's house and told the story of Jesus. To Peter's amazement the Holy Spirit fell upon these Gentiles while he was speaking without any interme-

21. Ibid., 79.
22. Ibid., 101.
23. Ibid., 121–22.
24. Ibid., 135.

diacy on his part such as he had practiced in Samaria. Peter was dumb-founded and realized that nothing should hinder these Gentiles from re-ceiving water baptism. They had believed the same gospel, had received the same Spirit, and therefore were entitled to receive the same water baptism received by believing Jews. Peter was learning a new dimension of the words of Joel, "I will pour out my Spirit on *all* people" (Joel 2:28, italics added; see Acts 2:16–21). He returned to Jerusalem to report this cataclys-mic event. However, the Jerusalem Christians were not pleased with the news about the Gentiles. Some caught him by his tunic and angrily re-torted, "You went into the house of uncircumcised men and ate with them" (11:3). After a full account from Peter about Cornelius, the majority of the Jerusalem church concluded, "So then, God has granted even the Gentiles repentance unto life" (11:18). According to Tannehill, the theolog-ical perspective that dominates Luke-Acts as a whole is the messianic Lord-ship of Jesus, which brings peace to the Jewish people in fulfillment of scrip-tural promises, and applies to all peoples, for they are invited to share with Israel in this messianic peace.[25]

The persecution that resulted from Stephen's preaching caused a scatter-ing of Christians to Phoenicia, Cyprus, and Syrian Antioch. Some preached only to Jews, but others, men of Cyprus and Cyrene, went to Antioch and began speaking to Greeks. A large number of these Greeks believed and caused such a need for instruction that Barnabas was despatched to Anti-och. Barnabas found the challenge to be beyond his capacity and left for Tar-sus to enlist the help of Saul. The two spent an entire year in Antioch teach-ing considerable numbers, and here is where the followers of Jesus were first called Christians (11:26).

Two more dark clouds appeared. First, a great famine in the Mediterra-nean brought severe hardship to the Jerusalem church. Second, Herod Agrippa I had James the brother of John, both sons of Zebedee, put to death by the sword. This politically advantageous act brought such praise from the non-Christian Jews that Herod arrested Peter, intending to execute him, too. Stott calls the death of James and Peter's imprisonment "a serious setback."[26] If Herod were successful, this would be no little loss to the struggling Jerusalem church. An all-night prayer meeting was called. While the church was praying, God performed a miracle. He opened the gates of the prison and Peter escaped. The church was shocked when Peter knocked at the door of Mary's house. They really had not thought that the prayers of righteous men availed that much! But they had received an answer to prayer and Peter had been spared. Peter disappeared from Jerusalem and Luke turned his literary spotlight on Paul, the central figure from Acts 13–

25. Ibid., 140.
26. Stott, 207.

28. While Acts 12 had opened with James dead, Peter in prison, and Herod triumphing, it closed with Herod dead, Peter free, and the word of God triumphing.[27]

The picture was much brighter in Antioch. The church was growing by leaps and bounds. The Holy Spirit moved on the church there to send Barnabas and Saul westward on the first missionary journey (Acts 13:4–14:28). The pair visited Seleucia and then Cyprus. In Paphos of Cyprus the proconsul, Sergius, believed despite opposition from Elymas, the magician. From Paphos the missionary team moved up to Perga in Asia Minor. The new prospects there were somewhat tarnished by the defection of John Mark, who left and returned to Jerusalem. Barnabas and Paul moved on to Pisidian Antioch where Luke recorded the second lengthy discourse by Paul in the synagogue.

In his discourse Paul stressed Jesus as the fulfillment of the prophets, showing that his death and resurrection were the fulfillment of Israel's hope of salvation. From the Old Testament Paul affirmed the promise of the messianic kingdom for the Jewish people and acknowledged that this promise was firmly rooted in Scripture. The mission was universal, but it must follow a prescribed order. The Jews must be addressed first. This priority was due to God's election of Israel and God's promise of a Messiah for Israel. Paul's preaching reflects a view that characterizes Luke-Acts from the beginning: Jesus is the Davidic Messiah who fulfills specific promises of God to the Jewish people.[28] The sermon brought a request for further details about this Jesus. A week later, an ugly confrontation occurred between Paul and those Jews who had heard Paul the previous Sabbath and had concluded that he was a heretic. Paul made a significant decision: "We had to speak the word of God to you first. Since you reject it and do not consider yourselves worthy of eternal life, we now turn to the Gentiles" (13:46). Tannehill notes that the speakers were making the important affirmation that Gentiles could be God's people (Gk. λαός) in the same full sense as Israel.[29] The Gentiles in Antioch of Pisidia responded favorably to Paul's message and a church was established there. But the Jews did not concede. Instead they instigated a persecution against Paul and Barnabas and drove them out of their district.

Mixed acceptance and rejection of the message followed in Iconium, so Paul and Barnabas had to flee to Lystra and Derbe. At Lystra they received an unexpected response, as some of the people believed Paul and Barnabas to be Greek gods who had come down to earth! While Paul was trying to dispel that notion, Jews from Antioch and Iconium arrived and initiated a

27. Ibid., 213.
28. Tannehill, 2:171, 73–74.
29. Ibid., 187.

stoning, which injured Paul badly. The next day he and Barnabas left for Derbe where they apparently experienced no incidents. After preaching the gospel and seeing many accept the message, Paul and Barnabas established a church. Then they left Derbe and returned to Lystra, Iconium, and Antioch. Along the way they encouraged the Christians and appointed elders in each church. Then they returned to Antioch and gave an encouraging report about how the Gentiles were responding to the gospel.

The euphoria did not last very long, however. Certain ones from Jerusalem came down to Antioch and insisted that the Gentiles must be circumcised according to the law of Moses if they were to be included among God's people. The Antioch church decided to send a delegation to Jerusalem so that the first church council could rule on the matter. Kee feels that Acts 15 marks the midpoint of Acts—literarily, conceptually, and theologically.[30]

After much heated discussion and debate, Peter stood up and argued that the Gentiles had heard the gospel through his mouth. The message had moved from Israel to the Gentiles rather than the Gentiles moving to Israel as the nation into which they had to be incorporated. The proof of the soteriological equality of the Gentiles was their reception of the Holy Spirit. Both Jews and Gentiles were saved by the grace of the Lord Jesus, and there was no need to add any further requirements. Paul confirmed Peter's mission practice and theology: God had also done signs and wonders through Barnabas and himself among the Gentiles. The new movement was *to* the Gentiles *from* Israel.

James, the new leader of the Jerusalem church, built upon Peter's argument that Paul had reinforced. The Old Testament prophets had prophesied this same movement that the church was seeing fulfilled before their eyes. Amos's prophecy was representative of the other prophets: Israel would be rebuilt *so that* the Gentiles could call upon the name of the Lord [Jesus]. The fallen house of David was being rebuilt in the remnant of Israel who had acknowledged Jesus as the Messiah of Israel raised from the dead. As Kee observes, Luke's omission of "as in the days of old" ("as it used to be," NIV) from Amos 9:11 is significant because the fulfillment of Amos involved a transformation rather than merely a restoration of the Israelite monarchy.[31] God had raised up this restored remnant to preach the good news of Jesus to the Gentiles so that the Gentiles would seek the Lord and have his name invoked upon them. Since the movement was outward to the Gentiles, it was unnecessary to add requirements for the Gentiles, such as circumcision, the sign of incorporation into Israel. The Gentiles needed to observe only the laws for Gentiles outlined in Leviticus 16, 17, and 18 to avoid unnecessary

30. Kee, 57.
31. Ibid., 59.

offense to Jews still steeped in Mosaic traditions. The Gentiles' compliance with these restrictions would facilitate Jewish evangelism. Such small concessions indicated no soteriological difference between Gentiles and Jews. The restrictions were a practical matter, not a soteriological matter. Also, this allowed the Jews to continue freely practicing their religious culture.[32]

One might assume that Paul and Silas's second missionary journey would proceed more smoothly than the first. On the contrary, Jewish missions became ever more difficult with growing resistance and persecution. The Christian movement was no longer looked upon as another variation within the spectrum of Jewish sects but as an entirely new religion. This new message could not be tolerated any longer as just a different way of interpreting the Old Testament. It had to be stopped. Consequently the missionaries were repeatedly thrown out of the Jewish synagogues.

Difficulties for the Christians arose even among the Gentiles. As pagan Greeks and Romans converted to the Christian faith, the commerce created by the manufacture of silver shrines and images for pagan worship began to decline (see Acts 19:23–27). External nonentities were no longer needed when one had the "Reality" within oneself. The affected merchants began to complain to the police that their business was being adversely affected by this new movement. Paul wound up in jail in Philippi and was nearly executed. The providential earthquake secured his release and resulted in the conversion of the jailer. An appeal to the police based upon Roman citizenship produced a public apology from the club-wielders (Acts 16:35; ῥαβδοῦ-χοι, "policemen").

The second missionary journey (Acts 15:39–18:22) extended the church into Greece as churches were founded in Thessalonica, Berea, Athens, and Corinth. Another influential city, Ephesus, heard the gospel and a church was established there, too. Things did not go smoothly, however. The Jews stirred up opposition in Thessalonica. The Bereans were skeptical about Paul's gospel (the optative mood is used in 17:11 in a deliberative sense to indicate doubt on their part) and only believed after a thorough search of the Old Testament supported the truth of Paul's gospel. Jews came from Thessalonica to Berea and stirred up the crowds against Paul. At Athens only a few believed the gospel. The intelligentsia in the Court of Areopagus considered Paul's doctrine of the resurrection as nonsense. Paul's preaching was basically a call to repentance, a call for the Greco-Roman world to break decisively with its religious past in response to the one God who now invited all to be part of the renewed world.[33] At Corinth Jewish opposition caused Paul to withdraw from the synagogue and use Titius Justus' house as a base for his work. Another crisis arose when the Jews

---

32. Tannehill, 2:191–92.
33. Ibid., 218.

brought charges against Paul before Gallio, the proconsul of Achaia. Gallio, however, realized that Paul was not guilty of any Roman crime and dismissed the charges.

After escaping a riot at Ephesus during his third missionary journey (Acts 18:23–21:17), Paul returned to Jerusalem to see how things were going with the church there. When he arrived, James informed him that Paul was persona non grata among the Jews of Jerusalem because of his "liberal" teaching and practices. However, James told Paul that he could convince his critics that he was a good Jew if he would take a vow that would prove his full compliance with the law of Moses. Paul agreed to the proposal and went to the temple to undergo the necessary procedure. The Jews were not impressed. Instead they used the fact that Paul had been seen with a Greek from Ephesus, Trophimus, to prove their thesis: Paul was an apostate who associated freely with pagans and who had the audacity to bring a Gentile into the Court of Israel! (Of course, one of the underlying premises of Paul [and Luke] was that the Gentiles now had full access to the privileges and covenants of Israel through Christ [Eph. 2:11–22].) The Jews dragged Paul out of the temple and shut the doors (21:30). Bruce feels that this verse is climactic.[34] The statement is a subtle Lucan suggestion that from this point forward Jerusalem and the temple were shut to Christianity. From this point forward the church will be comprised mainly of the uncircumcision, with only a few of the circumcision becoming Christians. What a turn of events! From an original completely Jewish entity the church had become almost a completely Gentile entity. Had God cast away his people? Or had they cast away him? The latter answer is Paul's solution to the dilemma in Romans 9–11.

Paul was arrested and subjected to trials by a Jewish court, Felix, Festus, and Agrippa. In his defense speeches he steadfastly maintained that his gospel was in direct continuity with the Old Testament and the hope of Israel. Before Felix he said, "I believe everything that agrees with the Law and that is written in the Prophets, and I have the same hope in God as these men, that there will be a resurrection of both the righteous and the wicked." (Acts 24:14–15). To Festus he said, "I have done nothing wrong against the law of the Jews or against the temple or against Caesar." (25:8). Finally, while before King Agrippa, Paul stated, "I am saying nothing beyond what the prophets and Moses said would happen—that the Christ would suffer and, as the first to rise from the dead, would proclaim light to his own people and to the Gentiles" (26:22–23).

Seeing that his words were falling on deaf ears and the situation was getting worse, Paul appealed to Caesar. He was then put on a grain ship from Egypt headed for Rome. En route Paul almost lost his life in the Mediterra-

34. Bruce, 659. See also Stott, 336.

nean Sea during a severe storm. Washed ashore on the island of Malta, Paul
would have died from a snake bite if the Lord had not, once again, worked
a miracle on his behalf.

The Book of Acts concludes with Paul in Rome where he still had an opportunity to preach the gospel. The same mixed response to his message resulted: some believed; some rejected. Using Isaiah 6:9–10 Paul castigated
those Jews who rejected his message for their unbelief. Paul concluded,
"Therefore I want you to know that God's salvation has been sent to the
Gentiles, and they will listen!" (Acts 28:28). Stott observes, "Three times
before, stubborn Jewish opposition has led Paul to turn to the Gentiles—in
Pisidian Antioch (13:46), in Corinth (18:6), and in Ephesus (19:8–9). Now for
the fourth time, in the world's capital city, and in a yet more decisive manner, he does it again (28)."[35] By this statement Paul [and Luke?] gave an explicit declaration of the shift from Israel (but not rejection of Israel) to the
Gentiles. Paul spent two years in his own rented house receiving all who
came to see him (including Jews?), preaching the kingdom of God and
teaching things about Jesus with all confidence.

Of the greatest importance for the salvation history of Luke-Acts is the
very last word in the Greek text of Acts—"unhindered" (ἀκωλύτως; "without hindrance," NIV). From the beginning of Luke's Gospel to the end of the
Book of Acts, the plan and purpose of God, as promised in the Old Testament and in the process of realization through the first advent of Jesus
Christ and the inauguration of the church, has triumphed despite opposition
and setbacks. The crucifixion of Jesus appeared to be the fatal blow to Israel's hopes: "We had hoped that he was the one who was going to redeem
Israel" (Luke 24:21). The very end to their hope was the real beginning of
their hope as Jesus responded, "How foolish you are, and how slow of heart
to believe all that the prophets have spoken! Did not the Christ have to suffer these things and then enter his glory?" (24:25). The death and resurrection of Jesus were the prophetic sine qua non for the fulfillment of redemption for both Israel and the Gentiles. Jesus told his disciples, "This is what
is written: The Christ will suffer and rise from the dead on the third day, and
repentance and forgiveness of sins will be preached in his name to all nations, beginning at Jerusalem. You are witnesses of these things" (24:46–48).

The same two polarities of fulfillment of purpose and hindrance to purpose have been surveyed in Acts. The church experienced progress and hindrance as it preached the gospel first to Israel and then to the Gentiles. Several times it appeared as though the church would split into Jewish and
Gentile factions. It seemed as though Gentiles would become nothing more
than proselytes to Judaism, celebrating the Jewish holidays, eating kosher
food, keeping Sabbath, and circumcising their children in obedience to the

---

35. Stott, 399.

law of Moses. At other times it seemed that the heroes of the church would be lost through imprisonment, execution, shipwreck, and poisonous snakebite. But despite the troubles, uproar, obstacles, debates, temporary setbacks, famine, persecution, and trials before courts, the gospel and the church were ultimately unhindered. The gates of Hades had *not* prevailed against Christ's church!

So what does Lucan salvation history show? First, the change from Jerusalem to Rome in Acts was very significant. All the earth was being blessed in Abraham's seed. Luke's universalism was never lost from the early chapters of the Gospel of Luke to the end of the Book of Acts. Second, the transethnic movement showed that Christ had died for all people and any who believed on him could be included in his church. Third, even though the church suffers temporary setbacks and roadblocks, it is invincible and God's plan cannot be thwarted. The whole process of world evangelization is deemed by Luke to be *unhindered*.[36] John Squires concluded his investigation of the plan of God in Luke-Acts by isolating two key events in the narrative: (1) the necessity and centrality of the passion of Jesus is asserted and expounded, in opposition to the deed of the Jewish leaders and the misunderstanding of the disciples, as being central to the plan of God; (2) the integral role of the mission to the Gentiles, as an important part of the plan of God is asserted and expounded in opposition to Jewish objections and misgivings on the part of certain Christians. Each of these events is central to the plan of God; each of them is explained by recourse to divine providence.[37]

The application of this to today's church is clear. The church will always have problems. The parables in Matthew 13 show that the interadvent age is a time of mixed response to the gospel. Accordingly, the church will never be entirely successful in mission. It will encounter delays, obstacles, interchurch dissensions, and conflicts. But the building of Christ's church will and must go on. At times the light may grow dim and flicker, but it will never go out. The church must always keep in view the larger perspective: the message and the plan of God will go forth . . . *unhindered!*

---

36. The preceding exposition takes a different approach than J. Bradley Chance, *Jerusalem, the Temple, and the New Age in Luke-Acts* (Macon, Ga.: Mercer University Press, 1988), who argues that Luke is at odds with the other New Testament writers and does not consider the city of Jerusalem and the temple superseded by Christ and the church. While the New Testament may reflect diversity, having variant theologies competing with one another is incongruent with the inerrancy of Scripture and unacceptable to this writer.

37. Squires, 194.

For Further Study

Kee, Howard Clark. *Good News to the Ends of the Earth: The Theology of Acts.* Philadelphia: Trinity Press International, 1990.

Kee has written a brief yet helpful survey of the theology of Acts.

Marshall, I. Howard. *Luke: Historian and Theologian.* Grand Rapids: Zondervan, 1971.

This is a standard treatment of Acts by an evangelical scholar who develops both the historicity and theology of Acts.

Stott, John. *The Spirit, the Church, and the World.* Downers Grove, Ill.: InterVarsity, 1990.

This is one of Stott's best expositional commentaries. His discussion of Acts not only discusses the interpretive problems, but shows the significance of Acts for the church and the Christian life.

Tannehill, Robert. *The Narrative Unity of Luke-Acts.* Volume 1: The Gospel According to Luke; Volume 2: The Acts of the Apostles. Minneapolis: Fortress, 1986, 1990.

These volumes are essential reading for any student of Luke-Acts. Tannehill's theological insight into Luke and Acts is among the best available treatments.

[handwritten notes:]

Dr. Hook.

Gives us a gunshot view of the beginning of the Book of Acts.

Main pts — Pg 3'

1.) Jerusalem to Rome

2) Christ died for all people

3) Church is invincible

The Passion of Jesus is Central in the Messages

Pg 31 good summary.

2

Distinctive Nature of Pentecost

*T*he words of John the Baptist in the synoptic Gospels and Acts anticipate Jesus' future work and emphasize the change that the Spirit would effect in salvation history (Matt. 3:11; Mark 1:7; Luke 3:16; Acts 1:5; see also Luke 24:49; John 1:26–27). In fact, when compared with Jesus' work, the work of John the Baptist is almost insignificant .

The first thing to note is the direct parallelism in the Greek text between the baptism of John and the baptism of Jesus as recorded in the synoptic Gospels:

| I baptize | you in water |
| he will baptize | you in Spirit and fire |

The pronouns "I" and "he" are in juxtaposition and are added for emphasis in the Greek text. The presence of "baptize" (present tense) with "will baptize" (future tense) contrasts the present ministry of John with the future ministry of Jesus. While the object of both baptisms is "you," the critical distinction between the two baptisms is the mode: *water* versus *Spirit.*

The phrase "Spirit and fire" has been widely discussed, resulting in divergent interpretations.[1] It seems best to link Spirit and fire closely together because of the presence of only one preposition before the two

---

1. For a representative discussion, see W. D. Davies and Dale C. Allison, Jr., *A Critical Exegetical Commentary on the Gospel According to Saint Matthew,* vol. 1 (Edinburgh: T. & T. Clark, 1988), 316–18. Critical commentaries on Matthew and Luke provide additional discussion.

nouns.[2] This construction does not mean that the two nouns are equal, as in the Granville-Sharp rule. What it does mean is that a radical separation between the two is not possible, such as the view that relates the Spirit to the day of Pentecost and fire to the millennium.[3] Rather the thought seems to be that Jesus will baptize either "with" or "in" the Spirit so that his people will be purified and live righteous lives (see Mal. 3:2–3).[4]

In Acts 1:6 the disciples question Jesus whether he will restore (ἀποκαθίστημι) the kingdom to Israel at this point in history (χρόνος). The verb ἀποκαθίστημι is the cognate verb for the noun ἀποκατάστασις, "restoration," used in Acts 3:21. According to Oepke, the Septuagint translation (LXX) used ἀποκαθίστημι in Jeremiah 16:15; 23:8; Hosea 11:11; and Malachi 4:6 as a technical term for the restoration of Israel to its own land by Yahweh. In the New Testament the noun does not denote the conversion of persons, but only the reconstitution or establishment of things.[5] F. F. Bruce suggests that ἀποκατάστασις is identical with the παλιγγενεσία of Matthew 19:28.[6] Stott adds that ἀποκατάστασις is more naturally understood as the eschatological restoration when nature will be liberated from its bondage to pain and decay and God will make a new heaven and earth. This final perfection awaits the return of Christ.[7] It is important to note, therefore, that Jesus did not dispute the fact of the restoration of the kingdom to Israel, but he did take issue with the *chronology* involved. Tannehill emphasizes that Jesus corrected their curiosity about times, but he did not reject the possi-

2. James D. G. Dunn, *Baptism in the Holy Spirit* (Naperville, Ill.: Allenson, 1970), 11.

3. John F. Walvoord, *The Holy Spirit* (Findlay, Ohio: Dunham, 1958), 148–49.

4. As Dunn points out, many scholars interpret the preposition ἐν instrumentally ("by") instead of locally ("in"). But Dunn opts for the locative sense denoting the element of baptism (Dunn, *Baptism*, 128). Dunn's view is supported by A. T. Robertson (*A Grammar of the Greek New Testament in the Light of Historical Research* [Nashville: Broadman, 1934], 520), and cautiously by Nigel Turner (Turner, *Syntax*, vol. III of *A Grammar of New Testament Greek*, ed. James Hope Moulton [Edinburgh: T. & T. Clark, 1963], 252), as well as by the commentators listed in Dunn's note.

5. Albert Oepke, "ἀποκαθίστημι, ἀποκατάστασις," in *Theological Dictionary of the New Testament*, ed. Gerhard Kittel, Gerhard Friedrich, and Geoffrey W. Bromiley, trans. Geoffrey W. Bromiley, 10 vols. (Grand Rapids: Eerdmans, 1964), 1:388, 391. This writer is not convinced by the arguments of Parker that the church is the fulfillment of the "restoration of all things" (James Parker, III, *The Concept of Apokatastasis In Acts* [Austin: Schola Press, 1978]). Obviously, more is involved than word studies. One's eschatological views, ecclesiology, and position on the relationship between Israel and the church are also important for interpreting the evidence. Nevertheless, these issues are too complex to settle here. The reader should read John S. Feinberg's *Continuity and Discontinuity* (Westchester, Ill.: Crossway, 1988) to observe how theological systems control exegesis in many cases.

6. F. F. Bruce, *The Book of Acts*, rev. ed. (Grand Rapids: Eerdmans, 1988), 84–85 note.

7. John Stott, *The Spirit, the Church and the World* (Downers Grove, Ill., InterVarsity, 1990), 7, 94.

Chronology – (1) witness not ~~restoration~~

bility of a restored kingdom for Israel. After receiving the Spirit, Peter still holds out the hope of the "restoration of all the things which God spoke through the mouth of his holy prophets from of old" (Acts 3:21), provided the people of Jerusalem repent. Both Acts 1:6 and Luke 1:69–70 indicate that the messianic kingdom is among the things promised by God through his holy prophets of long ago (Luke 1:70; Acts 3:21).[8] Thus Jesus' point in Acts 1:6 is that the interim between the two advents (NIV "times or dates") *key* would be a period of witness, not restoration.

Since Paul makes such a close association between the kingdom of God and righteousness, peace, and joy in the Holy Spirit (Rom. 14:17), the presence of the Spirit among God's people must be related to the advance of the kingdom. The Holy Spirit seems to be the initial installment of the forthcoming restoration to be established when the kingdom of God is here de facto. Boyd Hunt observes that all redemption is eschatological, so that the kingdom, as the Bible's most comprehensive term for God's pursuit of his redemptive purpose, is inescapably an eschatological concept.[9] It is important to note that the "Spirit passages" in Ezekiel 11, 36, and Jeremiah 31 also include references to "the land." Although references to the land do not prove the premillenial view regarding Christ's thousand year reign upon the earth, the mention of land does not show a disjunction between the Spirit and the earthly kingdom.

Jesus' reply to his disciples in Acts 1:6 leaves the present status of the kingdom in the ambiguous status that it must have as long as the king is absent. According to Acts 3:21, all things will be restored as the Old Testament prophets prophesied. At that time the de facto rule of Jesus will no longer be ambiguous, temporarily inactive, and indistinct. Then the kingdom (βασιλεία) will blossom and all things will be disclosed, but this restoration will not occur at this point in history (χρόνος). Those who are ruled must be gathered together before the realm can be established. So the emphasis is not on the de facto reign, but on the mission responsibility of the kingdom citizens before the kingdom is fully established with the Ruler, the ruled, and the realm. The Holy Spirit will provide the dynamic that is necessary for witness. Only through witness can the ruled be gathered so

---

8. Robert Tannehill, *The Narrative Unity of Luke-Acts*, Volume 1: The Gospel According to Luke (Philadelphia: Fortress, 1986), 1:35–36.

9. Boyd Hunt, *Redeemed! Eschatological Redemption and the Kingdom of God* (Nashville: Broadman and Holman, 1993), 83. Hunt's other perceptive comments should be noted: "Through two mighty acts, the incarnation and Pentecost, God inaugurated the presence in history of the promised kingdom and constituted the new covenant with His new people" (p. 14). "The Holy Spirit is the effecter of God's comprehensive kingdom purpose as revealed through the crucified yet risen Christ" (p. 15). "The incarnation and Pentecost are the decisive events in the biblical drama of redemption." (p. 31). "The power of the kingdom is redemptive, not merely political, national or military." (p. 41).

that the Ruler may return to rule over those who have submitted to his rule in a new realm in which righteousness dwells (see 2 Pet. 3:13).

Jesus gives a centrifugal outline for the mission to Israel and to the nations. The Old Testament mission was intended to be centrifugal also, but it had become centripetal because of the failure of Israel to evangelize. Therefore Zechariah spoke of many Gentiles coming up to Jerusalem to take hold of the garment of one Jew (Zech. 8:23). Jesus restores the original intention of God—his people are to be witnesses *to* the nations.[10] This witness is to extend to the whole earth, beginning in Jerusalem and then moving out concentrically to Judea, Samaria, Antioch, Asia Minor, Greece, Rome, and ultimately the ends of the earth! Of course, the Book of Acts ends with Rome; but the last word, *unhindered,* as discussed in the previous chapter, shows that further progress is expected.

Acts 2:1 begins with a very significant verb, συμπληρόω. The addition of σύν to πληρόω intensifies the meaning of the verb with the compound now meaning "to fill completely," or in the passive, "to become quite full."[11] Συμπληρόω occurs three times in the New Testament, all in Lucan writings: Luke 8:23; 9:51; and Acts 2:1. The form of the verb in this text, συμπληροῦσθαι, is either a present middle or passive infinitive. Luke 8:23 is theologically insignificant, but Luke 9:51 is extremely important for Acts 2:1, since Luke 9:51 marks a major break in the text of Luke as Jesus now "moved steadily toward Jerusalem with an iron will" (LB).[12] The time is approaching for Jesus to suffer and die, rise from the dead, and return to heaven. According to Luke there is a "filling up" of the days when his ascension would take place. In Acts there is a coordinate "filling up" of another day, the day of Pentecost when the Spirit will descend. The ascension of Jesus and the descent of the Spirit appear to be two aspects of a time program of God that will result in a new phase of the kingdom program. The rare compound verb συμπληρόω therefore suggests that the day of Pentecost was about to come to the fullest expression possible.

Leviticus 23 discusses the major feasts of Israel which the Lord gave to Israel through Moses. Verses 15–21 describe Pentecost as occurring fifty days after the Feast of the Passover. Two loaves of bread for a wave offering were to be offered as a firstfruits of the coming harvest to the Lord as well as many animal sacrifices for burnt offerings. Pentecost was to be a perpet-

---

10. Richard R. DeRidder, *Discipling the Nations* (Grand Rapids: Baker, 1975), 153–55.

11. William F. Arndt and F. Wilbur Gingrich, *A Greek-English Lexicon of the New Testament and Other Early Christian Literature* (Chicago: University of Chicago Press, 1979), 787.

12. For the significance of the Lucan "travel narrative" (i.e., Luke 9:51–19:44) for Lucan theology, see David Moessner, *Lord of the Banquet* (Philadelphia: Fortress, 1989).

ual reminder to Israel of God's faithfulness and a pledge of an abundant harvest.[13]

When Luke wrote that Pentecost was coming to its fullest expression, it would appear that he meant to imply that all prior Pentecosts would fade into insignificance by comparison. This day would be the supreme Pentecost, a beginning which would culminate in a great harvest in the future. This great event would be the advent of the Spirit and a subsequent great harvest of people who would acknowledge Jesus as Savior and Lord and who would become an ever-enlarging body known as the church.[14]

The word *all* occurs seventeen times in Acts 2.[15] This suggests that Luke is earnestly trying to emphasize the universal nature of the new covenant. No longer will there be Jew or Gentile (an ethnic division), male or female (a sexual division), bond or free (a socioeconomic division). All of them will now be soteriologically equal and part of one body, the church of Jesus Christ who breaks down all divisions resulting from the alienation produced by the Fall (see Gal. 3:28; Eph. 2:11–22).

The coming of the Spirit is compared with wind and fire (Acts 2:2–3). These two terms have an Old Testament background and show that a fulfillment of the Old Testament is taking place. The sounds and the visual phenomena show that the experience is external, and hence, objective and real rather than internal and mystical. Texts such as 1 Samuel 3:4 (sound), 1 Kings 19:11 (wind), 1 Samuel 6:1 (filling the house), and Exodus 3:2; 19:18 (tongues) show that the Lord is present.[16] His mighty acts demand expression and proclamation. The tongues sit on each follower of Jesus, enabling him or her to speak aloud with great fervor. The Holy Spirit kept energizing (Acts 2:4, iterative imperfect) the group so that their witness was sustained.

Considering what the Holy Spirit's advent actually effected presents somewhat of a problem. In Acts 2:4 Luke wrote that the followers of Jesus were all "filled" (from πίμπλημι) with the Spirit. Although Acts 1:5 said that they would be "baptized," Acts 2 gives no indication that this happened. Also, when Peter reported in Acts 11:16 what had happened in Cornelius's household, Peter referred directly to the statement of Jesus Christ in Acts 1:5, "you will be baptized with the Holy Spirit." Consequently, the absence of "baptized" in Acts 2 has led two recent writers to conclude that

13. Charles L. Feinberg, "Pentecost", *The Zondervan Pictorial Encyclopedia of the Bible*, ed. Merrill C. Tenney and Steven Barabas (Grand Rapids: Zondervan, 1975) 4:692–94.

14. For the eschatological or typological significance of Israel's feasts, see Terry C. Hulbert, "The Eschatological Significance of Israel's Annual Feasts" (Th.D. diss., Dallas Theological Seminary, 1965). On the Feast of Pentecost, see pp. 191–210.

15. See Acts 2:1, 4, 5, 7 (twice), 12, 14, 17, 21, 25, 32, 36, 39, 43 (twice), 44, 45.

16. J. H. E. Hull, *The Holy Spirit in the Acts of the Apostles* (Cleveland: World, 1968), 57–58.

being "baptized" and being "filled" are synonymous and that both terms connote a "prophetic anointing" with the Holy Spirit.[17] The question that immediately arises in this writer's mind is why John the Baptist would make such a great contrast between his ministry of baptizing in water and Jesus' ministry of baptizing in Spirit if baptizing in Spirit were synonymous with filling and both terms were an indication of a prophetic anointing. Was not John himself "filled with the Holy Spirit even from birth"? (Luke 1:15). Was he, therefore, also baptized in Spirit? What, then, is so special about Pentecost? Were not gifted Israelites in the Old Testament "filled" with the Spirit?[18]

A concordance shows that πίμπλημι occurs twenty-four times in the Greek New Testament.[19] The two occurrences in Matthew are unrelated to the Spirit and thus are irrelevant to the topic. The rest of the uses all occur in Luke-Acts. It is not difficult to conclude that the association of the verb πίμπλημι with the Holy Spirit is a Lucan device (Paul uses the cognate πληρόω in Eph. 5:18, but never uses πίμπλημι. It is also unclear whether the πνεῦμα in Eph. 5:18 is the Holy Spirit).[20]

The best exegesis of the relationship of the verb πίμπλημι to the noun that follows it is a genitive of content: people are filled with the content of something—fear, amazement, wonder, the Spirit. The filling causes the person so filled to overflow with the content. The effect of the filling cannot be hidden, since it is observable in outward acts or emotions.

It is important to notice that every reference to filling with the Spirit in the Lucan writings is closely linked with some type of verbal expression: John will be filled with the Holy Spirit from his mother's womb and will turn [verbally] many to the Lord (Luke 1:15); Elizabeth cried out when filled with the Holy Spirit (1:41); Zechariah prophesied when filled with the Holy Spirit (1:67); the disciples spoke in tongues when filled with the Holy Spirit (Acts 2:4); the disciples who had already been filled with the Spirit are re-filled when boldness is needed—Peter in Acts 4:8 and "the brethren" in

17. See Roger Stronstad, *The Charismatic Theology of St. Luke* (Peabody, Mass.: Hendrickson, 1984), and Kilian McDonnell and George T. Montague, *Christian Initiation and Baptism in the Holy Spirit* (Collegeville, Minn.: The Liturgical Press, 1991).

18. The verb πίμπλημι occurs in the Septuagint text of Exod. 28:3; 31:3; and 35:31 in reference to the skilled craftsmen who worked on the tabernacle.

19. Matthew 22:10; 27:48; Luke 1:15, 23, 41, 57, 67; 2:6, 21, 22; 4:28; 5:7, 26; 6:11; 21:22; Acts 2:4; 3:10; 4:8, 31; 5:17; 9:17; 13:9, 45; 19:29. See W. F. Moulton, and A. S. Geden, *A Concordance to the Greek Testament* (Edinburgh: T. & T. Clark, 1963), 803.

20. For a full discussion of the filling with the Spirit in Acts, see Timothy D. Crater, "The Filling of the Spirit in the Greek New Testament" (Th.M. thesis, Dallas Theological Seminary, 1971). For a study of Ephesians 5:18, see William E. Arp, "An Interpretation of 'Be Filled in Spirit' in Ephesians 5:18" (Th.D. diss., Grace Theological Seminary, 1983).

Acts 4:31; Paul preached when filled with the Spirit (9:17; see v. 20) and rebuked Elymas (13:9).

Now we can give more accurately a definition of "filling" with the Holy Spirit: *the filling of the Spirit is a distinctively Lucan phrase which connotes the sovereign activity of God through the Holy Spirit in so empowering his people that they are able to bear witness to God's mighty acts, rebuke sin, praise God, and preach the gospel.* These two functions of praising God and rebuking sin are basic to evangelism. This is why filling with the Spirit is so necessary to the growth of the church. The church must preach the gospel to extend itself in the world. The texts imply that the power of the Spirit is available to all who ask for it. However, no prerequisites are needed other than faith.

From the preceding we can conclude that only in the broadest sense can the filling of the Spirit be related to a doctrine of spiritual life. The Bible offers no texts that list confession of sin, promises of obedience, surrender, or anything else as requirements for filling, which is a very common theme in many works dealing with the Holy Spirit and the Christian life.[21] Everyone who asks the Lord for power in witness will be and is filled with the Spirit. Without this filling Christian mission is impossible. It also follows that there are not two levels of Christians: the filled (who are spiritual and more sanctified) and the unfilled (who are unspiritual, in need of repentance, and either "backslidden" or less sanctified).

This does not mean that the New Testament does not distinguish between those who are godly and those who are ungodly. Paul does delineate between walking "according to the Spirit" and walking "according to the flesh." But one must not confuse the need to live according to the Spirit's standard (κατά with the accusative case) with the "filling with the Spirit," for they are not synonymous. The New Testament does emphasize a "deeper Christian life," but filling with the Spirit is not a part of its vocabulary.

Paul's use of πληρόω with πνεῦμα in Ephesians 5:18 presents a special problem exegetically and theologically. Growing out of the redemptive-historical exposition in Ephesians 1–3, chapters 4–6 comprise a parenetic section in which Paul exhorts his readers to implement what Jesus has done historically into their lives existentially. They are to walk (i.e., live) circumspectly, which includes not becoming drunk with wine. Since they are

---

21. Arp lists Chafer, *He That Is Spiritual* (Findlay, Ohio: Dunham, n.d.), 44; Pache, *The Person and Work of the Holy Spirit* (Chicago: Moody, 1954), 118; Pentecost, *The Divine Comforter* (Chicago: Moody, 1965), 158; Ryrie, *The Holy Spirit* (Chicago: Moody, 1965), 93; Stott, *Baptism and Fulness* (Downers Grove, Ill.: InterVarsity, 1976), 57; Walvoord, *The Holy Spirit* (Findlay, Ohio: Dunham, 1954), 195; and Wood, *The Holy Spirit in the Old Testament* (Grand Rapids: Zondervan, 1976), 71, as advocates of this theology.

children of light they need to live lives of light, which can reprove the unfruitful works of darkness. Since opportunities to shine are limited and the
times are evil, they must take advantage of every opportunity and understand the Lord's will.

Instead of his usual contrast between flesh and spirit (σάρξ and πνεῦμα),
Paul uses wine and spirit. Why Paul departs from his usual practice of contrasting flesh and spirit is curious, but many writers assume that he wants
to make a point about control: a drunk person is controlled by wine, but a
spiritual person should be controlled by the Spirit. However, this proposal
has several problems. First, no lexicon of the Greek language lists control
as a meaning for πληρόω. Second, it is uncertain whether Paul even intended the Holy Spirit by πνεῦμα. Paul used πνεῦμα a total of fourteen times
in Ephesians. In two passages he uses the adjective *holy* with the noun
(1:13; 4:30). Once it refers to Satan (2:2). Four texts could refer either to the
human spirit or to the Holy Spirit (1:17; 4:23; 5:18; 6:18). The other seven
texts are most likely a reference to the Holy Spirit (2:18, 22; 3:5, 16; 4:3, 4;
6:17). Easley's chart of the New Testament use of πνεύματι designates 4:23
as the human spirit, and 1:13; 2:18; 2:22; 3:5; 5:18; and 6:18 as the Holy
Spirit. His summary of other Pauline usage shows a variety of meanings for
πνεῦμα, including human spirit, Holy Spirit, spiritual gift, and breath.[22] If
the meaning is human spirit, could the contrast between wine and spirit be
one of intoxication? A person who is intoxicated is usually verbally unin-
hibited.[23] Likewise a person who is intoxicated with the redemptive work
of God will verbalize that euphoria with praise and thanksgiving (these expressions follow in Eph. 5:19–20). Arp thinks Paul is citing Proverbs 23:31
LXX. According to this Old Testament text, drunkenness precludes walking
wisely.[24] Furthermore, wine does six things: (1) it prevents a man from
walking accurately; (2) it causes a man to waste away; (3) it robs a man of
understanding; (4) it causes a man to scoff at wise things; (5) it leads to
wastefulness; and (6) it prevents one from knowing God's will.[25]

22. Kendall H. Easley, "The Pauline Use of Pneumati as a Reference to the Spirit of
God," *Journal of the Evangelical Theological Society*, 27, no. 3 (September 1984): 300–
301.

23. This insight was forcefully reinforced in this writer's mind when he toured the
Corning Glass Museum in Corning, New York. In the Jerome Strauss exhibit a card had
a quote from the *Egyptian Book of the Dead* reading: "Do not overindulge when drinking
beer; for when you speak, something quite different will spring from your mouth." The
significance of this passage for Paul's imperative is staggering: the ancients attributed the
source of excessive verbiage to fullness within, especially alcohol! It is interesting that
the outsiders present on the day of Pentecost drew the same conclusion: Peter and the
other disciples were drunk because they were speaking in tongues (Acts 2:11–15).

24. Arp, 127.

25. Ibid., 175.

Since human spirit and divine spirit are so closely linked in both testaments, it may be unnecessary to separate the two. Man functions only because he has the divine πνεῦμα energizing him. In the Old Testament, a person who is lethargic, sad, or very sick is described as one "from whom the רוּחַ/πνεῦμα has gone forth" (1 Sam. 30:12; 1 Kings 10:5). By contrast the one who is "full of רוּחַ/πνεῦμα is energetic and productive. The human spirit energized by the divine spirit would produce the divine verbal fluidity.

In Ephesians 5:18 the Christian who is full in his personal spirit expresses verbally his internal fullness by praising the Lord in psalms, hymns, and spiritual songs. Of course, the Holy Spirit motivates him to give external expression of this internal joy since joy is a fruit of the Holy Spirit (Gal. 5:22). In either case, the result of the fullness is external verbal expression. Therefore, Paul's concept of filling would approximate Luke's.

Pentecost is a distinctive event because it calls the church to universal witness to the risen Christ. It accomplishes this through the poured out Spirit who fills Christians so that they are verbally empowered to bear that witness. But Pentecost is also distinctive because it is the birthday of the church. Even though the Spirit's filling is an important ingredient in evangelism, this filling is not unique to the New Testament age. In this writer's opinion, another work of the Spirit is unique to the New Testament age—baptism in the Spirit. In fact baptism in the Spirit creates the church and makes it the distinctive organism it is in salvation history.

Defining the precise nature of baptism in the Spirit faces a great obstacle, however. All of the texts that contrast John's baptism with Jesus' baptism give little indication of the actual details of this baptism. The preceding discussion of filling with the Spirit in Luke-Acts indicated that Luke mentioned baptism in the Spirit only twice in Acts (both as quotes of the risen Christ) with no exposition of the nature of this baptism. In this writer's opinion, however, one text aids immeasurably in defining the precise theological content of baptism in the Spirit, 1 Corinthians 12:13. This text not only clearly indicates what the baptism entails, but it allows the interpreter to formulate a close coherence with the material in Acts 2, 8, 10, and 19.

In order to facilitate the reader's understanding of the following exposition, this writer offers the following as a definition of baptism in the Spirit: *Baptism in the Spirit is a redemptive-historical complex of events whereby the universal church is created by the risen Christ as he pours out his Spirit, so that all who believe in Jesus and invoke his name for salvation are incorporated into his body, the church, regardless of their ethnic, sexual, or socioeconomic status.*

As such, baptism in the Spirit is to be placed alongside the other redemptive-historical events, such as the incarnation, death, resurrection, ascension, exaltation, and second coming of Jesus Christ. After Acts 19 believers are incorporated into this baptism in the Spirit by faith just as they are incorporated into Christ's death, resurrection, ascension, and exaltation. The New Testament has no evidence of individual baptism in the Spirit. Rather each pouring forth of the Spirit is upon a group who need to be incorporated into the church, for example, the disciples in Acts 2, the Samaritans in Acts 8, the Gentiles in Acts 10, and followers of John the Baptist at Ephesus in Acts 19. After Acts 19 no more groups need to be added. The divisions that were potentially destructive to the unity of the church were resolved. Henceforth, no more outpourings of the Spirit are needed. Baptism in the Spirit as a redemptive-historical complex is a *fait accompli*.

In 1 Corinthians 12 Paul exhorts the Corinthians to stop abusing the gifts of the Spirit because they are all part of one body. While gifts may differ, the Trinity is the source of all gifts, and every Christian has been energized and given a manifestation of the Holy Spirit. The diversity and unity of the Trinity set a pattern for diversity and unity in the church.

Since the synoptic Gospel texts[26] uniformly state that Jesus will baptize in the Spirit, exegetes like Walvoord mistakenly render ἐν πνεύματι instrumentally as "by the Spirit." The Spirit is *not* the instrument or source of the baptism. Jesus is. Rather the Spirit is the sphere of the baptism. This exegesis has important consequences for the Christian life. The Christian has been placed into the Holy Spirit so that the Spirit serves as the parameter within which the Christian lives. In a sense the Christian lives within the boundaries set by the Spirit. While there is great freedom in this life lived under the Spirit, there are also definite limitations if one is to live according to the Spirit and not according to the flesh.

If "baptism in the Spirit" is an immersion into the Spirit, what are the results of this Spirit baptism? Paul gives a number of clues in 1 Corinthians 12:13. First, this is *one* Spirit. The one Spirit produces the one body. Also, the Spirit produces a unity of all Christians in Christ.[27] Second, all Christians are included in this baptism. Paul uses the adjective *one* a total of five times in verses 12 and 13. The many are one and the all are one. Baptism in the Spirit is not for a spiritual elite—all Christians are recipients. Third, this baptism is a redemptive-historical event rather than an existential one. Paul uses two aorist passive indicatives with the verbs *baptized* and *caused to drink*. Although the aorist tenses themselves would not demand a redemptive-historical meaning, Pauline theology supports such an interpretation. Paul usually links the major redemptive deeds of God such as the cross, the resurrection, and the creation of the church together with aorist tenses (see 1 Cor. 6:11; 12:24; Eph. 1:3, 6, 10, 11; 2:5, 6, 10, etc.). Fourth, prior historical barriers have been torn down through the work of Christ.

---

26. Matthew 3:11; Mark 1:7; and Luke 3:16.
27. In Ephesians 4:3 the genitive of ἑνότητα πνεύματος is probably subjective, thus making it the "unity produced by the Spirit."

This result of Spirit baptism confirms that Paul is thinking redemptive-historically rather than existentially. The ethnic barrier between Jews and Gentiles is no longer in place (see Eph. 2:11–22). The economic and social barriers between slaves and freemen, Barbarian, and Scythian no longer exist (Col. 3:11), and the sexual superiority of the male has given way to equality for the female in Christ (Gal. 3:28). Fifth, the Spirit is now a source of spiritual vitality to all who believe (see John 7:37–39).

On the basis of the preceding discussion we can state the following. If baptism in the Spirit is a redemptive-historical event whereby Christians are immersed into the Spirit so that the Spirit now becomes the parameter for Christian ethical behavior and forms all believers into one body, regardless of race, sex, or station in life, then the church was given birth on the day of Pentecost, because this immersion and equality were not a historical reality prior to this time.

In order to distinguish filling with the Spirit from baptism in the Spirit, we list the following major differences: (1) filling with the Spirit is repeated as needed for power in witness; (2) baptism in the Spirit is a redemptive event that created the church; (3) after the creation of the church, the baptism was no longer repeated; (4) filling is existential; (5) baptism is redemptive-historical; (6) one can pray for filling; (7) one does not pray to be baptized; (8) filling recognizes differences in individual need; and (9) baptism resolves all individual differences.

A further implication of the baptism in the Spirit event is that humanity's former state of alienation has been changed to reconciliation. By his redemption Jesus Christ restored the relationships broken by the Fall. In the Fall human beings lost two indispensable, basic axes of relationship: (1) the vertical axis of relationship with God; and (2) the horizontal axis of relationship with one's fellow human beings. Alienation produced hostility between people and their neighbors. This alienation and hostility are dramatically captured in Cain's heated retort to the Lord, "Am I my brother's keeper?" (Gen. 4:9). People displayed their alienation through murder, greed, anger, theft, adultery, and through the endless quest for personal privacy and peace rather than service and generosity to others. Jesus' work was to remove the alienation legally; the Holy Spirit's work is to restore harmony practically. Thus life in the Spirit becomes the central affirmation of New Testament ethics.[28]

The next step is to show how this understanding of baptism in the Spirit drawn from 1 Corinthians 12:13 harmonizes with Acts 2 and provides a rationale for the interpretive enigmas raised by Acts 8, 10, and 19. The first

28. Wolfgang Schrage, *The Ethics of the New Testament* (Philadelphia: Fortress, 1988), 178.

line of harmony is Luke's repeated emphasis on unity and universality in Acts 2. Note the following:

1. The disciples were *all* together in the same place (v. 1).
2. The wind filled the *whole* house where they were gathered (v. 2).
3. The tongues sat on *every one* of them (v. 3).
4. They were *all* filled with the Holy Spirit (v. 4).
5. The Jews living in Jerusalem were from *every* nation of the nations under heaven (v. 5).
6. They heard *every one* of the disciples speaking in *their own* language (v. 6).
7. They asked, "*All* these who are speaking are Galileans, aren't they?" (v. 7).
8. They also asked, "How do we hear *every one*?" (v. 8).
9. The nations represented are drawn from a circle around the entire Mediterranean basin. Peter's address is to *all* who are living in Jerusalem (v. 14).
10. God will pour forth his Spirit upon *every kind* of flesh (v. 17).
11. The Spirit does not make distinctions but comes upon sons (males) and daughters (females); young men and old men receive revelations; male servants and female servants prophesy; wonders and signs occur in heaven and upon earth and above and below; sun and moon will be changed; *every one* who calls upon the name of the Lord will be saved (v. 21).

The pouring out of the Spirit resulted in an ability to speak foreign languages. There is hardly a commentator who does not make some remark about Pentecost possibly being a reversal of the Tower of Babel. By giving public expression to the mighty acts of God and carrying on what Jesus had taught and done, every individual became a spokesperson and representative for the living Lord.

The second line of harmony is Peter's handling of the Old Testament text of Joel. Using the pesher method of interpretation,[29] Peter adds to and deletes from the Old Testament text to show the fulfillment of Joel's oracle in Peter's community, the church. First, he changes "in that day" to "in the last days." There is little need to prove that the apostolic church considered the era inaugurated by the first coming of Christ as "the last days." A text like 1 Corinthians 10:11 is representative of the viewpoint: Jesus has inaugurated the end of the ages. The culmination of history was imminent.

---

29. For a discussion of the pesher method of interpretation, see Joseph A. Fitzmyer, *Essays on the Semitic Background of the New Testament* (Missoula, Mont.: Scholars Press, 1974), 299.

According to Jewish eschatology, time was divided into two ages: the present age (עוֹלָם הַזֶּה) and the age to come (עוֹלָם הַבָּא). The Jews were fervently anticipating this age to come because it would bring the restoration of the land of Palestine to Israelite autonomy. They based their hopes of the defeat of the Gentile nations, a tremendous outpouring of the Holy Spirit, and a universal knowledge of the God of Israel on Old Testament prophecies such as Joel 2 (the Spirit), Zechariah 8–13 (restoration and Gentile salvation), and Jeremiah 31 (a new covenant). Their eschatology also maintained that God would dwell in the midst of his people (Ezek. 37:11), the Anointed One would establish his covenant (Dan. 9:24–27), and the resurrection of the dead would take place (12:1–2).

With the coming of Jesus the fulfillment of these prophecies had begun: the Spirit was poured out on Pentecost; Gentiles would soon join Israel in experiencing Christ's redemption; the new covenant had been announced at the Last Supper and had been sealed with Jesus' blood when he was crucified; God was taking up residence in his new temple, the church; the dead had been and were being raised; and all these things were now a reality because the Messiah had come! Thus it comes as no surprise that the early church believed that the age to come had dawned; the last days were here! Peter underlined the importance of the fulfillment of prophecy by adding "God said" (Acts 2:17). It was God who had engineered all this!

The pesher changes in the text emphasize the universality of the gospel and the new age. Every level of humanity would now be a part of the people of God. All people would be involved in speaking the Word of God. All would minister to one another and spread the gospel in the world. All would have a strategic prophetic ministry. In one moment of time all of the old structures so basic to Israel's service for God would come crashing down. No more would there be a temple made of stone, animal sacrifices, a holy city, an elite priesthood set apart from the rank and file, or a human monarch. The people would be the temple; Christ's sacrifice was the final one; wherever the people of God gathered together the Lord would be present in their midst; all were priests before God; and there was only one monarch, the Lord Jesus Christ, who had been exalted to the right hand of the Father.

Of course, it seems probable that Peter did not understand the full implications of Joel or his own statements. He probably understood "every flesh" as "every *Jewish* flesh." It would take a forceful divine appearance and the conversion of Cornelius to awaken him to the dimensions of "every flesh."

The additions of "prophesy," "above," "signs," and "below" to Joel's text show that Peter is applying the pesher method. The emphasis is on the new prophetic activity of these who have been filled with the Holy Spirit.

The tongues appearing as fire are the wonders "above" and the speaking in tongues are the "signs" "below."

The fact no immediate fulfillment of the last half of verse 19 and all of verse 20 occurred should not blind one to the significant fulfillment of the rest of Joel's prophecy. After all, Peter had no awareness that the astral phenomena would not take place immediately. As far as he was concerned, these phenomena could take place that very afternoon! He did not have the privilege of a later historical perspective that the modern reader enjoys. Interpreters miss the point, however, when they argue, as some do, that no fulfillment at all occurred because no fulfillment of the astral phenomena occurred on that day. The prophetic activity by those filled with the Spirit provided a base for verse 21: now those who listened could call upon the name of the Lord [Jesus] and be saved! Without this prophetic witness accompanied by the signs and wonders that authenticated it, evangelism would not take place. People would continue on in life as if nothing had ever happened!

Earl Richard has provided great help to this writer in understanding how chapters 8, 10, and 19 fit into the picture of Acts and how they relate to the baptism in the Spirit. The first thirteen chapters of Acts show a concentration of Spirit texts,[30] which shows that the Spirit is crucial to Luke's conception of beginnings.[31] The major Pentecost scenes in Acts 2, 8, and 10 show an "iterative unity."[32] In Jerusalem, Samaria, and Caesarea, the apostle Peter and the twelve are involved in the opening of new mission areas. Hence, the Spirit receives concentrated attention because the Spirit is indispensable to merging these groups into the one church. The reason for the strange episode in Acts 19 is to unite the followers of John with the followers of Jesus. Thus Acts 2, 8, 10, and 19 are unique and underscore the "iterative unity" of the Spirit.[33]

The writer has chosen to call this "iterative unity" a redemptive historical event or complex. This complex may explain Luke's reluctance to restrict baptism in the Spirit to Acts 2, because at that point the church was not unified in relationship to the four groups that were potential independent Christian groups. The ministry of the Spirit unifies. Therefore, a "Jerusalem church," a "Samaritan church," a "Gentile church," and a "John the Baptist church" are unthinkable. The *one* Spirit baptizes *all* into *one* Body.

In conclusion, the day of Pentecost is distinctive for two major reasons. First, the Holy Spirit is poured out as the power necessary for evangelizing the

---

30. Earl Richard, "Pentecost as a Recurrent Theme in Luke-Acts," in *New Views on Luke-Acts*, ed. Earl Richard (Collegeville, Minn.: The Liturgical Press, 1990), 133.
31. Ibid., 134.
32. Ibid., 137.
33. Ibid., 144, 148.

world. Second, the Holy Spirit is the one who unifies all alienated peoples and groups into the new redemptive organism, the church of Jesus Christ. The universal gospel yielding a universal church is certainly new to the new age.

For Further Study

Arp, William E. "An Interpretation of 'Be Filled in Spirit' in Ephesians 5:18." Th.D. diss., Grace Theological Seminary, 1983.

Arp shows why "filling with the Spirit" as traditionally understood in dispensationalism's exegesis of Ephesians 5:18 is not a correct assessment of Paul's thought.

Crater, Timothy D. "The Filling of the Spirit in the Greek New Testament." Th.M. thesis, Dallas Theological Seminary, 1971.

Crater argues exegetically that "filling with the Spirit" is a Lukan doctrine and should be related to Christian ministry rather than to the popular Christian life approach.

DeRidder, Richard R. *Discipling the Nations.* Grand Rapids: Baker, 1975.

This is a wonderful treatment of missions as a theme in biblical theology throughout both testaments.

Dunn, James D. G. *Baptism in the Holy Spirit.* Philadelphia: Westminster, 1970.

Although Dunn's book has been heavily criticized by Pentecostal scholars, it remains one of the best discussions of "baptism in the Spirit."

Hull, J. H. E. *The Holy Spirit in the Acts of the Apostles.* Cleveland: World, 1968.

This is one of the best studies of the Holy Spirit in Acts.

Hunt, Boyd. *Redeemed! Eschatological Redemption and the Kingdom of God.* Nashville: Broadman and Holman Publishers, 1993.

Hunt's analysis of the relationship of the Holy Spirit to the kingdom of God is indispensable to a proper understanding of the relationship between these two.

McDonnell, Kilian and George T. Montague. *Christian Initiation and Baptism in the Holy Spirit.* Collegeville, Minn.: The Liturgical Press, 1991.

This book presents the Catholic approach to the relationship between the filling and baptizing work of the Spirit and water baptism. McDonnell's survey of the interpretation of the work of the Holy Spirit by the church fathers occupies 259 pages of the book.

Richard, Earl. *New Views on Luke-Acts.* Collegeville, Minn.: The Liturgical Press, 1990.

   This book was of great help to this writer in grasping the "baptism in the Spirit" as a redemptive-historical complex within Luke-Acts.

Stronstad, Roger. *The Charismatic Theology of St. Luke.* Peabody, Mass.: Hendrickson, 1984.

   This is probably one of the best Pentecostal treatments of the theology of the Holy Spirit in Luke-Acts. Stronstad argues that baptism and filling are synonymous and should be interpreted as a "prophetic anointing."

Part 2

The Configuration
of Newness

3

New Wineskins

*T*he next part of this book will develop twelve new things that Jesus inaugurated and that serve as a theological cluster around which other New Testament themes are developed, including: (1) new wineskins; (2) new teaching; (3) new covenant; (4) new commandment; (5) new creation; (6) new man; (7) new name; (8) new song; (9) new Jerusalem; (10) new heavens; (11) new earth; and (12) all things new. We will achieve a better understanding of these new things that Jesus inaugurated after a study of the occurrences of three specific New Testament Greek words: καινός ("new"), νέος ("new"), and παλαιός ("old").

According to most studies, καινός implies something recent in relation to time. Νέος connotes something fresh in contrast to something of lesser quality. However, Harrisville has shown that such distinctions are artificial in the koine Greek and that the two words are used synonymously.[1] Both words are related to time. According to Harrisville, the time aspect of New Testament newness is eschatological newness.

This newness has four distinctive features: *continuity, contrast, finality,* and *dynamic.* The parable of the garments and the wineskins will illustrate each of these features: the garments and the wineskins imply some continuity with the old; the fact that there are old garments and old wineskins versus new garments and new wineskins indicates a contrast between the old and the new; the impossibility of combining the old and the

---

1. Roy A. Harrisville, "The Concept of Newness in the New Testament," *Journal of Biblical Literature*, 74 (June 1955): 69–79; *The Concept of Newness in the New Testament* (Minneapolis: Augsburg, 1960), 1–11.

new garments and skins shows the finality of the new; and the fact that the new wine will explode the old skins shows the dynamic character of the new.

The occurrences of καινός reveal a stark contrast with the old as indicated by the following list:

1. New wine must be poured into new skins (Matt. 9:17).
2. A man instructed in the kingdom of heaven is like someone who brings new things and old things out of his treasure (13:32).
3. Jesus will drink new wine in the kingdom of the Father (26:29).
4. Jesus' followers placed his body into a new tomb (27:60).
5. In comparison with the teaching of the scribes, Jesus' teaching is regarded as new (Mark 1:27).
6. Jesus' followers will speak with new tongues (16:17).
7. The third cup of the Passover meal represented the new covenant in Jesus' blood (Luke 22:20).
8. Jesus gave his disciples a new commandment—love one another (John 13:34).
9. Although the Athenians viewed it in a negative sense, Paul's teaching was also regarded as new (Acts 17:19).
10. The cup of the Lord's meal represents the new covenant in Jesus' blood (1 Cor. 11:25).
11. God qualified Paul as a servant of the new covenant (2 Cor. 3:6).
12. If anyone is in Christ, there is a new creation (5:17).
13. In Christ neither circumcision nor uncircumcision is anything; the new creation is everything (Gal. 6:15).
14. Jesus created one new man out of Jew and Gentile (Eph. 2:15).
15. Christians have put on the new man that is renewed in righteousness and true holiness (4:24).
16. God promised and has inaugurated a new covenant with Israel and Judah (Heb. 8:8).
17. Jesus is the mediator of a new covenant that has been established on better promises (9:15).
18. Christians await the advent of the new heavens and the new earth (2 Pet. 3:13).
19. The apostle John exhorted his readers to practice the new commandment (1 John 2:7; 2 John 5).
20. Jesus will give a new name to the overcomer (Rev. 2:17).
21. The new Jerusalem will descend from heaven to the earth and become the eternal home of God's people (3:11; 21:5).
22. The redeemed sing a new song before the throne of God (5:9).
23. John saw a new heaven and a new earth (21:5).
24. God will ultimately make all things new (21:5).

The νέος texts add further information, as seen below:

1. No one places a new patch of unshrunken cloth on an old garment (Matt. 9:17).
2. Paul exhorted the Corinthians to purge out the old leaven so that they may be a new lump (1 Cor. 5:7).
3. Christians have stripped off the old man and put on the new man (Col. 3:10).
4. Jesus is the mediator of the new covenant which is built upon better promises (Heb. 12:24).

The παλαιός texts, while not as numerous as the καινός texts, nevertheless show the negative assessment of that which is old compared to that which is new. Note the occurrences of παλαιός below:

1. No one pours new wine into old skins (Matt. 9:16).
2. The Christian's old man has been crucified with Christ (Rom. 6:6).
3. The Corinthians were not to keep the feast of the Christian life with the old leaven of malice and wickedness but with the unleavened bread of sincerity and truth (1 Cor. 5:8).
4. A veil remains on the face of unbelieving Jews when the old covenant is read (2 Cor. 3:14).
5. Christians have put off the old man corrupted with deceitful lusts and practices (Eph. 4:2; Col. 3:9).
6. The new commandment is in reality an old commandment (1 John 2:7).

These texts show that the advent of Jesus Christ introduced a dynamic newness. The degree to which this newness is not recognized is the degree to which one will not recognize the distinctiveness of the coming of Christ, the day of Pentecost, the church, and the new covenant. The discontinuity between the old and the new covenants will be ignored or minimized.

The hard question that needs to be answered is, How new is new? Does the coming of Jesus Christ mark a radical change in salvation history or does his coming not really make that much difference? Should the Old Testament be christianized and the New Testament Judaized so that they really do not differ substantially from one another? This question is critical and greatly influences one's views of ecclesiology, eschatology, and Christian ethics. A minimizing of the change can lead to various results, such as seeing very little difference between Old Testament saints and New Testament saints, equating Israel with the church, equating the Old Testament temple with the church building, transferring the Old Testament priesthood to the clergy of the church, replacing circumcision with infant baptism, using the Mosaic Law as the rule of life for Christians, and calling Sunday the Christian Sabbath.

On the other hand, a maximizing of the change can lead to little continuity between the testaments. It can result in two testaments as two Bibles. It can erect insurmountable barriers between the old and the new so that the old is not foundational or preparatory for the new. The new becomes a parenthesis that interrupts the old program. It can create a radical breach between Israel and the church so that there is no fulfillment of Old Testament promises and covenants in the church. The nation of Israel becomes a strictly earthly people while the church becomes a strictly heavenly people. It can so compartmentalize the two Testaments that the Old Testament is seen only as "law" and the New Testament only as "grace." The result is a baffling conundrum: the Old Testament is law and yet it is the real center of biblical revelation and the ultimate hope eschatologically for Israel. The New Testament is grace and yet it is only temporary and an interruption of the real program of Israel and the law! If the law is bad and grace is good, then it would follow naturally that the good grace would never return to something worse, namely, the law.

This writer believes that neither extreme is necessary in articulating the significance of newness. A continuity does exist between the Testaments and needs to be spelled out carefully. On the other hand, the writer believes that Pentecost, the baptism in the Spirit, the beginning of the church as the new man in Christ, the inauguration of the new covenant, and the expectation of the new heavens and the new earth mark a radical difference in salvation history.

As will be argued later, the new covenant is *new* and is not a renewed or revamped old (Mosaic) covenant. Jesus and Paul's teaching contain genuinely new material, far beyond what Palestinian Judaism believed and taught during the first century and beyond what had been revealed in the Old Testament. The new creation is *cosmic*, characterized by universality, involving not only a new humanity but also new heavens and a new earth. In fact, according to Revelation 21:5, God will eventually make *all* things new!

The issue is really whether the first and second advents of Jesus Christ are the fulcrum of all history or whether they are merely steps along the way. Is the old primarily associated with Adam and the new primarily associated with Christ in Pauline thinking? Did Christ come to patch up or to change? To bandage man's superficial cuts or subject him to radical surgery? Unfortunately, there has been some very unclear thinking on these questions. For example, some conclude that the Fall only *stunned* man, or that Christ is nice, but not critical. Nearly 2000 years of Christian history have bred contempt for the central contentions of the New Testament such as the need for Christ's death for Adam's sin and man's need to live a transformed existence by the power of the Holy Spirit. Some scholars write as though the real need is to have the Arabs evicted from Israel so that the Jews can have full possession of the land and the temple mount. Others write with the hope that technology will eventually eliminate sickness and death and the problems of human beings will disappear! Such shallow views of the Fall lead to a shallow view of redemption. Accordingly, redemption is only forensic: it sets the record straight. On the contrary, redemption is also functional: it sets man straight!

Newness is centrally important to the New Testament. That is why the New Testament is called the "new testament" or "covenant" (Gk. καινή διαθήκη). This radical newness is the reason why the teaching of Jesus has been rejected (even though it is new) by so many and why many wish to diminish that newness. The parable of the new garments and new skins begins the significance of this newness. It exposes the folly of saying, "The old is good enough!"

This parable is found in the triple tradition, that is, in all three synoptic Gospels. Since all three Gospel writers included this parable, they must have considered it of considerable significance. The parable has been recorded in Matthew 9:14–17; Mark 2:18–22; and Luke 5:33–39. The following discussion will focus on the Lucan pericope.

The setting for the parable is unclear because Matthew speaks of the disciples of John, Mark describes the disciples of John and the Pharisees, whereas Luke simply says "they" came to Jesus. But the issue is clear: Jesus is being accused of inappropriate practice because he and his disciples do not fast, whereas the disciples of John the Baptist and the Pharisees do fast. The parable, therefore, is Jesus' reply to his critics and a defense of his practice.

Jesus began by using the analogy of a bridegroom: there is joy and celebration when a bridegroom is about to get married. As long as the bridegroom is in the midst of the bridal party, there is joy and feasting. Sorrow and fasting follow only after the bridegroom leaves the presence of his friends.

Next Jesus used two common illustrations from Palestinian peasant life to teach the significance of his presence and the program he was introducing: wineskins and garments. The translation of ἀσκούς as "bottles" in the KJV is misleading since bottles are made of glass in Western culture. Glass is impervious to whatever liquid it holds and would not require a different bottle for each new liquid. Instead Jesus was referring to containers made from animal skin, usually a goat-skin. To make these skin bags suitable for holding the wine, the goat was skinned and the hide cleaned. The legs were tied off and the neck of the skin was used as the pouring spout for the liquid inside the skin bag. Fresh grape juice was poured into the skin bag and as the juice fermented, gases were generated which in turn expanded and stretched the goat skin. The skin would stretch almost to the limit after the first filling and subsequent stretching. If fresh wine were added to this stretched skin it would burst. This would be disastrous because both the skin and the wine would be lost.[2] Therefore, the dynamic new contents needed a new elastic holder to accommodate the contents and enable the new wine to reach its full potential.

From the second illustration we learn that no one would think of patching an old garment with a patch from a new piece of material. Matthew 9:16 and Mark 2:21 use the word ἄγναφος in describing the new cloth being considered for a patch. For the meaning of ἄγναφος, Arndt and Gingrich list "unshrunken," "unbleached," "unsized," and "new."[3] From this it is unclear whether the point is that the new unshrunken cloth would tear the old garment when it shrunk at first washing, or that the colors would not match, or the fibers of the old and the new garments would be of different size. Unfortunately, we cannot determine with certainty the exact nuance of ἄγναφος in this context. The use of συμφωνέω in Luke 5:36 is probably flexible enough to allow all three previously mentioned meanings. The main point of the parable is still clear: Both items do not match and combining them together destroys both.

Through these two analogies Jesus seems to be saying that there is a fundamental incompatibility between his ministry and the "old."[4] This is not to deny that there is no continuity between Judaism and Christianity.[5] But the old containers and old coverings that were good for their day are not capable of containing the dynamic new content that Jesus is introducing. Luke is just as concerned as the other Evangelists to promote the radical newness of the gospel.[6] The old skins of Judaism accommodated the old wine of the old covenant. But the time has come for a change. The old forms have been extended to the limits of their elasticity. Initially the old coverings looked good, but now new clothes are needed. To try to patch the old would only cause a worse tear and also ruin the new cloth.

2. J. A. Thompson, *Handbook of Life in Bible Times* (Downers Grove, Ill.: InterVarsity, 1986), 159–63.

3. William F. Arndt, F. Wilbur Gingrich, and Frederick Danker, *A Greek-English Lexicon of the New Testament and Other Early Christian Literature* (Chicago: University of Chicago Press, 1979), 10.

4. Joseph A. Fitzmyer, *The Gospel According to Luke I–IX*, eds. William F. Albright and David N. Freedman, in *The Anchor Bible*, vol. 28 (Garden City, New York: Doubleday, 1981), 601.

5. John Nolland, *Luke 1–9:20*, eds. David A. Hubbard and Glenn W. Barker, in *Word Biblical Commentary*, vol. 35A (Dallas: Word, 1989), 249.

6. Craig L. Blomberg, *Interpreting the Parables* (Downers Grove, Ill.: InterVarsity Press, 1990), 125.

What is the significance of this parable? Jesus is teaching that the new age that he is inaugurating requires new forms. The new age that he is introducing is so dynamic that it will require an elasticity far beyond the capacity of the old age. Jesus did not come to patch up Judaism but to establish something new. While similarities and continuities may exist between the new and the old, the discontinuities are so radical and explosive that the old will need to be replaced (see Heb. 8:13). The new will both surpass and replace the old.

Luke includes a statement not found in Matthew and Mark: "No one after drinking old wine wants the new, for he says, 'The old is better.'" (Luke 5:39). By this statement Jesus revealed that there would be resistance to his new teachings and ultimate rejection not only of his program but his person. According to Fitzmyer, "The proverb used by Jesus is a wry comment on the effect that clinging to the old has on those who have closed their minds to his message about the new economy of salvation."[7] Jesus recognized that he did not meet the expectations of men. In effect, he "burst their balloons"! The gradual growing antipathy would eventuate in his death. In a sense he would be ruined, but his program would not be ruined. The reason why this parable is included in all three Gospels is probably because the writers knew that Jesus had introduced such radical newness that he had to be "poured out" in death. But the new forms he prepared during his lifetime would be inaugurated after his death and not a drop of gospel wine would be lost!

What were some of these new forms that Jesus would introduce? Since the transition from Judaism to Christianity is no longer the bombshell it was during the first century, it is hard to appreciate the radical newness of Jesus' teaching. Nearly 2000 years of church history have numbed Christians to the changes that he made. So what were some of these changes? We list six major changes in the following paragraphs.

First, the temple in Jerusalem would be replaced by a building not made with hands. Not only did Jesus predict the destruction of the temple in Jerusalem, he completely transformed the concept of temple: the new temple would be God's people who would worship him in spirit and truth (John 4:23). This temple would form the residence of the Holy Spirit and would offer up spiritual sacrifices, acceptable to God through Jesus Christ (1 Cor. 3:16; 1 Pet. 2:5). What did this change of "forms" facilitate? It allowed the worship of God by God's people anywhere on the earth in any structure available: cathedral, church building, school building, Quonset hut, grass thatched pavilion, or even in the woods!

Second, animal sacrifices would be replaced. Since the blood of bulls and goats could not take away sin (Heb. 10:4), Jesus offered himself up once

---

7. Fitzmyer, 602.

for all as the final and sufficient sacrifice (10:10–18). The significance of this change is that Christians can draw near to God with full assurance without having to ever offer an animal sacrifice again. No altars or sacrifices were required any longer because Jesus himself was both altar and sacrifice (13:10–16).

Third, the priesthood would be universalized. No longer would a select group of men within Israel be needed to intercede between men and God. Now only one Mediator stood between God and men (1 Tim. 2:5–6). Those who believed on that mediator were made priests to God (Rev. 5:10) and constituted a corporate royal priesthood (1 Pet. 2:9). Access to God was immediate and direct.

Fourth, the city of Jerusalem would no longer serve as the only legitimate city of God. Although Jerusalem would be the hub for the spreading of the Good News, it would, like the temple, be set aside after it had served its purpose. No longer was the goal to gather everyone into the city but to reach everyone from the city.

Fifth, the middle wall of partition separating Jew from Gentile would be destroyed and both would have equal access to God. Centuries of rigid separation between Jews and Gentiles would end with their joining as fellow partakers and coheirs in the body of Christ, the church (Eph. 2:11–22; 3:1–7).

Sixth, freedom of forms of worship would replace detailed prescriptions of forms. Under the leading of the Spirit, believers could gather in Jesus' name and exercise complete spontaneity in worship anywhere in the earth. The gospel required elasticity so that believers would not need certain "props" before they could worship God. From Jerusalem to Irian Jaya, igloos to tents, all who believed on Jesus could approach God as long as it was in Spirit and truth. The inflexibility of Judaism through its ethnic exclusivity, geographic centrality, and socioeconomic provinciality could not be used if the gospel were to expand to the far corners of the earth. People of every nation would now be included among God's people; no one needed to travel to Jerusalem to approach God; doctor, lawyer, and Indian chief would all stand side by side as they "gathered together" in Jesus' name.

All these new "skins" were necessary if the gospel were to achieve its goals. It was not that Judaism and the Mosaic Law were inherently bad; they were simply limited in their potential and incapable of adjusting to an ever-changing culture, although Pharisaism and post-A.D. 70 Judaism tried to change by means of reinterpretation of its tenets.[8] Jesus knew the struggle of Pharisaism. He knew that it was futile to patch up the system. He had to change the system entirely since it had failed so miserably in Israel.

8. See James D. G. Dunn, *The Partings of the Ways Between Christianity and Judaism and Their Significance for the Character of Christianity* (Philadelphia: Trinity Press International, 1991).

In the light of the exhilaration brought by such liberating change, it is lamentable that the church has reverted to constructing more and more forms like those that characterized Judaism. Although no church buildings were erected until the second century,[9] the church has become so building-centered that in the minds of many people today the church and the building are synonymous. It is almost impossible to teach that the church is *people*, not a building. Other rigidly fixed forms include Wednesday evening prayer meeting, two Sunday services, a strict order of service printed in the bulletin that never changes, the ubiquitous pulpit, the fixed pews, the organ console, and many more items. They have become such fixed forms that any suggested change or innovation brings the familiar censure: "We never did it that way before." This is even more surprising in light of the practice earlier in this country. According to A. G. Matthews, "the Puritans set little store by sacred buildings, many of them indeed rejected the idea of such consecration as superstitious."[10]

In reality the radical nature of this newness incited the Jews to try to stamp out Christianity because its freedom and flexibility tore at the heart of Judaism. This is why Paul "breathed threats and slaughterings" against the church (Acts 9:1 KJV). Paul recognized (especially because of Stephen's speech) that things were "going to seed." When Paul converted to Christianity, he made a complete about-face and recognized the implications of the newness. He learned that pagan Gentiles didn't have to change a thing except their life-style of sin. He witnessed the "explosive" wine of the gospel transform people from darkness into light and recognized the need to fight to the death for the Gentiles lest the Judaizers impose the old form of circumcision on the Gentiles.

If the church is to continue being the church, it will always need new forms to accommodate the changing needs of society as the gospel breaks down every barrier and penetrates deeper and deeper into the nations of this world. "Red and yellow, black and white, *all* are precious in his sight." Contextualization of the gospel is not an option; it is an indispensable requirement. The church cannot wear the fashions of days gone past. Rather it requires a "new wardrobe" for every new period of its history! May the procrustean bed of "the old is good enough" not stymie the advance of the gospel a day longer!

9. J. G. Davies, "Architectural Setting," in *The Westminster Dictionary of Worship*, ed. J. G. Davies (Philadelphia: Westminster, 1972), 22; Edward M. Blaiklock, "Dura Europos," in *The New International Dictionary of Biblical Archaeology*, ed. Edward M. Blaiklock and R. K. Harrison (Grand Rapids: Zondervan, 1983), 165.

10. A. G. Matthews, "The Puritans," in *Christian Worship*, ed. Nathaniel Micklem (New York: Oxford University Press, 1936), 184.

For Further Study

Dunn, James D. G. *The Parting of the Ways Between Christianity and Judaism and Their Significance for the Character of Christianity.* Philadelphia: Trinity Press International, 1991.

   Dunn's work is a thorough study of how Christianity started in Judaism but eventually separated from it.

Fitzmyer, Joseph A. *The Gospel According to Luke I–IX.* Vol. 28 of *The Anchor Bible.* Ed. William F. Albright and David N. Freedman. Garden City, New York: Doubleday, 1981.

   Fitzmyer's commentary on Luke is a very detailed exegetical analysis of the text and a gold mine of information on the background and culture of the New Testament.

Harrisville, Roy A. *The Concept of Newness in the New Testament.* Minneapolis: Augsburg, 1960.

   While Harrisville's book (a revision of his Princeton dissertation) is primarily a lexical study of the two Greek adjectives translated "new," it is the only full-length study of "newness" known to this author.

4

New Teaching

ccording to Mark 1:21–22, when Jesus Christ was teaching in the synagogue at Capernaum, the people were amazed at his teaching because he was teaching as one having authority and not as their scribes. Again, after Jesus healed the man with the unclean spirit, all were amazed and concluded that his teaching was new teaching with authority (Mark 1:27). This chapter will explore Jesus' new teaching. This writer believes that it is unnecessary to insist that all of Jesus' teaching is brand new without parallels or antecedents either in Judaism or the Old Testament. But much of the teaching is new and distinctive and underscores the central importance of newness for New Testament theology. Paul and other New Testament writers will build on and develop Jesus' teaching in their Epistles. We will discuss Jesus' new teaching under the following seventeen topics.

New Teaching about Abraham and His Seed

First-century Judaism believed that all the physical seed of Abraham through the line of Jacob were God's people by election.[1] The rabbis discussed among themselves whether or how one could "get out" of the elect group after he started "in." As a result of their query, they produced a list in the Mishnaic tractate, *Sanhedrin*, specifying those who would be excluded from the age to come.[2] The list of the excluded is very interesting.

1. E. P. Sanders, *Paul and Palestinian Judaism* (Philadelphia: Fortress, 1977), 85.
2. Philip Blackman, *Mishnayoth*, 2d ed., 7 vols. (New York: Judaica, 1963), 4:285–89.

It includes any who do not think the Law teaches resurrection (e.g., the Sadducees); he who says the Law is not from heaven; a skeptic or atheist; one who reads heretical books; one who utters the Divine Name according to its letters; Jeroboam, Ahab, and Manasseh; Balaam, Doeg, Ahitophel, and Gehazi; the generation of the Flood; the generation after the Tower of Babel; the men of Sodom; the men who brought an evil report about the land; the generation of those who died in the wilderness; the sons of Korah, and the inhabitants of an apostate city. In contrast, the rabbis assumed that all Israel was the seed of Abraham by birth unless one excluded oneself from the age to come through various sins.

Jesus' teaching revoked this theology by declaring that all would perish unless they repented (Luke 13:1–5). He castigated those who boasted in their Abrahamic lineage, calling them murderers and children of the devil (John 8:44). Paul argued that none were righteous and both Jew and Gentile were "under sin" (Rom. 3:9–18). According to Jesus and Paul, membership in the seed of Abraham was determined by exercising the same kind of faith that Abraham exercised (John 8:39; Rom. 4:1–25). Physical descent from Abraham was no guarantee of inclusion in the seed that would become the children of God. In fact, according to Jesus, the Gentiles would recline at table in the kingdom of God and the unbelieving Jews would find themselves on the outside (Matt. 8:11–12). To add insult to injury, Paul argued that pagan Gentiles through faith in Jesus Christ were Abraham's spiritual seed and heirs according to the promise made to Abraham (Gal. 3:29).

New Teaching about the Source of Authority

Jesus presented *himself* as the source of absolute authority, appealing to no authority other than his Father. Jesus' word was true and absolute. He spoke the words of the Father and the Father spoke his words through Jesus, the Son (Matt. 11:25–27). Jesus' authority arose out of his relationship with the Father, a relationship shared by no other being in the universe. A number of biblical texts indicate the extent of Jesus' authority, showing that he had:

1. authority over unclean spirits (Mark 1:27);
2. authority to forgive sins (2:10);
3. authority to cast out demons (3:15);
4. authority to cleanse the temple (11:28–30);
5. all authority in heaven and earth (Matt. 28:18);
6. authority to execute judgment (John 5:27);
7. authority to lay down his life and take it up again (10:18);
8. authority over all men (17:2);
9. authority over Pilate (19:1–11).

Who could make these claims in the first century? In that day the rabbis and scribes based their authority on tradition and the teachings of former sages. The approach in the Mishnah is to cite famous rabbis, giving their opinion on each legal matter (the previously cited list from the Mishnah contains the names of rabbis with dissenting views). In contrast, Jesus grounded all of his authority in the statement, "I say unto you."

This absolute sense of authority astounded the people because they recognized immediately that Jesus did not appeal to some theological consensus established over centuries of discussion. His continual claim to be the absolute authority and to speak the words of the Father prompted his enemies to attempt stoning him for blasphemy (John 8:59; 10:31–33; 11:8).

New Teaching about Baptizing in the Spirit

Water flowed freely in first-century Judaism. According to Scobie, it is impossible to ascertain the extent of baptist sects within Palestine during the first century A.D. as they were too numerous to count.[3] The Pharisees and the Dead Sea sect were obsessed with water and cleansing rites. Even where water baptism was a part of Jesus' ministry, John notes that Jesus himself did not baptize but his disciples baptized (John 4:2). As we demonstrated in chapter 2, all four Gospels and the Book of Acts anticipate the time when Jesus would baptize in the Holy Spirit. It was this baptism in the Spirit that created the church (1 Cor. 12:13). This is not to say that water baptism was abandoned or considered unnecessary, but the early church gave baptism in water its proper place, as the pledge of a good conscience to God (1 Pet. 3:21) rather than a means for providing the needed inner cleansing.

Jesus' Use of "I Am" Statements

According to Philip Harner, Jesus used "I am" statements in two different ways: (1) In an absolute sense where no predicate follows. The background of this usage is Exodus 6:2–3; 3:14; and Isaianic passages where the Hebrew phrase אֲנִי הוּא, "I am he," is used. The absolute use of "I am" reveals Jesus Christ as deity; and (2) the predicate sense where some predicate noun follows the linking verb "am." For example, Jesus calls himself the way, the truth, and the life; the bread of life; the good shepherd; the resurrection and the life; and others.[4]

Twenty centuries of Christian theology and tradition have blunted the force that these statements had on the first-century hearers. These state-

3. Charles H. H. Scobie, *John the Baptist* (London: SCM, 1964), 33–34.
4. Philip B. Harner, *The 'I Am' of the Fourth Gospel* (Philadelphia: Fortress, 1970).

ments were extremely disturbing, even blasphemous, to those who had been raised in a strictly monotheistic milieu. In Muslim or Jewish cultures today, the idea of Jesus as God is inconceivable and tremendously offensive. Such an idea denies all that they believe about the oneness of God. Jesus' claims to deity truly scandalized his listeners and caused the Jews to resolve to eliminate Jesus. When Jesus said, "Before Abraham was born, I am" (John 8:58), the Jews were immediately offended and took up stones to kill him, because he, a man, was making himself equal with God.

Jesus claimed to be the resurrection and the life (John 11:25). Pharisaic Judaism believed in the resurrection of the dead. But God would raise the dead and he would do it at the last day. Jesus not only claimed the authority to raise the dead but also raised people during his life on earth. The Jews also held that life belonged to God alone. To claim to be *the life* was blasphemy. McDowell is correct when he argues that Jesus' claims were either the claims of a liar, a lunatic, or of one equal with God.[5]

Jesus claimed to be the way, the truth, and the life (John 14:6). The first-century Jew would have agreed that God sent many spokesmen who spoke for him and were his channels of revelation. But no prophet had ever claimed to be the only way to God, the truth incarnate, and certainly not the life (of the age to come). Jesus claimed that he was the only way to God and the very embodiment of truth. He claimed that all life was resident in himself so that no one can have eternal life except through him.

Jesus' exclusive claims are the offense of Christianity, especially in a pluralistic world. No other world religion has a leader or founder who made such exclusive and sweeping claims as those made by Jesus. Access to God in other world religions is generally taught as coming through following the practices or teachings of the founder or leaders. Jesus taught that access to God is to be gained through him. His *teachings* are not the means of salvation; *he* is!

New Teaching about What the Messiah Has Come to Do

The fact that there is little or no evidence for a suffering Messiah as part of the Jewish messianic hope may explain why first-century Judaism had no emphasis on a suffering Messiah. Isaiah 53 was simply not interpreted in a messianic sense.[6] Many studies have been done on the theology of the Samaritans, Sadducees, and Essenes, but none of these groups had any conception of a suffering Messiah. Suffering was related to individuals, groups, or

5. Josh McDowell, *Evidence That Demands a Verdict* (Arrowhead Springs, Calif.: Campus Crusade For Christ, 1972), 107–13.

6. A. Neubauer and S. R. Driver, *The Fifty-Third Chapter of Isaiah According to the Jewish Interpreters* (New York: KTAV, 1959).

Israel, but not to the Messiah.[7] Since Deuteronomy 21:43 had stated that everyone who was hanged upon a tree was under the curse of God, it was unthinkable that the Messiah of the world would be crucified! According to this line of reasoning, crucifixion and messiahship are irreconcilable with one another. Hengel's study of crucifixion shows the reprehensible image that this method of capital punishment had in the first century.[8] It was the ultimate way to humiliate someone. Although various means were available to kill someone, none of them humiliated a person as crucifixion. The person not only hung naked before the public, but was forced to endure a slow, agonizing death. In fact even Rome realized the connotations that crucifixion had and spared its citizenry from such an ignominious form of execution.

Thus to suggest that the Messiah *must* suffer for his people's sins through crucifixion was the ultimate scandal, an insulting and despicable suggestion. Christians can glory in the cross, but they must be forever mindful of the terrible suffering that their Lord endured to purchase their salvation.

According to first-century expectations, the Messiah would deliver Israel from foreign control. In the first century the Zealots were the most fanatical group committed to reaching this goal.[9] When Jesus said that he had come to seek and save the lost and to give his life as a ransom for many, many Jews must have felt a tremendous letdown. Surely the temple sacrifices were sufficient to take care of the sin problem! What needed resolution was the military and political problem! If Jesus was the Messiah, why didn't he do something about that? Why didn't he mobilize an army, lead it first to the castle Antonia, capture it, march on to Caesarea and take Pilate's headquarters, then move up to Antioch to defeat the Roman legion there, and then head westward to Rome to defeat Tiberius himself?

Only a study of New Testament historical background can help someone to grasp the ethos of Jesus' times.[10] The Jews had often been under the rule of a foreign oppressor. For example, in 722–21 B.C. the Assyrians had taken the northern kingdom captive. In 606, 597, and 586 B.C. the Babylonians sacked Jerusalem. Then came the Persians in the fifth century B.C., followed by the Greeks in the fourth century B.C., and the Romans in 63 B.C. The Jews were thoroughly frustrated with foreign oppression and rule and longed for a person who would mobilize Israel, lead them to victory, and rid

7. See James D. G. Dunn, "Messianic Ideas and Their Influence on the Jesus of History," in *The Messiah*, ed. James H. Charlesworth (Minneapolis: Fortress, 1992), 378ff.

8. Martin Hengel, *Crucifixion* (Philadelphia: Fortress, 1977).

9. Martin Hengel, *The Zealots* (Edinburgh: T. & T. Clark, 1989).

10. Suggested books with which to start include Everett Ferguson, *Backgrounds of Early Christianity*, 2d ed. (Grand Rapids: Eerdmans, 1993); and James D. Newsome, *Greeks, Romans, Jews* (Philadelphia: Trinity Press International, 1992).

the land of the hated occupying troops. For centuries the Jews had been dreaming of a time when they would finally be free.

Therefore, when Jesus spoke of the necessity that the Son of man be crucified, buried, and rise again, no one, including Jesus' disciples, was receptive to this kind of message! His fixation on death simply did not match their theology. Consequently, his continual mention of death, burial, and resurrection was viewed as absolute nonsense. Some people suggested that Jesus was demented (John 10:20), and Peter even called for God to grant mercy to Jesus for such thoughts (see the Greek text of Matt. 16:22 where Peter says, "May God show mercy to you, Sir!").

Today Christians must remember that they have a far greater perspective on Jesus' words because they know the end of the story. They know that the cross changed from a means of rejection, ignominy, defeat, and humiliation to *the* symbol of victory and grace (Gal. 6:14). But those in Jesus' audience saw only the ugliness and degradation in Jesus' death. Paul recognized that the cross was an offense to the Jew and foolishness to the Greek (1 Cor. 1:23). Only Christians who stood on the resurrection side of the cross viewed it as the power of God and the wisdom of God (v. 24).

Only when one recognizes the indispensable requirement of God for payment for sin and the substitutionary nature of Christ's death can one understand God's wisdom in the cross. Once this wisdom is believed, Christ becomes wisdom, righteousness, sanctification, and redemption to that believer (1 Cor. 1:30). But in the process all human wisdom and confidence in man's resources is repudiated (1:26–31).

Jesus' whole orientation toward his death, his hour, his appointment, from the point of conception until the time he died as the Lamb of God bearing the sins of the world, ran contrary to the messianic conceptions of his generation. Since his substitutionary death was completely ruled out by everyone who heard him, his prediction of this event was indeed new teaching.

New Teaching about His Relationship with God

In John 10:30 Jesus declared that he and the Father were one in essence. The Jews caught the significance of the claim (even though Jehovah's Witnesses cannot), and took up stones to kill him because they considered it blasphemy (and it was, given their premises). By definition, God is God and man is man. To make God man and man God confuses mutually exclusive categories. And yet the New Testament makes it clear that Jesus is God incarnate.[11] Christian theology has wrestled with the problem of the Trinity,

11. For a thorough study of the evidence supporting this claim, see Murray J. Harris, *Jesus As God* (Grand Rapids: Baker, 1992). Appendix II is "An Outline of the New Testament Testimony to the Deity of Christ."

not because the doctrine is foreign to the New Testament, but because it is a necessary inference from numerous New Testament texts. Contrary to what Jehovah's Witnesses claim, Christian theologians have not sought to create the doctrine of the Trinity; rather they have labored to *clarify* it.

New Teaching about the Church

In Matthew 16:18–20 Jesus claimed that his mission would not end with his death. He also intended to build his church. This church would be built on the confession of his person as the Messiah and the Son of God.[12]

The hope of first-century Judaism was that the Messiah would regather Israel from among the nations and establish her in her land, Palestine, secure and independent of the Gentiles. The Jews had no concept of a flock comprised of both Jewish and Gentile Christians incorporated into a single new fold (John 10:16). Paul called this Jew-Gentile equality in Christ a "mystery" and stated that the mystery had not been made known in other generations to the sons of men (Eph. 3:1–8). If the church existed prior to the resurrection of Christ and the pouring forth of the Spirit on the day of Pentecost, then that church had no Head (1:22); no apostles, prophets, evangelists, and pastor-teachers (4:7–16); and no equality of Jew and Gentile. One wonders how definitions can be so manipulated that the essential content of something is not essential to the definition.[13]

Jesus taught that he would build his church on those who would confess him. Peter's quotation of Joel 2:28–32 in Acts 2:17–21 shows that everyone who called upon the name of Jesus would be saved. Gentiles eventually called upon that Name and were added to the church.

It took Israel fifty years to recognize that Jesus' teaching was radically new. At first Jews viewed Christianity as merely a subsection of Judaism. Only the final breach between the church and the synagogue, which occurred sometime after A.D. 85, showed the newness of the church. While the synagogue retained its *religio licita* status, the church's status changed to *religio illicita*.[14] The result was a persecution against the church that

12. For an excellent study of the reference(s) to "rock" in Matt. 16:18, see Alfred Kuen, *I Will Build My Church* (Chicago: Moody, 1971), 107–18.

13. Marten H. Woudstra wrote that the post-Reformation confessions state that the church exists from the beginning of the world to the end thereof. The First Scottish Confession, written in 1560, states, "We maist constantly believe, that God preserved, instructed, multiplied, decored, and from death called to life, his Kirk in all ages fra Adam till the cumming of Christ Jesus in the flesh." See Marten H. Woudstra, "Israel and the Church: A Case for Continuity," in *Continuity and Discontinuity*, ed. John S. Feinberg, (Westchester, Ill.: Crossway, 1988), 221.

14. James Parkes, *The Conflict of the Church and the Synagogue* (Cleveland: World, 1961), 85–92.

lasted until the time of Constantine in the fourth century. The church was regarded by church fathers like Justin Martyr as the replacement for Israel.[15] While such evaluations go beyond the New Testament evidence (see Appendix A), they underscore the fact that Jesus' teaching concerning the church was new.

New Teaching about the Paraclete

Various attempts have been made to clarify the work of the Holy Spirit in the Old Testament.[16] Such efforts have revealed the difficulty of determining the precise ministries of the Holy Spirit during the period before Pentecost. After studying all the references to the Hebrew term רוּחַ, "breath, wind, spirit," in the Old Testament and reflecting on Jesus' statement to Nicodemus that no one could see the kingdom of God without being born of the Spirit, this writer concluded that the Holy Spirit performed all the works described in the New Testament during the Old Testament age except the baptism in the Spirit. We have already argued that Pentecost is distinctive because that event creates the church through the baptism in the Spirit. Although scholars disagree over the range of ministries the Holy Spirit had during the Old Testament period, they all recognize the frequent references to the Spirit and extensive development of pneumatology in the New Testament. Some would go so far as to call the New Testament period "the age of the Spirit."

All would agree that Jesus Christ brings a significant dimension to pneumatology. Jesus' teaching concerning the Paraclete in John 14–16 reveals that the role of the Holy Spirit would change significantly after Jesus returned to heaven. These changes include the following:

1. The Spirit would be with Jesus' disciples forever (John 14:16).
2. The world would not be able to receive this Spirit (14:17).
3. The Spirit would continue to stay with the disciples and be in their midst (14:17).
4. Jesus would come to them in the Spirit so that they would not be left orphans (14:18). (This is neither Jesus' only "coming" nor a replacement for the second "coming"; nevertheless, it is a true "coming.")[17]

15. Peter Richardson, *Israel in the Apostolic Church* (Cambridge: Cambridge University Press, 1969), 9–14.
16. For a full-length treatment, see Leon J. Wood, *The Holy Spirit in the Old Testament* (Grand Rapids: Zondervan, 1976).
17. Charles Augustus Briggs, *The Messiah of the Gospels* (Edinburgh: T. & T. Clark, 1894), 292–94.

5. The Father would send the Spirit in Jesus' name (14:26).
6. The Spirit would teach the disciples the significance of all that Jesus had said and bring to mind all that Jesus had taught them. Jesus would send the Spirit from the Father. The Spirit is the Spirit of truth and proceeds from the Father. The Spirit's task would be to testify concerning Jesus (15:26).
7. Jesus must leave the earth in order for the Spirit to come to his disciples (15:7).
8. When the Spirit arrived he would have a strategic ministry, convicting the world of its sin, its lack of righteousness, and its judgment (16:8–11).[18]
9. The Spirit would progressively guide Jesus' disciples into all the truth about Jesus (16:13).
10. The Spirit would continue the revelation Jesus began by acting as the Announcer of all that he "hears" from the Father and the Son (16:13–15).
11. The supreme task of the Spirit would be to glorify Jesus (16:14).

Compared with the Old Testament material and the awareness of first-century Judaism, no writer would deny that this was new teaching about the Holy Spirit.[19]

New Teaching about Love for Enemies

One of the most offensive teachings of Jesus must have been his command to love enemies.[20] The Jews of Jesus' day did not differ from the common sentiment today where it is axiomatic that a person loves his friends and hates his enemies. Centuries of foreign domination had not given the Jews any reason to adopt any different attitude toward the enemies of Israel. The Pharisees and Zealots, especially, kept priming the pump of national patriotism and instilling hatred for the Romans into every Israelite.

In stark contrast Jesus was teaching his disciples to turn the left jaw to anyone who struck them on the right jaw and to pray for persecutors who despitefully use and abuse (Matt. 7:38–42; Luke 6:27–36). Such teaching must

18. D. A. Carson, "The Function of the Paraclete in John 16:7–11," *Journal of Biblical Literature*, 98 (1979): 547–66.
19. When he begins discussing the New Testament material on the Holy Spirit, George Montague writes that the Old Testament and intertestamental literature are dwarfed by the kind of Mount Everest that looms ahead in the New Testament. See his *The Holy Spirit: Growth of a Biblical Tradition* (New York: Paulist, 1976), 126.
20. John Piper, *'Love Your Enemies'* (New Rochelle: Cambridge University Press, 1979).

have caused many people to shake their heads and lose confidence in Jesus' role as Messiah to deliver his people from oppression (see Luke 1:69–73).

New Teaching about Foods

Mark's editorial comment in Mark 7:19, "cleansing all foods," must have been another bombshell for any Jew listening to Jesus' teaching. For centuries the Jews had adhered to strict dietary practices based upon the lists in Leviticus 11. Jesus retracted covenantal stipulations that had been one of the four identifying badges of membership in Israel: circumcision, Sabbath, feasts, and abstinence from unclean foods.[21] For 1500 years the Jews would not eat forbidden foods. Their dietary restrictions served as one of the main barriers to association with Gentiles. Even in the later church, the problem of foods seemed to have been a point of contention between Jewish Christians and Gentile Christians (Rom. 14:1–15:13).

Now Jesus proclaimed that what entered a person's mouth did not matter that much (see 1 Cor. 6:13). Rather it was a person's heart that counted. Paul probably reflects this teaching of Jesus when he wrote, "For everything God created is good, and nothing is to be rejected if it is received with thanksgiving, because it is consecrated by the word of God and prayer" (1 Tim. 4:4).

If Jesus had not been crucified for blasphemy, it appears that his teaching concerning diet would have been on the list of other heretical teachings worthy of death.

New Teaching about Gentiles

Although the Gospels have no explicit texts about Gentiles having an equal place with Israel in Jesus' teaching, in numerous places he lays the groundwork for this later Pauline development of the "mystery" concerning Jew-Gentile equality in Christ. One of the key texts is Matthew 8:11–12, which the Living Bible paraphrases, "And I tell you this, that many Gentiles [like this Roman officer], shall come from all over the world and sit down in the Kingdom of Heaven with Abraham, Isaac, and Jacob. And many an Israelite—those for whom the Kingdom was prepared—shall be cast into outer darkness, into the place of weeping and torment." Such teaching is amplified and reconfirmed in Jesus' parables like the parable of the great banquet (Luke 14:15–24). It is also implied in the "other sheep" in the good shepherd discourse in John 10:16. It is suggested in Jesus' concession to the Syrophoenician woman's use of humor to persuade Jesus to exorcise the

21. James D. G. Dunn, *Romans 1–8*, eds. David A. Hubbard and Glenn W. Barker, in *Word Biblical Commentary*, vol. 38A (Dallas: Word, 1988), lxxi.

demon from her daughter (Mark 7:24–30). Although the Old Testament looked forward to Gentile salvation in the future (see esp. Zech. 8:20–23; 14:16–21), no Jews in the first century interpreted the place of Gentiles vis à vis Israel as radically as Jesus and Paul did.

New Teaching about God as Father

Joachim Jeremias has written extensively on the term *Abba*.[22] Although some of his contentions have been challenged,[23] one of his points does seem valid, namely, the word *Abba* reflects a close, intimate relationship between God and the disciples of Jesus. Although Jesus does not include his disciples on the same level as his relationship with the Father (he does not include himself in calling God "our Father" but uses "my Father" and "your Father"), Jesus' statements about the relationship between his disciples and God the Father (esp. Matt. 11:25–27), show the reality of a bond between Father and children established through the Son that was not possible prior to the Son's appearance. This bond is intensified through the work of the Holy Spirit (Rom. 8:15; Gal. 4:6).

New Teaching about Hell

The Old Testament doctrine concerning life after death is very indistinct with the concept of "Sheol" serving as a catchall for everything beyond death.[24] Later Judaism began to develop the concepts of resurrection, immortality, and eternal life in more detail.[25] Terms like "Abraham's bosom" and "Gehenna" became a part of Jewish vocabulary, but Judaism did not develop these doctrines like Jesus did.[26] Second Timothy 1:10 must be recognized as an important commentary on the dramatic difference Jesus made: "Christ Jesus, who has destroyed death and has brought life and immortality to light through the gospel." Alongside Jesus' teaching about entering

22. Joachim Jeremias, *New Testament Theology* (New York: Scribner's, 1971), 61–68; *The Prayers of Jesus* (Philadelphia: Fortress, 1978), 11–65.

23. See Robin D. Mattison, "God/Father: Tradition and Interpretation," *Reformed Review*, 42, no. 3 (Spring 1989): 189–206.

24. See the excellent discussion of "Death and Beyond" in Ralph L. Smith, *Old Testament Theology* (Nashville: Broadman & Holman, 1993), 373–97.

25. See George W. E. Nickelsburg, Jr., *Resurrection, Immortality, and Eternal Life in Intertestamental Judaism*, Harvard Theological Studies XXVI (Cambridge, Mass.: Harvard University Press, 1972).

26. Discussions of the evidence vary: Rene Pache, "Hell," in *The Future Life* (Chicago: Moody, 1962), 279–325 (Conservative); William Strawson, "The Fate of the Lost," in *Jesus and the Future Life* (Philadelphia: Westminster, 1959), 137–55 (Mediating); and Alan E. Bernstein, "Damnation," in *The Formation of Hell* (Ithaca: Cornell University Press, 1993), 228–47 (Noncommittal).

the kingdom of God and inheriting eternal life were his stern warnings about the punishment of the wicked in Gehenna, the eternal fire, and outer darkness (Matt. 5:22, 29, 30; 8:12; 10:28; 18:8–9; 22:13; 23:33; 25:30, 41; Luke 12:5).

New Teaching about the Destruction of Jerusalem

In the Olivet discourse Jesus taught the disciples not to be overly impressed with the stones of the temple because there would not be one stone upon another which would not be dismantled (Matt. 24:2). This was an unacceptable statement since no Jew then believed that the Lord God Of Israel would permit the destruction of Jerusalem again after the return from Exile and all the work that had gone into rebuilding the temple. As one reads Josephus' account of the *Jewish War*, he feels the conviction in the hearts of the Jews defending the temple against Titus that God would somehow, miraculously if necessary, deliver the temple from the Romans.[27] When the porch of the temple fell, the Zealot defenders felt tremendous disillusionment and loss of hope. Some Jews completely lost their faith and from that day forward no longer anticipated the fulfillment of the Old Testament promises. The Old Testament prophets like Haggai, Zechariah, and Malachi had prophesied the future glory of Jerusalem, not its destruction. Again, Jesus' teaching was radically new.

New Teaching about Judgment

All Jews of the first century looked forward to some judgment of sinners by God (usually the sinner was someone separate from your group!). Jesus' teaching was new in that he taught that this judgment would come through him, the Son (John 5:22). No one would be exempted from his judgment. Judgment would be on an equal basis. Furthermore, judgment would be on the basis of each man's relationship to Christ himself (John 5:21–22).

New Teaching about the Kingdom of God

Jesus gave a new dimension to the kingdom of God when he taught his "theology of reversal," that is, the kingdom does not belong to those who are the rich, the powerful, the masters, the first. Instead the kingdom of God belongs to the poor, the weak, the servants, the last.[28]

27. Gaalya Cornfeld, ed., *Josephus: The Jewish War* (Grand Rapids: Zondervan, 1982), 428–29.
28. Donald B. Kraybill, *The Upside-Down Kingdom* (Scottdale, Pa.: Herald, 1978).

As Paul would later emphasize, the kingdom of God consisted not of externals like meat and drink, but of internal qualities such as righteousness, peace, and joy in the Holy Spirit (Rom. 14:17). The kingdom was present in the person of Jesus. As he taught he expounded the character of the kingdom and the type of people who would enter it or be excluded from it. In fact, the kingdom belonged to little children (Mark 10:14). Such teaching was diametrically opposed to the ideals of first-century Jews. For them the image was Daniel 2:44 where Daniel pictured the kingdom of God as a stone that would crush and put an end to all other kingdoms. For first-century Jews this meant a cataclysmic end to the Gentile nations and the exaltation of Israel. For Jesus the kingdom meant the inclusion of the Gentiles in God's kingdom if they "will produce its fruits" and the exclusion of Jews who rejected him (Matt. 21:43).

New Teaching about Eternal Life

Eternal life in Jewish thinking was equated with the kingdom of God and the age to come (compare Matt. 19:16 with vv. 23–24 and with v. 28). Eternal life, the kingdom of God, and the age to come were all future realities that would be present in "the last day." Jesus taught that eternal life was both a present possession and a future inheritance (Matt. 25:46; John 5:24). This was true because life was something he gave as the way, the truth, and the life. Life was a relationship with God the Father available now only through God the Son. Although the kingdom, eternal life, and the age to come had a future aspect, many of their eschatological blessings such as salvation and resurrection were already available through Christ. Jesus had come so that his people might have life, and experience it more abundantly through a right relationship with God through him (John 10:10).

These seventeen new teachings are not the only new teachings of Jesus, but they are indicative of the newness of his teaching.[29] Jesus planted the seed ideas and presented the new teachings in embryonic form. Later Paul, Peter, James, and John elaborated on and developed them. But they were not the first to propose them. Indeed, the Author of Christianity was Jesus.[30]

---

29. The reader may want to consult the following books for other "new teachings" of Jesus: W. S. Harris, *A Complete Index to the Thought and Teachings of Christ* (Nashville: Cokesbury, 1939); Ernest DeWitt Burton, *A Source Book for the Study of the Teaching of Jesus in its Historical Relationships* (Chicago: The University of Chicago Press, 1923); Thomas Walker, *The Teaching of Jesus and the Jewish Teaching of His Age* (New York: George H. Doran Co., 1923).

30. The classic defense of Jesus as the true founder of Christianity and Paul as a disciple of Jesus who built upon Jesus' teachings is J. Gresham Machen, *The Origin of Paul's Religion* (Grand Rapids: Eerdmans, 1947). The most recent presentation of this same thesis is Seyoon Kim, *The Origin of Paul's Gospel* (Grand Rapids: Eerdmans, 1982).

For Further Study

Harner, Philip B. *The 'I Am' of the Fourth Gospel.* Philadelphia: Fortress, 1970.

    A very thorough study of the "I Am" sayings of Jesus in the Gospel of John.

Harris, Murray J. *Jesus As God.* Grand Rapids: Baker, 1992.

    A careful exegetical study of the deity of Christ in the New Testament.

Hengel, Martin. *Crucifixion.* Philadelphia: Fortress, 1977.

    Hengel's study on crucifixion in the first century is required reading for Christians who "glory" in the cross and what the death of Christ accomplished redemptively but fail to recognize the revulsion that crucifixion caused in the minds of people living under Roman rule.

Kraybill, Donald. *The Upside-Down Kingdom.* Scottdale, Pa.: Herald, 1978.

    A stimulating study of how Jesus inverts human values.

Kuen, Alfred. *I Will Build My Church.* Chicago: Moody, 1971.

    An exegetical and historical study of ecclesiology.

Piper, John. *'Love Your Enemies.'* New Rochelle: Cambridge University Press, 1979.

    A revision of Piper's doctoral dissertation on the unique aspects of Jesus' command to "Love your enemies."

Hoel discusses New teachings in the N.T. point to Christ as the originator.

5

New Covenant

The Nature of the Old Covenant

Although scholars have been engaged in a heated debate over the form-critical classification of the Mosaic (old) covenant, especially conservative and liberal Old Testament scholars, a large percentage of evangelical scholars (but not all) consider the Mosaic covenant to be a suzerainty-vassal treaty modeled after the Hittite treaties of the second millennium B.C.[1] These treaty covenants had five major sections with additional elements that were not always included. The five major sections were: (1) the *preamble*, in which the suzerain identifies himself to the vassals; (2) the *historical prologue*, in which the suzerain reviews for his vassals his past deeds of faithfulness to them; (3) the *stipulations* or requirements that the vassals must obey if they are to continue in a proper and favorable relationship with the suzerain; (4) a *cursings* section that outlines the penalties that will be enacted upon the vassals by the suzerain if they break the covenant; (5)

1. Meredith G. Kline, *Treaty of the Great King* (Grand Rapids: Eerdmans, 1963); *By Oath Consigned* (Grand Rapids: Eerdmans, 1968); K. A. Kitchen, *The Bible in Its World*, Ch. 5, "The Birth of a Nation" (Downers Grove, Ill.: InterVarsity, 1978), 75–85. The leading liberal criticism of this hypothesis is Ernest W. Nicholson, *God and His People* (Oxford: Clarendon Press, 1986). The debate is colored by the agendas of the two sides: (1) the conservatives find that the Hittite hypothesis supports a Mosaic authorship, or at least date, of the Pentateuch; (2) the liberals, wishing to avoid any Mosaic associations with the Pentateuch and holding numerous source-, form-, and redaction-critical positions concerning the entire Old Testament are not willing to yield much ground to conservative Old Testament exegetes.

a *blessings* section that promises rewards and good things to the vassals if they keep the covenant. In the following paragraphs we will observe how this fivefold structure is applied to the Mosaic covenant.

The Preamble

This is found in Exodus 20:2a and is reduced simply to the words: "I am the LORD your God." Since the LORD is now known as the God of redemption because of his great might he displayed in leading Israel out of Egypt and through the Red Sea, no further identification of this suzerain is necessary. The redeemer of Israel is the author of this covenant!

The Historical Prologue

This is found in Exodus 20:2b where the words are added: "who brought you out of the land of Egypt, out of the land of slavery." Although this is an extremely brief prologue in comparison with the Hittite treaties, it was sufficient at this point in Israel's history. The sole proof of Yahweh's past deeds of faithfulness to Israel was the Exodus. After Yahweh had led Israel through the wilderness and brought her to the banks of the Jordan forty years later, however, this prologue was greatly expanded in Deuteronomy. The historical prologue is even longer in Joshua 24 and attained its longest form in Nehemiah 9. In fact the longer that history unfolded, the longer the list of Yahweh's deeds for the benefit of Israel became. But initially the Exodus from Egypt was sufficient proof and served as the point of reference for all the later relationships between Yahweh and his people. According to Eakin, "The exodus event is the *sine qua non* for understanding the existence of Israel as a people and the Old Testament as their literary record."[2] Further, "In each major section of the canonical Hebrew Scriptures (law, prophets, writings), from the major periods of Israel's history (pre-exilic, exilic, post-exilic), and from every type of literature (with the possible exception of the wisdom literature), Israel strongly emphasized the mighty deed of Yahweh that precipitated her deliverance."[3] Eakin then lists a number of texts that reflect on the centrality of the Exodus.[4]

---

2. Frank E. Eakin, Jr. *The Religion and Culture of Israel* (Boston: Allyn and Bacon, 1971), 51.

3. Ibid., 53–54.

4. Ibid., 54. Verses listed by Eakin include: Exod. 12:17; 13:16; 16:32; 17:3; 20:2; 32:4; Lev. 11:45; 23:43; 26:13; Num. 15:41; 23:22; Deut. 1:17; 5:6; 16:1; 26:8; Josh. 24:5–6; Judg. 6:8, 13; 1 Sam. 8:8; 10:18; 12:8; 2 Sam. 7:6; 2 Kings 17:36; 1 Chron. 17:21; 2 Chron. 6:5; Neh. 9:18; Ps. 80:8; 81:10; 105:37; Isa. 11:16; Jer. 2:6; 7:22; 11:7; 16:14; 23:7; Ezek. 20:6, 9; Dan. 9:15; Hos. 11:1; 12:13; Amos 2:10; 3:1; 9:7; Mic. 6:4; Hag. 2:5.

The Stipulations

The first three stipulations should be regarded as obligations of the vassals to the suzerain, Yahweh. The fourth stipulation, the Sabbath command, is the sign or seal of the covenant. The last six stipulations regulate the relationships of the vassals to one another.

THE FIRST THREE STIPULATIONS (EXOD. 20:3–7)

Since Yahweh is the only true God, he is to be both the spiritual and political ruler of his people. To worship other gods and make images is a rejection of Yahweh as the only true and spiritual ruler. To enter into foreign alliances not only rejects Yahweh's political headship, but also is tantamount to an acceptance of that nation's gods. Therefore, idolatry is directly forbidden and foreign alliances are indirectly forbidden. The Israelites are not to swear by Yahweh's name in an empty manner.

THE FOURTH STIPULATION (EXOD. 20:8–11)

Since covenants in the extrabiblical treaties were written in their entirety on both sides of one table[t], Kline concluded that the two tablets Moses had were duplicate copies of the covenant, a common practice in the secular treaties. Kline also noted that the suzerain's dynastic seal was found in the midst of the front side of the international treaty documents; therefore, he maintains that the Sabbath was the "sign of the covenant" since Yahweh would not permit a representation of himself on his seal. The Sabbath signified the perfection of creation and Yahweh's absolute sovereignty over people. It was therefore uniquely given to Israel as the seal of Yahweh's ownership and authority.[5]

THE LAST SIX STIPULATIONS (EXOD. 20:12–17)

According to Mendenhall, these stipulations were designed to resolve internal conflicts and were found in ancient law codes outside of Israel. These stipulations regulate the relationships between the vassals as fellow subjects of the king.[6]

ADDITIONAL STIPULATIONS

The basic "ten words" (Exod. 34:28; Deut. 4:13; 10:4) are expanded throughout the rest of the Pentateuch in great detail (see Figure 5.1). These stipulations attempt to cover every phase of life within Israel. This writer has attempted to summarize the various categories that these other stipulations cover (see Figure 5.2).

5. Kline, *Treaty,* 18–19.
6. George E. Mendenhall "Covenant," in *IDB,* ed. George Buttrick et al., 4 vols. (New York: Abingdon, 1962), 1:720.

Figure 5.1

The Laws of the Pentateuch

1. Israel is to worship no other gods than Yahweh (Exod. 20:3; 34:14; Lev. 19:4; Deut. 5:7).
2. Israel is not to make any graven image (Exod. 20:4; Deut. 4:15–24; 5:8–9).
3. Israel is not to take Yahweh's name in vain (Exod. 20:7; Lev. 19:12; Deut. 5:11).
4. Remember the Sabbath day and keep it holy (Exod. 20:8; 23:12; 34:21; 35:2–3; Lev. 19:3; Deut. 5:12–15).
5. Honor your father and mother (Exod. 20:12; Lev. 19:3; Deut. 5:16).
6. Do not commit murder (Exod. 20:13; Deut. 5:17).
7. Do not commit adultery (Exod. 20:14; Lev. 18:20; 20:10; Deut. 5:18; 22:22).
8. Do not steal (Exod. 20:15; Lev. 19:11; Deut. 5:19).
9. Do not give false testimony (Exod. 20:16; Lev. 19:11; Deut. 5:20).
10. Do not covet (Exod. 20:17; Deut. 5:21).
11. You shall make an altar of earth (Exod. 20:24).
12. You shall not make an altar of cut stones (Exod. 20:25).
13. You shall not go up an altar by the steps (Exod. 20:26).
14. Slaves shall serve for six years (Exod. 21:2).
15. Slaves shall be released the seventh year (Exod. 21:2).
16. A slave shall be released in the same state as he was in when he became a slave (Exod. 21:3).
17. If a master gives a slave a wife, . . . (Exod. 21:4–6).
18. If a man sells his daughter as a slave, . . . (Exod. 21:7).
19. If a master doesn't like the daughter, . . . (Exod. 21:8).
20. If the master saves the girl for his son, . . . (Exod. 21:9).
21. If a master has another wife in addition to the slave girl, . . . (Exod. 21:10).
22. If a master does not provide food, clothing, and marital rights, . . . (Exod. 21:11).
23. He who strikes a man (Exod. 21:12).
24. If it is not premeditated, . . . (Exod. 21:13).
25. If it is premeditated, . . . (Exod. 21:14).
26. If a man strikes his father or mother, . . . (Exod. 21:15; Lev. 20:9).
27. Kidnapping (Exod. 21:16; Deut. 24:7).
28. If a man curses his father or mother, . . . (Exod. 21:17).
29. If men have a quarrel and death doesn't result, . . . (Exod. 21:18–19).
30. If a slave owner strikes his slave with a rod, . . . (Exod. 21:20–21).
31. If a woman has a miscarriage, . . . (Exod. 21:22).

32. If a man strikes the eye of a slave, . . . (Exod. 21:26).
33. If a man knocks out a tooth, . . . (Exod. 21:27).
34. If an ox gores, . . . (Exod. 21:28).
35. If a man opens a pit, . . . (Exod. 21:33).
36. If one ox hurts another ox, . . . (Exod. 21:35).
37. If a man steals an ox or a sheep, . . . (Exod. 22:1).
38. If a thief is caught, . . . (Exod. 22:2).
39. If a man allows a field to be grazed bare, . . . (Exod. 22:5).
40. If a fire breaks out, . . . (Exod. 22:6).
41. If a man entrusts money, . . . (Exod. 22:7; Lev. 6:2–7).
42. If a man entrusts an animal, . . . (Exod. 22:10).
43. If a man borrows, . . . (Exod. 22:14).
44. If a man seduces a virgin, . . . (Exod. 22:16).
45. Sorceress (Exod. 22:18).
46. Bestiality (Exod. 22:19; Lev. 18:23; 20:15–16).
47. He who sacrifices to a god other than the Lord (Exod. 22:20).
48. Don't wrong a stranger (Exod. 22:21; 23:9).
49. Don't afflict widows or orphans (Exod. 22:21).
50. You shall not charge the poor interest (Exod. 22:25; Lev. 25:35–37).
51. If you take a cloak as a pledge, . . . (Exod. 22:26).
52. You shall not curse God (Exod. 22:28; Lev. 24:15).
53. You shall not curse a ruler of your people (Exod. 22:28).
54. Don't delay the harvest or vintage offering (Exod. 22:29).
55. Give Yahweh your firstborn sons (Exod. 22:29; 34:19).
56. Give Yahweh your eight-day old oxen and sheep (Exod. 22:30; Lev. 22:27).
57. Eat no meat torn to pieces in the fields (Exod. 22:31).
58. Bear no false rumors (Exod. 23:1).
59. Don't run in a pack (Exod. 23:2).
60. Don't pervert justice (Exod. 23:2; Deut. 16:18–20).
61. Don't be partial to the poor in a lawsuit (Exod. 23:3).
62. Return a wandering ox or donkey (Exod. 23:4).
63. Donkey with a heavy load (Exod. 23:5).
64. Don't be partial to the needy in a lawsuit (Exod. 23:6).
65. Acquit the innocent (Exod. 23:7).
66. Don't take bribes (Exod. 23:8).
67. Seventh-year Sabbath (Exod. 23:10–11; Deut. 15:1–18; Lev. 25:1–7).
68. Celebrate a feast three times a year (Exod. 23:14–17; 34:23; Deut. 16:16).
69. Feast of Unleavened Bread (Exod. 34:18; Lev. 23:6–8; Deut. 16:1–8).
70. Pentecost (Exod. 34:22a; Lev. 23:10–20; Num. 28:26–31; Deut. 16:9–11).

71. Feast of Tabernacles (Exod. 34:22b; Lev. 23:34–44; Num. 29:12–40; Deut. 16:13–15).
72. Do not sacrifice with leavened bread (Exod. 23:18; 34:25).
73. Do not allow the fat of the feast to remain overnight (Exod. 23:18; 34:25).
74. Bring choice firstfruits into house of Lord (Exod. 23:19; 34:26).
75. Do not boil a kid in its mother's milk (Exod. 23:19; 34:26; Deut. 14:21).
76. Break down the Canaanite altars (Exod. 23:24; 34:13).
77. Make no covenant with the Canaanites (Exod. 23:32; 34:12).
78. Build a dwelling for Yahweh (Exod. 25:8).
79. Construction of ark (Exod. 25:10–16).
80. Construction of mercy seat (Exod. 25:17).
81. Construction of cherubim (Exod. 25:18–20).
82. Table of the bread of the presence (Exod. 25:23–30).
83. Golden lampstand (Exod. 25:31–40).
84. Curtains (Exod. 26:1–14).
85. Boards (Exod. 26:15–18).
86. Sockets (Exod. 26:19–25).
87. Bars (Exod. 26:26–30).
88. Veil (Exod. 26:31–33).
89. Position of furniture (Exod. 26:34–35).
90. Screen for doorway (Exod. 26:36).
91. Pillars for doorway (Exod. 26:37).
92. Bronze altar (Exod. 27:1–8).
93. Court (Exod. 27:9–19).
94. Lamp (Exod. 27:20–21; Lev. 24:1–4).
95. Garments of priests (Exod. 28:2–43).
96. Consecration of priests (Exod. 29:1–44).
97. Incense altar (Exod. 30:1–10).
98. Census (Exod. 30:11–16).
99. Bronze laver (Exod. 30:17–21).
100. Anointing of tabernacle (Exod. 30:22–33; 40:1–15).
101. Incense (Exod. 30:34–38).
102. Sabbath (Exod. 31:12–17; Lev. 19:30; Lev. 23:1–3).
103. Burnt offering (Lev. 1:2–17; 6:9–13; 7:8).
104. Grain offering (Lev. 2:1–16; 6:14–18; 7:9).
105. Peace offering (Lev. 3:1–17; 7:11–21; 7:29–34; 19:5–6).
106. Sin offering (Lev. 4:2–5:5; 6:25–30).
107. Guilt offering (Lev. 5:6–19; 7:1–7).
108. Priest's offering (Lev. 6:19–23).
109. Rules for fat and blood (Lev. 7:23–27; 17:6–16; 19:26).
110. Wine and strong drink (Lev. 10:9).

111. Clean animals (Lev. 11:2–3; 20:25; Deut. 14:4–6).
112. Unclean animals (Lev. 11:4–8; 20:25; Deut. 14:7–8).
113. Clean fish (Lev. 11:9; Deut. 14:9).
114. Unclean seafood (Lev. 11:10–12; Deut. 14:10).
115. Unclean fowl (Lev. 11:13–19; 20:25; Deut. 14:12–19).
116. Unclean insects (Lev. 11:20,. 23).
117. Clean insects (Lev. 11:21–22).
118. Unclean contacts (Lev. 11:24–43).
119. Unclean people (Lev. 12:1–8; 13:1–59; 14:1–32; 15:1–33; Num. 5:2–4; 19:11–22).
120. Unclean houses (Lev. 14:34–57).
121. Day of Atonement (Lev. 16:1–34; 23:27–32).
122. Slaughter of beasts (Lev. 17:1–5).
123. Uncovering nakedness (Lev. 18:6–19; 20:17–21).
124. Infant sacrifice (Lev. 18:21; 20:1–5).
125. Homosexuality (Lev. 18:22; 20:13).
126. Leftover gleanings from harvest (Lev. 19:9–10; 23:22; Deut. 24:19–22).
127. Wages (Lev. 19:13; Deut. 24:14–15).
128. Deaf and blind (Lev. 19:13).
129. Justice (Lev. 19:15).
130. Slander (Lev. 19:16).
131. Hate (Lev. 19:17).
132. Vengeance (Lev. 19:18).
133. Love your neighbor (Lev. 19:18).
134. Don't breed two kinds of cattle (Lev. 19:19).
135. Don't sow two kinds of seed (Lev. 19:19; Deut. 22:9).
136. Don't wear a garment of two kinds of material (Lev. 19:19; Deut. 22:11).
137. Intercourse with a slave (Lev. 19:20–22).
138. Don't eat of newly planted trees for three years (Lev. 19:23–25).
139. Divination and soothsaying (Lev. 19:26).
140. Rounding off sideburns and trimming beard (Lev. 19:27).
141. Cuts and tattoos on body (Lev. 19:28; Deut. 14:1).
142. Prostitution (Lev. 19:29; Deut. 23:17–18).
143. Mediums and spiritists (Lev. 19:31; 20:6, 27; Deut. 18:9–14).
144. Honor the aged (Lev. 19:32).
145. Strangers in the land (Lev. 19:33–34).
146. Just weights and measures (Lev. 19:35–36; Deut. 25:13–16).
147. Incest (Lev. 20:11–12; Deut. 22:30).
148. Polygamy (Lev. 20:14).
149. Cleanness of priests (Lev. 21:1–24; 22:1–16).
150. Cleanness of sacrifices (Lev. 22:18–25).

151. Passover (Lev. 23:5; Num. 9:2–3; 28:16–25).
152. Feast of Trumpets (Lev. 23:24–25; Num. 29:1–11).
153. Presentation loaves (Lev. 24:5–9).
154. Blasphemy (Lev. 24:16).
155. Lex Talionis (Lev. 24:17–22; Deut. 19:21).
156. Jubilee Year (Lev. 25:8–34).
157. Treatment of slaves (Lev. 25:39–55).
158. Vows (Lev. 27:1–33; Num. 30:1–16; Deut. 23:21–23).
159. Sin and restitution (Num. 5:6–8).
160. Gifts to priest (Num. 5:9–10).
161. Trial by ordeal (Num. 5:11–31).
162. Nazirite vow (Num. 6:1–21).
163. Cleansing of Levites (Num. 8:6–26).
164. Law of shophar (Num. 10:1–10).
165. Law of burnt, special vow, freewill, sin offerings (Num. 15:1–31; 28:1–15).
166. Tassels (Num. 15:37–41; Deut. 22:12).
167. Priests' food (Num. 18:8–20).
168. Tithes for Levites (Num. 18:21–24).
169. Tithes from Levites (Num. 18:25–32).
170. Red heifer (Num. 19:1–10).
171. Law of inheritance (Num. 27:6–11; 36:1–9).
172. Cities of refuge (Num. 35:1–34; Deut. 19:1–13).
173. Love the Lord (Deut. 6:5).
174. Destroy the high places (Deut. 12:1–4).
175. Worship at a central sanctuary (Deut. 12:5–28).
176. False prophets and seducers (Deut. 13:1–17).
177. Clean fowl (Deut. 14:11).
178. Dead creatures (Deut. 14:21).
179. Tithe of produce (Deut. 14:22–29).
180. Firstborn (Deut. 15:19–23).
181. Asherahs and pillars (Deut. 16:21–22).
182. Blemished sacrifices (Deut. 17:1).
183. Capital punishment of transgressors (Deut. 17:2–7).
184. Lawsuits (Deut. 17:8–13).
185. King (Deut. 17:15–20).
186. Portion of the Levites (Deut. 18:1–8).
187. Prophets (Deut. 18:9–22).
188. Landmarks (Deut. 19:14).
189. Two or three witnesses (Deut. 19:15).
190. False witness (Deut. 19:16–20).
191. Military exemption (Deut. 20:1–9).
192. Law of Herem (Deut. 20:10–20).

193. Purification from unknown murder (Deut. 21:1–9).
194. Marriage to captive women (Deut. 21:10–14).
195. Loved and unloved wives (Deut. 21:15–17).
196. Rebellious son (Deut. 21:18–21).
197. Hangings (Deut. 21:22–23).
198. Straying animals (Deut. 22:1–4).
199. Dressing like the other sex (Deut. 22:5).
200. Bird's nests (Deut. 22:6–7).
201. Parapets on houses (Deut. 22:8).
202. Don't yoke an ox with a donkey (Deut. 22:10).
203. Nonvirgin wives (Deut. 22:13–21).
204. Premarital fornication (Deut 22:23–29).
     A man and an engaged girl (22:23–27)
     A man and an eligible girl (22:28–29).
205. Persons excluded from the assembly (Deut. 23:1–8).
206. Purity for warfare (Deut. 23:9–11).
207. Latrines (Deut. 23:12–14).
208. Escaped slaves (Deut. 23:15–16).
209. No interest on loans to any Israelite (Deut. 23:19–20).
210. Grapes in neighbor's vineyard (Deut. 23:24).
211. Plucking grain in a field (Deut. 23:25).
212. Divorce (Deut. 24:1–4).
213. Newly-married man (Deut. 24:5).
214. Pledges of millstones (Deut. 24:6).
215. Leprosy (Deut. 24:8–9).
216. Pledges (Deut. 24:10–13).
217. No substitute punishment (Deut. 24:16).
218. Aliens, orphans, widows (Deut. 24:17).
219. Forty stripes (Deut. 25:1–3).
220. Don't muzzle an ox treading out grain (Deut. 25:4).
221. Law of Levirate marriage (Deut. 25:5–10).
222. Wife grabbing genitals of husband's attacker (Deut. 25:11–12).
223. Offering of firstfruits (Deut. 26:1–11).
224. Third-year tithes (Deut. 26:12–15).

Figure 5.2

Categories of Laws

1. Monotheism
2. Idolatry
3. Swearing
4. Rest

 5. Respect for parents
 6. Murder
 7. Adultery
 8. Theft
 9. Lying, perjury
10. Covetousness
11. Approach to God
12. Slavery
13. Provision of basic necessities
14. Assault
15. Kidnapping
16. Manslaughter
17. Miscarriage
18. Justice
19. Reparation
20. Trust
21. Fornication
22. Occult
23. Bestiality
24. Widows and orphans
25. Usury
26. Leaders
27. Offerings
28. Dedication
29. Slander
30. Lawsuits
31. Compassion
32. Bribery
33. Festivals
34. Sacrifices
35. Pagan practices
36. Foreign alliances
37. Tabernacle
38. Priests
39. Proper, improper foods
40. Infectious diseases
41. Cleanliness
42. Homosexuality
43. Welfare
44. Wages
45. Handicapped
46. Hate
47. Vengeance

48. Love of neighbor
49. Mixtures
50. Conservation
51. Disfigurement
52. Aged
53. Strangers
54. Weights and measures
55. Incest
56. Polygamy
57. Blasphemy
58. Vows
59. Gifts
60. Dress
61. Inheritance
62. Asylum
63. Love for God
64. True and false prophets
65. Capital punishment
66. King
67. Landmarks
68. Verification
69. Military exemption
70. Holy War
71. Guilt
72. Equality
73. Hanging
74. Safety
75. Mismatching
76. Purity
77. Sanitation
78. Divorce
79. Marital adjustment
80. Perpetuity of property

In an attempt to reduce these single stipulations (the Pharisees counted a total of 613: 365 negative and 248 positive) into categories and then to reduce the categories to umbrella topics, this writer has subsumed all stipulations under two main topics: relationship with God and relationship with neighbor (following Matt. 22:34–40); and five subtopics: worship, service, family, government, and business (see Figure 5.3). These five subtopics may not be all-inclusive or may be inaccurate in terms of specific stipulations, but they seem to cover the gamut of Israelite life in the world. The important truths to learn are the comprehensive nature of the legislation and the detailed instructions given. These stipulations are very detailed so that there are specific procedures to be followed (to the letter!) in every area covered. To this writer, this indicates that the Lord God of Israel was interested in the "fine print" of what life before him involved.

Figure 5.3

Hierarchy of Laws

Relationship with God

Worship	Service
Monotheism	Rest
Idolatry	Leaders
Swearing	Dedication
Occult	Priests
Offerings	Prophets
Festivals	King
Sacrifices	Holy War
Pagan practices	
Foreign alliances	
Tabernacle	
Blasphemy	
Vows	
Gifts	

Relationship with Neighbor

Family	Government	Business
Parents	Murder	Trust
Sex	Theft	Usury
Adultery	Perjury	Wages
Fornication	Assault	Weights

No division between Church/State in Israel.

Family	Government	Business
Bestiality	Kidnapping	Measures
Homosexuality	Manslaughter	
Incest	Justice	
Polygamy	Reparation	
Divorce	Usury	
Slaves	Slander	
Widows	Lawsuits	
Orphans	Sanitation	
Aged	Public health	
Property	Welfare	
Inheritance	Conservation	
	Disfigurement	
	Asylum	
	Capital punishment	
	Leaders	
	King	
	Landmarks	
	Military	
	Hanging	
	Safety	

The Cursings and the Blessings (Consequences)

While Exodus does not have a separate section of blessings and cursings, Leviticus 26 and Deuteronomy 27–28 do have very detailed lists. The prophets, who serve as prosecutors of Yahweh's controversy or lawsuit (רִיב) against Israel,[7] also have lists scattered throughout their writings. The cursings and blessings are very concrete and related to life on this earth: famine

7. Julien Harvey, "Le 'Rib-Pattern,' requistoire prophetique sur la rupture de l'alliance," *Biblica*, 43, no. 2 (1962): 172–96.

and fertility; disease and health; defeat and victory; utter destruction and peace.

Although some scholars may find the preceding form-critical classification of the Mosaic covenant unacceptable, the theological truth behind each of the five basic treaty elements still stands. It is really unimportant whether any of the elements in the Pentateuch have a Hittite origin or some other origin in the ancient Near East. These preceding five elements are simply a convenient way to organize the extant pentateuchal materials. Thus it matters little whether the Hittite empire or the treaties even existed!

This means that one does not need a preamble to posit that Yahweh became the God of Israel through a covenant that he established at Mt. Sinai through Moses. One does not need a historical prologue to recognize the emphasis in the text on the Lord's faithfulness to Israel in delivering them with great power from the Egyptians, guiding them through the wilderness, and giving them the land of Canaan as an inheritance in fulfillment of the covenant he made with Abraham. One does not need "stipulations" to acknowledge that the Pentateuch is filled with apodictic ("thou shalt not . . .") and casuistic ("if . . . then . . .") commands. The total number of commands is irrelevant. The label that one assigns to a command is irrelevant. The commands stand in the text. One does not need "cursings" and "blessings" to feel the force of the consequences of obedience or disobedience to the Mosaic covenant. Finally, one does not need the terms "suzerain" and "vassal" to develop the nature of Yahweh's relationship to Israel: he is their king and they are his people! First Samuel 12:12 clearly states that the Lord God was the king of Israel and the request for a king "like the nations" was a slap in his face as King. A simple concordance study is enough to establish the axiomatic character of Israel as God's people in both Old and New Testaments. Regardless of whether the old covenant is a suzerainty-vassal treaty, the nature of it is clear: it is a pact between Yahweh and Israel, based upon Yahweh's deliverance of Israel from Egypt. This pact involves commitments on the part of Yahweh and on the part of Israel. Yahweh's commitments are stated in terms of his acts. Israel's commitments are stated in terms of her expected response. The response is minutely defined in terms of covenantal obligations that cover every aspect of Israelite existence. When the commitments are violated, clearly stated penalties will result; when the commitments are kept, clearly stated rewards or benefits will result.

The Purpose of the Old Covenant

John Walton has written a provocative study of the purpose of the biblical covenants (he actually prefers subsuming all the covenants under the rubric, "The Covenant").[8] Walton adduces texts from all over the Old Testament to prove that the purpose of the covenants is revelatory so that people might know him.[9] Walton argues that while the covenant is characteristically redemptive, and ultimately soteric, it is essentially revelatory.[10] His important statement concerning the interrelationship of covenant, salvation, and kingdom follows:

> In my proposal both salvation and kingdom are important aspects of the covenant-revelation program, but neither is the primary focus. They are both subsumed under the aegis of an overarching of God's revealing his character, his will, and his plan. In so doing, God provides a foundation for relationship with him (knowing God and being like him), a means by which that relationship might be achieved (salvation), and the structure that will define that relationship (kingdom).[11]

Walton states boldly that the Pentateuch and the Former Prophets comprise not a history of Israel, but a history of the covenant![12]

The Reasons for Keeping the Old Covenant

This writer has found eighteen reasons for Israel to keep the stipulations of the Mosaic covenant:

1. To show that Israel is Yahweh's possession (Exod. 19:5; Deut. 4:20; 7:6);
2. That Israel might serve as a kingdom of priests (Exod. 19:6);
3. That Israel might live as a holy nation (Exod. 19:6; Deut. 4:8; 6:25);
4. That Israel might live long lives (Lev. 18:5; 25:18; Deut. 4:1, 40; 5:33; 6:2; 8:1; 11:9; 30:16, 20; 32:47);
5. That Israel might not be like the pagan nations around them (Lev. 18:3, 24);
6. That Israel might be able to distinguish between the holy and profane (Lev. 10:10);
7. That Israel might live securely in the land (Lev. 25:18; Deut. 4:1, 5, 14, 25–28; 5:33; 6:18; 8:1; 11:8, 31–32; 30:16);

8. John H. Walton, *Covenant: God's Purpose, God's Plan* (Grand Rapids: Zondervan, 1994).
9. Ibid., 24. Major texts that corroborate Walton's thesis include Exod. 6:2–8; Deut. 4:32–40; 7:7–9; Ps. 106:7–8; 2 Sam. 7:22–24; Ezek. 16:59–63; 20:5–14, 19–22, 26, 38–44; 34:22–31; 36:19–23, 26–28, 31–32, 36–38; 37:24–28; Isa. 43:10–15; 43:25–28; 48:9–11; Jer. 14:21. See p. 32 for a chart of significant texts.
10. Ibid., 25.
11. Ibid., 29.
12. Ibid., 44.

8. That Israel might not defile the land that Yahweh owns and where he dwells (Lev. 25:23; Num. 35:34);
9. That Israel might acquire wisdom and understanding (Deut. 4:6);
10. That Israel might show fear for Yahweh (Deut. 4:10);
11. Because God is a jealous God (Deut. 4:24);
12. That it might be well with Israel forever (Deut. 5:29, 33; 6:3, 18; 12:28);
13. That Israel might multiply greatly (Deut. 6:3; 8:1; 30:16);
14. That Israel might be greatly blessed (Deut. 7:12–14; 11:14; 29:9; 30:8–10, 16);
15. For Israel's own good (Deut. 10:13);
16. So that Israel might be strong (Deut. 11:8);
17. Because it is right and good to do so (Deut. 12:28);
18. That Israel might be exalted above all the nations of the earth (Deut. 28:1).

This writer could not find one verse that taught that an Israelite would be saved eternally by keeping the law of Moses. And we have no indication anywhere that the Mosaic covenant was a mistake in salvation-history.

The Results of Not Keeping the Old Covenant

The following results would accrue to anyone in Israel who broke the stipulations of the covenant:

1. He would be excluded from the land (Deut. 1:32–38).
2. He would be defeated in battle (Deut. 1:41–45).
3. His life on earth would be short (Deut. 4:23–26).
4. Israel would be scattered among the nations (Deut. 4:27–28).
5. His sin would be visited on his children (Deut. 5:9).
6. He would be punished (Deut. 5:11; 7:10).
7. The anger of the Lord would be kindled (Deut. 6:15; 7:4; 11:17; 29:14–28; 31:17–18).
8. The Lord will wipe Israel off the face of the earth (Deut. 6:15; 8:19–20; 11:17).
9. There would be no rain and crops would fail (Deut. 11:17).
10. Transgressors would be put to death (Deut. 17:2–7).
11. Numerous curses would fall on the transgressor (Lev. 26; Deut. 11:26–30; 27:9–26; 28:15–68).

These curses did not fall automatically on the guilty party. In mercy and grace God had instituted the sacrificial system to avert the curses and restore the vassal to a proper relationship with the suzerain (king). Yet

Yahweh was not obligated to forbear his wrath, for under the covenant he had every right to punish immediately. But because he is merciful and slow to wrath, he delayed the execution of the curses until years later when he finally executed them by deporting Israel to Assyria and Babylonia.

The Motives for Keeping the Old Covenant

People seem to have had two primary motives for keeping the covenant: love for Yahweh, the suzerain; and fear of Yahweh, the suzerain. These two motives are prominent throughout the text of Deuteronomy.[13] The biblical texts, however, do not suggest that the motives for keeping covenant were to acquire righteousness with Yahweh. The Apostle Paul knew that the purpose of the covenant was not to provide some kind of merit system: "For if a law had been given that could impart life, then righteousness would certainly have come by the law" (Gal. 3:21). Paul therefore appeals to Genesis 15:6 and Habakkuk 2:4 as the key texts to define how a person is justified before God: righteousness is imputed to the sinner who by faith appropriates God's promises (Rom. 1:17; 4:3, 9; Gal. 3:6, 11). The love texts stress gratitude to Yahweh for his past deeds of faithfulness. Obedience to covenantal stipulations is grounded in a desire to show love to the Lord for what he has done. The fear texts reveal that Yahweh is not a god made in the Israelite's image. He is not someone with whom one can trifle. He is holy and expects his people to adhere to the covenantal stipulations. He is holy; his people are to be holy (Lev. 11:44–45; 19:2; 20:7, 26; see also 1 Pet. 1:16).

The Nature of the New Covenant

Classification of the new covenant receives little discussion. In passing, Barker calls it a *royal grant* covenant.[14] McComiskey argues that the Abrahamic and Davidic covenants are *promissory* covenants, while the old and the new covenants are *administrative* covenants.[15] By "administrative" he means "the kind of obedience necessary to ensure the eternal relationship

13. The love passages are: Deut. 5:10; 6:6; 7:9; 10:12; 11:1, 13, 22; 13:3; 19:9; 30:6, 16, 20. The fear passages are: Deut. 4:10; 5:29; 6:2, 13, 24; 8:6; 10:12, 20; 13:4; 14:23; 17:19; 21:21; 25:18; 28:58; 31:12, 13. For an excellent discussion of the love theme in Deuteronomy, see W. L. Moran, "The Ancient Near Eastern Background of the Love of God in Deuteronomy," *Catholic Biblical Quarterly,* 25 (1963): 77–87.

14. Kenneth L. Barker, "The Scope and Center of Old and New Testament Theology and Hope," in *Dispensationalism, Israel and the Church,* ed. Craig A Blaising and Darrell L. Bock (Grand Rapids: Zondervan, 1992), 310.

15. Thomas E. McComiskey, *The Covenants of Promise* (Grand Rapids: Baker, 1985), 167.

of God's people to the promised inheritance."[16] However, a number of factors complicate the classification of the new covenant. Consider the following:

1. In what sense is the new covenant "not like" the old covenant (Jer. 31:32)?
2. Is the new covenant a "new" covenant or a "renewed" old covenant?[17]
3. Unlike the old covenant, you cannot point to a passage in the New Testament and say, "This is the new covenant in its entirety." This requires a hypothetical reconstruction of the new covenant form along the lines of the reconstruction of the old covenant form from the Old Testament materials. Such reconstructions are always subject to debate and criticism and cannot serve as absolute bases for further exposition.
4. Many interpreters make an equation of the old covenant with law and the new covenant with grace. To classify the new covenant as a suzerainty-vassal covenant poses dangers to the gracious nature of the new covenant and allegedly turns grace into law again.
5. Only a few passages in the New Testament use the term "new covenant."

Only one New Testament passage uses the terminology "old covenant" (2 Cor. 3:14). The Book of Hebrews does use the word "covenant" in connection with the old covenant, but never with the adjective "old." The writer calls the old covenant the "first" covenant (Heb. 8:7, 13; 9:1, 15, 18). While many passages in both Testaments are related to the new covenant, these passages must be carefully studied and evaluated in terms of the contribution they make to the theology of the new covenant. This occasional appearance of new covenant texts and the lack of a full systematic development of the new covenant as a covenant in the texts creates great obstacles to anyone seeking to systematize a biblical theology of new covenant.

In light of these limitations and questions concerning the new covenant, the following positions presented by this author should be taken as *suggestive*, rather than *dogmatic*. The intent is to stimulate further discussion and study leading to more insight into the nature of the new covenant.

16. Ibid., 166.
17. For a defense of the new covenant as a "renewed" old covenant, see Walter C. Kaiser, Jr., "The Old Promise and the New Covenant: Jer. 31:31–34," *Journal of the Evangelical Theological Society*, 15 (1972): 11–23.

This writer suggests that the new covenant is "not like" the old covenant in respect to content and enablement, not in nature, purpose, and motives for keeping covenant. Since the new covenant seems to be a replacement for the old covenant in Jeremiah 31, 2 Corinthians 3, and Hebrews 8, it would appear reasonable to assume that the new covenant is also a suzerainty-vassal covenant. One would expect the new covenant to have a preamble, historical prologue, stipulations, and cursings and blessings formulae like the old covenant.

As stated above, the problem with finding a preamble or any other component in the New Testament texts is the absence in the New Testament of any systematic and full development of the new covenant as covenant. It is important to realize that even the covenantal sections of the Old Testament were not presented so clearly that one could turn to a specific section and say, "There is the old covenant." It was necessary to reconstruct the various parts of the old covenant on the basis of the Hittite parallels from the fragmented portions scattered throughout the Pentateuch. Keeping this in mind this writer believes that it is possible to reconstruct a hypothetical new covenant form from the New Testament texts. The following is that proposed reconstruction.

The Preamble

Since the new covenant is a covenant based in the shed blood of Jesus Christ (Luke 22:20), he is the inaugurator of the covenant. His title is the Lord Jesus Christ. The preamble would designate him as, "I am the Lord Jesus Christ." This identifies the suzerain of the new covenant with his three primary titles—Lord (κύριος), Savior (Ἰησοῦς), and Messiah (Χριστός).

The Historical Prologue

One is unsure how much to include in this section, but it must surely begin with, "Who died for your sins according to the Scriptures, was buried, and was raised the third day according to the Scriptures." One should probably add, "who ascended to heaven and now sits at the right hand of God as Lord and High Priest to his church." Like the old covenant, this historical prologue could be extended throughout the apostolic age as the risen Christ acted benevolently toward his church and on into church history as each succeeding century brought fresh deeds of kindness to Christians.

The Stipulations

Just as the old covenant stipulations were scattered throughout the Old Testament literature, the new covenant stipulations are scattered throughout the New Testament literature. It is difficult to determine how many new covenant stipulations are contained in the Gospels due to the fact that the Gospels are part of the old covenant age historically, but were written by Christians who were living in the new covenant age redemptively. Each command in the Gospels must be evaluated as to whether it is strictly an old covenant stipulation, a strictly new covenant stipulation, or a transitional command given during the shift from the old age to the new age.

An example of an old covenant Gospel command would be, "But go, show yourself to the priest and offer the gift Moses commanded, as a testimony to them" (Matt. 8:4). An example of a new covenant Gospel command would be, "Therefore go and make disciples of all nations, baptizing them in the name of the Father and of the Son and of the Holy Spirit, and teaching them to obey everything I have commanded you" (Matt. 28:19–20). An example of a transitional Gospel command would be: "Go and make preparations for us to eat the Passover" (Luke 22:8). The Passover is an old covenant feast, but it becomes a transitional base for the new covenant meal celebrated in the Christian community as a memorial of the crucified Lord (1 Cor. 11:23–26).

As far as this writer knows, no one has attempted to publish a complete list of the new covenant stipulations. Several former students of this writer began the process by investigating and categorizing Pauline directives in Acts and in Paul's thirteen epistles. One student listed 304 stipulations in Acts and the Epistles of Paul.[18] A second student built upon the work of the former and developed "A Taxonomy of New Testament Stipulations in Acts and Paul."[19] While the list is incomplete, the stipulations included show several important facts. First, the new covenant is not without commands and directives. Second, the new covenant stipulations cover the same categories as the old covenant stipulations. The list, "A Taxonomy of New Covenant Stipulations" (Figure 5.4) summarizes the findings of Kelly. Figure 5.5 is a chart of "The New Man Under the New Covenant." The latter chart should be compared with the Old Testament "Hierarchy of Laws" chart (see Figure 5.3). Such a comparison should clearly show that the basic categories are the same for both covenants. The difference, however, is that the old covenant stipulations are not the same as the new covenant stipulations. Thus, while the categories are the same, the content is different. The difference in content is due to the redemptive-historical change brought about by the death of Christ and the inclusion of the Gentiles into God's people. The old content was limited to an ethnic people, Israel; to a geographically circumscribed territory, Palestine; and to a socioeconomic structure based in an agrarian

---

18. This was a project done by Duane M. Duhon for a course taught by this writer entitled, "The Law in Romans and Galatians."

19. This work was submitted by Joan Aronson Kelly for another course taught by this writer entitled, "New Testament Studies II: Acts and Paul." Neither student extended the list into Hebrews; James; 1 or 2 Peter; 1, 2, or 3 John; or Jude.

economy. The new covenant content is directed toward all nations, anywhere in the earth, and in all socioeconomic structures. But the categories
of "Relationship with God" and "Relationship with Neighbor" and the
subcategories of "Worship," "Service," "Family," "Government," and
"Business" are transcovenantal (see Figure 5.3). They are, therefore, common to both covenants. Figure 5.6 is an attempt on this writer's part to
list which of the 613 stipulations counted by the Pharisees carry over into
the new covenant stipulations. This list of 95 stipulations should provide
further help in determining the lines of continuity and discontinuity between the covenants.

Figure 5.4

A Taxonomy of New Testament Stipulations in Acts and Paul

Table of Contents by Topic

I. The Christian's Relationship to God
  A. Christian Doctrine
    1. Proper worship
    2. Orthodox doctrine
    3. Heresy
    4. Idolatry
    5. Hope for the future
  B. The Church
    1. Church leaders
    2. Teaching and preaching
    3. Learning
    4. Support of teachers
    5. Church discipline
    6. Church decorum
    7. Prayer
II. Outliving the Christian Life in the World
  A. Sanctification of the Individual
    1. The Christian's status in Christ
    2. Living in accord with the new status
    3. The fruit of the Spirit
    4. Joy and thankfulness
    5. Humility
    6. Speech and the tongue
    7. Wisdom
    8. The Christian and works
    9. Self-examination
    10. Honesty
    11. Perseverance

12. Adversity
13. Vengeance
14. Separation
15. Sin and evil
16. Sexual impurity
17. Clothes
18. Christian liberty
B. Life in the Christian Community
  1. Mutual submission
  2. Selflessness
  3. Charity
  4. Peace
  5. Unity
  6. Accepting one another
  7. Judging one another
  8. Masters and slaves
  9. Family relationships
 10. Women
 11. Authority in the church
C. The Christian Life in an Unregenerate World
  1. Peace and tranquility
  2. Government and citizenship
  3. Sanctity of individuals
  4. Employment and money
  5. Relationships with unbelievers

Figure 5.5

The New Man under the New Covenant

I. The New Man's Relationship to God: Freedom to Love Him

A. *Worshiping God*
  1. In Spirit
    Outward Forms
    Reading Scripture
    Music
    Prayer
    Exhortation
    Teaching
    Tongue
    Interpretation
    Lord's Supper
    Revelation

Inner Attitudes
Humility
Lowliness
Submission
2. In Truth
Orthodox doctrine
Heresy
Idolatry
B. *Serving God*
1. Edification of the Brethren
Shepherding
Teaching
Giving
Discipline
Order
Prayer
2. Extension of the Gospel

II. The New Man's Relationship to Neighbor: Freedom to Love Him

A. *Self*
1. Indicative
a. The new status
b. The new ethic
2. Imperative
a. Fruit
b. Thanksgiving
c. Humility
d. Wisdom
e. Good works
f. Speech
g. Perseverance
h. Adversity
i. No vengeance
j. Separation
k. Dress
l. Freedom
m. Impurity
B. *Neighbor (Christian)*
1. Church
a. Submitting
b. Love
c. Peace
d. Unity

      e. Acceptance
   2. Family
      a. Husband/wife
      b. Parent/child
      c. Slave/master
      d. Orphans
      e. Widows
      f. Aged
C. *Neighbor (Pagan)*
   1. Government
      a. Obedience
      b. Citizenship
      c. Respect
   2. Business
      a. Respect
      b. Hard work
      c. Unto Lord
   3. Society
      a. Rebuke
      b. Confront
      c. Live within

Figure 5.6

The 95 Commandments of the 613 Pharisaic Commandments of the Torah Found Also in the New Covenant

1. One must believe that God exists (Exod. 20:2).
2. Acknowledge his unity (Deut. 6:4).
3. Love God (Deut. 6:5).
4. Fear God (Deut. 6:13).
5. Serve God (Exod. 23:25; Deut. 11:13).
6. Cleave to God (Deut. 10:20).
7. Imitate God (Deut. 28:9).
8. Sanctify God's name (Lev. 22:32).
9. Study the Torah and teach it to others (Deut. 6:7).
10. God is to be praised after meals (Deut. 8:10).
11. Israel is to honor its priests (Lev. 21:8).
12. One must confess one's sins before God and repent for them (Num. 5:6–7).
13. The Sanhedrin (government) was to be obeyed (Deut. 17:11).
14. In case of division, the majority opinion would prevail (Exod. 23:2).
15. Stolen property must be restored to its owners (Lev. 5:23).

16. Give charity to the poor (Lev. 25:33, 36; Deut. 15:8).
17. Pay the worker his wage on time (Deut. 24:15).
18. He is also to be permitted to eat of the produce with which he is working (Deut. 23:25–26).
19. Lost property must be restored to its owner (Exod. 23:4; Deut. 22:4).
20. It is required to reprove the sinner (Lev. 19:17).
21. It is required to love one's neighbor as oneself (Lev. 19:18).
22. One must also love the proselyte (Gentile) (Deut. 10:19).
23. Weights and measures must be accurate (Lev. 19:36).
24. Respect the wise (Lev. 19:32).
25. Honor one's parents (Exod. 20:12).
26. Fear one's parents (Lev. 19:3).
27. Marriage is to be governed by the law (Deut. 24:1).
28. Judgment must be rendered in cases of trespass.
29. This is true in all other matters (Deut. 25:12).
30. One must not believe in any but the one true God (Exod. 20:3).
31. Do not practice necromancy (Lev. 19:31).
32. Do not resort to familiar spirits (Lev. 19:31).
33. Do not take the mythology of idolatry seriously (Lev. 19:4).
34. Do not encourage Jews (Christians) to worship idols (Deut. 13:12).
35. Do not use anything connected with idols or idolatry (Deut. 7:26).
36. It is forbidden to prophesy falsely in the name of God (Deut. 18:20).
37. Do not imitate the ways of idolaters or practice their customs (Lev. 20:23).
38. Do not indulge in impure thoughts or sights (Num. 15:39).
39. Do not intermarry with pagans (Deut. 7:3).
40. Do not fear your enemy (Deut. 7:24).
41. Do not blaspheme the holy name (Lev. 24:16).
42. Do not take God's name in vain (Exod. 20:7).
43. Do not profane it (Lev. 22:32).
44. Do not try the Lord God (Deut. 6:16).
45. Do not break your word (Num. 30:3).
46. Gluttony and drunkenness is prohibited (Lev. 19:26; Deut. 21:20).
47. Do not muzzle an animal working in a field to prevent it from eating (Deut. 25:4).
48. One may not leave the Levites without support (Deut. 12:19).
49. Do not deny charity to the poor (Deut. 15:7).
50. Do not delay payment of wages (Lev. 19:13).
51. Do not steal (Lev. 19:11).
52. Do not defraud (Lev. 19:13).

53. Do not deceive anybody in business (Lev. 25:14).
54. Do not mislead a man even verbally (Lev. 25:17).
55. Do not afflict the widow or the orphan (Exod. 22:21).
56. Do not misuse a Hebrew (any) slave (Lev. 25:39).
57. Do not covet another man's possessions (Exod. 20:17).
58. Even the desire alone is forbidden (Deut. 5:18).
59. Do not give false testimony (Exod. 20:16).
60. Do not pronounce judgment on the basis of the testimony of one witness (Deut. 19:15).
61. Do not murder (Exod. 20:13).
62. Do not leave a stumbling block on the way (Deut. 22:8).
63. Do not tell tales (Lev. 19:16).
64. Do not bear hatred in your heart (Lev. 19:17).
65. Do not shame a Jew (Christian) (Lev. 19:17).
66. Do not bear a grudge (Lev. 19:18).
67. Do not take revenge (Lev. 19:18).
68. Do not rebel against the transmitters of the tradition of the law (Deut. 17:11).
69. Do not add to the precepts of the law (Deut. 13:1).
70. Do not subtract from the precepts of the law (Deut. 13:1).
71. Do not curse a ruler (Exod. 22:27).
72. It is forbidden to have sexual relations with one's mother (Lev. 18:7).
73. This is true also with one's stepmother (Lev. 18:8).
74. This is true with one's sister (Lev. 18:9).
75. This is true with one's stepsister (Lev. 18:11).
76. This is true with one's daughter-in-law (Lev. 18:10).
77. This is true with a granddaughter (Lev. 18:10).
78. This is true with a daughter (Lev. 18:10).
79. This is also forbidden between a mother and daughter (Lev. 18:17).
80. It is forbidden between a mother and her daughter-in-law (Lev. 18:17).
81. It is forbidden between a grandmother and her granddaughter (Lev. 18:17).
82. It is forbidden between nephew and aunt (Lev. 18:12).
83. It is forbidden between niece and aunt (Lev. 18:13).
84. It is forbidden with one's paternal uncle's wife (Lev. 18:14).
85. It is forbidden with one's daughter-in-law (Lev. 18:15).
86. It is forbidden with one's brother's wife (Lev. 18:16).
87. It is forbidden with one's wife's sister (Lev. 18:18).
88. Do not commit adultery (Lev. 18:20).

89. A man shall not have sexual relations with an animal (Lev. 18:23).
90. Homosexuality is forbidden (Lev. 18:22).
91. Homosexuality is forbidden with one's father (Lev. 18:7).
92. Homosexuality is forbidden with one's uncle (Lev. 18:14).
93. It is forbidden to have any intimate physical contact with anyone except one's own wife (Lev. 18:6).
94. Harlotry is forbidden (Deut. 23:18).
95. A divorcee may not be remarried to her first husband if, in the meanwhile, she has married another (Deut. 24:4).

The Cursings

New covenant curses are not as obvious as old covenant curses because the New Testament does not include specific curse chapters like Leviticus 26 or Deuteronomy 28 in the Old Testament. But punishment for disobedience to new covenant commands is clearly indicated in many passages:

Do you want to be free from fear of the one in authority? Then do what is right and he will commend you. For he is God's servant to do you good. But if you do wrong, be afraid, for he does not bear the sword for nothing. He is God's servant, an agent of wrath to bring punishment on the wrongdoer.

(Rom. 13:3–4)

For we will all stand before God's judgment seat.

(Rom. 14:10)

Do you not know that the wicked will not inherit the kingdom of God? Do not be deceived: Neither the sexually immoral nor idolaters nor adulterers nor male prostitutes nor homosexual offenders nor thieves nor the greedy nor drunkards nor slanderers nor swindlers will inherit the kingdom of God.

(1 Cor. 6:9–10)

Do not be deceived: God cannot be mocked. A man reaps what he sows. The one who sows to please his sinful nature, from that nature will reap destruction; the one who sows to please the Spirit, from the Spirit will reap eternal life.

(Gal. 6:7–8)

Marriage should be honored by all, and the marriage bed kept pure, for God will judge the adulterer and all the sexually immoral.

(Heb. 13:4)

The question of whether any eternal penalties are attached to breach of covenant is hotly debated. In regard to this Judith Volf wrote an entire dissertation devoted to the subject of perseverance.[20] Wolf appeals to Romans

20. Judith M. Gundry Volf, *Paul and Perseverance: Staying in and Falling Away* (Louisville: Westminster/John Knox, 1990).

8:29–30 as the fundamental Pauline text guaranteeing the final salvation of the elect.[21] She also appeals to 2 Thessalonians 2:13–14 as grounding salvation in God's election in eternity.[22] She argues that God not only elects to salvation but also supplies the means to realize this purpose, namely, sanctification and faith.[23] The Holy Spirit is God's guarantee that he is committed to the Christian's full redemption.[24] Philippians 1:6 is another text reflecting Paul's confidence that God will finish the work of salvation begun in the Philippian Christians.[25]

In order to accommodate Pauline statements that warn about the eschatological consequences of certain sins and apostasy to her thesis that nothing can thwart God's election to salvation, Volf maintains that such texts (e.g., 1 Cor. 6:9–10; 10:1–22; Gal. 6:7–8) are directed to the unbeliever, the unrighteous, the nonelect.[26] Paul's words threaten only those who are not genuine believers.[27] Those whose lives are characterized by vices have never truly been converted. They are "brothers" in name only.[28] Wrong conduct can indicate only three things: (1) the person is not a true believer; (2) the true Christian will experience divine chastisement; (3) the true Christian's sanctification will be retarded.[29]

Yet Volf admits that perseverance in holiness is a necessary part of final salvation. Continuance is the test of reality.[30] The threat to the Galatians' perseverance in the true gospel amidst the solicitations of the Judaizers is most serious.[31] In spite of Paul's use of "I fear" in Galatians 4:11, Volf insists that Paul is certain that the Galatians will not finally turn away from the gospel.[32] Volf must further argue that ἀδόκιμος in 1 Corinthians 9:27 does not refer to the loss of salvation but to failing the test of faithful service[33] and that the γάρ connective in 10:1 following 9:27 is "loose."[34] Thus the Corinthians are not in the same danger as the Israelites of committing sins such as idolatry and fornication that excluded Israel from the land (see Heb. 3:7–19) and exclude professing

21. Ibid., 9–14.
22. Ibid., 15–27.
23. Ibid., 20.
24. Ibid., 30.
25. Ibid., 46–47.
26. Ibid., 126.
27. Ibid., 136.
28. Ibid., 140.
29. Ibid., 157.
30. Ibid., 197 n. 231.
31. Ibid., 214.
32. Ibid., 215.
33. Ibid., 220 n. 97.
34. Ibid., 239.

Christians from the kingdom of God (1 Cor. 6:9–10). Further, the prize (βραβεῖον) in 1 Corinthians 9:24 is the glory that comes from having made voluntary sacrifices in the Christian life out of love, but the prize (βραβεῖον) in Philippians 3:14 is final salvation.[35] In conclusion, Volf concedes that God's purpose to save Christians completely and finally does not mean that the process is "automatic."[36] Certainty of final salvation ought not and need not foster complacency and carelessness on the part of Christians.[37]

In contrast to Volf is the approach of I. Howard Marshall to the problem. His entire volume attempts to establish the thesis that the warnings in Scripture against falling away are not to be lightly explained away as hypothetical or unreal, but are meant to be taken with full seriousness as warnings against a real danger.[38] Marshall writes of a "tension" between being kept by the power of God and the threats to the Christian that jeopardize his faith.[39] Marshall maintains that God's promises always appear to be conditional on the faith and obedience of his people.[40] Marshall's analysis of the Gospels leads him to conclude that election in itself does not guarantee perseverance nor does it exclude the possibility of apostasy.[41] The condition of salvation is the steadfast endurance that does not give way under temptation but remains loyal to God and his will.[42] Marshall does not believe that the faithfulness of God rules out the faithlessness of people.[43] Marshall believes there is a direct link between 1 Corinthians 6:9–10 and 1 Corinthians 10.[44] The warnings to the Corinthians in chapter 10 are based on the experience of Israel and are not to be dismissed as hypothetical. Therefore, a "paradox" exists between God's care for the believer and the believer's need to persevere in the faith.[45] Marshall summarizes:

> Paul, then, did not regard grace as operating in such a mechanical fashion that the believer is inevitably carried on to perfection with no effort on his part. The paradox of grace and freewill is not to be solved by emphasizing the former to the exclusion of the latter. While Paul certainly anticipated the final perseverance of the vast majority of his converts, he never regarded this perse-

---

35. Ibid., 246 n. 74; compare with p. 259 in Gundry's work.
36. Ibid., 283.
37. Ibid., 284.
38. I. Howard Marshall, *Kept by the Power of God* (Minneapolis: Bethany, 1969), 12.
39. Ibid., 22.
40. Ibid., 34.
41. Ibid., 72.
42. Ibid., 74.
43. Ibid., 107.
44. Ibid., 116.
45. Ibid., 123.

verance as something predetermined and inevitable; always there pressed upon him 'the care of all the churches,' a care which involved him in constant prayer and effort lest any member should fall away and so cause him to have run his course in vain.[46]

It is possible to conclude that the curses of the covenant do include eternal consequences. It is legitimate to say that God's ends or purposes include God's means. God's means to eternal salvation are faith and endurance in covenantal stipulations. For Volf, true Christians will meet the means and thus arrive at the end because of their election by God. For Marshall, some Christians may apostatize and fail to arrive at the end because they did not meet the means of their own volition. Whichever interpretation is ultimately correct, the truth remains that God intends for the stipulations of the new covenant to be kept and that obedience and transgression are rewarded appropriately. Whether these covenant-breakers are true Christians or only "professing" Christians, eternal consequences await them.

The Blessings

Like new covenant cursings, new covenant blessings do not occur in whole chapters or specific sections. The blessings come in at the end of sections containing a list of stipulations: "a spirit of unity" (Rom. 15:5); "joy and peace . . . hope . . . power" (Rom. 15:13); "reward" (1 Cor. 3:14); "All things" (1 Cor. 3:21); "praise" (1 Cor. 4:5); "all grace" (2 Cor. 9:8); "thanks to God" (2 Cor. 9:12); "blameless and pure" (Phil. 2:15); "God is pleased" (Heb. 13:16). These blessings and cursings should be compared with the old covenant blessings and cursings. The major difference between the two covenants seems to be the material blessings and cursings of the old covenant versus the immaterial blessings and cursings of the new covenant.

The Purpose of the New Covenant

Based upon Walton's contention that the purpose of all covenants is revelatory so that people might know God, we maintain that the purpose of the new covenant is revelatory so that people might know God through the Lord Jesus Christ. This purpose will be developed more fully below when the various new covenant texts are examined.

At this point it is sufficient to note that a great number of texts in the New Testament stress "knowing," employing the two Greek verbs γιν-

46. Ibid., 125.

ὤσκω[47] and οἶδα.[48] According to Jeremiah 31:34, knowing God would be one of the major provisions of the new covenant.

The Motives for Keeping the New Covenant

The same two motives for keeping the old covenant seem to be the motives for keeping the new covenant: love for the Lord and fear of the Lord. In the new covenant the Lord is not only the God of Israel but the Lord Jesus Christ of the church. Probably because of the emphasis in the New Testament on the love of God and Christ for people and the love of the redeemed for the Redeemer, the love texts are more common than the fear texts.[49] But 1 John seems to teach that the ultimate motive is love. The one who has been perfected in love casts fear out as a motive.

Is the New Covenant a New Covenant or a Renewed Old Covenant?

Bozak represents many writers who opt for a renewed old covenant instead of a new covenant. She states that the content of the new covenant is the same as that of the old—same Torah, same partners. The newness appears not in the content but in the manner of establishing the relationship and in its consequences of unmediated knowledge of Yahweh.[50] The major strength of this view is that it observes the statement that Yahweh will write his Torah on the hearts of his people. The implication is that the Torah of the old covenant and the Torah of the new covenant are either identical or virtually synonymous.

This writer, however, believes that there are good reasons for believing that the new covenant is actually a new covenant and not a renewed old covenant. First, according to McComiskey, Jeremiah's use of "new" should be understood in the strictest sense of the word. The new covenant

47. For example, Matt. 13:11; Luke 24:35; John 8:28, 32; 10:14, 38; 13:35; 14:7, 17, 20, 31; 17:3, 8, 23, 25; Acts 2:36; 22:14; 1 Cor. 13:9, 12; 2 Cor. 5:16; 8:9; Gal. 4:9; Eph. 3:19; Phil. 3:10; Heb. 8:11; 10:34; 1 John 2:3, 5, 13, 14; 3:6, 16, 19, 24; 4:2, 6, 7, 8, 13, 16; 5:20; 2 John 1.

48. For example, 1 Cor. 2:2, 12; 3:16; 5:6; 6:2, 3, 9, 15; 6:16, 19; 8:4; 15:58; 2 Cor. 4:14; 5:1, 6, 11; Gal. 2:16; 4:8; Eph. 1:18; 5:5; Col. 3:24; 4:1; 1 Thess. 1:4; 4:5; 5:2; 2 Thess. 1:8; 2 Tim. 1:12; Heb. 8:11; 1 John 2:20, 21, 29; 5:20.

49. The key love texts are John 14:15, 21; 15:10; 1 John 2:5; 4:20–21; 5:2–3; 2 John 6. The fear texts are 1 Pet. 2:17; Rev. 19:5; Acts 5:5, 11; 9:31; 2 Cor. 5:11; 7:1; Eph. 5:21; 1 Tim. 5:20; 1 Pet. 1:17.

50. Barbara A. Bozak, *Life 'Anew': A Literary-Theological Study of Jer 30–31* (Rome: Biblical Institute Press, 1991), 121.

is not comprised of the complex structure of legal statutes given through Moses.[51]

Second, three perfectly good Greek words for "renew" or "renewal" are never used in conjunction with either the old or new covenants in the New Testament. Rather ἀνακαινίζω is used of repentance (Heb. 6:1); ἀνακαινόω is used of the inner man (2 Cor. 4:16) and the new man (Col. 3:10), and ἀνακαίνωσις is used of the mind (Rom. 12:2) and of the renewal produced in the Christian by the Holy Spirit (Tit. 3:5).

Third, the idea of renewal is foreign to the parable of the wineskins and garments as developed in chapter 3 of this book. The old would be "good enough" with a few adjustments.

Fourth, the writer to the Hebrews does not seem to consider the new covenant a renewed old covenant. In Hebrews 7:12 he argues that the change from the Aaronic priesthood to the Melchizedekian priesthood requires a change of law (νόμος). Jesus is the surety of a better covenant (7:22) and the mediator of a better covenant. The new covenant is established ("legally enacted" is the meaning of νομοθετέω in 8:6) upon better promises, and the new covenant has better sacrifices (9:23). The fact that the new covenant is called "new" implies that the first covenant is in an antiquated state. The old covenant is therefore worn out and about to vanish (8:13). The term "renewal" hardly seems to apply!

Fifth, those who argue for a renewed old covenant have to make all sorts of adjustments to the old covenant in order to make it applicable to the church. A common approach is to divide the old covenant up into moral, civil, and ceremonial stipulations. Then the civil and ceremonial are said to be fulfilled in the death of Christ. This leaves the moral as still obligatory. It is difficult to understand how this is a renewal of the old covenant along the lines of Deuteronomy, Joshua 24, and Nehemiah 9. Another approach is to adopt a so-called principle hermeneutic for applying the old covenant to the Christian. Interestingly, Kaiser, who is an advocate of the "renewed" view, ends up with his "principles" in the same place the new covenant stipulations end.[52] One wonders why others have such a desire to retain old covenant stipulations. Are new covenant stipulations inadequate? Or do Old Testament scholars have a proclivity to protect the Old Testament from retirement as a rule of life for Christians?

Sixth, even those who argue for a renewed old covenant write of "newness" and "radical change."[53] Anderson writes that "Jeremiah's oracle can-

---

51. McComiskey, 167.

52. Walter C. Kaiser, Jr., "How Can Christians Derive Principles from the Specific Commands of the Law?" in *Readings in Christian Ethics. Volume 1: Theory and Method*, ed. David K. Clark and Robert V. Rakestraw (Grand Rapids: Baker, 1994), 192–201.

53. Bozak, 128.

not be understood as reactualization of the past sacred history. He speaks of a new covenant, not a covenant renewal, and thereby assumes a radical break with the Mosaic tradition."[54]

Seventh, the fact that some old covenant stipulations are reincorporated into new covenant stipulations does not mean the new covenant is the same as the old covenant or that the new is a reworking of the old. The structural similarities previously developed as "Relationship with God" and "Relationship with Neighbor," along with their respective subcategories (see Figure 5.3), would certainly cause one to expect some directives common to both covenants. In fact, one would be surprised if the two covenants had nothing in common since God gave both of them! We conclude, therefore, that the new covenant *is* a new covenant, *not* a renewed old covenant. The character of the new covenant does not mean that there is complete discontinuity between the two covenants. But enough discontinuity exists to maintain the distinctiveness of each covenant.

The New Covenant Texts

There is a general agreement among scholars that Ezekiel 11:14–21, 36:22–32, and Jeremiah 31:31–34 are pertinent Old Testament texts in respect to the new covenant, and that Luke 22:20, 1 Corinthians 11:25, 2 Corinthians 3:1–18, and Hebrews 7–13 (esp. Heb. 8) are pertinent New Testament texts in respect to the new covenant. Also, Malatesta has shown that the Johannine literature is permeated with new covenant motifs, even though the term new covenant is not explicitly used.[55]

Ezekiel 11

Ezekiel speaks in a time of great distress to a people conquered by the Babylonians. He notes Israel's deliverance into the hands of foreigners who will execute the Lord's judgments on her. In 11:13 Ezekiel mourns and asks God whether he will bring the remnant to a complete end. God responds with a message of hope, promising to regather his people and give them the land of Israel again; the people will cleanse the land of all its abominations when they return to Palestine (11:17–18). In 11:19 Ezekiel speaks of God giving his people one heart and putting a new Spirit within them so that they may walk in his statutes and keep his ordinances. They will then be his people and he will be their God. According to Zimmerli, this is a firm promise of a new being that will transform the old evil one. He states, "The heart, the seat of both thought and of the will, must be changed. Its hard-

54. Bernhard W. Anderson, "The New Covenant and the Old," in *The Old Testament and Christian Faith*, ed. Bernhard W. Anderson (New York: Harper and Row, 1963), 232.
55. Edward Malatesta, *Interiority and Covenant* (Rome: Biblical Institute Press, 1978).

ness, described as a stony heart, must give place to a new genuine vitality, to a heart of flesh. The spirit must become new."[56]

Ezekiel 36

In this context Ezekiel reviews God's work of intervening for his people, causing them to experience deliverance and restoration. God has been acting to vindicate his holy name that Israel profaned (Ezek. 36:21–23), so that the nations will know Yahweh is Lord. But God will take Israel from among the nations and cleanse them, give them a new heart and a new spirit. He will put his Spirit within Israel and cause them to walk in his ways (36:26–27). Zimmerli observes that the heart, which until now has been hard as stone and has remained deaf to the call of obedience, will become alive. The heart will change as a result of Yahweh's new activity. What is new here is the obedience that is now possible with regard to Yahweh's commands and the new way of life.[57] According to Allen, Yahweh would remake their human natures so they would march to the music of the covenant terms that expressed Yahweh's nature and will. Only then could the covenant relationship become a living actuality rather than a doctrinal truth.[58] Wevers notes that the gift of the divine Spirit was characteristic of apocalyptic notions of the age to come (Ezek. 39:29; Joel 2:28–29; Acts 2:4–21, 33; 10:44–47; 15:8; 19:2–7).[59]

Jeremiah 31

Jeremiah moves beyond Ezekiel and actually mentions the new covenant in his prophecy. But the parallels among all three passages are numerous and form a core of truth about the new covenant: God will restore, cleanse, take away a stony heart, give a new heart of flesh and a new spirit, put his Spirit within his people so that his people will know him and walk in his ways, and establish an intimate relationship between himself and his people.

It is important to observe the significant statements that Jeremiah makes:

1. The new covenant was not a reality during Jeremiah's day but was to be a fervent expectation on the part of Israel.
2. These verses in Jeremiah 31 contain six "I's" and two "my's." Thus, the emphasis is upon what the Lord *himself* will do.
3. The covenant will be a new covenant.

56. Walter Zimmerli, *Ezekiel 1*, Hermeneia (Philadelphia: Fortress, 1979), 262.
57. Ibid., *Ezekiel 2*, Hermeneia (Philadelphia: Fortress, 1983), 249.
58. Leslie C. Allen, *Ezekiel 20–48*, WBC (Dallas: Word, 1990), 179.
59. John W. Wevers, *Ezekiel*, NCBC (Grand Rapids: Eerdmans, 1982), 193.

4. The covenant will be made with the house of Israel and with the house of Judah.
5. The new covenant will stand in contrast with the old covenant: it will not be like the covenant that God made with their fathers when he brought them out of the land of Egypt.
6. The old covenant will be replaced because of Israel's failure to keep it. The onus on Israel is particularly acute because Yahweh was a husband to Israel under the old covenant arrangement.
7. The Lord will put his Torah within his people by "writing" it on their hearts.
8. This writing activity will rejoin God with his people.
9. All who become a part of this new covenant community will know the Lord innately. No one will need to instruct the vassals in the knowledge of the suzerain because every vassal will know the suzerain from the least of them to the greatest of them—young/old; powerful/weak; servant/master; child/parent; leader/led; rich/poor; male/female.
10. The greatest gift of all will be the permanent forgiveness of sins.

According to Raitt, the new covenant is not a reaffirming of the terms of the old covenant. The Israel of the future is not the Israel of the past. It is freed from its sin and changed in order to relate to God in a new way. The people will be changed internally. This change is prerequisite to the realization of the kingdom of God within history.[60] Bright concurs: "The people of this covenant are the people of God's Kingdom, for they are the pure in heart who have been, as it were, born again. The old covenant thus points to a solution beyond itself—the creation of a new people."[61] Raitt articulates in what ways the new covenant is "old." It is "old" in so far as:

1. it is unilaterally initiated by God;
2. it requires knowledge of the people;
3. it carries "law" as its central structuring norm;
4. it is made with Israel and Judah.

He also lists how the new covenant is "new." It is "new" in that:

1. it will contain full and free forgiveness;
2. it effects an inner relationship between God and a person;
3. a new humanity is created that has a new level of obedience and knowledge of God required of and made possible for it;

60. Thomas M. Raitt, *A Theology of Exile* (Philadelphia: Fortress, 1977), 199–200.
61. John Bright, *The Kingdom of God* (Nashville: Abingdon, 1953), 126.

4. the covenant is inviolable;
5. it combines an unprecedented grace with traditional law;
6. it is based on a new act of divine deliverance;
7. God calls it "new."

Raitt thinks that it is also new in terms of "speech-genre." This seems to mean that he advocates a different type of covenant than the suzerainty-vassal form.[62] This writer has already stated previously in this chapter why he thinks that the new covenant is a suzerainty-vassal type covenant. Regardless of the form-critical identification of the new covenant, Raitt's seven observations regarding the new covenant are on target.

Ezekiel 11, 36, and Jeremiah 31 are the three basic Old Testament passages that speak of a future day after dispersion, judgment, and purging when God will restore his people. A tremendous renovation will result in their lives, transforming Israel from a rebellious people who have profaned Yahweh's name among the nations into a people who will reflect his character. This renovation will be due to the work of Yahweh's Spirit. A spiritual operation will take place in which the corrupt heart of stone will be excised and replaced by an implant of flesh that will be sensitive to God. As a result, Israel will manifest a proper orientation to the Lord.

Luke 22

Jesus celebrated the Passover in an upper room with his disciples according to Matthew 26:18; Mark 14:14; and Luke 22:11. John 13 is a thorough account of the proceedings before the meal. Luke 22 is the fullest account of the symbolism of the loaf and the cup: the loaf represented the Lord's body that he would offer on the cross, and the cup represented his blood that he would shed on the cross. This shed blood would be the sacrifice that would inaugurate the new covenant. Along with the new covenant, Jesus instituted a new memorial feast that would replace the old Passover feast. As the living Lamb, without blemish and without spot, Jesus would bear the sins of the world (John 1:29; 1 Pet. 1:19). The whole Passover feast would be summarized in him as Paul stated: "Christ, our Passover, was sacrificed for us" (1 Cor. 5:7). According to Ware, Jesus' death for sin would provide the basis for the new covenant's enactment. There could be no other way for the desired forgiveness of sin than the Lamb of God taking away the sin of the world. This sacrificial base for the new covenant is amply expounded in the Book of Hebrews.[63]

62. Raitt, 201.
63. Bruce A. Ware, "The New Covenant and the People(s) of God," in *Dispensationalism, Israel and the Church,* ed. Craig A. Blaising and Darrell L. Bock (Grand Rapids: Zondervan, 1992), 85–86.

First Corinthians 11

First Corinthians 11 follows on Paul's discussion in chapters 8–10 regarding eating meals in a pagan temple and eating meat purchased in the Corinthian meat market for meals at home. The close connection with chapter 11 is seen at 10:16–17 where Paul begins a series of rhetorical questions: "Is not the cup of thanksgiving for which we give thanks a participation in the blood of Christ? And is not the bread that we break a participation in the body of Christ? Because there is one loaf, we, who are many, are one body, for we all partake of the one loaf." In 10:21 Paul insists, "You cannot drink the cup of the Lord and the cup of demons; you cannot have a part in both the Lord's table and the table of demons."

The discussion in chapters 8–10 has prepared the way for the directives about another meal, the Lord's meal. The use of δεῖπνον in verse 11:20 shows that Paul is referring to a whole meal because the Old Testament Passover feast background and the Gospel tradition indicate that a whole meal was eaten and because the word δεῖπνον is the technical Greek word for dinner.[64] The fact that some of the Corinthians were becoming drunk and had overeaten (v. 21) proves that the observance included more than what we include today—a wafer and a small glass of grape juice.

So what was happening at Corinth? Theissen in his *The Social Setting of Early Christianity* provides a good background.[65] The church was gathering in houses comprised of two rooms: a small triclinium, where three couches were used for reclining while eating, and a larger atrium. Murphy-O'Connor estimates that the triclinium would hold a maximum of nine people and the larger atrium between thirty and forty.[66] Theissen proposes that wealthy Corinthian Christians were gathering in the triclinium and having a "private" meal. The poor in the church were consigned to the outer atrium. The wealthy probably arrived early and proceeded to consume almost all of the food and to become inebriated from imbibing too much wine. All of this took place prior to the arrival of the poor, leaving them with little food to eat and little wine to drink. This resulted in hard feelings and created a schism between the rich and the poor.[67]

Paul's response to the Corinthians was not a directive to stop eating together. Instead, it was a directive to really start eating together! So far the

64. William F. Arndt and F. Wilbur Gingrich, *A Greek-English Lexicon of the New Testament and Other Early Christian Literature* (Chicago: The University of Chicago Press, 1957), 172.

65. Gerd Theissen, *The Social Setting of Pauline Christianity* (Philadelphia: Fortress, 1982).

66. Jerome Murphy-O'Connor, *St. Paul's Corinth* (Wilmington, Del.: Michael Glazier, 1983), 156.

67. Theissen, 151.

Corinthians had turned a meal that was instituted by the Lord, based in his blood that inaugurated the new covenant, into a private, individualistic, hedonistic indulgence. Instead of unity in the assembly they had divisions. Instead of eating the *Lord's* supper each was eating *his own* supper. Instead of demonstrating covenantal love at the love feast (ἀγάπη), they were displaying terrible selfishness. Instead of satisfying their ravenous appetites at home, they were overindulging at the community meal. Instead of edifying one another, the rich were bringing shame on the poor. What they were doing was being done in an unworthy manner.

Their ungodly and reprehensible behavior was due to a lack of perception of the Lord's body and the nature of the new covenant. Commentators have devoted much discussion to whether the word "body" refers to the church or to the Lord's physical body that he offered on the cross, but it is unnecessary to determine exactly what Paul had in mind. Those who were eating selfishly really did not grasp the significance of the church or the covenantal relationship they had with one another. Also, these egotistical Corinthians had completely forgotten an important purpose of Christ's death: to demolish the barriers that separated people from each other and to reconcile all in one body to God (Eph. 2:15, 16; 2 Cor. 5:18; Col. 1:22)! In this new covenant community division and strife were out of order. The dichotomy between rich and poor was unacceptable. If one did not "discern the body," he slighted what Christ had accomplished in his death and slighted the church, Christ's mystical body. In 1 Corinthians 12 Paul will develop the theme of the unity of the body and the need for the members to have the same care for one another (12:25).

The Corinthians needed to come to their senses and eat in community. If they continued their present practice, they would continue to experience covenantal curses, such as the death and sickness already being experienced by some Christians at Corinth. They needed to wait until all were present before eating together, and they needed to share the food so that no one went home hungry feeling cheated. Paul would settle the other problems when he came to Corinth.

Second Corinthians 3

This is the longest passage in the Pauline literature devoted to the new covenant. Paul has been reminding the Corinthians that suffering necessarily accompanies the spread of the Gospel. Much can be learned through suffering. One of the brethren who had been disciplined had suffered enough and had learned his lesson. It was necessary, therefore, for the Corinthians to restore, forgive, and comfort this brother because he had repented and turned from his sin.

In 2 Corinthians 3 Paul begins an apologetic toward those who had questioned his credentials as an apostle of Jesus Christ. According to Stockhausen 2 Corinthians 3:1–4:6 is the doctrinal heart of 2 Corinthians.[68] Paul is drawing on an event in the life of Moses described in Exodus 34 and using Moses as a model for contemporary Christian Jews like himself.[69] Paul's argument unfolds through his use of two basic rabbinic exegetical rules: (1) lesser to greater (*kal va-homer*); and (2) hook words (*gezera shava*).[70] Apparently Paul's critics had demanded official papers legitimizing Paul as a genuine apostle of Jesus Christ. Paul responded to the demand by stating that the Corinthians were his "official papers," known and read by all people. If Paul's life and the lives of the Corinthians are seen as authentically Christian, then the existence of the Corinthian Christian community is a witness to Paul's effective apostleship.[71] This authentic life of Paul and the Corinthians is presented by using hook word connections centered around the new covenant as found in Jeremiah 31 and other Old Testament texts that interpret Exodus 34.[72] The hook words are: (1) new covenant; (2) hearts of flesh; (3) stone tablets; and (4) engraved on the heart. Each of these phrases has its source in the Septuagint.[73] Jeremiah 31 and 32 are connected through the word "covenant," while "spirit" is the most significant link between Ezekiel 11 and 36.[74] The interrelationship between the texts via the hook words would cause an individual or community familiar with the Septuagint to associate the Spirit with Jeremiah's new covenant in spite of the fact that Jeremiah does not mention the Spirit.[75] These hook words and Old Testament passages form a "covenant pool," which includes: (1) a new covenant; (2) written on hearts; (3) knowledge of God; (4) forgiveness of sins and divine mercy; (5) a reconstituted people of God; (6) the Spirit; and (7) spiritual reality.[76] Jeremiah 32:38–40 contributes the ideas of the eternity of the covenant and the fear of the Lord as a characteristic of God's renewed people to the conceptual pool.[77]

Paul's use of "written on our hearts" (2 Cor. 3:2) was new covenant terminology and led to the following comparison between the new and the old covenants. Written letters of recommendation fall implicitly on the side of superseded Mosaic writing, clearly inappropriate for a minister of the new covenant. For Paul the interior recommendation of a heart enlivened by the

68. Carol Kern Stockhausen, *Moses' Veil and the Glory of the New Covenant* (Rome: Biblical Institute Press, 1989), 6.
    69. Ibid., 24.
    70. Ibid., 25.
    71. Ibid., 37.
    72. Ibid., 41.
    73. Ibid., 43.
    74. Ibid., 56.
    75. Ibid., 62.
    76. Ibid., 63.
    77. Ibid., 65.

divine spirit suffices, along with the obvious existence of a new people of God created by that same spirit.[78] God had written his Torah on the hearts of the Corinthians. They knew the Lord. This was sufficient proof of the authenticity of Paul's gospel and his new covenant ministry. The gospel is known to be authentic because of what it accomplishes in the lives of people—regenerated lives that serve as living epistles, not external stone tablets or papyrus scrolls. The Corinthians were not just a document written with ink, but a living expression of the work of the Spirit of the living God. Because of God's regenerative work, Paul can present the Corinthians as trophies of God's grace. Paul is a liturgical minister of the new covenant in contrast to Aaron, the liturgical minister of the Sinai covenant.[79] Just as God had qualified Moses as an able servant of the old covenant (Exod. 4:10), God has now qualified Paul as an able servant of the new covenant.[80] Paul, therefore, sets himself as an equal beside Moses.[81]

Paul, however, is both like and unlike Moses. He is unlike Moses because he can be bold and does not veil himself in either shame or humility. He is like Moses because he also has a share in the glory that is given to the minister of God's covenant with Israel.[82]

The new covenant was one not of "letter" but of "Spirit." The contrast here is not a hermeneutical one of a "literal" versus a "spiritual" interpretation, but of something exterior versus something interior.[83] The letter kills, but the Spirit gives life. This ambiguous statement about letter and spirit needed explanation and Paul devotes the rest of 2 Corinthians 3 to an exposition of these terms. A chart of Paul's contrasts is helpful at this point (see Figure 5.7). These contrasts illustrate the radical newness and superiority of the new covenant to the old covenant. The old covenant must be canceled as a contractual arrangement between God and his people. Paul's word for this canceling is καταργέω (see also Rom. 7:2, 6; 2 Cor. 3:11, 13, 14; Eph. 2:15). The old covenant is null and void, no longer valid (see also Heb. 8:13).

Now the Holy Spirit gives life. He is a personal being who causes the change from a heart of stone to one of flesh. The letter of the old covenant was fixed and external. The stone tablets used by Moses were particularly symbolic of the intrinsic inflexibility of the Mosaic law. This inflexible code was so limited in its ability to deal with the dynamics of changing circumstances of life that the Pharisees and scribes devoted the major part of their lives to the contextualization of the code.

78. Ibid., 72.
79. Ibid., 80.
80. Ibid., 84–85.
81. Ibid., 85.
82. Ibid., 94.
83. Ibid., 105.

Figure 5.7

Comparison Between the Old and New Covenants in 2 Corinthians 3

Old Covenant	New Covenant
Letter	Spirit
Kills	Gives life
Engraved on stones	Engraved on hearts
Fading glory	Increasing glory
Ministry of condemnation	Ministry of righteousness
Despair	Hope and boldness
Veil put on	Veil removed
Bondage	Liberty
Moses	Christ
Impotent to transform	Potent to transform

People have recognized the inherent limitations of any external code that is fixed in writing. In order to contextualize the letter, it must be constantly qualified, expanded, deleted, emended, and even countermanded. Those involved in law enforcement have a continual problem with enforcing the letter because of "loopholes," gray areas, and special situations. Circumstances such as a father-to-be breaking the speed limit while rushing his expectant wife to the hospital require a less than literal application of the statutes regarding speed limit. People can easily provide reasons for why the "letter of the law" should be set aside and changed into a less rigid rule.

The letter is fine and good, but inherently limited because of the inflexible nature of its demands. Life is so dynamic and complex that all of the laws that people have ever devised are still insufficient to cover the variety of circumstances that the letter of the law must address. The legal courts of our country are in constant session attempting to interpret the application of codes to everyday life. The law student must not only memorize the laws, but the whole history of their interpretation. When the Pharisees attempted to do that, the result was the huge Babylonian Talmud!

The letter is always in tension between simplicity and complexity. If it is too simple, it cannot possibly cover all the cases. If it is too complex, people find it too difficult either to understand it or apply it. In contrast, the

Spirit is internal and flexible. He is an ever-present monitor who automatically adjusts to each situation and each individual.

This is not to imply that the indwelling Spirit makes no demands or that new covenant life sanctions antinomianism. The new covenant is not a relaxation of morals or ethics. It demands purity not only in actions but in intentions and thoughts. The Pauline approach to new covenant morality is not antinomian.[84] The Spirit personalizes the Torah or teaching of God by inscribing it inwardly. By no means does the Spirit give free reign to satisfying the lusts of the flesh; rather the Spirit is a constant indwelling guide and enabler who is flexible. Indeed, under the Spirit many things previously precluded under the old covenant are now permitted under the new covenant. For example, all foods are clean and no special days or weeks need to be esteemed above others. The Spirit may even permit freedom to one Christian while denying that freedom to another Christian. Interestingly, according to Romans 14, the strong brother can eat anything, while the weak brother can only eat what his conscience allows. To do otherwise is to sin. The Spirit is able to so tailor things that each Christian can be fully persuaded in his own mind that he is pleasing his Master. The Spirit is not an anarchist. He provides guidelines and directives that encompass the New Testament documents. But the fundamental difference is that the Spirit is not the inanimate, inflexible, impersonal letter of the law, but the living, intelligent, and personal monitor.

The new covenant not only has directives, but it also provides an example and a dynamic. The example is Jesus himself who serves as the model for doing the will of God. The dynamic is the Holy Spirit. Under the old covenant there was no intrinsic equipment providing enablement to overcome a person's basic inability incurred by the Fall to do the will of God. It is like a child's toy that has a statement on its package that says, "Battery not included." What a frustrating experience to discover on Christmas morning that the new toy truck purchased for Junior will not work because it lacks four "D" cells. Nice truck, but it won't run! This is not to say that the Holy Spirit had no *presence* during the old covenant period; but the Spirit provided no *power* as an intrinsic provision of that old covenant. The new covenant comes with "batteries included." The new covenant is functional from the start. It is not "weak through the flesh" (Rom. 8:3). The Spirit internalizes the new covenant so that the people of God are motivated to do God's will. By contrast, the old covenant stood over the people of Israel like a judge, demanding obedience, but providing no enablement.

The "written on the heart" terminology in Ezekiel, Jeremiah, and Paul seems to refer to regeneration. The beauty of the new covenant is that the

---

84. See T. J. Deidun, *New Covenant Morality in Paul* (Rome: Biblical Institute Press, 1981).

internalization produces a regenerate community. All individuals within such a community know God innately and have a relationship with him through this new birth. Christians cry out "Abba, Father" through the Spirit as the Spirit regenerates them and gives them an awareness of God so that they are sensitive to God. Believers are not immediately given a *complete* knowledge of God and all that God desires of them. Rather they have a *sufficient* knowledge of him to enable them to begin new covenant life and experience the transformation from glory to glory.

First John 2:27 says that believers have no need of teaching due to the anointing from the Holy One. Obviously, John is not saying that the church has no need for any teachers. If he were, then he was wasting his own time writing this letter to tell these Christians they had no need of him! John is teaching that the Spirit of God comes upon believers in regeneration and places them into a position with the living Lord in which they have no need for anyone to teach them how to know the Lord, for they know him intrinsically, although not exhaustively. Knowing more about him is accomplished progressively through teaching and continued growth (i.e., "abiding or remaining [μένω] in him").

When believers receive Christ, they participate in the new covenant and the Spirit writes this sensitivity to God upon each individual's heart (i.e., their intellect, sensibility, and will). The intellect is enlightened by the Spirit so that the noetic results of the Fall are overcome. Believers now have an understanding of God that they did not have when their minds were "darkened" (Eph. 4:17–19). Paul illustrates this change in perspective when he changed from a blasphemer and persecutor of the church into a person who cried out to Jesus on the road to Damascus, "What shall I do, Lord?" (Acts 22:10).

The sensibility is also renewed and transformed as the Spirit begins his work of emotional renewal in the one whose heart the new covenant is written. Paul calls this transformation a transformation from "glory to glory" (2 Cor. 3:18). This transformation liberates the Christian from his former bondage to sin and directs his emotional responses into "love, joy, peace, patience, kindness, goodness, faithfulness, gentleness and self-control" (Gal. 5:22–23).

The will is changed from "I won't" to "I will." Prior to conversion, the Christian is characterized by alienation from God, enmity toward God, and self-centeredness. But through the ministry of the Spirit the will is altered so that the person desires to do the will of the Lord (Rom. 12:2; Eph. 5:17; 6:6; Col. 1:9; 4:12; 1 Thess. 4:3; 5:18; Heb. 10:36; 13:21; 1 Pet. 4:2; 1 John 2:17; 5:14). The will is transformed so that the believer moves progressively from self-centeredness to God-centeredness. Now the Christian lives with the primary goal of adoring and magnifying the name of the Lord and loving one's neighbor. The new commandment given by Jesus is that his followers should love one another, and this change of orientation is enabled by the transformation of the intellect, sensibility, and the will.

A question that will surely arise at this point is whether Old Testament believers had the same changes effected in them as did new covenant believers. The answer is Yes, they did. But the difference between the two covenants is that nothing within the old covenant produced those things from the inside out. The old covenant lacked the person who facilitates this renewal, namely, the Holy Spirit. It is not that the Holy Spirit was not present during the old covenant age, but that the Holy Spirit was not an intrinsic part of the old covenant code. The old covenant was like a handbook, good and beneficial if followed, but with no inherent power to change anyone "under" the handbook. Laws and rules cannot change people one iota; in fact, laws often serve to increase sin and encourage people to devise ways and means to break the laws. As Paul said,

> What shall we say, then? Is the law sin? Certainly not! Indeed I would not have known what sin was except through the law. For I would not have known what coveting really was if the law had not said, 'Do not covet.' But sin, seizing the opportunity afforded by the commandment, produced in me every covetous desire. For apart from law, sin is dead. Once I was alive apart from law; but when the commandment came, sin sprang to life and I died. I found that the very commandment that was intended to bring life actually brought death. For sin, seizing the opportunity afforded by the commandment, deceived me, and through the commandment put me to death.
>
> (Rom. 7:7–11)

Laws, therefore, do not transform. At best, they only curtail. Sinful people instinctively rebel against constraints on their freedom to do as they please. They try deviously to get around the intent of the law even though they are not guilty of actual infraction of the letter. They rationalize, qualify, excuse, reinterpret, figure out ways the rule does not apply in their case, and break everything except the literal letter of the law. For example, when you tell your son to turn off the light in his bedroom and go to bed, you expect compliance to the spirit of your request. Instead, although the overhead light may be off in his room, you may find your son using a flashlight under the sheets doing what he wants to do past his bedtime. Laws do not change behavior. They limit behavior, condemn it, set controls and parameters around behavior, and serve as a basis for punishment of aberrant and errant behavior. But in and of themselves, the laws are powerless. This is why municipalities must hire police to patrol the neighborhoods and arrest those who are violating the laws.

The cure for all of this would be a moral monitor implanted in the brain of every person in the world that would motivate them to do good and deter them from doing evil. If everyone would live by this monitor, we would not need any laws, police, or courts. In the case of the new covenant, the "monitor" is the Holy Spirit. This is why Paul told the Galatians to walk by means of the Spirit and they would by no means fulfill the lust of the flesh (Gal. 5:16). If they would allow themselves to be led by the Spirit, they would not be under law (5:18). Thus the sine qua non of the new covenant is the Spirit of God because he makes transformation possible by enabling the individual to conform to the will of God. The Spirit is an internal agent who transforms from within, where the trouble lies. The old covenant shouted, "You shall not covet!" The new covenant also shouts, "You shall not covet!" But this time, the Holy Spirit creates in the new covenant Christian a desire to stop coveting and to start being content.

What thrills Paul is the fact that the Holy Spirit has come as the great gift of the risen Christ to God's people. The Spirit is such an intrinsic part of the new covenant that wherever Paul preaches the gospel, the Holy Spirit comes upon people, regenerates them, gifts them, places them into the body of Christ, and produces his fruit in their lives. Paul saw that the Holy Spirit could accomplish more in the lives of pagan Gentiles who were previously alienated from and ignorant of God than the old covenant could produce in the lives of many Israelites over fifteen centuries of old covenant history.

The old covenant is not only inscribed on stone, symbolizing its inflexibility and fixed character, but it also kills by declaring everyone who breaks it as guilty before God (Rom. 3:19). Thus it ministers death even to those who try to keep it! Transgression brought severe penalties with it. Yet the law could not give life because of the total depravity of the human race. Unlike the Judaism of his day, Paul's fundamental contention is that people are in a state of alienation from God as a result of the Fall (5:12–21). People are dead in trespasses and sins, also. Thus totally depraved people will only have death ministered to them through the Mosaic covenant. Try as they will, people cannot overcome their magnetism to sin because they are "in Adam" positionally and a descendant of Adam constitutionally. Adam's sin has been imputed to them so that they are under God's condemnation. Their only hope is a transfer into a position of reconciliation with God and the imputation of a perfect righteousness. Under the new covenant this transfer is "in Christ" and the righteousness is his righteousness (3:21–26).[85]

The New Testament writers never consider the old covenant to be bad. The old covenant was simply ineffective. In fact, as a covenant from God, it was holy, righteous, and good (Rom. 7:12). The old covenant had glory as a revelation of God's righteous requirements for Israel. But the new covenant is far more glorious due to its far greater results and accomplishments. The old covenant was good during the temporary period for which it was designed as a guardian of God's people (Gal. 3:24; 4:1–5). But when Christ

---

85. See John Murray, *The Imputation of Adam's Sin* (Nutley, N.J.: Presbyterian and Reformed, 1977) and S. Lewis Johnson, Jr., "Romans 5:12—An Exercise in Exegesis and Theology," in *New Dimensions in New Testament Study*, ed. Richard N. Longenecker and Merrill C. Tenney (Grand Rapids: Zondervan, 1974), 298–316.

came, the old covenant had to be exchanged for a new covenant that would be appropriate for the new adult position of God's people (4:4–6).

The new covenant serves as a ministry of righteousness. It acquits people of their forensic unrighteousness by Christ's payment for their sins. But it also promotes their functional righteousness by the Holy Spirit that is the "battery" of the new covenant. The opposite was true with the old covenant. It declared people forensically unrighteous and under God's condemnation. It had no ability to promote functional righteousness other than stipulations accompanied by either blessings or cursings. The failure of people under the old covenant was due to their total depravity and their inability to live righteously without the power of the Holy Spirit (Rom. 8:3–4).

As a result, people groaned under the guilt-producing character of the old covenant that ministered death due to its fixed character. The new covenant gives people a clean conscience (Heb. 9:9, 14; 10:22). This is not because new covenant people are any better than old covenant people, but because the penalty has been paid by Jesus Christ and God "will remember their sins no more" (Heb. 8:12, quoting Jer. 31:34). People were under terrible bondage under the old covenant because of its demands and the inability of people to meet its demands. The new covenant frees people from the guilt of their inability and frees people through the Holy Spirit to begin meeting the covenantal stipulations. New covenant stipulations require many of the same actions that old covenant stipulations required. Stealing, adultery, coveting, and other vices are still wrong under the new covenant, which demonstrates that the freedom of the new covenant is not a freedom to sin. It is a freedom to love the Lord as one should love him and to love one another. The topic of freedom will be developed in more detail in chapter 12, "Newness and the Individual Christian."

The new covenant regards people at a higher level of spiritual maturity and thus able to discern how godly principles should be worked out. New covenant freedom results in discriminating how God's will can be followed in a variety of circumstances as the Spirit tailors his guidance to meet the exigencies of individual existence. Each believer can be fully persuaded individually about the particular will of God for him or her. A new covenant stipulation such as loving one's neighbor can be carried out in any number of ways. New covenant people, therefore, have no airtight rules telling them who to love, how to love, or when to love. The neighbor is not ethnically, sexually, or socioeconomically defined, but includes anyone in need. The church adds a new legalism when it begins to set boundaries on how such a directive ought to be fulfilled in the life of each Christian.

New covenant freedom enabled the early church to do what was necessary to advance the Gospel. Neither Peter nor Paul negated cultural differences. The braiding of hair and covering of the head were accommodations to cultural sensitivities because of the storm of controversy that the violation of these sensitivities would bring. Paul was also careful to maintain peace, order, and tranquillity within the church. He wanted to avoid those things that would needlessly tear the church apart. But if any requirements, such as circumcision, were demanded in order to qualify a Gentile as a Christian, Paul reacted strongly to the point of calling all such additions false gospels (Gal. 1:6–7).

Along with new covenant freedom comes new covenant responsibility. Christians must determine how they will work out the new covenant stipulations in their own lives. Every situation must be judged on its own merits because all of life is a part of the new covenant ethic and every circumstance must be judged individually. This is not ethical anarchy because many lists in Paul and other New Testament writers spell out what sins a Christian must stop doing or avoid doing. But many moral acts in the Christian life are not directly addressed. These areas must be handled as the Spirit directs and guides the individual Christian conscience. Christians are not to judge other Christians' consciences. Each Christian must be "fully convinced in his own mind" (Rom. 14:5). Thus the Spirit leads every Christian. The Christian is to be sensitive to the Spirit's leading and be fully convinced of his direction. What the church does not need are people who feel they have been hired by the Spirit to judge the behavior of other Christians, especially when the check-list is self-compiled and cannot be found in the New Testament. Christians must stop promoting rules and regulations for each other that go beyond the covenantal document, the New Testament. As long as a Christian does not violate any new covenant directive, that Christian is free in Christ to live as the Spirit guides him or her.

The old covenant glory was a temporary glory because it was provisional until the Seed would come to whom the Abrahamic promise had been made. Moses' action in veiling himself was a deliberate one, aimed at concealing not only the glory of his face but the end of that glory, his ministry and his covenant.[86] In contrast, the new covenant is an open glory because God will never cause its glory to diminish. To see this glory, one must become a Christian by "turning to the Lord." This "turning" is a turning of repentance and conversion. But it is a turning that at least some of the sons of Israel will not perform, according to the prophet Isaiah (Isa. 6:9–10, interpreting Exod. 34).[87] The inability to "see" the glory of the new covenant on the part of unbelieving Israel is linked by Paul through the words "heart," "Spirit," and "eye" to Isaiah 6, Isaiah 29, and Deuteronomy 29.[88] Christians are not like Moses when he veiled his face. They are like Moses when he did not veil his face.[89] Christ's revelation of God's glory opens up all of the

86. Stockhausen, 126.
87. Ibid., 138.
88. Ibid., 142–43.
89. Ibid., 151.

newness that this study is pursuing. As the Christian responds to this newness, he enters into all of the potential that the new covenant holds. This
is "possibility thinking" with a capital P!

Hebrews 7–13

Although the writer to the Hebrews does not explicitly express it, he has
the new covenant in the back of his mind from the beginning to the end of
his epistle. This is due to the fact that he often refers to the old covenant as
the *first* covenant (Heb. 8:7, 13; 9:15, 18) and that the law ultimately becomes synonymous with the old covenant in the writer's mind.[90] Throughout the letter, the author is stressing the superiority of Christ to everything
that preceded his coming within the Old Testament economy. Christ is
better than the prophets, the angels, Moses, Aaron, Abraham, Levi, the old
covenant, and the entire Old Testament cultus. Nowhere do we hear of a
"new" or "better" law.[91] Christ has brought in a better hope (7:19), a better
covenant (7:22), better promises (8:6), better sacrifices (9:23), better possessions (10:34), better homeland (11:16), better resurrection (11:35), and better blood (12:24). In so doing the author of Hebrews reminds his readers of
the superiority and finality of the new covenant over against the old covenant. Any retreat back to the old covenant is apostasy and will result in
eternal loss (10:39; see also 12:25–29). The entire argument for the author
of Hebrews is to try to move his readers away from any inclinations of re-
treating and giving up their professed allegiance to Christ and embracing
the old covenant (i.e., the Mosaic system).

The author of Hebrews contends that the old covenant has been superseded by the new covenant. Therefore, the old is obsolete and no longer
valid. A salvation-history change has taken place. The old covenant is to be
shelved. Although the old covenant served its purpose during its divinely
designated period, it has been replaced due to the far superior work of
Christ. When the writer uses "new" and "old" or "first" and "second" the
word *covenant* should be supplied to properly grasp his contrast: "If that
first [covenant] had been faultless, there would have been no occasion
sought for a second [covenant]" (8:7). "When he said, 'A new [covenant],' he
has made the first [covenant] obsolete. But whatever is becoming obsolete
and growing old is ready to disappear" (8:13). "Now even the first [cove-
nant] had regulations of divine worship and the earthly sanctuary" (9:1).
"Therefore even the first [covenant] was not inaugurated without blood"
(9:18). "He takes away the first [covenantal system] in order to establish the
second [covenantal system]" (10:9). It is clear from these texts that the

90. Susanne Lehne, *The New Covenant in Hebrews* (Sheffield: Sheffield Academic
Press, 1990), 22.
91. Ibid., 27.

writer is contrasting two whole covenantal systems: the old [Mosaic] covenant and the new [Christ] covenant.

In the author's discussion Hebrews 7:12 is a key text: "For when there is a change of the priesthood, there must also be a change of the law." The argument is that the order of Melchizedek has replaced the order of Aaron. Since it was the old Mosaic covenant that instituted the Aaronic priesthood and the order of Melchizedek was not instituted until Psalm 110, the new order belongs to a different law than the old order. To change Aaron is to change Aaron's system. If Aaron goes, the covenant that designates him as its high priest also goes. The new covenant replaces the order of Aaron with Christ as High Priest after the order of Melchizedek. According to Hebrews 7:18, the reason the former order of Aaron has been replaced is because that order [and its system] were weak (ἀσθενής) and useless (ἀνωφελής). The problem with the old covenant law was that it perfected nothing, serving only to introduce a better hope by which Christians now draw near to God (Heb. 7:19).

In the Book of Hebrews the word *perfection* means that all requirements for salvation are met.[92] In contrast, the law made nothing perfect because it could not save anyone. It was wonderful in its statements, declaring many things that were indeed needful, holy, righteous, and true. But the law had a built-in problem since it was weak in a person's flesh, it used the blood of animals that could never take away sins (10:4), and ultimately it was useless for cleansing the conscience from guilt (9:9, 14). The law could condemn, but not justify; it could command, but not sanctify.

Jesus is therefore the guarantee of a better covenant (7:22). His blood purges the conscience from dead works to serve the living God (9:14). Note the emphasis: the old covenant was unable to cleanse the conscience. Although gallons of animal blood were offered, the conscience of the offerers still felt guilty. If the animal sacrifices had taken away guilt, then the priests would have ceased to offer them. But the Aaronic priests had to make offerings for both their own guilt and the guilt of the people repeatedly. This was because the animal blood never really removed sin.[93]

Because the blood of Christ was of infinite value, he needed to die only once. His death brought in a better hope, a better resurrection, and a better inheritance. The total ineffectiveness of the old covenant system in contrast to the total effectiveness of the new covenant system is clear. Jesus is the mediator of the new covenant (9:15) because his death provides an eternal inheritance for his people. Not even the first covenant was renewed apart from blood, for the blood of bulls was sprinkled on the people, on the scroll, on the tent, and on all the vessels of the ministry. All things need to

---

92. David Peterson, *Hebrews and Perfection* (New Rochelle: Cambridge University Press, 1982).

93. See Lehne's chart of the contrasting cultic features of both covenants (pp. 98–99).

be cleansed with blood; apart from the shedding of blood there is no forgiveness (9:22). Lehne considers the elaborate theological expositions of the
Christ event as a kind of historical prologue for the stipulations governing
life under the new covenant. The Exodus from Egypt is the foundation of
the old covenant. Christ's death and exaltation are the foundation of the
new covenant.[94]

When Jesus came to do God's will, he took away the first system in order
to establish the second system. God's people are now sanctified because
Christ fulfilled God's will (10:9–10). Quoting Jeremiah's prophecy of the
new covenant, the author of Hebrews concludes that where there is forgiveness of sins, there is no longer an offering for sin (10:16–18).

Coming to the close of his argument, the author warns his readers that
if there was punishment under the Mosaic law, how much more worthy of
greater punishment would they be considered if they become guilty of insulting the Spirit of grace and trampling under foot the Son of God, considering the blood of the new covenant by which they have been sanctified as
a common thing. Only vengeance from the living God awaits such apos-
tates (10:26–31).

In two concluding passages the author of Hebrews contrasts the former
covenant with the new covenant. The old covenant was associated with
Mt. Sinai, which could not be touched because of the fire, darkness, gloom,
and whirlwind connected with it. No beast could touch that mountain
without being stoned. Even Moses was full of fear and trembling at that
mountain (12:18–21). In contrast, the new covenant is associated with the
heavenly Zion, the city of the living God, the heavenly Jerusalem, a myriad
of angels, a festal gathering, the church of the firstborn, and the spirits of
righteous people (probably Old Testament saints) who have been now included in Christ's perfection (12:22–23). The new covenant reality is all
based upon the work of Jesus who is the mediator of this new covenant
(12:24). Finally, this new covenant is an everlasting covenant because it is
not only guaranteed by Christ's blood but also by his everlasting resurrection (13:20).

These scattered references to the new covenant in Hebrews 7–13 underscore the centrality of Hebrews 8 in the discussion of the new covenant. In
this chapter the author of Hebrews quotes Jeremiah 31:31–34 in full. According to 8:1, the main idea of the author's exposition up to this point in
the epistle has been that Christians have a high priest who sits at God's
right hand, a minister of the true tabernacle in heaven pitched by the Lord,
not people. Although it was the function of the high priest to offer up gifts
and sacrifices according to the law, Jesus is after a different order and does
not offer up a sacrifice according to the law. Those Old Testament sacrifices

94. Lehne, 107.

served only as a pattern (8:5, ὑπόδειγμα) and a shadow (v. 5, σκιά) of heavenly things. Moses was told to make all things according to the type (v. 5, τύπος) that God showed him on the mountain. Thus Christ is now the mediator of a better covenant that has been founded on better promises. Why is this new covenant so superior? It is because it enables the people to fulfill it. If the old covenant had been faultless, God would not have changed it. But because of the people's continual breaking of the covenant, God declared through Jeremiah that he would enact a new covenant with Israel and Judah that would be inscribed on the hearts of his people. The word *new* in the Jeremiah passage causes the author of Hebrews to detach it and draw emphasis to it. The very word *new* is in contrast to something *old*. It does not take much imagination to know what is old: it is the old covenant. That old covenant is not only old, but it is worn out so that it is no longer usable and is about to disappear as a base of relationship between God and his people.[95]

The greatest problem with the Old Testament Israelite, other than his sense of guilt, was his murky future. Death was a dark door. Sheol offered little hope as a place of shade and darkness. At best, one would be said to be gathered to his ancestors. All real life was to be lived here on the earth. But even Abraham realized that there must be something beyond the land of Canaan. He therefore looked for a city with foundations, whose builder and maker was God (11:10). He realized that God had prepared for him an eternal city. Abraham looked forward to the time when his seed, Christ, would make all of this a reality (John 8:56).

The new covenant brings a better hope, an entrance into the realm of ultimate reality, while the old covenant was simply a shadow, pattern, and type of the new. The new covenant was needed to solve the dilemma of death and the problem of guilt. Only in the new covenant is the believer able to approach God with full assurance because of the once-for-all sacrifice of Jesus (Heb. 4:14–16).

The old covenant has served its purpose and run its course from the time of Moses to Jesus. But now that Christ has come and the Holy Spirit has been poured out, the guide (the old covenant) has retired because it is no longer needed. Christians are full partakers in Christ's inheritance as his adopted brothers and sisters. Therefore, argues the author of Hebrews, don't trade the new for the old; don't go back to the old system with its sacrifices. Christ has purchased a much better inheritance. All of the Old Testament saints, who looked for a better inheritance but did not experience it during their lifetimes, also enter the heavenly Jerusalem because the death of Jesus

95. Compare these last few thoughts with the parable of the wineskins and garments. Also, see chapter 3, "New Wineskins," in this book.

includes those old covenant saints, too. What God has effected and inaugurated, he will consummate when Christ appears the second time (9:28).

What a glorious covenant! Only a fool would listen to those who would urge abandonment of so great salvation and a retreat to the blood of bulls and goats. The readers of this epistle apparently had lost confidence in Christ and Christianity due to persecution (10:32–39). God did not seem to be responding to their misery, so some (many?) were considering rejoining Judaism since at this point in history Judaism was still a legitimate and protected religion. But in a few short years Jerusalem would fall, animal sacrifices would cease, and the unbelieving Jews would have to find their identity in the study of the Torah itself rather than in the activities and structures that it commanded.

The Johannine Writings

Although the expression *new covenant* never occurs in the Johannine writings, Malatesta has shown that the concept and terminology permeate the Johannine writings.[96] Two constructions express the theme of interiority, a major new covenant emphasis: εἶναι ἐν, "to be in," and μένειν ἐν, "to remain, live in."[97] According to Malatesta, the Old Testament promise, "I will be your God, and you shall be my people," has become a reality in the new covenant as expressed in the affirmation, "God is Love and he who remains in love remains in God and God remains in him" (1 John 3:24; 4:13, 15, 16).[98] The interiority expressions are found throughout 1 John and are concentrated in the last discourses in the Gospel of John.[99] The last interiority expression in the Gospel highlights the glorified Jesus as being in his disciples (17:26), while the last in 1 John stresses that Christians are in God and in Jesus (5:20).[100]

This presence of God is intimately related to the new covenant, for the whole purpose of the covenant is communion and communion is unthinkable without presence.[101] Communion is unthinkable without obedience. Therefore, *all* the promises of the new covenant contain more or less explicit mention of a new fidelity to God's laws. An essential aspect of the knowledge of God proper to the new covenant is that communion with the Lord that consists in loving obedience to his commandments.[102] It is God's will that his revelation transform us interiorly, that the thoughts, decisions, and conduct that proceed from within be inspired by God's own wis-

96. Malatesta, 1–90.
97. Ibid., 3.
98. Ibid., 24.
99. Ibid., 32.
100. Ibid.
101. Ibid., 45.
102. Ibid., 76–77.

dom.[103] The major criteria for judging the presence or absence of communion with God are observance or nonobservance of his commandments, epitomized in the new commandment of fraternal love.[104]

The new covenant was given because Israel had not remained in the old covenant. The implication is that God's people will remain in the new covenant to the degree that the new interior gift remains in them. This new interior gift is the Holy Spirit. The Christian is to remain in the Spirit and the Spirit's teaching is to remain in the Christian.[105]

Malatesta's study shows that the words "new covenant" do not have to be used by a writer for him to have the new covenant in view. Words drawn from the Old Testament texts (particularly the Septuagint version) speaking of the new covenant (and the words "new covenant" do not occur in all of these texts!) can so permeate the vocabulary and conceptuality of the writer that the new covenant plays a central role in his thinking. This type of study needs to be done in both Testaments to provide a full exposition of those portions of Scripture where the concept of the new covenant is in view, although the actual words, "new covenant," are absent.

The Problem of Paul and the Law

The topic of Paul and the law has become a very complex discussion in recent years. The literature is enormous and seems to have no end.[106] The problem is acute for a number of reasons. We list four of them in the following paragraphs.

103. Ibid., 115.
104. Ibid., 160.
105. Ibid., 220.
106. The following list is basic reading on the subject of the Law and Paul and the Law: Robert Badenas, *Christ the End of the Law* (Sheffield: JSOT, 1985); Greg Bahnsen, *Theonomy in Christian Ethics* (Nutley, N.J.: Craig, 1977); Greg Bahnsen, Walter C. Kaiser, Jr., Douglas J. Moo, Wayne G. Strickland, and Willem A. Vangemeren, *The Law, the Gospel, and the Modern Christian* (Grand Rapids: Zondervan, 1993); William S. Barker and W. Robert Godfrey, eds., *Theonomy: A Reformed Critique* (Grand Rapids: Zondervan 1990); John Drane, *Paul: Libertine or Legalist?* (London: SPCK, 1975); James D. G. Dunn, *Jesus, Paul and the Law* (Louisville: Westminster, 1990); *The Partings of the Ways* (Philadelphia: Trinity Press International, 1991); Daniel P. Fuller, *Gospel and Law* (Grand Rapids: Eerdmans, 1980); Lloyd Gaston, *Paul and the Torah* (Vancouver: University of British Colombia Press, 1987); H. Wayne House and Thomas Ice, *Dominion Theology: Blessing or Curse?* (Portland, Ore.: Multnomah, 1988); Hans Hübner, *The Law in Paul's Thought* (Edinburgh: T. & T. Clark, 1984); Bruce Kaye and Gordon Wenham, eds., *Law, Morality and the Bible* (Downers Grove, Ill.: InterVarsity, 1978); Ernest F. Kevan, *The Grace of Law* (Grand Rapids: Baker, 1976); Brice L. Martin, *Christ and the Law in Paul* (Leiden: Brill, 1989); Douglas J. Moo, "The Law of Moses or the Law of Christ," in *Continuity and Discontinuity*, ed. John S. Feinberg (Westchester, Ill.: Crossway, 1988); Heikki Räisänen, *Paul and the Law* (Philadelphia: Fortress, 1986); C. Thomas Rhyne, *Faith Establishes the Law* (Chico, Calif.: Scholars, 1981); Rousas John Rushdoony, *The Institutes of Biblical Law* (Nutley, N.J.: Craig, 1973); E. P. Sanders, *Paul and Palestinian*

First, the Books of Romans and Galatians contain a concentration of law (νόμος) texts. Paul uses νόμος a total of 121 times.[107] Out of 121 occurrences, 88% of them appear in Romans (74 times) and Galatians (32 times).[108] Regardless of whether Galatians is dated in the late 40s or middle 50s with Romans, it seems that for a ten-year period (A.D. 47–57), Paul was confronted with a great problem over the relationship between the law of Moses and Christians, particularly Gentiles. The cause of this problem was Judaizers who were dogging Paul's footsteps and attempting to convert the Gentiles to their theology of law. Their primary contention was that Gentiles needed to be circumcised in order to become full Christians (Acts 15:1). Galatians and Romans are polemical against these Judaizers. When polemics are employed, however, one needs to be very careful, because all aspects of an issue are not always addressed, and the heat of debate causes both sides of the controversy to target certain arguments in order to win the debate and to be somewhat unbalanced in argumentation. This means that occasional statements in Galatians and Romans about the law are not necessarily a systematic theology of law. The occasional statements were written to combat Judaizers and should be used cautiously when attempting to build a biblical theology of law. As we demonstrated above in the discussion about "The Reasons for Keeping the Old Covenant," nothing in the Old Testament indicates that the law was a means of salvation or that the Mosaic covenant was a mistake in salvation-history. The statements about the law covenant in the Old Testament are very positive. Paul's very negative statements about the law must be evaluated over against the Judaizers' contentions and the statements about the law in the Old Testament itself.

Second, the problem of Paul and the law is acute because Paul held a seemingly ambivalent position about the law. According to Schreiner, "one of the most difficult issues in Pauline theology is the question of the permanence of the law."[109] Paul makes a series of fifteen positive statements about the law. On the other hand, he makes twenty-seven negative statements about it (see Figure 5.8). Did Paul think that the law was something

---

Judaism (Philadelphia: Fortress, 1977); *Paul, The Law, and the Jewish People* (Fortress, 1983); *Jesus and Judaism* (Fortress, 1985); *Jewish Law from Jesus to the Mishnah* (Philadelphia: Trinity, 1990); *Judaism: Practice and Belief 63 BCE–66 CE* (Trinity, 1992); Thomas R. Schreiner, *The Law and Its Fulfillment* (Grand Rapids: Baker, 1993); Peter J. Tomson, *Paul and the Jewish Law* (Minneapolis: Fortress, 1990); Stephen Westerholm, *Israel's Law and the Church's Faith* (Grand Rapids: Eerdmans, 1988); N. T. Wright, *The Climax of the Covenant* (Minneapolis: Fortress, 1992).

107. Robert Morgenthaler, *Statistik des neutestamentlichen Wortschatzes* (Zürich: Gotthelf-Verlag, 1973), 123.

108. The remaining occurrences are: 9 times in 1 Corinthians; none in 2 Corinthians; once in Ephesians; three times in Philippians; none in Colossians, 1 Thessalonians, 2 Thessalonians, 2 Timothy, and Titus; and only twice in 1 Timothy.

109. Thomas R. Schreiner, *The Law and Its Fulfillment* (Grand Rapids: Baker, 1993), 123.

Table 5.8

Negative Statements	Positive Statements
1. By the works of the law no flesh shall be justified (Rom. 3:20).	1. Christians establish the law through faith (Rom. 3:31).
2. Through the law is the knowledge of sin (Rom. 3:20; 7:7).	2. The law is holy and the commandment is holy and righteous and good (Rom. 7:12).
3. The promise to Abraham was not through law (Rom. 4:13).	3. The law is spiritual (Rom. 7:14).
4. The law brings about wrath (Rom. 4:15).	4. The law is good (Rom. 7:16).
5. The law came in that transgressions might increase (Rom. 5:20).	5. I serve the law of God with my mind (Rom. 7:25).
6. Christians are not under law but under grace (Rom. 6:14).	6. The law is fulfilled in us who walk according to the Spirit (Rom. 8:4).
7. Christians died to the law (Rom. 7:4).	7. He who loves his neighbors has fulfilled the law (Rom. 13:8).
8. The law aroused sin (Rom. 7:5).	8. Love is the fulfillment of the law (Rom. 13:10).
9. Christians have been released from the law (Rom. 7:6).	9. Paul became as "under the law" to those who were "under the law" (1 Cor. 9:20).
10. I was alive apart from the law (Rom. 7:9).	10. Women should be submissive as the law says (1 Cor. 14:34).
11. The law was weak through the flesh (Rom. 8:3).	11. The law is not contrary to the promises of God (Gal. 3:21).
12. The mind does not submit to the law of God (Rom. 8:7).	12. The law was a custodian (Gal. 3:23).
13. Christ is the end of the law (Rom. 10:4).	13. The law has become our guardian unto Christ (Gal. 3:24).
14. The power of sin is the law (1 Cor. 15:56).	14. If you are led by the Spirit you are not under the law (Gal. 5:18).

15. Through the law I died to the law (Gal. 2:19).

15. The law is good if used lawfully (1 Tim. 1:8).

16. If righteousness comes through the law, Christ died in vain (Gal. 2:21).

17. As many as rely on the works of the law are under a curse (Gal. 3:10).

18. The law is not of faith (Gal. 3:12).

19. Christ redeemed us from the curse of the law (Gal. 3:13).

20. If the inheritance is based on law it is no longer based on promise (Gal. 3:18).

21. The law was added because of transgressions (Gal. 3:19).

22. Righteousness that leads to eternal life cannot be based on law (Gal. 3:21).

23. Circumcision demands keeping the whole law (Gal. 5:3).

24. If you seek to be justified by law you have fallen from grace (Gal. 5:4).

25. Christ abolished the enmity which is the law of commandments (Eph. 2:15).

26. Law righteousness is opposed to Christ righteousness (Phil. 3:9).

27. The law was not made for a righteous man (1 Tim. 1:9).

good, or did he consider it a mistake? One set of texts implies that the law was a disaster and that God made a mistake (or, to take Scofield's suggestion, Israel made a mistake in accepting the law[110]) in giving it to Israel because it was a monster that devoured Israel. The only value of the law was to show how sinful people were. On the other hand, the fifteen positive statements seem to show that Paul considered the law to be a good thing. Paul does indicate that the law is applicable to Gentile Christians. As Schreiner observes, Paul expects believers to honor their parents (Eph. 6:2); not covet, commit adultery, murder, or steal (Rom. 7:7; 13:9); love their neighbor as themselves (Rom. 13:9; Gal. 5:14); and abstain from idolatry (1 Cor. 10:14). Also, Paul commends Gentile Christians for keeping the law (Rom. 2:26), says that the purpose of Christ's death was that the law should be fulfilled in Christians (Rom. 8:4), and praises the keeping of God's commandments (1 Cor. 7:19).[111] The problem with Paul is further exacerbated by Paul's statements that the law has been canceled (καταργέω; see Rom. 7:2, 6; 2 Cor. 3:7, 11, 13; and Eph. 2:15). Has the law been canceled or not? Schreiner says that Paul's view of the law is complex. In one sense the law has passed away, but in another sense it remains authoritative for the church of Christ.[112] Schreiner has clear texts to compile a list of old covenant norms that have been canceled: animal sacrifices, feasts of Israel, food laws, purity laws, circumcision, and Sabbath observance. However, the "moral norms" have not been canceled.[113]

The idea of "moral norms" leads to the third problem with Paul and the law. What are these "moral norms"? No one is sure. They are differently defined by those who are advocates of a particular theological viewpoint. Reformed theologians have historically divided the law up into "moral," "civil," and "ceremonial" categories. Most Reformed thinkers believe that the "civil" and "ceremonial" commands in the law have been canceled. Only the "moral" carry over for the church. Theonomists contend that the "civil" are still obligatory along with the "moral." Only the "ceremonial" have been "fulfilled" in Christ. But all who believe that the "moral," including theonomists, are still obligatory for Christians sooner or later revert to the vague "principle" as the way of applying the "moral" norms to different cultures and contexts in the twentieth century. There does not seem to be any objective way of defining these "principles." Each theologian or ethicist has his own list. The list is persuasive proportionately to the rhetorical abil-

---

110. The famous quote is, "Israel rashly accepted the law . . .; they exchanged grace for law"; see Rev. C. I. Scofield, *The Scofield Reference Bible* (New York: Oxford University Press, 1909), 20 n. 1.

111. Schreiner, 171.

112. Ibid., 160.

113. See his discussion of "The Fulfillment of the Law by Christians", 145–178.

ity of the one developing the list. Each group, therefore, has its "gurus" who articulate the norms for the church based on what they think are directly carried over "moral" commands and what they think are "principles."

Fourth, another problem with Paul and the law is the plethora of views regarding the meaning of Paul's phrase, "not under law." After surveying the literature, Duhon found that the nine occurrences of this Pauline phrase had received ten different interpretations:

1. Christians are not under the law as a condemning judge;
2. Christians are not under the ceremonial regulations of the law;
3. Christians are not under the "letter" of the law but are under its "spirit";
4. Christians are not under the law as a legalistic system of works-righteousness;
5. Christians are not under the law as that law serves as a provocative power to sin;
6. Christians are not under the law as a demonic force;
7. Christians are not under the law as a soteriological instrument;
8. Christians are not under law any longer as a barrier between Jew and Gentile;
9. only Christians who are immature are under the law;
10. Christians are no longer under the Mosaic law in its entirety as a regent code of behavior.

Duhon devotes his thesis to a critique of the first nine views and a defense of the tenth view.[114] Competent scholars defend each of these ten views. With such diversity of viewpoint, one is reminded of Schreiner's statement that Paul's view of the law is "complex."

Chris Miller has suggested another solution to the problem of Paul and the law. Miller traces the relationship of Jewish Christians to the law through Acts and Paul to the law through Galatians. He concludes that Acts and Galatians present Jewish Christians as "law-abiding." Not until the writing of the Book of Hebrews is there a clean break with the law. This later New Testament book is at the end of an era of progressive revelation and is the culmination of almost a century of difficulties concerning the role of the law in the lives of Christians, especially Gentiles. Paul was a Torah-keeping Jew up until the end of his life. Paul only taught that Gentiles were "not under law." Thus, between A.D. 30 and 70 Jewish believers observed the law while Gentiles did not.[115]

---

114. The writer is indebted to Duane Duhon, a former student, for the study of this phrase in his study, "The Referent for the Pauline Phrase 'Not under Law'" (Th.M. thesis, Grand Rapids Baptist Seminary, 1990).

115. Chris A. Miller, "The Relationship of Jewish and Gentile Believers to the Law Between A.D. 30 and 70 in the Scripture" (Ph.D. diss., Dallas Theological Seminary, 1994).

This is an interesting proposal and notes the clear position of Hebrews on the relationship between the old and the new covenants. One wonders, however, how such an abrupt change took place in the apostolic church. Miller dates Hebrews between A.D. 65 and 70.[116] Under any proposed chronology for the life of Paul, he was martyred sometime during the 60s in the first century A.D. Did this sudden "revelation" that Jewish Christians were also no longer "under law" take place within the space of five to ten years? Such a brief period seems to be too short a time for such an intense issue to be suddenly resolved.

Conclusion

All writers agree that the new covenant is a covenant stressing the role of the Holy Spirit in enabling Christians to fulfill the will of God. The emphasis in the new covenant is on forgiveness of sins and on the internalization of the "Torah" in the lives of Christians. The work of Jesus Christ is basic and central to the inauguration of this covenant. This covenant is in vogue for the church and Paul regarded his ministry as a new covenant ministry.

At this point writers begin to disagree and diverge from one another in terms of the new covenant's relationship to the old covenant and the role of the law in the lives of Christians today. No consensus has emerged and it appears that the debate among scholars intensifies with the publication of new works on either the new covenant or on Paul and the law. At this juncture, there apparently is no way of resolving all of the issues pertaining to the new covenant. But the core emphases of the new covenant should cause all Christians to rejoice in what Christ has inaugurated in the new covenant and pray that the Holy Spirit will guide scholars toward greater unanimity over the place of the new covenant in the life of the church and the Christian.

For Further Study

Anderson, Bernhard W. "The New Covenant and the Old." In *The Old Testament and Christian Faith.* Ed. Bernhard W. Anderson. New York: Harper and Row, 1963.

   Anderson's study is one of the seminal works on the relationship between the new and the old covenants.

Deidun, T. J. *New Covenant Morality in Paul.* Rome: Biblical Institute Press, 1981.

   This is an exciting study of the application of the new covenant to the Christian life in Paul.

116. Ibid., 41.

Lehne, Susanne. *The New Covenant in Hebrews.* Sheffield: Sheffield Academic Press, 1990.

A revised doctoral dissertation, this is a full-length monograph on the new covenant in Hebrews.

McComiskey, Thomas E. *The Covenants of Promise.* Grand Rapids: Baker, 1985.

A basic and indispensable study of the biblical covenants.

Malatesta, Edward. *Interiority and Covenant.* Rome: Biblical Institute Press, 1978.

A comprehensive investigation of the Johannine concepts of "being in" and "remaining in," especially with reference to the new covenant.

Marshall, I. Howard. *Kept By the Power of God.* Minneapolis: Bethany, 1969.

An exegetical study of perseverance and falling away in the New Testament.

Master, John R. "The New Covenant." In *Issues in Dispensationalism.* Ed. Wesley R. Willis and John R. Master. Chicago: Moody, 1994.

A presentation of the "classical dispensational" view that there are two new covenants: one with Israel and one with the church.

Miller, Chris A. "The Relationship of Jewish and Gentile Believers to the Law Between A.D. 30 and 70 in the Scripture." Th.D. diss., Dallas Theological Seminary, 1994.

This study argues that the understanding of the new covenant as a distinct covenant from the old covenant was a late development within first-century Christianity since the earlier Jewish Christians were "law-abiding."

Saucy, Robert L. "The New Covenant and the Salvation of the Gentiles." In his *The Case for Progressive Dispensationalism.* Grand Rapids: Zondervan, 1993.

Without equating the church with Israel, Saucy has written a fine study of the new covenant as presently operative in the church.

Schreiner, Thomas R. *The Law and Its Fulfillment.* Grand Rapids: Baker, 1993.

A carefully nuanced study of Paul and the law showing the difficulty of reconciling Paul's statements about the cancellation of the law with his statements about the continuing validity of the law.

Stockhausen, Carol Kern. *Moses' Veil and the Glory of the New Covenant.* Rome: Biblical Institute Press, 1989.

A brilliant study of 2 Corinthians 3 showing how Paul's treatment of the relationship between the Mosaic covenant and the new covenant is perfectly consistent when approached from the standpoint of first-century Jewish hermeneutics.

Volf, Judith M. Gundry. *Paul and Perseverance: Staying in and Falling Away.* Louisville: Westminster/John Knox, 1990.

A revised doctoral dissertation that argues that Romans 8 should be the control text for Pauline texts suggesting the possibility of a true believer "falling away." The conclusion is a reaffirmation of the Reformed doctrine of the perseverance of the saints.

Walton, John. *Covenant: God's Purpose, God's Plan.* Grand Rapids: Zondervan, 1994.

A stimulating study that argues that all covenants of Scripture are revelatory of God and are directed toward a person knowing God.

Ware, Bruce A. "The New Covenant and the People(s) of God." In *Dispensationalism, Israel and the Church.* Ed. Craig A. Blaising and Darrell L. Bock. Grand Rapids: Zondervan, 1992.

A "progressive dispensational" argument that there is one new covenant that is presently operative in the church but still has aspects that will be fulfilled only eschatologically that distinguish the church from Israel. The discussion focuses on four areas in which the new covenant is "new."

6

New Commandment

J ohn 13 introduces the new commandment as a part of the teaching of Jesus Christ. This passage occupies a critical place in the Gospel of John. In chapters 1 through 12, John has presented certain signs that Jesus performed to show that he was the Messiah. Chapters 13 through 21 are the "book of the glory" where Jesus will be lifted up as the Son of God.[1] The aim of the whole Gospel is that people might believe that Jesus is the Christ, the Son of God, and that by believing they will have life in his Name (John 20:31).

Jesus' Teaching about the New Commandment

Background to the New Commandment

Scholars usually call John 13–17 "the upper room discourse." Jesus is alone with his disciples and discloses to them what will transpire after his death, burial, resurrection, exaltation, and ascension. Jesus attempts to prepare his disciples for his imminent death, but the disciples seem to be unable to grasp this idea because of their typical Jewish understanding of a Messiah who would deliver them from the power of Rome.

Several times in the first eight chapters John inserted the editorial comment, "his [Jesus'] time had not yet come" (John 7:30; 8:20; see also 2:4).

---

1. George Mlakuzhyll, *The Christological Literary Structure of the Fourth Gospel* (Rome: Biblical Institute Press, 1987). See also Raymond E. Brown, *The Gospel According to John I–XII* (Garden City, New York: Doubleday, 1966) and *The Gospel According to John XIII–XXI* (Garden City, New York: Doubleday, 1970) who designates the first twelve chapters as "The Book of Signs" and the last nine chapters as "The Book of Glory."

ain Greeks asked to see Jesus, Jesus responded, "The hour has
or the Son of Man to be glorified" (12:23). This *hour* is central in
n's theology of the cross because it is the point in history for which Jesus
has come to the earth (12:27). The hour is the climax of Jesus' ministry, the
sine qua non of his existence, driving him and motivating him throughout
the whole course of his ministry. This hour of Jesus' glorification had arrived. The time had come for him to leave this world and return to the Father. Having loved his own who were in the world with him to this point,
he loved them εἰς τέλος (John 13:1). This phrase is difficult to translate because the noun τέλος may have the following meanings: (1) end, in the sense
of termination or cessation; (2) the last part, close, conclusion; (3) end or
goal toward which a movement is being directed, outcome; (4) finally; (5) to
the end, to the last; (6) in the end, finally; (7) rest, remainder; or (8) tax, customs, duties.[2] According to Brown, within the context of John 13:1 we can
reduce these meanings to two possibilities: "utterly, completely," or "to
the end of life," that is, to the death.[3] The first sense would describe the intensity of Jesus' love; the second sense would describe the temporal extent
of his love. Both views are theologically tenable. Jesus' love for his disciples
never abated. It continued in a steadfast affirming and confirming manner.
Jesus never ceased to love his disciples but kept giving himself for them (intensity) up to the close of his earthly ministry (longevity). His love for his
disciples had no limit in terms of how fervently he loved them and how
long he loved them. By using this ambiguous phrase, John may have intended both aspects of Jesus' love.[4]

While the meal was in progress (reading the present rather than an aorist
participle in John 13:2), Jesus arose from the couch on which he was reclining and wrapped a towel around his waist. This action bore a symbolic
meaning because it was the task of Gentile servants to wash and dry the
feet of those who had entered a house for a meal. Beasley-Murray notes that
the Mishnah includes the menial task of foot washing among those works
which Jewish slaves were not required to perform.[5] Jesus was therefore performing a humiliating service that symbolized his messianic role as servant. When Jesus came to Simon Peter, Peter asked Jesus whether he was
going to wash his feet. Jesus replied that Peter would not recognize the significance of what Jesus was doing now, but after he arose from the dead
Peter would see the significance of what Jesus was doing prior to his death

2. William F. Arndt and F. Wilbur Gingrich, *A Greek-English Lexicon of the New Testament and Other Early Christian Literature* (Chicago: University of Chicago Press,
1957), 818–20.
3. Brown, *The Gospel According to John XIII–XXI*, 550.
4. So Leon Morris, *The Gospel According to John* (Grand Rapids: Eerdmans, 1971),
614 n. 8.
5. George R. Beasley-Murray, *John* (Waco, Tex.: Word, 1987), 233.

(see also John 2:22; 12:16). Peter objected to the washing in a boisterous, blundering manner: "You shall never wash my feet!" Peter recognized the incongruity of the role reversal where the master had become the servant. Jesus gently reminded Peter that unless he allowed Jesus to wash his feet, Peter would not have a part with him. These verses contain a play on words for the verbs νίπτω (13:6, 8, 9, and 10) and λούω (13:10). The verb λούω means "to wash the whole body, to bathe,"[6] while the verb νίπτω means "to wash a part of the body."[7]

Peter responded to the rebuke, "Sir, if you are going to wash me, wash not only my feet, but also my hands and head!" Again Jesus replied that those who had taken a bath had no need of another bath but needed only to cleanse the part of the body that had become dirty. The symbolism is that the disciples who had believed on Jesus had the bath of regeneration and needed only the washing of the feet as their "walk" involved sin.[8] All the disciples except Judas had experienced the bath of regeneration and were "clean" forensically. All they needed was functional cleansing. Since Judas was unregenerate, Jesus declared, "Not every one was clean" (13:11).

When Jesus had washed their feet he again reclined on the couch and asked whether the disciples now realized the significance of what he had just done. He continued, "You call me 'Teacher' and 'Lord,' and rightly so, for that is what I am. Now that I, your Lord and Teacher, have washed your feet, you also should wash one another's feet" (13:14). Then he clarified the significance of what he had just done: he had left them a pattern (ὑπόδειγμα) so that they would do what he had done. These sentences are filled with various forms of the verb "do" (ποιέω). The servant must be like his master. If the Master has *done* something, then the servant must *do* something also. As servants, the disciples were not greater than Jesus, their Master. As messengers whom Jesus would send forth to preach his Gospel, they were not greater than Jesus, whom the Father had sent to be "lifted up" on the cross and offered as a ransom for many (Matt. 20:28; Mark 10:45). If the disciples recognized the significance of what Jesus had done, then God would bless them if they would *do* also.

The next few verses develop the character of Judas as the betrayer, using a typological approach to Psalm 41.[9] The disciples are aghast over Jesus'

---

6. Arndt and Gingrich, 481.

7. Ibid., 542.

8. See the discussion in D. A. Carson, *The Gospel According to John* (Grand Rapids: Eerdmans, 1991), 463–66. Carson does not think there is any real semantic difference between λούω and νίπτω in Johannine use (p. 465). But he does distinguish between the cleansing provided by the "fundamental cross-work of Christ" and the cleansing from "subsequent sins." The two verbs may not be distinguishable, but the two aspects of cleansing certainly are!

9. Ibid., 470.

statement that one of them will betray him. They try to unmask the person who would be party to such a foul deed. Jesus again defers to their ignorance by giving a clue to the betrayer: he is one who will dip a piece of bread in the charosheth sauce with him.[10] Since all the disciples were dipping into the dish, this clue was not unambiguous. When Judas dipped his piece of bread, Jesus apparently said quietly to him, "Whatever you *do* [ποιέω], *do* [ποιέω] quickly." Judas would do, but his doing was a diabolical doing. His type of doing was the antithesis of the type of doing the true disciple must do and his act forms the antithesis to the new commandment that Jesus will give to his disciples after Judas has left the room.

The Gospels wrap Judas' motivation in obscurity. Perhaps he had been wondering over a long period of time whether Jesus was truly the Messiah of Israel. He may have had a Zealot orientation and thought that if Jesus were truly the Messiah he would soon deliver Israel from Roman domination and oppression. Over the years Judas may have waited for Jesus to fulfill what Judas presumed was the messianic mission, yet Jesus had not shown any political inclinations. Also, Judas may have had a growing disaffection because he had joined up with Jesus hoping to be a part of the great liberation movement. Jesus' teaching on servanthood may have been the final disillusionment for Judas. What kind of deliverer would descend to that level?! Further, Judas may have thought that he could force Jesus' hand by making a pact with Jesus' enemies. If a showdown came, Jesus would need to reveal his true colors. Judas would be on the winning side and he would also have thirty shekels of silver! But Judas' plan backfired on him and he died totally disillusioned and devastated (see also Matt. 27:4). None of his plans had materialized successfully. Although Satan had planted the ideas in Judas' mind and energized him to betray Jesus, Judas was responsible for all he did. Probably Satan also energized Judas to hang himself.

No one reclining at the tables perceived what Jesus had said to Judas. Some were thinking that because Judas had the reed flute box (γλωσσόκο-μον, John 12:6; 13:29),[11] which he used to store the communal money, that Jesus had told Judas to go and buy what was needed for the Passover or that Judas had left to give the customary offering for the poor. Interestingly, at this point the disciples viewed Judas as a giver (servant?) and did not suspect his diabolical plan. When Judas left, it was night. This simple word "night" is typical of Johannine double entendre: it is not only nighttime; it is the darkest hour of world history! Then Jesus turned to the eleven and said,

10. For an outline and discussion of the Passover ritual, see William Barclay, *The Lord's Supper* (Philadelphia: Westminster, 1967), 22–24.

11. Arndt and Gingrich, 161.

Now is the Son of Man glorified and God is glorified in him. If God is glorified in him, God will glorify the Son in himself, and will glorify him at once. My children, I will be with you only a little longer. You will look for me, and just as I told the Jews, so I tell you now: Where I am going, you cannot come.

(13:32–33)

Jesus' Command to Love One Another

In John 13:34 Jesus gave the new commandment: "Love one another." This directive was not without a source. The emphasis throughout John 13 that we just surveyed has been on the servanthood of Jesus Christ. Interestingly, almost every commentary on the Gospel of John points out the parallels between John 13 and Philippians 2:5–11. In Philippians 2 Paul exhorts the Philippians to have the mind of Jesus, the mind of a servant. Each is not to look on his own interests, but on the interests of others (Phil. 2:4). This mind-set is the essence of servanthood and is the essence of love. Therefore, the best approach to John 13 is to regard it as an acted parable or didactic lesson of what it means to be a servant and what it means to love εἰς τέλος.[12] When John records that Jesus put his garments on again and reclined again, this is the parabolic equivalent to Paul's statement that Jesus took upon himself the form of a servant and after he became obedient to death, God highly exalted him and granted him the name that is above every name— Lord. For a period of time Jesus surrendered his rights for the benefit of others. This is core of what love entails. Therefore, we may define love as *the voluntary giving of oneself for the benefit of another person so that the will of God can be fulfilled in that person's life.*

After Jesus had completed his task of loving his own, he put on his normal garments and resumed his divine status. The garments are then equal to the τὸ εἶναι ἴσα θεῷ (living in a manner of equality with God) of Philippians 2:6. The emptying of himself and taking the nature of a servant, despite being the very nature of God, is equivalent to taking off the garments. Jesus represents the exaltation back to the realm of the Father by putting his garments back on and reclining again. His reclining symbolizes his finished work (see also Heb. 1:3). John 13 thus shows that the new commandment involves action, service, interaction, and giving of oneself for the benefit of others. The emphasis is on *doing,* not *feeling.* Due to the emphasis on romance in contemporary culture, Christians have the misconception that love is feeling. Biblical love, however, is doing. Thus feeling must become secondary; action must become primary.

At this point the problem that we must address is how the new commandment is new. After all, this commandment occurs in the Old Testa-

---

12. J. N. Sanders, *A Commentary on the Gospel According to St. John* (New York: Harper and Row, 1968), 316.

ment in Leviticus 19:18. Later in the New Testament Jesus declared to the lawyer that the whole law of Moses ultimately depended on two commandments: loving God and loving neighbor (Matt. 22:34–38). Jesus also declared that it was fundamental for all horizontal ethics. But how can Jesus call this idea of loving one another "new" when it was as old as Moses? This writer suggests that the new commandment has five aspects making it something new for the new age[13]: (1) a new model; (2) a new motive; (3) a new motivator; (4) a new mission; (5) and a new milieu.

Five Aspects of the New Commandment

1. The New Model

The new commandment is new because it has a new model: Jesus. He himself has set the example.[14] The disciples are to love one another as Jesus has loved them (John 13:34). As the Servant of the Lord He is the pattern for their service and love. Jesus demonstrated what it meant to love, and he is the preeminent example of what love is and what love entails, as well as being the embodiment of love. Love reaches its pinnacle in him, being demonstrated in and through him most potently through his own actions of sacrifice, care, continually meeting the needs of all who came to him, and ultimately pouring out himself in death for them so that they might live. Not only did Jesus command love, he modeled it.

2. The New Motive

The new commandment is new because it has a new motive: the love of Jesus for lost people. The First Epistle of John contains the greatest exposition of this motive. The first mention of the new commandment in 1 John follows John's statement, "Whoever claims to live in him must walk as Jesus did" (1 John 2:6). The Christian must follow the model established by Jesus. First John 3:16a repeats the model: "This is how we know what love is: Jesus Christ laid down his life for us." Then the motive follows in 3:16b: "And we ought to lay down our lives for our brothers." John expands on this motive:

> Dear friends, let us love on another, for love comes from God. Everyone who loves has been born of God and knows God. Whoever does not love does not know God, because God is love. This is how God showed his love among us:

---

13. Raymond F. Collins, "'A New Commandment I Give to You, That You Love One Another . . .'," in *Christian Morality* (Notre Dame, Ind.: University of Notre Dame Press, 1986), 115 . This chapter can also be found in Raymond Collins, *These Things Have Been Written* (Grand Rapids: Eerdmans, 1990), 217–56.

14. Morris, 633.

He sent his one and only Son into the world that we might live through him.
This is love: not that we loved God, but that he loved us and sent his Son as
an atoning sacrifice for our sins. Dear friends, since God so loved us, we also
ought to love one another. No one has ever seen God; but if we love one
another, God lives in us and his love is made complete in us. . . . We love,
because he first loved us.

(1 John 4:7–12, 19)

People have no greater motive to love one another than God's love for
them.

3. The New Motivator

The extensive exposition of the new covenant passages in chapter 5 has
shown the central role the Holy Spirit plays in this new covenant. According to Galatians 5:22 the first fruit of this Spirit is love. Paul learned from
Epaphras the Colossians' love in the Spirit (Col. 1:8). The Living Bible captures the nuance well when it renders this verse, "And he is the one who
has told us about the great love for others which the Holy Spirit has given
you." The Holy Spirit is the great motivator for the church. He works to
produce the fruit of love in Christians so that they can fulfill the new commandment.

4. The New Mission

The new commandment is new because of the new mission of the
church. All people will know Christ's disciples by their love for one another
(John 13:35). It is instructive to compare the text of John 1:18 with 1 John
4:12. Both verses start with the statement, "No one has ever seen God." The
second half of John 1:18 says that Jesus has revealed God. The second half of
1 John 4:12 suggests that Christians reveal God by loving one another. Can
one conclude that Jesus and Christians have similar missions—to reveal
God to lost people? If so, then the new commandment is doubly important
because it is a major evangelistic tool for reaching a lost world with the gospel. Even though the new commandment is as old as Leviticus 19:18, it is
new in terms of mission. Leviticus 19:18 is sandwiched in between many
other covenantal stipulations, including the following commands:[15]

1. To be holy as God is holy (v. 2);
2. To respect one's mother and father (v. 3);
3. To observe Sabbaths (v. 3);
4. To shun idols (v. 4);
5. To make peace (fellowship) offerings properly (vv. 5–8);

---

15. Sanders calls it "swamped in a mass of miscellaneous legislation" (p. 316).

6. To leave behind provisions for the poor and the aliens from the harvest of the fields and vineyards (vv. 9–10);
7. To refrain from stealing (v. 11);
8. To be honest (v. 13);
9. To treat the handicapped properly (v. 14);
10. To show impartiality in judgment (v. 15);
11. To refrain from slander (v. 16);
12. To plant only one kind of seed in a field (v. 19);
13. To wear garments made from only one kind of material (v. 19);
14. To refrain from eating meat with blood in it (v. 26);
15. To refrain from soothsaying (v. 26).

Buried in the middle of these and many other diverse regulations is the command to "love your neighbor as yourself" (Lev. 19:18). In effect the command to love one's neighbor was a summary statement for these other directives. To love one's fellow Israelite as oneself meant implementing this command in all the activities commanded in the chapter, including for example, not defrauding hired workers of their wages, not harvesting a field so completely that the poor had nothing to glean, not becoming involved in lying and hatred, not being disobedient to parents, not carrying on illicit sexual relationships, and various other stipulations. Love in this Old Testament context meant concern for a proper relationship with one's fellow human being. This relationship was very practical and concrete, involving specific practices that benefited other people, protected their rights, and guaranteed that their needs would be met. Jesus extricated this love command and made it central to Christian new covenant ethics and mission. Just as loving God is the all-embracing vertical command, loving one's neighbor as one's self is the all-embracing horizontal command.

After nearly twenty centuries of history the church has unfortunately seen so little practice of the love command among Christians. The world is well aware of the terrible things that have been done in the name of Christ, especially the reprehensible acts perpetrated by the Nazis who sought to justify such by referring to Jews as "Christ killers." The recent film *Schindler's List* drew huge crowds to the theater and created a great impact on all who viewed it. The brutality of Hitler's army was placed in sharp relief to Oskar Schindler's benevolent treatment of Jews. Viewers will remember the risks Schindler took to show compassion to his fellow human being. This is the type of compassion that must be a witness to the world that Jesus loves them and wishes to save them from their sins. One can only wonder what impact the gospel could have on the world if Christians would consistently and unconditionally show love to one another and those around them. As Carson remarks, "Orthodoxy without principal obedience to this characteristic command of the new covenant is merely so much humbug."[16]

5. The New Milieu

The last reason the new commandment is new is because Christ has introduced a new milieu. All commentators on the Gospel of John mention that Jesus gave the new commandment at the Last Supper when he announced that the new covenant was in his blood. According to Beasley-Murray, "The newness of the command springs from the eschatological reality of Christ's redemption, which is an eternal reality and holds its people in the eternal order."[17] The new situation created by the sacrifice of Christ anticipates in the present the conditions of the age to come. The mutual love of the disciples is therefore the rule for the new era.[18] Thus the new commandment is in perfect harmony with all of the other aspects of newness addressed within this book.

The new commandment is the sine qua non of the Christian life.[19] "It is simple enough for a toddler to memorize and appreciate, profound enough that the most mature believers are repeatedly embarrassed at how poorly they comprehend it and put it into practice."[20] Can any more be said?

For Further Study

Collins, Raymond F. "'A New Commandment I Give to You, That You Love One Another. . . .'," in *Christian Morality*. Notre Dame, Ind.: University of Notre Dame Press,1986. This chapter can also be found in his *These Things Have Been Written*. Grand Rapids: Eerdmans, 1990.

 This is one of the few studies outside of commentaries on the Gospel of John that discusses the New Commandment.

---

16. Carson, 485. Carson notes Tertullian's testimony of the pagans of his day who marveled at the love of the Christian fellowship, especially as it faced sometimes ferocious persecution: "See how they love one another! . . . how are they ready even to die for one another!"

17. Beasley-Murray, 248.

18. Barnabas Lindars, *The Gospel of John* (Greenwood, S.C.: Attic, 1972), 464.

19. Sanders, 317.

20. Carson, 484.

New command.
   Model Christ
   love one another

7

New Creation

*O*ne of the most important themes of newness is the new creation. This theme is expressed in the Pauline phrase καινὴ κτίσις used in 2 Corinthians 5:17 and Galatians 6:15. Although these are the only two occurrences of the phrase in the New Testament, there are other uses of the Greek verb "create" (κτίζω) where the theme of new creation is in the background (see Eph. 2:10, 15; 3:9; 4:24; Col. 3:10). Parallel expressions like "regeneration" (παλιγγενεσία) and "restoration" (ἀποκατάστασις) are also part of the larger semantic domain of "new creation." Further, the literature of the Old Testament and Judaism offer a significant background to the whole theme.[1] Although commentators make sparse comments on "new creation" and only one full-length book written in difficult German explores this theme, the commentaries and the German work by Ulrich Mell,[2] which is of great value, provide sufficient development of the theme of the "new creation."

The Background of the New Creation in the Old Testament

There are three major texts in the Old Testament that provide a basis for the theme of the new creation. The first is Isaiah 43:16–21, which says:

---

1. See, e.g., Isa. 42:9; 43:18–19; 48:6; 65:17–25; 66:22; 1 Enoch 45:4–5; 72:1; 90:28–29; 91:16; 2 (Syriac) Bar. 32:6; 44:12; 57:2; Jub. 1:29; 4:26; 1QS iv 25; 1QH iii 19–23b; xi. 10–14; xiii 11–12; xv 13b–17a ; 11QTemple 29:7b–10; Joseph and Asenath 15:4; 1 Enoch 91:15ff.; Liber Antiquitatum 3:10.

2. Ulrich Mell, *Neue Schöpfung*, Beiheft zur Zeitschrift für die neutestamentliche Wissenschaft und die Kunde der alteren Kirche, ed. Erich Grasser, vol. 56 (Berlin: de Gruyter, 1989).

> This is what the Lord says—
>   he who made a way through the sea,
>   a path through the mighty waters,
> who drew out the chariots and horses,
>   the army and reinforcements together,
> and they lay there, never to rise again,
>   extinguished, snuffed out like a wick:
> Forget the former things;
>   do not dwell on the past.
> See, I am doing a new thing!
>   Now it springs up; do you not perceive it?
> I am making a way in the desert
>   and streams in the wasteland.
> The wild animals honor me,
>   the jackals and the owls,
> because I provide water in the desert
>   and streams in the wasteland,
> to give drink to my people, my chosen,
>   the people I formed for myself
>   that they may proclaim my praise.

Isaiah speaks of God's liberation of the Jews from Babylon as similar to God's deliverance of them from Egyptian bondage: it will be a "new exodus."[3] A new, miraculous act of God lay ahead of Israel.[4] This new event that the Lord would accomplish demanded Israel's undivided attention and thought.[5] According to Young, the contrast is not merely between the redemption from Egypt and the deliverance from Babylon, but between the redemption from Egypt and the redemption that the servant will perform. In Isaiah 42:9 the author had contrasted the former things and the new things, and had declared that the new things had not yet sprouted forth. Therefore, the new thing is the work of redemption that God will do for his people. This redemption culminates with the death of the promised Messiah on the cross. The revolutionary change is so all-embracing that the entire world is affected.[6]

The second text is Isaiah 65:17, which says, "Behold, I will create new heavens and a new earth. The former things will not be remembered, nor will they come to mind." Although commentators point out the parallelism between this text and 2 Peter 3:13 and Revelation 21:1, they do not

3. John T. Willis, *Isaiah* (Austin, Tex.: Sweet, 1980), 372.
4. Claus Westermann, *Isaiah 40–66*, OTL Library (Philadelphia: Westminster, 1969), 128.
5. Edward J. Young, *The Book of Isaiah*, 3 vols. (Grand Rapids: Eerdmans, 1972), 3:155.
6. Ibid., 154–57.

agree on whether the language is to be taken in a cosmological sense of re-creation. Barnes insists that the passage is not to be interpreted literally. It is "picture language" for the glorious future of the people of God.[7] Grogan, however, states that the whole created order is to be renewed. References to "new heavens" and "new earth" presuppose the advent of God's new order, in which all will be perfect and which, according to Revelation 21–22, lies beyond the millennium.[8]

The third text is Isaiah 66:22, which says, "'As the new heavens and the new earth that I make will endure before me,' declares the LORD, 'so will your name and descendants endure.'" Although Young interprets this promise as a prediction of the "true Israel of God," he does make a number of significant statements. First, he notes that the prophet purposely uses the Hebrew word בָּרָא, "shape, create," in 65:17, which is the same word that appears in Genesis 1:1. The almighty power that was displayed at the original creation will be displayed again in a new work of creation. Second, with the advent of the Messiah, the blessing to be revealed will in every sense be so great that it can be described only as the creation of a new heaven and a new earth. Third, according to the prophet's concept, time and eternity are not sharply distinguished. The conditions of paradise are to be restored, but the new age will surpass paradise.[9] Mell concludes his study of the theme of the "new creation" in the Old Testament by saying that according to these passages in Isaiah, Yahweh as the Creator and Lord of history brings a new future to Israel. Implied is a realistic understanding of a renewed world as the destruction of the old world and creation of a new world. This interpretive tradition of a hope of a new creation is the same tradition followed in the literature of early Judaism.[10]

The Background of the New Creation in Early Judaism

The Use of New Creation in the Qumran Literature

There are a number of texts that are relevant to the new creation motif at Qumran. The first text is 1QH iii 19–23b. This text is a part of the community hymns of the Qumran sect. The text reads as follows:

> I give thanks unto Thee, O Lord, for Thou hast freed my soul from the pit and drawn me up from the slough of hell to the crest of the world. So walk I on

7. Albert Barnes, *Notes on the Old Testament: Isaiah*, 27 vols. (Grand Rapids: Baker, 1971), 2:418

8. G. W. Grogan, "Isaiah" in *The Expositor's Bible Commentary*, ed. Frank E. Gaebelein, 12 vols. (Grand Rapids: Zondervan, 1986), 6:351, 15.

9. Young, *Isaiah* 3:513–15.

10. Mell, 66–67.

uplands unbounded and know that there is hope for that which Thou didst
mold out of dust to have consort with things eternal. For lo, Thou hast taken
a spirit distorted by sin, and purged it of the taint of much transgression, and
given it a place in the host of the holy beings, and brought it into communion
with the sons of heaven. Thou hast made a mere man to share the lot of the
Spirits of Knowledge, to praise Thy name in their chorus and rehearse Thy
wondrous deeds before all Thy works.[11]

The second text is 1QH xi 9a–14a. This text reads as follows:

. . . and Thy mercies are shed upon all who do Thy will. For thou hast made
them to know Thy deep, deep, truth and divine Thine inscrutable wonders;
and, for Thy glory's sake, Thou hast granted it unto man to be purged of transgression, that he may hallow himself unto Thee and be free from all taint of
filth and all guilt of perfidy, to be one with them that possess Thy truth and
to share the lot of Thy Holy Beings, to the end that this worm which is man
may be lifted out of the dust to the height of eternal things, and rise from a
spirit perverse to an holy understanding, and stand in one company before
Thee with the host everlasting and the spirits of knowledge and the choir
invisible, to be for ever renewed with all things that are.[12]

The third text is 1QH xv 13–17a. This text reads as follows:

I know that in Thy hand is the shaping of each man's spirit, and ere Thou didst
create him Thou didst ordain his works. And how can any man change what
Thou hast decreed? Thou alone it is that hast created the righteous, condition-
ing him from the womb to rank among the favored at the end of days, to be
safeguarded ever by covenant with Thee, to walk always [undaunted] through
the moving of Thy compassion, to open all the straitness of his soul to everlasting salvation and perpetual peace unfailing. Thou hast raised his inner
glory out of the flesh.[13]

The fourth text is 1QH xiii 11–12. This text reads as follows:

For when the first world began Thou didst so order them and appoint the work
of each that they would spell out Thy glory throughout Thy dominion, making known thereby what none would else have seen, how ancient things pass
over, and new things are ever created, how Thou doest away with outworn
forms, yet [main]tainest eternal nature, for Thou art a God everlasting, and
Thou wilt endure for all time.[14]

11. Theodor H. Gaster, *The Dead Sea Scriptures*, 3d rev. ed. (Garden City, N.Y.: Doubleday, 1976), 154.
12. Ibid., 187.
13. Ibid., 199.
14. Ibid., 194.

The fifth text is 1QS iv 23b–26. This passage is part of the so-called Manual of Discipline, which was a formal set of "rules" that governed the community. This text reads as follows:

> Thus far, the spirits of truth and perversity have been struggling in the heart of man. Men have walked both in wisdom and folly. If man casts his portion with truth, he does righteously and hates perversity; if he casts it with perversity, he does wickedly and abominates truth. For God has apportioned them in equal measure until the final age, until 'He make all things new'. He foreknows the effect of their works in every epoch of the world, and He has made men heirs to them that they might know good and evil. But [when the time] of Inquisition [comes], He will determine the fate of every living being in accordance with which of the [two spirits he has chosen to follow].[15]

The last text is 11QTemple 29:7b–10. This text reads as follows:

> And I will be there for them in eternity [and] I will dwell with them always and forever, and I will fill my holy shrine with my glory, there I will cause my glory to dwell around it . Until the day of the (new) creation when I will create (new) my shrine to prepare it for me (myself) all days in accordance with my covenant which I have concluded with Jacob in Bethel.[16]

According to Ulrich Mell's study, the Qumran texts emphasize the acquisition of salvation through the purified life of the community. Some of the texts emphasize the life of the group, which constitutes in itself a new world. But there is also an end-time, eschatological dimension. 1QS 4:25 parallels Isaiah 43:19 and 1QH 13:11ff. parallels Isaiah 65:17. The use of "create anew" in 1QH 13:11ff. is of interest for Pauline exegesis because the Hebrew בָּרָא חֲדָשָׁה is basic Hebrew terminology for the Greek καινὴ κτίσις. Thus, the Qumran community expected an eschatological change at the end of time. God's eschatological new creation is the end-time goal of his dealings with his creation. The completion possesses an eternal quality. The new creation limits the time of the old creation. The expectation of a new temple also underscores the expectation of an earthly future. One can therefore see that the concept of a new creation is pre-Pauline, even though Paul may not employ the phrase in the same way as these texts.[17]

15. Ibid., 51.
16. Author's translation of the German translation of the Hebrew text in Mell, 106.
17. Mell, 110–112.

The Use of New Creation in the Apocalyptic Literature

A number of texts in the apocalyptic literature also present the theme of the new creation. The first text is from the "Apocalypse of Weeks" as recorded in 1 Enoch 91:15–16. This text reads as follows:

> Then, after this matter, on the tenth week in the seventh part, there shall be the eternal judgment; and it shall be executed by the angels of the eternal heaven—the great (judgment) which emanates from all of the angels. The first heaven shall depart and pass away; a new heaven shall appear; and all the powers of heaven shall shine forever sevenfold.[18]

This passage follows a description of the ninth week where the righteous judgment shall be revealed to the whole world. All the deeds of sinners shall depart from upon the whole earth and be written off for eternal destruction; and all people shall direct their sight to the path of uprightness.

The second text is Revelation 21–22. We will examine this passage in chapter 10 when we discuss the new heaven and new earth.

The third text is Pseudo-Philo's *Biblical Antiquities* 3:10, a work which is often referred to by its Latin title, *Liber Antiquitatum Biblicarum*. This text reads as follows:

> But when the years appointed for the world have been fulfilled, then the light will cease and the darkness will fade away. And I will bring the dead to life and raise up those who are sleeping from the earth. And hell will pay back its debt, and the place of perdition will return its deposit so that I may render to each according to his works and according to the fruits of his own devices, until I judge between soul and flesh. And the world will cease, and death will be abolished, and hell will shut its mouth. And the earth will not be without progeny or sterile for those inhabiting it; and no one who has been pardoned by me will be tainted. And there will be another earth and another heaven, an everlasting dwelling place.[19]

The fourth text is 2 Peter 3:13, a well-known passage: "But in keeping with his promise we are looking forward to a new heaven and a new earth, the home of righteousness." Even though Peter actually uses the plural οὐρανούς, "heavens," according to Mell this is a Hebraic plural with a singular, collective sense.[20]

18. James H. Charlesworth, ed., *The Old Testament Pseudepigrapha, Volume 1, Apocalyptic Literature and Testaments* (Garden City, N.Y.: Doubleday, 1983), 73.

19. James H. Charlesworth, ed., *The Old Testament Pseudepigrapha, Volume 2, Expansions of the "Old Testament" and Legends, Wisdom and Philosophical Literature, Prayers, Psalms, and Odes, Fragments of Lost Judeo-Hellenistic Works* (Garden City, N.Y.: Doubleday, 1985), 307.

20. Mell, 142–43.

The fifth text is 1 Enoch 72:1. This text reads as follows:

The Book of the Itinerary of the Luminaries of Heaven: the position of each and every one, in respect to their ranks, in respect to their authorities, and in respect to their seasons; each one according to their names and their places of origin and according to their months, which Uriel, the holy angel who was with me, and who (also) is their guide, showed me—just as he showed me all their treatises and the nature of the years of the world unto eternity, till the new creation which abides forever is created.[21]

The sixth text is Jubilees 1:29. This text reads as follows:

And the angel of the presence, who went before the camp of Israel, took the tablets of years from the time of the creation of the law and testimony according to their weeks (of years), according to the jubilees, year by year throughout the full number of jubilees, from [the day of creation until] the day of the new creation when the heaven and earth and all of their creatures shall be renewed according to the powers of heaven and according to the whole nature of earth, until the sanctuary of the Lord is created in Jerusalem upon Mount Zion. And all of the lights will be renewed for healing and peace and blessing for all of the elect of Israel and in order that it might be thus from that day and unto all the days of the earth.[22]

The seventh text is Jubilees 4:26. This text reads as follows:

For the Lord has four (sacred) places upon the earth: the garden of Eden and the mountain of the East and this mountain which you are upon today, Mount Sinai, and Mount Zion, which will be sanctified in the new creation for the sanctification of the earth. On account of this the earth will be sanctified from all sin and from pollution throughout eternal generations.[23]

According to Mell, seven other texts speak of the renewal of creation, the Renewer (God) of the world, and the hope of a new world. These texts are 4 Esdras 7:75; 2 (Syriac) Baruch 32:6; 57:2; Liber Antiquitarum 32:17; 16:3; Apocalypse of Abraham 17:14; and (Syriac) Baruch 44:12. Translations of these texts can be found in the Charlesworth volumes.

These apocalyptic texts explore various themes in relation to the new creation introduced in the passages in Isaiah. "New creation," "day of the Lord," "new heaven and new earth," "new Jerusalem," and "restoration of the temple" are all phrases that express a pessimism about the present reality within history and anticipate a time when Yahweh will act to bring

21. Charlesworth, *The Old Testament Pseudepigrapha* 1:50.
22. Ibid., 2:54–55.
23. Ibid., 63.

about the total transformation of the world. Of all the above-mentioned texts, Jubilees 4:26 is the most important as it employs the phrase "new creation" as a technical term for a new world order.[24]

The Use of New Creation in the Tannaitic Literature

According to Mell, rabbinic Judaism does not emphasize eschatology but fidelity to the law. It is unnecessary, therefore, to develop the use of the theme of "new creation" in the Tannaitic literature. The terminology and perspective therefore diverge from that of the Old Testament and early Judaism and from Paul. The formula, "Always begin anew with the beginning," best expresses the credo of rabbinic theology. Readers interested in the details of this approach may refer to Mell.[25]

The Use of New Creation in the Literature of the Hellenistic Synagogue

The discussion of this literature by Mell does not contribute substantially to what can be gleaned from the Old Testament and early Judaism texts in terms of providing any background for Paul. In Slavonic Enoch the orientation is toward a repression of the future-cosmic eschatology in favor of an individualistic hope of an afterlife. The perspective changes from a linear one in the texts of Isaiah and texts of early Judaism to a vertical one where new birth replaces new creation. The influence of Hellenistic dualism of two worlds—the earthly and the heavenly—is especially strong in this literature. The book of Joseph and Asenath, especially 8:9 and 15:2–6, stresses the difference between the Jew and the Gentile. Conversion to Judaism is a "new creation." Conversion of proselytes to Judaism is therefore the necessary precedent to an individual participation in an eschatological salvation existence.[26]

Mell concludes that "the Pauline idea of καινὴ κτίσις turns out to be a pre-Pauline consensus-idea of early Jewish eschatology for the initiative of God reserved for an overwhelmingly-worthy future end-salvation. This abstract idea is not one-sided in early Jewish theology, i.e. cosmological or fixed, but is open to a soteriological fulfillment. An anthropological and present-eschatological development of the idea as the motive for the new creation could not be detected in the literature of early Judaism."[27]

24. Mell, 172–78.
25. Ibid., 179–203.
26. Ibid., 205–51.
27. Ibid., 257.

The New Creation in the New Testament

The next step in our study is to examine the concept of the new creation in the New Testament literature. Several key passages mention new creation explicitly, namely, 2 Corinthians 5:17 and Galatians 6:15. We will now turn our attention toward these two passages.

Second Corinthians 5:17

THE WIDER CONTEXT

In order to interpret 2 Corinthians 5:17 correctly, we must examine it within the wider context of Paul's letter. Beginning at 2 Corinthians 3:1, Paul states that he has no need to commend himself with letters of recommendation to convince people that his apostleship is authentic. The Corinthians themselves were Paul's epistle, being known and read aloud by all people. The proof of the genuineness of Paul's gospel and his personal "credentials" was the changed lives of these formerly pagan Corinthians. They had been transformed by the "writing" of God! This "writing" was an inscription made not with ink, but with the Spirit of the living God!

Because the new covenant brings the promise of the Holy Spirit, Paul's new covenant ministry is a ministry of the Holy Spirit. Paul is a minister of a covenant that gives life through the Spirit, not one that brings death through the letter. This new covenant brings such great hope to Christians that Paul and other servants of God respond with great boldness. Obscured from unbelieving Jews, the new covenant glory is revealed for Christians because they have returned to the Lord (Jesus) for salvation. To embrace the Lord (Jesus) results in a transforming work of the Holy Spirit who introduces the Christian to ever higher levels of glory.

Because Christians have this new covenant ministry, they dare not give up. God will continue to sustain his servants as they serve him. Paul and other servants of Christ do not have to resort to fraud in order to survive. Paul has renounced the hidden things of dishonesty; he does not walk in craftiness or adulterate the gospel message so as to make it more palatable to people. The final proof of the power of the gospel is its effect on every person's conscience.

Once again Paul admits that the effect of the gospel is not uniform. It is hidden from those whose minds are darkened. They do not see the uncovering of this glorious gospel about Christ. Satan has been very active in the lives of these unbelievers so that the light of the gospel cannot shine in their minds. They simply do not comprehend what the gospel implies nor do they perceive its significance and greatness.

At this point Paul's reference to new creation in 2 Corinthians 5:17 receives its Old Testament setting. Second Corinthians 4:6 says, "For God, who said, 'Let light shine out of darkness,' made his light shine in our hearts to give us the light of the knowledge of the glory of God in the face of Christ." Here Paul is referring to Genesis 1 and is saying that the same God who created the cosmos is now working in and through Jesus Christ to establish a new creation. The same God who created the old creation has also created the new creation through Jesus Christ. Through faith in Jesus Christ the redeemed are now heirs to that new creation that will be finalized when Jesus is Lord of all. The same God who effected the old creation by fiat and called light out of darkness is now active in the hearts of his people who are a part of his new creation. This God provides the light of the gospel that results in knowledge about the glory of God in the presence of Jesus Christ.

Paul's ministry results in death within himself but life in those to whom he ministers. Paul knew that the fragile "vessel" would shatter one day. It might be soon or it might not be for years. But the shattering would come to all. This prospect did not hinder Paul for a moment. He was confident that the God who raised up Jesus would raise up all believers in Jesus also. Paul and the Corinthians would all appear before God. Nothing would be lost. All of the things that Paul did were for the benefit of the Corinthians. In terms of his body Paul saw the operation of the law of inverse proportions: the more his body lost, the more those whom he served gained. The resurrection power that raised Jesus would also raise Paul. Even if Paul died, the Corinthians could thank God for his grace to them through Paul's ministry. Therefore Paul refused to quit. He had this tremendous new covenant ministry. Even though his outer person was dying, his inner person was being renewed daily. Paul was not depressed by this prospect, but he considered his momentary light afflictions as producing an exceeding and eternal weight of glory.[28]

The present age is a time of affliction and a time when death is operative. But this present situation will give way to a time of exultation and life when God's new creation will be established in all its fullness. Therefore, Christians do not concentrate on the things they can see, but on the things they cannot see. The things that can be seen are only temporary (Gk. πρόσ-καιρος, "lasting only for a time, temporary, transitory"). The things that cannot be seen—the glories of the new creation—are eternal.

Second Corinthians 5 is a separate chapter in the English versions but it is clear from the Greek text that Paul did not intend a break after 4:18 since 5:1 begins with the conjunction γάρ, "for." What follows the conjunction explains the statement made by Paul in 4:18, namely, the things that can be seen are temporal, but the things that cannot be seen are eternal. Paul

---

28. See Romans 8:18, where the sufferings of the present time are not worthy of comparison to the glory to be revealed.

knew that his body was subject to death (4:16). If the Lord did not return before Paul died, Paul would experience physical death. His present body was temporal.

What Paul intended in 5:1–5 is unclear. In his book on eschatology, *The Bible and the Future*, Anthony Hoekema presents and discusses four views held by various writers: (1) the "building" is an intermediate body that God gives a Christian at death, which prevents a state of "nakedness" until the Lord raises him at the resurrection and gives him a permanent resurrected body;[29] (2) another view is that the building is heaven;[30] (3) the third view is that the building is the resurrection body that a Christian receives at death;[31] (4) the last view is that the present tense ἔχομεν in verse 1 should be interpreted as a futuristic present and translated "we will have." Thus the building is the resurrection body that Christians receive at Christ's parousia. Many writers, including this one, prefer this view.[32] Whatever the correct interpretation may be, clearly Paul looked forward with certainty to a permanent "building" from God that he and other Christians would receive, which motivated them to faithful service for Christ in the interim. The Holy Spirit is God's pledge that he intends to fulfill this promise to his people.

Paul's eschatological orientation in this section of 2 Corinthians must be considered in any interpretation of new creation in 5:17. Is this eternal building from God another piece of the new creation that Christ has inaugurated? The old creation was characterized by death. The new creation will be characterized by life. Life includes not only spiritual life, but resurrection life. According to 1 Corinthians 15:26 death is one of the last enemies that Christ must destroy.

Paul can be of great cheer because he knows that death will not be the end of existence. On the contrary, to be absent from the body is to be present with the Lord. While Paul is at home in the body his aim is to please God. All Christians must appear before the judgment seat of Christ (another eschatological motif) to receive either reward or rebuke from him based on the things they have done through their bodies, whether good or worthless. Because the Lord holds Christians accountable, they must be faithful in new covenant ministry of extending the church in the world. Whatever the Corinthians think of Paul is ultimately unimportant. He must please God.

29. This is the view held by theologian Lewis Sperry Chafer. See his *Systematic Theology*, 8 vols. (Dallas: Dallas Seminary Press, 1975), 4:414–15.

30. Anthony A. Hoekema adopts this view. See his *The Bible and the Future* (Grand Rapids: Eerdmans, 1979), 104–6.

31. See Murray J. Harris, "2 Corinthians," in *The Expositor's Bible Commentary*, ed. Frank E. Gaebelein, 12 vols. (Grand Rapids: Zondervan, 1976), 10:349–50 n. 1. Harris also allows for the reception of the spiritual body at the parousia (see p. 350 n. 1).

32. Representatively, Philip E. Hughes, *Paul's Second Epistle to the Corinthians*, NICNT (Grand Rapids: Eerdmans, 1962), 160–67.

Paul's love for Christ motivates him to keep preaching the gospel. Christ demonstrated his love toward people by dying for all people who, in Adam, were dead in trespasses and sins (see Rom. 5:6–21; 1 Cor. 15:22). Christ's redemptive love for people calls for a reciprocal love for him from those who live by faith in him. Those who live through him should no longer live for themselves but for him who died for them and was raised again.

This is the whole reason why Paul preaches the gospel. The old creation was marred by Adam's transgression and the reign of death. All people have Adam's sin imputed to them so that they stand condemned before God whether or not they have sinned.[33] Of course, all people have sinned personally. But because Adam's relationship with God was severed (this is what the Bible means by "death"), so every one of his descendants has the same severed relationship with God at birth. Yet that severed relationship has been restored by Christ through his work of reconciling people to God. Paul will develop that reconciliation theme in 2 Corinthians 5:16–21.[34]

THE NARROWER CONTEXT

This redemptive death of Christ has changed Paul's perspective toward the old created order. Before Paul came to faith in Christ as the Savior of Israel, he looked at Christ as an impostor and failure. If Jesus were the Messiah, Paul had reasoned, then Jesus was a miserable failure. He had failed to deliver Israel from Rome and bring her to the place where she could enjoy the old order without any further hassle. As a Christian Paul came to realize that such a perspective on Christ was "after the flesh." Although scholars debate the meaning of κατὰ σάρκα, "after the flesh," in 2 Corinthians 5:16, Bruce's paraphrase seems to come close to Paul's meaning:

> . . . an appreciation of Christ crucified involves a transvaluation of values and in particular the turning upside down of secular canons of wisdom and power. No man presents the same appearance when viewed from the vantage-point of the new order ("according to the Spirit") as he does when seen "according to the flesh"; and this is pre-eminently true of one's assessment of Christ.[35]

Paul's argument in this entire section of 2 Corinthians now comes to a climax in 5:17. The ὥστε at the beginning of verse 17 draws a conclusion from the preceding contrast between death in Adam and life in Christ and

---

33. See S. Lewis Johnson, Jr., "Romans 5:12—An Exercise in Exegesis and Theology," in *New Directions of New Testament Study*, ed. Richard Longenecker and Merrill C. Tenney (Grand Rapids: Zondervan, 1974), 298–316; and John Murray, *The Imputation of Adam's Sin* (Nutley, N.J.: Presbyterian and Reformed, 1977).

34. See David L. Turner, "Paul and the Ministry of Reconciliation in 2 Cor 5:11–6:2," *Criswell Theological Review*, 4 (Fall 1989): 77–95.

35. F. F. Bruce, *1 and 2 Corinthians*, NCB (Greenwood, S.C.: Attic, 1971), 208.

the changed perspective brought by the death of Christ. Although scholars vary in their opinions on what Paul means by the terms he uses in verse 17, they agree that the phrase "in Christ" is a significant component of Pauline theology. Barrett says,

> "In Christ" is itself a Pauline phrase of central but disputed significance. It is best explained as originating neither in mysticism nor in the realistic ideas of sacramental communion, nor in the idea of the church as an institution, but in primitive Christian eschatology. The death and resurrection of Jesus were eschatological events, effecting the transition from this age to the Age to Come. Believers could take advantage of this transition, but the transference from the one age to the other could take place only "in Christ."[36]

All scholars dispute the exact nuance of καινὴ κτίσις, "new creation." The majority favor the translation of κτίσις as "creation" rather than "creature." Hughes argues that "redemption in Christ is nothing less than the fulfillment of God's eternal purposes in creation, so radical in its effects that it is justly called a new creation (see 4:6). . . ."[37] Since Paul is using the phrase in an eschatological sense, new creation is preferred to the rabbinic sense of new creature.[38] Furnish points out that in Paul's letters κτίσις virtually always refers to creation in its entirety (see Rom. 1:20, 25; 8:19, 20, 21, 22).[39]

But is this new creation only soteriological or is it also eschatological? If it is eschatological, how inclusive is this eschatology? Once again, scholars have reached no consensus. Mell devotes his entire book to arguing that new creation for Paul is a christological new order where people are redeemed from the old order of sin and death. The background of Paul is not apocalyptic Judaism. Therefore, ideas of new heaven and new earth and renewal of the cosmos are not part of his theology. Plummer states quite bluntly, "The very essence of the new creation is that it is moral and spiritual, not, as is often pictured in prophetic and apocalyptic literature, an actual new heaven and new earth."[40] On the other hand, Furnish believes that Paul is indebted to apocalyptic Judaism. The apostle's use of the phrase derives from the general apocalyptic tradition and designates the totality of creation. Parallels to Paul's thought are 2 Peter 3:10 and Revelation 21:4–5.

36. C. K. Barrett, *A Commentary on the Epistle to the Romans*, HNTC (New York: Harper & Brothers, 1957), 127.

37. Philip E. Hughes, *Paul's Second Epistle to the Corinthians*, NICNT (Grand Rapids: Eerdmans, 1962), 202.

38. Ralph P. Martin, *2 Corinthians*, WBC (Waco, Tex.: Word, 1986), 152.

39. Victor Paul Furnish, *II Corinthians*, AB (Garden City, N.Y.: Doubleday, 1984), 314.

40. Alfred Plummer, *A Critical and Exegetical Commentary on the Second Epistle of St Paul to the Corinthians*, ICC (Edinburgh: T. & T. Clark, 1915), 181.

Paul is "clearly indebted" to the apocalyptic tradition that conceives of a total replacement of the old by the new.[41] Bruce writes that a believer anticipates the new heaven and new earth of which Isaiah spoke in Isaiah 65:17 and 66:22.[42] Strachan goes even further and says that Paul shared the belief of the early Christian church in the imminent advent of Jesus to inaugurate his kingdom on earth.[43]

This writer believes that Paul is thinking neither individually nor existentially. He is thinking redemptive-historically. The old redemptive-historical order has been replaced by a new redemptive-historical order in Christ. This new order moves forward to the glorious period in the history of the world when all things will be subjected to Christ as creator and redeemer (see 1 Cor. 15:20–28; Rev. 4:11; 21–22). God's new revelation in Christ has completely changed the perspective—the old creation will not be restored because the new creation has been inaugurated. The new activity of God will involve the resurrection body, a new city (the new Jerusalem that descends from heaven), and the new heaven and the new earth. Seven keys to understanding 5:17 include the following:

1. the background in Isaiah and early Judaism;
2. the use of the creation motif in 4:6;
3. the change of perspective concerning God's redemptive purposes (5:16);
4. the conjunction of result (ὥστε) in 5:17;
5. the dynamic and eschatological sense of "in Christ" in Paul's writings;
6. the contrast between "the old" and "the new" in the last part of 5:17;
7. the parallel between Paul's terminology in this passage and Romans 8, where Paul speaks of the freedom of the creation that will be introduced at the resurrection of Christians (Rom. 8:18–25).

Two problems that any interpretation of 5:17 must face, however, include the absence of a finite verb in 5:17a and the textual problem in 5:17b. Should "he is" be supplied in 5:17a? Should "all things" be included in 5:17b? This writer suggests that the answer to both questions should be "No." He believes that 5:17a should be translated as "so then, if any person [is] in Christ, new creation [becomes his perspective]." And 5:17b should be

41. Furnish, 314–16.
42. Bruce, 209.
43. R. H. Strachan, *The Second Epistle of Paul to the Corinthians*, MNTC (London: Hodder and Stoughton, 1935), 114.

rendered "the things of the old [order] have passed away; behold, the new [order] has come." To insert "he is" in 5:17a leads to the interpretation of καινὴ κτίσις as "new creature" and narrows the scope. Sufficient reasons have been given so far to regard the "new creation" as cosmic in orientation.

To add "all things" to "new" in 5:17b is an error. The reading "all things" is a corruption of the text that probably arose by copying those words from 5:18 through a process known as dittography. The shorter reading is supported by the earliest manuscripts, whereas the longer reading is supported by later manuscripts. Therefore, the editors of the fourth revised edition of the United Bible Societies' text give the shorter reading an "A" rating, indicating a high degree of certainty.[44]

It is important to note the tenses Paul uses in terms of the two orders. The old order has "passed away" (aorist tense) as a redemptive-historical category. The new order has begun and is now present (perfect tense) as a new redemptive-historical category. Since the interim between the cessation of the old order and the culmination of the new order has already lasted 2000 years, modern Christians have difficulty in believing that the new order has really come. Since Christians do not actually observe much newness, they doubt seriously whether the new things are present. What Christians need to do today is recapture Paul's perspective: all the old things that were a part of the condemnation upon Adam brought by the Fall—sin, rebellion, alienation, and judgment—have been remedied through the work of Christ. In Paul the counterpoint to "in Christ" is "in Adam." As Cranfield has pointed out, Genesis 1–3 is never far from Paul's thought.[45] Paul never left the fundamental premise that Adam's sin set the stage for all subsequent human history, bringing alienation between people and God.

Christ's death was not just some insignificant footnote within history but the central event that resolved man's dilemma. God has reconciled people to himself through Christ. He no longer imputed their transgressions to them. His righteousness becomes their righteousness. This was Paul's gospel and this gospel drove him as a qualified servant of the new covenant to preach to people about their need to respond in faith to God's reconciliation through Christ. Only divinely effected reconciliation can resolve the problem that people face; only through the blood of Christ's cross can people experience peace with God (see Rom. 5:1).

Adam is associated with the old creation, which involves three realms: people, angels (both good and evil), and the cosmos. These three realms must be brought under the sovereignty of God when his kingdom is final-

44. For a discussion of the textual phenomena, see Bruce M. Metzger, *A Textual Commentary on the Greek New Testament* (New York: United Bible Societies, 1971), 580.
45. C. E. B. Cranfield, *The Epistle to the Romans*, ICC, 2 vols. (Edinburgh: T. & T. Clark, 1975), 1:294.

ized and two of the realms must be redeemed: people and the cosmos. The new creation cannot be established in all its fullness until all of this work is done.

Redeeming people seems to be the first phase of God's program. The work of Christ on the cross was needed first to secure the redemption of people. The second phase of the program will be the total subjugation and elimination of evil angelic activity from the creation. Without question Christ dealt Satan a preliminary, yet decisive defeat in the cross, as Cullmann argues.[46] Colossians 2:14–15, Ephesians 4:8, and 1 Peter 3:22 confirm this preliminary defeat, but the defeat will not be final until Satan and his hosts are confined to the lake of fire (Rev. 20:20; see 2 Pet. 2:4 and Jude 6). The third phase will be the redemption of the cosmos. This is third in order and follows chronologically on the redemption of people and the banishment of Satan. According to Revelation 21:1, the new heaven and new earth appear after the two preceding phases have been completed. The last use of "new" in the New Testament canon is Revelation 21:5 where God declares that he will make "all things new."

When all three phases are finally completed, then the new creation will be established in all its fullness. A clean and clear break will take place between the lost and the saved. The Holy City will contain only those who have washed their robes and made them white in the blood of the Lamb; all others will be excluded from that city (Rev. 22:14–15). Mourning, pain, death, and illness will also be removed (Rev. 21:4). This whole future work of God has its redemptive base in the cross of Christ. Hughes notes that the verb παρέρχομαι in 2 Corinthians 5:17 is used elsewhere in the New Testament in connection with the passing away of the old order and its replacement by a new order (Matt. 24:35; 2 Pet. 3:10).[47] Thus, Paul may legitimately say that the old order has passed away and the new order is present.

Galatians 6:15

THE WIDER CONTEXT

The other New Testament text where the phrase "new creation" occurs is Galatians 6:15. Throughout Galatians, Paul has been arguing that the work of Christ and the Mosaic law are two distinct phases of redemptive history. The law was given to Israel, a particular nation, until the time when Christ would come and provide the perfect redemption from sin for all people. With his sacrifice the law ended as the basis for a proper relationship with God. The law had served its interim function as a παιδαγωγός, or "instructor, teacher, or guide," for children growing up toward adulthood.

---

46. Oscar Cullmann, *Salvation in History* (New York: Harper and Row, 1967), 242.
47. Hughes, 203 n. 42.

Christ has brought adulthood, which carries inheritance with it. The new phase of adulthood means that the function of the παιδαγωγός is no longer necessary. The παιδαγωγός can now retire and allow the adults to function as adults.

On the other hand, Paul's opponents argued that the Mosaic covenant had not been canceled, and that the Mosaic law was as much in effect as it ever had been, with the possible exception of animal sacrifices. Israel was God's *only* people. If Gentiles were to experience salvation, they must be circumcised, keep Sabbath, and celebrate the Jewish festivals just as any member of the covenant people had done since Moses delivered the Torah at Sinai.

Paul referred to these Mosaic requirements imposed upon the Gentiles as "works." If Gentiles really needed to become Jews in order to be saved, then Christ's death was a waste. Gentile proselytes to Judaism were nothing new and were a long-standing phenomenon before Christ was ever born. If Gentiles had to add these Jewish "works" to their faith in Christ, the gospel Paul preached was false. He preached that Gentiles were justified by faith and authenticated by the Holy Spirit. If Paul's gospel were true, then his opponents' gospel was false. They not only had compromised the efficacy of Christ's death but placed law above promise.

Paul therefore showed the subordination of law to promise. The law of Moses was added alongside the promise to Abraham until the seed should come to whom the promise had been made. Now that the seed had come, the law had served its purpose. Adoption into the family of God was now direct, by faith. All sons receive the promised inheritance of the Abrahamic covenant, that is, the promise of great soteriological and ecclesiological realities. With the coming of Christ, the Heir, those affiliated with him (not with Israel) are joint-heirs in the inheritance. They were *all* sons of God through faith in Christ. The great evidence of this sonship was not circumcision of the flesh, but circumcision of the heart by the Holy Spirit. The Spirit enabled the sons to cry out to the Father: Abba!

The Galatians had two choices. They could follow the Judaizers and their teaching or they could follow Paul and his teaching. To follow the Judaizers meant they would align themselves under one paradigm: Hagar–Ishmael–the old Mosaic covenant–the earthly Jerusalem with its bondage to the cultus. To follow Paul meant they would align themselves with another paradigm: Sarah–Isaac–the new covenant–the heavenly Jerusalem–promise and freedom. Since these were two diametrically opposed paradigms, one could not belong to both. One had to choose one or the other. Which would it be? Bondage or freedom? The Judaizers or Paul? For Paul the choice was obvious.

Christ had freed Christians to freedom. These Gentile Galatians needed to avoid the trap of Jewish legalism that would bring them back into terrible bondage. Circumcision would only bring greater obligation to the entire old system of law. Reliance on these Jewish works instead of on Christ and the Spirit would alienate them from Christ and grace.

If the Galatians really wanted to be under law, a law was readily available for them. This law was the law of love. This law was true freedom and fulfilled the ultimate intent of the Mosaic law. Their present squabbling would lead to their consumption if they continued to follow the Judaizers. But if they adopted the new commandment of love, they would experience the unity and peace it creates.

The choice of paradigm was also a vote either for the flesh or the Spirit. The conflict between Ishmael and Isaac symbolized an even greater conflict: flesh against Spirit. The solution to the flesh problem was certainly not the bondage of the Mosaic law, which had never freed anyone. In fact, it only stirred up the works of the flesh (see Rom. 7:7–25). Only release from sin and transformation by the Spirit would produce the "fruit" that the law required in the first place (see Rom. 8:4). Furthermore, only those who produced this fruit of the Spirit would inherit God's kingdom.

To avoid the inference that life according to the Spirit meant sinlessness, Paul gave directives in Galatians 6 for handling those who fell into sin and described the restorative process. Christians who were led by the Spirit needed to restore the fallen brother or sister. Pride had no place in the restoration process because temptation was not a problem for only a few. By bearing the burdens of one another, Christians would fulfill the law of Christ, the law of love. Yet each one had to realize that the sharing of burdens did not mean absolution from individual responsibility before the Lord. The gospel does not lead to antinomianism. There is a law of Christ. God is not mocked; whatever one sows, one will reap—either corruption or eternal life. Christians must persevere in well-doing. In God's eschatological season Christians will reap eternal life, if they do not drop out in the interim. One new covenant directive is to do good to all people, but especially to Christians.

THE NARROWER CONTEXT

Paul concludes the letter in his own hand—why he does this is uncertain (Gal. 6:11). Perhaps he desired to add more authority to the letter. He does not want the Judaizers to win. So once more he warns the Galatians about his opponents. They have ulterior motives in urging circumcision—they want to make a good impression so they will not be persecuted by (unbelieving?) Jews because of the cross of Christ. Not even those who are going around circumcising keep the law.[48] They wish others to be circumcised so

48. It seems better to take the present participle περιτεμνόμενοι as the proper reading in 6:13. Also, see the discussion in Peter Richardson, *Israel in the Apostolic Church* (Cambridge: Cambridge University Press, 1989), 84–97.

that they may boast about their accomplishments. Paul, however, wants no other confidence than the cross of Christ, through which [whom?] the world has been crucified to him and he to the world.

In verse 14 the meaning of the term "world" is a critical problem. Guthrie suggests that the meaning is "the order of material creation and everything under its sway, independent of the control of the Holy Spirit."[49] If this definition were correct, it would have important consequences for the meaning of "new creation" in verse 15. Other commentators suggest other definitions for the term "world" here, including "the mode of life which is characterised by earthly advantages, viewed as obstacles to righteousness";[50] "this age, in sharp opposition to God";[51] and "the comprehensive designation for everything that is connected with the law."[52] Thus, for Paul the world consists in "Israelitish descent, circumcision, the rank and dignity of a Pharisee, the righteousness that is in law."[53] The cross of Christ has severed Paul's relationship with this world. Therefore, circumcision is of no salvific value nor is uncircumcision of any salvific value. The new creation is the only redemptive work of God that has ongoing value.

At this point, scholars struggle once again to define "new creation." Fung suggests "new order."[54] For Bruce it means "life in Christ" and everything which that entails eschatologically.[55] For Luhrmann it means "righteousness, life, blessing, freedom, Spirit, love—in Christ as the crucified One (see 2 Cor. 5:17)."[56] For Betz the expression is tantamount to a "new religion."[57] For Mell it refers to the crucified Lord as eschatological reign of salvation, a pre-Pauline formula with a new soteriological orientation, the annulling of the soteriological privilege of the synagogue, and a new soteriological basic rule for the world.[58] The new creation in Christ does not rule out a future fulfillment of God's promise to Israel as the texts in the Book of Romans reveal. But this is part of a Pauline dualism between present and future that Paul himself does not resolve.[59]

49. Donald Guthrie, *Galatians*, CB (Greenwood, S.C.: Attic, 1974), 150–51.

50. Ernest De Witt Burton, *A Critical and Exegetical Commentary on the Epistle to the Galatians* (Edinburgh: T. & T. Clark, 1921), 514.

51. Frank J. Matera, *Galatians*, SP (Collegeville, Minn.: The Liturgical Press, 1992), 231.

52. Dieter Luhrmann, *Galatians: A Continental Commentary* (Minneapolis: Fortress, 1992), 121.

53. Burton, 354.

54. Ronald Y. K. Fung, *The Epistle to the Galatians* (Grand Rapids: Eerdmans, 1988), 308.

55. F. F. Bruce, *The Epistle to the Galatians*, NIGTC (Grand Rapids: Eerdmans, 1982), 273.

56. Luhrmann, 121.

57. Hans Dieter Betz, *Galatians*, Hermeneia (Philadelphia: Fortress, 1979), 320.

58. Mell, 285–318.

59. Ibid., 318–25.

Commentators point out the close relationship among three Pauline texts in Galatians: "For you are all one in Christ Jesus" (Gal. 3:28); "For in Christ Jesus neither circumcision nor uncircumcision has any value. The only thing that counts is faith expressing itself through love" (Gal. 5:6); "Neither circumcision nor uncircumcision means anything; what counts is a new creation" (Gal. 6:15). Also, the verbal parallels between the texts in Galatians with 2 Corinthians 5:17 and the conceptual patterns in 2 Corinthians and Galatians of new covenant replacing old covenant argue well for a unity of Pauline theology concerning the "new creation." The new creation brings a reconciliation of the horizontal fractures characteristic of the old creation and old order. Instead of the great difficulties that have divided people since the Fall, Christ has brought unity to his people and ultimately to the universe. The new creation brings reconciliation to the ethnic, sexual, and socioeconomic barriers that have divided people and enables them to love one another once more.[60]

Just as there are two persons in Pauline anthropology and soteriology (Adam and Christ), there are also two creations (old and new). Due to the Fall, the old creation was marred by divisions and enmity. But Christ's cross heals the division and enmity and introduces new creation. As part of this new creation Christians should work hard to maintain the unity created by the Holy Spirit in the bond which is Christ's peace. There is one body, one Spirit, one hope of our calling, one Lord, one faith, one baptism, one God and Father of all who is above all, and through all, and in all (Eph. 4:3–4).

Redemption is ultimately cosmic in scope. God has acted in Christ to unify people once more. The church should be the primary example of the reconciliation that Christ has brought. The body of Christ should be completely free from prejudices based on race, intelligence, sex, wealth, status, or privilege. All Christians should receive one another and no barriers should exist that separate people from one another and recreate alienation. The blood of Christ's cross has canceled all of these divisions and has paved the way for peace and love. Faith must operate through love. The new creation has begun in Christ. But it must be functionally implemented. Even though the subjugation of Satan and the redemption of the cosmos have an eschatological dimension, during the interim believers must strive to achieve the reconciliation of people. If diligence is not maintained, the body will consume itself through backbiting (Gal. 5:15).

Since new creation starts with the reconciliation of people, the Pauline anthropology of the new man will now become our focus. We will develop that theme next in chapter 8.

---

60. This emphasis upon reconciliation recalls a frequent contrast in Paul between two (δύο) and one (εἷς). Key texts for this include 1 Cor. 12:4, 5, 12, 13, 14; Eph. 2:14, 15, 16, 18; and Phil. 1:27; 2:2.

For Further Study

Minear, Paul S. *Christians and the New Creation*. Louisville: Westminster/ John Knox Press, 1994.

While this book does not deal with the new creation per se, it does show the influence of Genesis 1–4 on the New Testament. Topics include: "Peace on Earth: The Promise of the Covenant in Luke"; "Jesus and Satan: The Sealing of the Covenant in Luke"; "Adam and Christ: Death and Life in I Corinthians 15"; "Works of God: The Two Families in John's Gospel"; and "From One Covenant to Another: Metaphors of Transition."

Mell, Ulrich. *Neue Schöpfung*. Beiheft für die neutestamentliche Wissenschaft und die Kunde der alteren Kirche. Ed. Erich Grasser. Berlin: de Gruyter, 1989.

While this doctoral dissertation is limited to those who can read difficult theological German, it is the most comprehensive treatment of the new creation motif in 2 Corinthians 5:17 and Galatians 6:16 and non-Pauline literature. It is worthy of translation into English so that it can be available to a wider readership.

New Creation deals with the Redemptive-historical plan for the world. It includes

Man.
Angels. } *creatures*

World } *Universe.*

Journal Search

NEW MAN — (especially Ethical structure)

Eph 4:17 – 6:9

Col 2:20 – 4:6

N.T. — Ethical imperatives

NEW MAN.

relationship   status ———> Not ontological

Anthropological   Ecclesiological   Ethical

8

Structures

see pg 52
Trans 14
15

The New Man

O ne of the difficulties in interpreting the Bible is understanding what a writer means by the terms that the writer uses. This difficulty is especially prominent in Paul's use of the Greek word ἄνθρωπος. In Ephesians 4:24 the NIV and the NASB render this word "self" and the RSV translates it as "nature." Such translations can be misleading and can introduce concepts foreign to the New Testament. When Paul means "nature" he uses φύσις. The fact that he used ἄνθρωπος when writing about the "old man" and the "new man" should alert the interpreter to investigate carefully what Paul meant when he used these phrases. Paul also wrote about the "inner man" and "outer man" in 2 Corinthians 4:16 (see also Rom. 7:22 and Eph. 3:16 for other texts where "inner man" is used). Are all these ἄνθρωπος texts referring to the same thing? Are they looking at something internal or external to the individual? Are they describing a relationship, a status, or an ontology? The writer believes that when Paul uses the phrases "old man" or "new man" he is describing relationship and status rather than ontology. Further, the concepts of relationship and status involve three structures: (1) an *anthropological* structure, (2) an *ecclesiological* structure, and (3) an *ethical* structure. We will discuss these three structures in the following pages.

The Anthropological Structure

J. Sidlow Baxter correctly states what Paul meant by "old man" when he used this phrase as an anthropological structure: it is a Paulinism for the whole human race "in Adam."[1] The phrase old man describes a person's status in Adam: under God's condemnation and judgment, alienated from God, and destined for death and hell. Alternately, the phrase "new man" is a Paulinism for the status of the redeemed "in Christ": reconciled to God through Christ, regenerated by the Holy Spirit, and destined for heaven. Neither phrase is descriptive of the popular "old nature" and "new nature" in the believer.[2] This understanding views the terms as descriptive of a person's ontology. But for Paul they are redemptive-historical expressions for an individual or corporate status before God.

The two phrases old man and new man are related to the old creation and the new creation. They relate to the program of redemption. The Fall damaged the position of the human race before God drastically and altered the course of the cosmos. The work of God in history is to extricate people from their status of alienation and transfer them to a status of reconciliation. The work of Christ accomplished this transfer. Adam's transgression had implications in every dimension. People were not only alienated from God, but from their neighbors, from the cosmos, and from themselves. Christ's redemption had to repair all of these broken relationships. People needed reconciliation to God, love for their neighbors, the lifting of the curse from the cosmos, and the ability to begin living the way God designed them to live.

Christ's redemptive work, therefore, involved a transfer of status from in Adam to in Christ. When Paul used ἄνθρωπος he probably used it deliberately to describe humanity. Humanity stood condemned in Adam. In Christ, humanity can be reconciled. "In Adam" and "in Christ" are categories of relationship. All people are in Adam by birth and under God's wrath, because Adam's sin is imputed to them. Christ effected a redemptive-historical transfer by dying for a person's sin. The new status ("in Christ") is created by his death. People appropriate this new status when they believe on Christ. The transfer then becomes personal and efficacious. When Paul writes of the old man or the new man in an anthropological sense (Rom. 6:6; Eph. 4:22; Col. 3:9), he is using terms to describe a person's status in Adam or in Christ.

One must understand that the change of status is a *legal* one. The status of the human race in Adam was effected legally when the Fall occurred. A person's status in Christ was effected legally when Christ's death occurred. Romans 5:12–21 is the major passage in the New Testament describing this

1. J. Sidlow Baxter, *A New Call to Holiness* (Grand Rapids: Zondervan, 1973), 92, 94.
2. Lewis Sperry Chafer states, "Those who are regenerate have two natures. The old nature abides with the Christian as an active principle in his life, and his experimental victory over it will be realized only through a definite reliance upon the indwelling Spirit" (*Systematic Theology*, Vol. II, Angelology, Anthropology, Hamartiology [Dallas: Dallas Seminary Press, 1947], 348).

change of status. No attempt will be made here to develop that passage.[3] The legal change cannot be altered by individual knowledge or response. One does not have to know that he is in Adam to be lost. One's rejection of Christ does not nullify his work.

Theologians have struggled for centuries over how to explain the lack of strict parallelism between the two halves. All people are condemned in Adam but all people are not justified in Christ. The New Testament does not teach universalism. People must believe the gospel in order to be saved. All people are a part of the old man, but only those who have placed faith in the redeeming work of Christ are a part of the new man. While Adam's sin was imputed to all people, Christ's righteousness is imputed only to those who believe. The parallelism is not strict. Nevertheless, the objective historical events of the Fall and the Cross are realities.

Another problem is the relationship of Old Testament believers to the new man and to the transfer. Theologians have found this to be another difficult problem. The best solution seems to be that the redemptive work of Christ was always anticipated in the divine mind so that Christ was the Lamb of God who was foreordained from the foundation of the world (1 Pet. 1:20). Christ's redemptive work has retroactive efficacy for all who responded in faith to God from Abel through the Cross. Although individual Old Testament believers did not historically believe on Jesus Christ, they did experience his perfection when he made atonement for their sins as well as for the sins of believers who lived after his death (Heb. 11:39–40).[4] Perhaps an analogy will help here. Consider an employee who receives an advance on his paycheck. Although the employer does not actually owe the employee any money, the employer pays the employee for work that he has not yet done. Similarly, Christ earned redemption for people. In a sense Old Testament believers received an advance on what Christ would accomplish. Christ's death was an event in history that had implications both for believers before the Cross as well as believers after it. Thus the Cross functions as the fulcrum of divine activity in history.

The change of legal status does not necessarily coincide with a change in the way a person lives. It is necessary to separate the relational status based on the redemptive-historical work of Christ from the performance status based on the person's life in the Spirit. Paul recognizes a proclivity toward sin

3. For further exegetical details, this writer encourages the reader to consult the following: John Murray, *The Imputation of Adam's Sin* (Nutley, New Jersey: Presbyterian and Reformed, 1977); S. Lewis Johnson, Jr., "Romans 5:12—An Exercise in Exegesis and Theology," in *New Dimensions of New Testament Study*, ed. Richard N. Longenecker and Merrill C. Tenney (Grand Rapids: Zondervan, 1974), 298–316.

4. The difficulties with this topic are well-discussed by Fred Klooster and Allen P. Ross in chapters 6 and 7 of *Continuity and Discontinuity*, ed. John S. Feinberg (Westchester, Ill.: Crossway, 1988), 131–78.

in the Christian, which he calls "flesh" (*not* "nature"). The flesh is a residue left from a Christian's former status in Adam. However, a Christian is not to "walk according to the flesh" but "walk according to the Spirit." The ethical change is part of the anthropological change as *obligation*. It is not part of the anthropological change as *function*. Again the parallelism is not strict. In Adam the anthropological change automatically brought an ethical change. People were not only accounted sinners; they sinned and continued sinning since the Fall. In Christ the anthropological change brings a *potential* ethical change. Christians do not automatically stop sinning and live righteously. If they are to become what they need to become in Christ, they must respond to the Spirit in his ministry of transformation. Romans 6 is the major Pauline passage on this truth. Christians must consider themselves (λογίζομαι) to be dead to sin and alive to God in Christ Jesus (Rom. 6:11).[5]

A very popular doctrine in conservative Christian circles is the idea of the "two natures" in the believer. While this theology correctly recognizes the proclivity toward sin in the Christian, it confuses Pauline categories and has an improper emphasis. Baxter points out that the two-nature theology is deficient because the new nature is presented as subservient to the old nature.[6] The analogy usually pictures two dogs fighting inside: a large, vicious black dog against a small, helpless white dog. The obvious verdict seems to be "no contest." Actually Paul's emphasis is that the Holy Spirit will enable the Christian, the white dog, to win victoriously in the battle against the flesh, the black dog (Gal. 5:16). In this discussion we have attempted to demonstrate that the two-nature theology has nothing to do with Paul's terms old man and new man. If there is any "nature" in the believer, however, Paul's term for that is the "flesh."

The Ecclesiological Structure

The major passage in Paul that expounds the ecclesiological structure of the new man is Ephesians 2:11–22. This writer has done a detailed exegesis of this passage in published form,[7] and the reader is referred to that work for a more thorough treatment. The present discussion will only outline the contours of the ecclesiological structure.

It is important to read Paul redemptive-historically rather than existentially. Much misunderstanding of Paul's vocabulary and theology is due to

---

5. See the very helpful discussion of the "tension" in Christian existence in James D. G. Dunn, *Jesus and the Spirit* (Philadelphia: Westminster, 1975), 308–18.

6. Baxter, 104.

7. Carl B. Hoch, Jr., "The New Man of Ephesians 2," in *Dispensationalism, Israel and the Church*, ed. Craig A. Blaising and Darrell L. Bock (Grand Rapids: Zondervan, 1992), 98–126.

reading him existentially in terms of personal salvation instead of redemptive-historically in terms of God's work in space and time. Paul looks at what God has done redemptively and the results of that redemption. In Ephesians Paul continually contrasts the two periods of salvation history. He writes of what people were before Christ accomplished redemption (ποτέ, "formerly") and what they are now since Christ died on the cross (νῦν, "now"). To use Cullmann's analogy, D-Day is the work of Christ on the cross where he paid the penalty for sin and dealt Satan a preliminary, yet decisive defeat. The Christian awaits V-Day when Christ will establish his kingdom de facto and all things will be made new.[8] Paul describes the present interim period between D-Day and V-Day as "now" (νῦν).[9] He describes V-Day as "then"(τότε).[10] So, while Christians are in the "now" period, they await the "then" period to come.

What happened in the "former" period? This period was characterized by enmity between Jews and Gentiles. God had chosen Israel as a people of privilege and advantage (Rom. 3:1–3; 9:4–6). On the other hand, Gentiles had no status before God. They were totally estranged from the commonwealth of Israel and were strangers from the covenants of the promise. They had no messianic hope, no hope of eternal life, and no knowledge of the one and true God (Eph. 2:12).

Paul wrote of how God has acted redemptively to fulfill his covenants and promise to Israel and extend his grace to the Gentiles. In Genesis 12 God called Abraham and promised him that he would make a great nation from Abraham. In Abraham's seed all the families of the earth would be blessed. During the entire Old Testament period, the Gentiles had little blessing from the seed of Abraham. For the most part the Gentiles were at war with Israel and became hated enemies of Israel. Israel longed for the day of freedom from Gentile domination. Israel also longed for the freedom to serve the Lord and enjoy the promised land without foreign interference and invasion. In this "former" period God was in the process of revealing himself to Israel and making the covenants that would serve as the basis for his future work in Christ, not only to Israel but also to the Gentiles.

The death of Christ changed the "former" period into the "now" period. Paul became the primary apostle to the Gentiles, preaching to them the gospel of acceptance before God through faith in Jesus Christ. In Ephesians 1:7 Paul reminds these Gentiles that for the first time redemption is available to them in Christ's blood. They also have forgiveness of sins. God has

8. Oscar Cullmann, *Christ and Time*, trans. Floyd V. Filson, rev. ed. (Philadelphia: Westminster, 1964), 84.
9. See Rom. 3:26; 5:9, 11; 8:1, 18, 22; 11:5, 30, 31; 16:26; 2 Cor. 5:16; 6:2; Eph. 3:5, 10; Col. 1:26; 2 Thess. 2:6; 1 Tim. 4:8; 6:17; 2 Tim. 1:10; 4:10; Tit. 2:12.
10. See 1 Cor. 4:5; 13:12; 15:28, 54; Gal. 6:4; Col. 3:4; 1 Thess. 5:3; 2 Thess. 2:8.

made known the mystery of his will. The "former" period lacked clarity about the Messiah, but "now" God has revealed that all things are headed up in Christ. The previous succession of time periods (καιροί) led up to the fullness of time. The patriarchs, Moses, the conquest, the judges, Saul, David, Solomon, the divided kingdom, the exile, the restoration, and the intertestamental periods were all moving toward the climax—the coming of Jesus as the Messiah who would fulfill all God's covenants and promise to Israel. In the fullness of time God sent forth his Son, born of woman, born under the law economy so that he might grant adoption as his sons first to Israel and then to the Gentiles (Gal. 4:4). The purpose of this work of God was that those Jews who believed in Jesus might be to the praise of God's glory because they first hoped in Christ back in the "former" period.

Now the Gentiles also were included in this grand redemptive plan and were sealed with the promised Holy Spirit. With the coming of Christ, believing Jews experienced the fulfillment of their redemptive hope. Gentiles shared in this hope and also received the promise of the Spirit simply because they were "in Christ."

In Ephesians 2:1 Paul begins to contrast the status of the Gentiles prior to the death, burial, and resurrection of Christ. They were legally dead to God in the realm of trespasses and sins. They lived according to the course of this world and were under the dominion of Satan who continues to energize unbelievers. In Ephesians 4:17–19 Paul will describe in detail what kind of life-style this existence entailed.

Jews were not exempt from the sinful effects of the Fall, however. They also lived in the desires produced by the degenerate orientation they received from Adam. They followed their own desires and were ontically (i.e., by nature) objects of God's wrath just as the Gentiles were (see Rom. 3:9–20). Even though the Jews had the revelation of God, they rebelled against God's covenant and were guilty of the same idolatry that was characteristic of Gentiles.

But God in his love was merciful to both Jew and Gentile. He gave both ethnic groups eternal life through Christ. By God's grace both Jew and Gentile were saved. Their position in Christ enabled them to be identified with his resurrection and exaltation in the heavenly realm. They would become God's exhibit in coming ages of the surpassing riches of his grace in his kindness to sinners in Christ Jesus. Salvation was entirely by grace without any human merit. No creature could boast of his achievements before God. However, this new creative act of God entailed a new ethic: people should no longer live in trespasses and sins; the redeemed were to fulfill God's redemptive intention by doing good works. Christ made a decisive change when he transferred people from the "former" period to the "now" period. In this historical change, a person's status changed from alienation to reconciliation, from a life of condemnation to a life of justification, from a life dead in transgressions and sins to a life of righteousness, holiness, goodness, and truth.

The three σύν compounds in Ephesians 2:5–6 indicate that Jews and Gentiles have jointly experienced a change in status. Christ is the key. Without him one cannot escape the predicament of sin. He is the person in whom Jews and Gentiles share in his salvation.

Paul has come full circle and probably intended an inclusio with the verb "walk" (περιπατέω) in Ephesians 2:2 and 2:10. Whereas the Gentiles walked formerly in trespasses and sins in the "former" period, "now" they are able to walk in good works that God has prepared from eternity. This transfer in the anthropological structure leads to transfers in the ecclesiological and ethical structures. Through the work of Jesus Christ, God effected a new creation (ποίημα, κτίζω in 2:10) so that good works would be the result of his redemptive activity just as he had desired good works to be the result of his original creation with Adam. The death of Jesus Christ provides the base for the transfer from the old creation to the new creation, from the old man to the new man, and from in Adam to in Christ.

Paul wants to remind the Gentiles of their tremendous alienation and their inferior status redemptively in the "former" period. It is Christ's cross that makes the definitive redemptive-historical transfer. But the benefits of Christ's work are not realized in an individual's life until that person existentially appropriates by faith what Christ has accomplished objectively and historically. Until each person comes to Christ in faith, the merit of Christ is not imputed to the person's account. Faith is the sine qua non for appropriation, not for provision.

In Ephesians 2:11 Paul contrasts the "former" status of the Gentiles with their "now" status described in verses 13–22. In that period before Christ, the Jews, a privileged people who boasted in their circumcision made with a surgical instrument, referred to the Gentiles with the pejorative term "uncircumcision." The status of the Gentiles was one of total alienation from any access to God.

The "now" period has changed that "former" period completely. The Gentiles have a changed status because they are now in Christ. Previously, Gentiles were "far off" (μακράν); now they are "near" (ἐγγύς). The blood of Christ has changed their status. During the "far off" period the Gentiles had only general revelation; there was only occasional witness to them by Jews such as Jonah; they were involved in abominations and ungodly practices, effectively apart from God's redemptive activity with Israel. Except for proselytes and "God-fearers," Gentiles at that time had no interest in the God of Israel and looked upon Israel as odd. But now Gentiles were near, near to Christ, and hence near to the covenants of Israel, to the hope of eternal life, and to the true God. Although the Pauline σύν compounds in Ephesians show that they share *with* Israel, Paul never said that they are incorporated *into* Israel, making them a "new Israel" or "spiritual Israelites."

The emphatic "he" (αὐτός) in Ephesians 2:14 shows that Christ is the peace who has resolved the enmity between Jew and Gentile. Because of his coming the reconciliation takes place that creates the new humanity and ecclesiological structure. This coheres with the definition of "baptism in the Spirit" as that act by which God, by pouring out his Spirit on every level of flesh, created a new entity, the church, in which all former distinctions are soterically leveled.[11] Peace is the opposite of alienation. Jesus has eliminated the hostility that existed previously. He did this by "making" both groups one and by "creating" the two groups into one new man (note the new creation language in vv. 14–15).

From the language that Paul has used in the various texts examined in this book, one can begin to understand Paul's thought structures. As the following table indicates, he thinks in pairs:

The first man	the second Man
the first Adam	the last Adam
the old man	the new man
the old creation	the new creation
the old covenant	the new covenant
the Jew	the Gentile
"formerly"	"now"
"far off"	"near"
two	one
both	one
enmity	peace

A rereading of the above table shows his orientation: it is redemptive-historical rather than existential. The movement is from one to the other.

For Paul only two segments of humanity exist: a person is either a Jew or a Gentile. "Both" describes the two divisions of humanity. Paul was not interested in numbers or proportions, but in redemptive-historical priorities, privileges, and status. Back in the former period, the Gentiles had nothing

---

11. Refer to the discussion in chapter 2, the "Distinctive Nature of Pentecost."

ONE NEW ἄνθρωπος

compared to the Jews. But in Christ these two great groups are united so that both are created by God through Jesus Christ into one unit, one new organism, one new man, that is, the body of Christ, the church!

Christ has broken down the wall that divided the Jew and the Gentile. While Ephesians 2:14 may contain some distant allusion to the balustrade in Herod's temple separating the Court of the Gentiles from the Court of Israel, the contextual definition of the wall is the Mosaic law. The law, with its minute stipulations, was what separated Israel from the Gentiles. That law had to be canceled (καταργέω) and replaced by the new covenant (see the discussion in chapter 7, "New Covenant") before the enmity between Israel and the Gentiles could be resolved and peace be created. "Hostility" (ἔχθρα, v. 14) and "law" (νόμος, v. 15) are accusatives of apposition and define more closely what the "middle wall" is.

The law of Moses was canceled so that God could create (κτίζω, a new creation word) one new man of the Jew and the Gentile. Thus, the new man is an ecclesiological structure, not an individual structure. It certainly is not an ontological structure, as implied by the translation of ἄνθρωπος as "nature." Paul uses this phrase to describe the new united humanity in Christ that he calls the "church" in Ephesians 3:10.

The Jews in the former period were in Adam just as much as the Gentiles were. But because of God's election of Israel as a kingdom of priests, a holy nation, and a people for his possession (see Exod. 19), they had a place of privilege in redemptive history that Gentiles did not have. They were near to God; Gentiles were far off. God's grace to Israel was an attempt to protect them and to preserve them as the channel of his blessing until the time when Christ would come and confirm the promises made to the fathers. Once the Gentiles were also brought near through Christ, the soteric position of both Israel and Gentiles was equalized. However, Israel retained the privileges Paul lists in Romans and Ephesians and served as the channel of witness to the Gentiles. Israel also had the priority in mission. The gospel was preached to the Jew first, and then to the Gentile.

The role of the Holy Spirit in the creation of the new man is as vital as the role of Christ. He provides access for both groups to God the Father. All of these New Testament realities cohere: because of the baptism in the Spirit, the new creation, the new humanity, and the work of Christ, the church has come into existence with no soteric divisions and all people stand before God on an equal salvific basis. The result is that they can approach God with full confidence because the alienation and enmity no longer exist. Peace is effected so that the Gentiles are no longer transients and aliens, but fellow citizens with their fellow Jewish brothers and sisters and equal members of God's household.

This one new organism is built upon the foundation of the apostles and prophets with Jesus Christ as the cornerstone.[12] The Gentiles are being built up together with Israel to become a dwelling place in which God lives by his Spirit. This ecclesiological structure is the second structure of the new man. The anthropological structure looked at the transfer from Adam to Christ; the ecclesiological structure looked at the transfer from two to one, as Gentiles and Jews became a part of the new united organism, the church. The ethical structure will develop the need to live righteously in light of the transfer anthropologically and ecclesiologically.

The Ethical Structure

The two major passages on the new man as ethical structure are Ephesians 4:17–6:9 and Colossians 2:20–4:6. It is significant that both of these passages are in the so-called Pauline imperative sections of these letters. They follow and grow out of the Pauline indicative. The transfer from in Adam to in Christ and from two to one are redemptive-historical and are developed in the Pauline indicative. But the transfer implies and demands a corresponding change in the behavior of those who have appropriated the transfer by faith. So Paul moves to the imperative after he has expounded the indicative. The imperative is not optional because it is second. Some Christians have a tendency to believe that the indicative is essential and the imperative is optional, or that ethics are nice but not necessary. This tendency, however, is a serious misunderstanding of the intent of God in the indicative. God's intent in redemption is that his people might produce good works. Ephesians 2:10 is just as much a part of God's redemptive work as Ephesians 2:8–9. Christians quote Ephesians 2:8–9 frequently. But how many know Ephesians 2:10? Similarly, Titus 3:5–7 is often quoted. But is it ever quoted along with Titus 3:8?

In Ephesians 4 Paul begins his exhortation (παράκλησις) to his readers. Paul has spent three chapters developing the anthropological and ecclesiological structures of the new man. Now he will spend three more chapters developing the ethical structure. He exhorts his readers to live in a manner that is commensurate with God's calling in Christ. His readers need to practice certain virtues if the church is to experience the unity subjectively that Christ has created objectively. These virtues are humility, gentleness, patience, forbearance, and love. Only a diligent exercise of these virtues toward fellow Christians will preserve the unity of the church created by the Holy Spirit in the bond which is the peace that Christ has brought (see

---

12. For the sake of the argument here, it is unnecessary to decide whether the cornerstone is a stone in the base or the top of the temple. The point is that the new temple is a holy temple in the Lord.

Free from sin
Slave to righteousness } pg 208

2:14). The objective unity is stressed by seven "ones": (1) one body; (2) one Spirit; (3) one hope; (4) one Lord; (5) one faith; (6) one baptism; and (7) one God and Father. But the objective unity can quickly become subjective schism if they fail to exercise diligently the gifts that the ascended Christ gave to his church.

In Ephesians 4:11–16 Paul expounds how the gifts of apostle, prophet, evangelist, and pastor-teacher were designed by Christ to perfect the church in unity. The unity of the church enables the church to function holistically and to grow up in Christ to the place where it is perfect in love.

In verses 17–19 Paul reverts to a description of the life-style of these Gentiles before they had appropriated the anthropological new man. Their old life in Adam was characterized by vanity of mind, darkened understanding, estrangement from the life of God, ignorance of God, hardness of heart, loss of all sensitivity to God, debauchery, and the performance of every type of sexual perversion. Their new life in Christ had brought a change because those who preached the gospel to them originally taught them about the need to put off the old man and put on the new man. The aorist infinitives in verses 22 and 23 imply that this "putting off" (ἀποθέσθαι) and "putting on" (ἐνδύσασθαι) was an accomplished fact. When these Gentiles were converted they subjectively appropriated the anthropological new man and discarded the anthropological old man.

Paul uses clothing imagery to describe this change. These Gentiles in Christ had received a new wardrobe. The old wardrobe had to go to the dump. Their transfer from in Adam to in Christ brought them a new status before God: coheirs, members of the same body, and fellow sharers in the promise in Christ Jesus through the gospel (3:6). But the new status brought a new demand: they had been created in righteousness and true holiness. Therefore, they needed to be renewed (the infinitive ἀνανεοῦσθαι, "to renew," in v. 23 is present, indicating a process) in the spirit of their mind. In verses 17–19 Paul has just described what that mind was in Adam. In the rest of the letter he will describe what the renewed mind of the new man entails ethically.

Instead of working through every verse from 4:25 to the end, we have provided the following list to illustrate the contrasts between the ethical deeds of the old man and the ethical deeds of the new man.

Ethical Deeds of the Old Man	Ethical Deeds of the New Man
lying	telling the truth
held anger	forgiveness

Ethical Deeds of the Old Man	Ethical Deeds of the New Man
stealing	sharing
destructive speech	constructive speech
bitterness	sweetness
losing one's cool	controlling oneself
shouting	normal voice
slander	praise
harsh	kind
hard-hearted	compassionate
holding grudges	forgiving injuries
self-centeredness	love
immorality	morality
lewd and coarse language	thanksgiving
evil	goodness
unrighteousness	righteousness
error	truth
pleasing oneself	pleasing the Lord
participating in sins of unregenerate	rebuking unregenerate
wasting time	judicious use of time
ignorance of Lord's will	knowledge of his will
drunkenness	fullness of spirit
silence	song
complaining	thanksgiving
rebellion	submission
abusing one's wife	loving one's wife
dishonoring one's husband	respecting one's husband
disobeying one's parents	obeying one's parents
angering one's children	training one's children
disobeying one's masters	obeying one's masters

Ethical Deeds of the Old Man	Ethical Deeds of the New Man
clock-watchers	hard workers
pleasing people	pleasing the Lord
winning by intimidation	treating people as equals

Clearly the preceding list shows that the new ethical wardrobe contains many articles of clothing. Since many of the articles from the old ethical wardrobe have been worn for years, Christians may find it difficult to put them off permanently. Perhaps that is why Paul used "become" (γίνομαι; NIV "be") so many times in this ethical section (4:32; 5:1, 7, 17), as well as many other present imperatives. Paul knew that the life-implementation of the ethical structure would not be easy. Sinful people have practiced by the deeds of the old man for a long time! It will take time to renew the mind and live according to the new ethical structure!

Since Ephesians and Colossians are sister epistles, Colossians 2:20 begins a parallel to the ethical structure in Ephesians: "Since you died with Christ [anthropological structure] to the basic principles of this world, why, as though you still belonged to it, do you submit to its rules [ethical structure] . . . ?" Why, asks Paul, are you allowing people to control you, saying that you should not touch this or taste that? Since this legalism is according to the commands and teachings of people, it will simply disappear. Such regulations have an appearance of wisdom with their self-imposed worship, their false humility, and their harsh treatment of the body; but they lack any value in restraining sensual indulgence.

In Colossians 3:1–4 Paul exhorts his readers to seek the things "above." They have been raised with Christ [anthropological structure]; therefore, they need to "seek" [ethical structure]. They are to set their minds on things above, not on earthly things [ethical structure] because they have died and their life has now been hidden with Christ in God [anthropological structure].

Paul employs a chiastic pattern (i.e., A-B-B-A; see diagram below) in the next section to develop what he means by "things above" and "things upon the earth." First, he mentions "things above," then he mentions "things upon the earth." In verse 5 he begins his list of "things upon the earth" and continues it through verse 11. In verse 12 he begins his list of "things above." Failure to recognize this pattern has resulted in all sorts of speculation and individually concocted lists of what "things above" and "things upon the earth" entail.[13]

13. Rather than making a list of the contrasting practices of the old man and the new man in Colossians, as the writer did for Ephesians, we will simply mention that such a list will overlap considerably with the list in Ephesians because of the great amount of material common to the two letters.

(A) Things above (v. 2a)
(B) Things upon the earth (v. 2b)
(B) Things upon the earth (vv. 5–11)
(A) Things above (vv. 12–14)

In Colossians Paul inserts the statement about the old man and the new man in the middle of the lists of the ethical structure (3:9–10), while in Ephesians he placed his comments about the old man and new man at the beginning. Nevertheless, Paul uses the same verb tenses in Colossians that he used in Ephesians: both "taken off" and "put on" are aorist and "being renewed" is present. Also, the theology is the same: the old man as anthropological structure has been put off through the work of Christ and the new man has been put on. The new ethical structure is a process of renewal whereby the practices of the old man are replaced by knowledge that is according to the image of Christ who created the new man.

According to Romans 1, sin has a cumulative effect. As the behavior of people worsened, God progressively gave them up to their profligacy. However, the unregenerate human race did not descend to the depths of depravity instantaneously. It happened slowly as people gradually surrendered themselves to sinful practices. A progressive hardening of the heart developed in the process of sinning so that sinning became easier and spread into other areas. For example, to cover up his theft the thief found it necessary to lie, and then the thief had to lie to more and more people to keep his deeds secret.

Just as sin is not static, so righteousness is not static. Righteous deeds lead to more deeds of righteousness and a pattern of righteous behavior develops that begins to characterize one's life. The pattern becomes habitual. The old man was corrupted because this became a pattern of life. Centuries of human history spread and compounded sin, making it so complex that no one could ever unravel all the sins in order to get back to the source. Thus the whole pattern of the old man had to be "put off." Jesus Christ could not "patch up" the old man because the old man was totally corrupt and under God's wrath and condemnation.

Reforming people by reorganizing and improving the political, economic, educational, and social environment in which they live has never been a realistic possibility. People constantly place false confidence in reform movements, presuming that economic prosperity or equitably distributed power will end class hatred and that more education will solve the problems of people. All of these philosophies mistakenly assume that people are basically good and that the solution to the problems of the world lies in altering a person's external circumstances in one way or another. The recent failure of communism in Europe clearly illustrates the fact that sooner or later the most ethereal goals of people will abort. Simply stated, people

Look @ Body of W. II - "Conn"

are sinners. They do not need a band-aid; they need a blood transfusion from Jesus Christ. Ultimately, if people are to experience the happiness that only God can give, they need the regenerating power of the gospel and the transforming power of the Holy Spirit.

Just as the "degeneration" of the old man took place over time, so too the renewal of the new man must take place progressively over time. Unfortunately, many Christians are looking for a formula for spiritual success, some kind of "secret," and the Christian book market is full of these "secrets." But the renewal process involves a time for growth and development. Renewal is developmental, and progress is incremental. Each day the Christian is brought more and more into conformity with the image of Christ. The fact that books continue to offer another "secret" should prove that there is no "secret." If there were, then one book would reveal it, Christians would use it, and the struggle would be over.

Christian leaders have allowed people to think that holiness is something that comes instantly. Becoming holy, however, is a slow process of renewal, replacing the old practices of the old man with the new practices of the new man. That is why Paul instructed the Colossians to put on compassion, kindness, humility, and gentleness, with patience, forbearance, and forgiveness. They needed to put on love and let the peace of Christ rule in their hearts. They must permit the Word of God to dwell richly in them in all wisdom, teaching and admonishing one another in psalms, hymns, and spiritual songs, singing with grace in their hearts to the Lord. Whatever they did, they needed to do all in the name of the Lord Jesus, giving thanks to God the Father by him. Then Paul gave special instructions to wives and husbands, children and parents, slaves and masters so that they would live godly lives and please the Lord. All this was to be done in fear of the Lord and heartily, knowing that they would receive the promised inheritance from the Lord.

The other ethical imperatives in the New Testament Epistles show the extensive treatment that the writers give to the ethical structure for the new man. Some letters alternate indicative and imperative. Others reserve an entire section for indicative and an entire section for imperative. Sadly, one of the things that the church today has lost is the ethical structure of the new man. Instead the church has concentrated on externals. For example, American Fundamentalism has been particularly guilty of preaching against practices such as smoking, drinking, dancing, and card-playing, but ignoring greed, slander, backbiting, strife, and enmity. By devoting so much effort preaching against these practices, Fundamentalism has actually promoted one of the sins of the old man that Paul lists in Galatians 5:19–21: dissension. Fundamentalists seem to cause splits continually. To make matters worse, such splits are dignified as necessary to preserve the "truth." In reality, however, the only thing that is preserved is the fact that schism in the church of Jesus Christ is a work of the flesh rather than a fruit of the Spirit.

The world's value system teaches you that the sins of the old man are "the only way to go." Its wisdom teaches you to get all you can, make it to the top, climb over everyone, use everybody you can, and don't let anybody push you around. Being a "winner" justifies any means of getting there.[14] This type of philosophy views humility, patience, toleration, forbearance, and love as the characteristics of wimps. To be kind, tender-hearted, and compassionate is to court disaster.

For Christians, however, the ethical structure demands that they live differently and distinctively. Their new status "in Christ" should result in a new life-style, a new orientation, and new practices. The New Testament is not ambiguous about the identity of these practices, but names them explicitly. These are the practices that are important in God's sight, and the church needs to teach and preach them, instead of focusing on legalistic teachings that have been the standard for Christian ethics for the last 100 years. God's program for true holiness must replace the teachings of people! Many Christians who would never consider smoking don't even hesitate to slander fellow Christians. Other Christians who would never touch a drop of alcohol seem oblivious to the brutal way that they treat people. The ethical structure of the new man is in need of urgent exposition! The church must cease to stress externals and begin to walk in the ways of true holiness.

For Further Study

Baxter, J. Sidlow. *A New Call To Holiness*. Grand Rapids: Zondervan, 1973.

While this writer cannot accept all of Baxter's conclusions in this book, his discussions of "The 'Old Man' Crucified," "Transfiguration of Character," and "What Does Paul Mean By 'The Flesh'?" are very helpful and support many of the conclusions drawn by this writer from the Pauline data.

Cullmann, Oscar. *Christ and Time*. Trans. Floyd V. Filson. Rev. ed. Philadelphia: Westminster, 1964.

While this book is not about the "new man," it has helped this writer greatly in comprehending the redemptive-historical nature of the New Testament and the need for reading Paul linearly.

14. A most blatant example of this philosophy is that of Robert J. Ringer, *Winning Through Intimidation* (New York: Funk & Wagnalls, 1974).

Hoch, Carl B., Jr. "The New Man of Ephesians 2." In *Dispensationalism, Israel and the Church.* Ed. Craig A. Blaising and Darrell L. Bock. Grand Rapids: Zondervan, 1992.

This is a wider exegetical discussion of the "new man" in Ephesians 2 than the discussion in this chapter and should be read for the detail it provides.

9

New Name, New Song, New Jerusalem

*I*t is fitting that the climax of newness occurs in the last book of the present canonical arrangement, the Book of Revelation. Ladd considers Revelation as characterized by newness,[1] and Charles observes that Revelation dwells on newness.[2] Revelation reflects on six different aspects of the grandeur of newness:

1. a new name (2:17; 3:12);
2. a new Jerusalem (3:12; 21:2);
3. a new song (5:9; 14:3);
4. a new heaven (21:1);
5. a new earth (21:1);
6. and "everything new" (21:5).

The last reference is particularly striking since it is the last occurrence of καινός in the New Testament. The climax of newness is God making all things new! This is a most exciting hope for all Christians.

Unfortunately, scholars demonstrate very little agreement in the exegetical literature concerning the meaning of each of these six new things in Revelation. This is quite frustrating because one would like to end a study of newness in the New Testament with certainty and clarity as to the final

1. George E. Ladd, *A Commentary on the Revelation of John* (Grand Rapids: Eerdmans, 1972), 90.

2. R. H. Charles, *A Critical and Exegetical Commentary on the Revelation of St. John*, 2 vols. (Edinburgh: T. & T. Clark, 1920), I:146.

form of newness. The diversity of views on each of the six is due not only to the apocalyptic nature of Revelation with its pervasive symbolism, but also to the eschatological commitments of scholars. For example, an amillennialist simply does not approach the symbolism and structure of Revelation in the same way as the premillennialist. A preterist interpretation of the book differs widely from a futurist interpretation. But despite their disagreement over the exact form of the end reality, all interpreters agree that the goal of God in history is newness. God will make all things new!

The New Name

The first new thing in the Book of Revelation is the new name. Two texts mention this new name. In the letter to the church in Pergamum Christ says through John his servant, "To him who overcomes, I will give some of the hidden manna. I will also give him a white stone with a new name written on it, known only to him who receives it" (Rev. 2:17). And in the letter to the church in Philadelphia Christ promises, "Him who overcomes I will make a pillar in the temple of my God. Never again will he leave it. I will write on him the name of my God and the name of the city of my God, the new Jerusalem, which is coming down out of heaven from my God; and I will also write on him my new name" (3:12).

Smith refuses to try to interpret the new name. For him, it is "folly to seek to interpret what *no man knows.*"[3] Other interpreters attempt to identify the name in 2:17 and 3:12 either separately or both together. The majority opt either for the person of Christ or for the new life and relations that he brings. Commentators interpret the new name as either "the glory and majesty of Christ,"[4] "the fuller glories of Christ's Person and character,"[5] "all that Christ is,"[6] or "Christ's new state of completed Messianic work."[7] In regard to the Christian, the new name is either the "believer's new name or changed character through redemption (Isa. 62:2; 65:15),"[8] "the personal heritage of the glories that are beyond this world and assurance of eternal salvation,"[9] "the transforming experience of entrance into the marriage supper of the Lamb,"[10] "the totality of a Christian's new relationship with

3. J. B. Smith, *A Revelation of Jesus Christ* (Scottdale, Pa.: Herald, 1961), 74.
4. Ladd, 64.
5. Henry Barclay Swete, *The Apocalypse Of St. John* (Grand Rapids: Eerdmans, 1908), 58.
6. Homer Hailey, *Revelation* (Grand Rapids: Baker, 1979), 155.
7. Isbon T. Beckwith, *The Apocalypse of John* (Grand Rapids: Baker, 1967), 486.
8. Alan F. Johnson, "Revelation," in *The Expositor's Bible Commentary*, ed. Frank E. Gaebelein and J. D. Douglas, 12 vols. (Grand Rapids: Zondervan, 1981), 12:442
9. John F. Walvoord, *The Revelation of Jesus Christ* (Chicago: Moody, 1966), 71.
10. Robert H. Mounce, *The Book of Revelation* (Grand Rapids: Eerdmans, 1977), 100.

Christhim,"[11] or "individual identity."[12] Ford believes that the new name denotes a new person.[13]

A synthesis of the preceding views would suggest that the new name connotes the new status that Christians have in Christ. Because Christ has changed the Christian from the inside out, the Christian can be renamed a name that denotes the new character he or she possesses in Christ. This new character allows Christians to overcome evil in the present,[14] and gives them the right to a glorious inheritance with their Redeemer throughout eternity.

The New Song

The Book of Revelation contains several texts that refer to a "new song." The texts of these passages are as follows:

And they sang a new song:
"You are worthy to take the scroll
   and to open its seals,
because you were slain,
   and with your blood you purchased men for God
   from every tribe and language and people and nation.
You have made them to be a kingdom and priests to serve our God,
   and they will reign on the earth."

(5:9–10)

And they sang a new song before the throne and before the four living creatures and the elders. No one could learn the song except the 144,000 who had been redeemed from the earth.

(14:3)

In the first passage the identity of the singers is obscured by a textual problem in 5:9–10. The KJV follows the Byzantine text and reads "us" and "we" in 5:9–10. This reading seems to equate the singers with the twenty-four elders in 5:8. The twenty-four elders are then interpreted as the church.[15] Other versions, such as the NIV, follow the eclectic text, which reads "they" and "them" in 5:9–10. This reading seems to differentiate the twenty-four elders from the redeemed. The twenty-four elders are then interpreted as angels.[16] So the singers in 5:9–10 are either the church or angels.

11. Hailey, 134.
12. Martin Kiddle, *The Revelation of St. John* (New York: Harper and Brothers, 1940), 35.
13. J. Massyngberde Ford, *Revelation,* AB (Garden City, N.Y.: Doubleday, 1975), 399.
14. Beckwith, 463.
15. Walvoord, *Revelation,* 118.
16. Ladd, 75.

In the second passage the identity of the singers is obscured by a reference to the 144,000 in 7:4. In 14:3 the singers are variously interpreted as either tribulation saints from ethnic Israel,[17] the church,[18] or angels.[19] Accepting the validity of Stonehouse's arguments that the elders and the living-beings in 14:3 are celestial beings who are of a rank superior to the angels in general, like the cherubim and seraphim,[20] this writer believes that the singers in 5:9–10, then, are the cherubim and seraphim. This writer also believes that the 144,000 in 14:3 comprise a remnant within ethnic Israel and has argued elsewhere for this identification.[21] Thus the singers in 14:3 are the faithful remnant of ethnic Israel who sing a song of gratitude for the new mercies of God in redemption and preservation.

Many commentators point out that the new song is based upon the Psalms and the Book of Isaiah. Frequently cited texts include Psalms 33:3, 98:1, 144:9, 149:1, and Isaiah 42:10. Songs of praise to God are not new. What is new is the reason for praise and the content of praise. Revelation 5 and 14 set forth the reasons and the content quite clearly. First, Yahweh is going forth to destroy his idolatrous foes.[22] Second, the new covenant is in process of completion.[23] Third, God is worthy as Creator and the Lamb worthy as Redeemer.[24] Fourth, a new era and order has been inaugurated.[25]

In a sense, the content of the song is a collation of the various praise sections in the Revelation, which are listed below:

Holy, holy, holy is the Lord God Almighty, who was, and is, and is to come.
(4:8)

You are worthy, our Lord and God, to receive glory and honor and power, for you created all things, and by your will they were created and have their being.
(4:11)

You are worthy to take the scroll and to open its seals, because you were slain, and with your blood you purchased men for God from every tribe and language and people and nation. You have made them to be a kingdom and priests to serve our God, and they shall reign on the earth.
(5:9–10)

---

17. Walvoord, 215.

18. Mounce, 268.

19. Beckwith, 652.

20. Ned B. Stonehouse, *Paul Before the Areopagus* (Grand Rapids: Eerdmans, 1957), 88–108.

21. Carl B. Hoch, Jr., "The Term 'Israel' in the New Testament" (Th.D. diss., Dallas Theological Seminary, 1971), 69–72.

22. Martin Rist, "The Revelation of St. John the Divine," in *The Interpreter's Bible*, ed. George Buttrick, 12 vols. (Nashville: Abingdon, 1957), 12:409.

23. G. B. Caird, *A Commentary on the Revelation of St. John the Divine* (New York: Harper and Row, 1966), 76; see also William J. Dumbrell, *The End of the Beginning* (Grand Rapids: Lancer Books, 1985), 116.

24. E. W. Bullinger, *The Apocalypse* (Greenwood, S.C.: Attic, 1972), 241.

25. Ladd, 90; see also Kiddle, 102.

Worthy is the Lamb, who was slain, to receive power and wealth and wisdom and strength and honor and glory and praise!

(5:12)

To him who sits on the throne and to the Lamb be praise and honor and glory and power, for ever and ever!

(5:13)

Salvation belongs to our God, who sits on the throne, and to the Lamb.

(7:10)

Amen! Praise and glory and wisdom and thanks and honor and power and strength be to our God for ever and ever. Amen!

(7:12)

The kingdom of the world has become the kingdom of our Lord and of his Christ, and he will reign for ever and ever.

(11:15)

We give thanks to you, Lord God Almighty, the One who is and who was, because you have taken your great power and have begun to reign. The nations were angry; and your wrath has come. The time has come for judging the dead, and for rewarding your servants the prophets and your saints and those who reverence your name, both small and great—and for destroying those who destroy the earth.

(11:17–18)

Great and marvelous are your deeds, Lord God Almighty. Just and true are your ways, King of the ages. Who will not fear you, O Lord, and bring glory to your name? For you alone are holy. All nations will come and worship before you, for your righteous acts have been revealed.

(15:3–4)

Hallelujah! Salvation and glory and power belong to our God, for true and just are his judgments. He has condemned the great prostitute who corrupted the earth by her adulteries. He has avenged on her the blood of his servants.

(19:1–2)

Hallelujah! The smoke from her goes up forever and ever.

(19:3)

Praise our God, all you his servants, you who fear him, both small and great!

(19:5)

Hallelujah! For our Lord God Almighty reigns. Let us rejoice and be glad and give him glory! For the wedding of the Lamb has come, and his bride has made herself ready. Fine linen, bright and clean, was given her to wear.

(19:6–8)

Amen. Come, Lord Jesus.

(22:20)

The New Jerusalem

Scholars widely debate the nature of the new Jerusalem and the new heaven and the new earth in Revelation 21–22. While many monographs, articles, and books have already been written on a variety of subjects relevant to these two chapters, a thorough treatment of all the issues involved would require an extensive study. Since the subject of this book is newness, it is not absolutely necessary to resolve the debate over what precise form the newness will take in respect to the new Jerusalem and the new heaven and the new earth. This writer will simply present the various viewpoints and choose one that best represents his understanding of biblical theology.

The immediate debate regarding the new Jerusalem is whether this phrase refers to people or a place. Adopting a viewpoint held by many writers, Robert Gundry argues that the new Jerusalem designates people as a place, not a place for people.[26] Other writers have identified the new Jerusalem as "the Christian society,"[27] "the church in its glorified existence,"[28] "the church in its perfected and eternal state,"[29] and "the fellowship of God with the elect."[30] For Walvoord, however, the city is just as literal as the new heavens and the new earth and is a satellite city suspended over the earth during the thousand-year reign of Christ that serves as the dwelling place for the resurrected and translated saints who also have access to the earthly scene.[31] Bullinger subscribes to this interpretation as well, stating flatly that the heavens, the earth, and the sea are literal. Then he asks, "Why is not the City to be literal?"[32] And Seiss maintains that when something is given all the attributes of a city, it is best to conclude that it is a city.[33]

Other writers take a mediating position. The city is both place and people. Ladd comments that if it is a city, it is located on the earth. On the other hand, it may refer to God's people.[34] Turner is probably the most recent advocate of a mediating view. Turner wants to avoid an insensitive approach to apocalyptic imagery and a spiritualizing, Platonic approach to redemption.[35] He opts for an approach that does justice to apocalyptic symbolism without evaporating the earthiness of biblical protology and eschatology.[36] According to Turner, the glory of the new

26. Robert H. Gundry, "The New Jerusalem: People as Place, Not Place for People," *Novum Testamentum*, 29 (1987): 254–64.

27. Swete, 276–77.

28. Johnson, 593–94.

29. Mounce, 370.

30. Abraham Kuyper, *The Revelation of St. John* (Grand Rapids: Eerdmans, 1963), 315.

31. Walvoord, 89, 312.

32. Bullinger, 647.

33. J. A. Seiss, *The Apocalypse* (Grand Rapids: Zondervan, 1964), 495ff.

34. Ladd, 276.

35. David L. Turner, "The New Jerusalem in Revelation 21:1–22:15: Consummation of a Biblical Continuum," in *Dispensationalism, Israel, and The Church*, ed. Craig A. Blaising and Darrell L. Bock (Grand Rapids: Zondervan, 1992), 265.

36. Ibid., 276.

Jerusalem far surpasses the language used to describe it.[37] Five occurrences of two words translated "like" or "as" (ὡς, ὅμοιος) in Revelation 21:2, 11(both words), 21; and 22:1 show that although the visionary detail corresponds to the physical object from everyday life, it is hardly to be equated or identified with that object.[38] But the earth cannot be etherealized into heaven. To take the vision of the new Jerusalem merely as an ideal symbol of the church's blessing fails to reckon with the earthly character of the Old Testament eschatological hope and the full cosmic effects of Christ's redemption.[39] The eschatological hope of the Bible is not for deliverance from the earth but from sin. Creaturehood inevitably involves physical existence, and the redemption of creatures includes the redemption of creation.[40] Further comments on this critical assessment of salvation history will be made in the next chapter on the new heaven and the new earth.

We will conclude this chapter with descriptions of the new Jerusalem furnished by Boring and Seiss. According to Boring,[41] the new Jerusalem will be:

1. a city;
2. a particular city, "Jerusalem";
3. a renewed city;
4. a big, inclusive city;
5. a beloved, beautiful, bridal city;
6. a Holy City; and
7. an active city.

Seiss[42] notes first the blessedness of the city:

1. every tear is wiped away;
2. death no longer exists;
3. sorrow then ceases;
4. all crying shall be hushed;
5. there shall be no more pain;
6. life is there;
7. a soul-satisfying worship is there;
8. there is the possession of God himself.

---

37. Ibid.
38. Ibid., 277.
39. Ibid., 278.
40. Ibid.
41. M. Eugene Boring, *Revelation* (Louisville: John Knox, 1989), 219–23.
42. Seiss, 489–90.

Next Seiss[43] observes the occupants and possessors of the city:

1. no cowardly, unbelieving, polluted, murderers, fornicators, sorcerers, idolaters, or false ones are there;
2. all saints are there;
3. the still ongoing race redeemed is there.

Finally, Seiss[44] presents eight attributes of the city:

1. its derivation: God;
2. its location: suspended near the earth;
3. its splendour: invested with glory, light, brightness and radiating splendour of God;
4. its amplitude: immense;
5. its system of illumination: the Light of God and the Lamb;
6. its lack of a temple: God and the Lamb are the temple;
7. its relation to the world at large: nations shall walk by means of the light of it; the kings of the earth bring their glory and honour to (or into) it; they shall bring the glory and reverence of the nations to (or into) it;
8. its superlative holiness.

Whether the new Jerusalem is just people or people and place, it certainly exceeds all previous places, including the Garden of Eden. The glory and joy characteristic of it will make all current arguments over its identity or location seem silly and misplaced. And all focus will be centered on the One who made it possible: the eternal triune God.

For Further Study

Gundry, Robert H. "The New Jerusalem: People as Place, Not Place for People," *Novum Testamentum*, 29, (1987), 254–64.

   Although this writer cannot accept Gundry's conclusion that people only are the "place," this is a stimulating article and worthy of study.

Johnson, Alan F. "Revelation." In *The Expositor's Bible Commentary*. Ed. Frank E. Gaebelein and J. D. Douglas. 12 vols. Grand Rapids: Zondervan, 1981.

   In this writer's opinion, Johnson's commentary on Revelation is one of the best premillennial commentaries on Revelation and should be consulted for detailed textual discussions.

---

43. Ibid., 491.
44. Ibid., 496–501.

Seiss, J. A. *The Apocalypse.* Grand Rapids: Zondervan, 1964.

Seiss is another excellent premillennial commentary on Revelation and contains rich theological insights into the portion of Scripture studied in this chapter.

Turner, David L. "The New Jerusalem in Revelation 21:1–22:15: Consummation of a Biblical Continuum." In *Dispensationalism, Israel, and the Church.* Ed. Craig A. Blaising and Darrell L. Bock. Grand Rapids: Zondervan, 1992.

Turner's work is a well-balanced study of the "new Jerusalem" and is, to some degree, a response to Gundry's argument for place as people.

10

The New Heaven and the New Earth

The interpretive issues surrounding the new heaven and the new earth are even more difficult to resolve than those surrounding the new Jerusalem. Three major questions face the interpreter: (1) Is there a millennium, and if so, what is the relationship of the new heaven and the new earth to this millennium? (2) Are the new heaven and the new earth a re-creation or a renovation of the old heaven and the old earth? (3) Is the earth a major factor in eschatology or is heaven the only ultimate concern? Since scholars are no closer to agreement now on these questions than they have been throughout the history of the church, it would be presumptuous for this writer to insist on dogmatic answers to these questions. He will simply present his own thoughts on these issues and relate them to the subject of newness.

From word statistics alone it would appear that the earth plays a prominent part in the Book of Revelation. While the Greek noun γῆ, "earth," occurs eighty-two times[1] in the Greek New Testament, the noun οὐρανός, "heaven," occurs fifty-two times.[2] While statistics alone can be misleading, the number of key texts in Revelation about the earth show that the earth cannot be regarded as peripheral to redemptive history. In support of this we read that the saints will reign upon the earth (5:10); God created the earth and the things in it (10:6; 14:7); and the kings of the earth bring their glory into the new Jerusalem (21:24). Ladd seems to be accurate when he

1. Robert Morgenthaler, *Statistik des neutestamentlichen Wortschatzes*, 2d ed. (Zürich: Gotthelf-Verlag, 1973), 85.
2. Ibid., 127.

writes, "Biblical thought always places man on a redeemed earth, not in a heavenly realm removed from earthly existence."[3]

An author who has impressed this writer with her comments on the perspective of the Revelation is Elisabeth Schüssler Fiorenza. According to Fiorenza, a key question addressed by Revelation is, "To whom does the lordship of the earth belong?"[4] She believes that the answer given by Revelation is as follows:

> John asserts that redemption involves liberation from bondage and slavery and that salvation gives new dignity to those who have been redeemed through the death of Jesus Christ. He expresses this new dignity through the titles *basileia* (kingdom) and *hiereis* (priests), which in antiquity designate the bearers of political power and sacral authority. The use of these two titles together is not surprising since in antiquity politics and religion were closely interrelated. Conceiving of redemption in political terms, the author asserts that final redemption and salvation are not now possible, but only when the state of dominion on earth is radically changed. Only when Satan and the concrete representation of demonic power, the Roman empire, no longer rule on earth is final salvation possible. Only when God and the Lamb reign on earth is salvation accomplished. Then a new, more humanized world shall be created by God where there shall no longer be weeping and mourning, hunger and thirst, pain and death.[5]

Fiorenza believes that established Christianity has more and more conceived of salvation as the spiritual salvation of the soul.[6] In contrast to this spiritualizing notion of kingdom and kingship, the author of Revelation stresses that Christ must be Lord over the world. Only when Christ establishes his kingdom on earth and only when the throne of God and the Lamb are found in the new Jerusalem on a new earth will Christians actively exercise their kingship and priesthood.[7] Fiorenza continues:

> Insofar as scholars have not taken into account that the "eschatological reservation" is made by Rev. also for the church, they have affirmed that the glorification and exaltation of the Christian community has already taken place and that the eternity of the New Jerusalem is already present on earth in the church. Consequently, the eschatological end is understood as nothing more than a manifestation and disclosure of what has already been realized in

---

3. George E. Ladd, *A Commentary on the Revelation of John* (Grand Rapids: Eerdmans, 1972), 275.

4. Elisabeth Schüssler Fiorenza, *The Book of Revelation: Justice and Judgment* (Philadelphia: Fortress, 1985), 124.

5. Ibid., 68.

6. Ibid., *The Apocalypse* (Chicago: Franciscan Herald Press, 1976), 60.

7. Ibid., *The Book of Revelation*, 75–76.

redemption. But this interpretation of Rev. is actually more similar to the self-understanding of the early Christian enthusiasts and gnosticizing elements than to the interpretation of Christian existence as explicated by Rev.[8]

Newport supports Fiorenza when he writes:

> Hoekema states that if the resurrection body were nonmaterial or nonphysical, the devil would have won a great victory. This is true because God would then have been compelled to change human beings with physical bodies, such as He had created, into creatures of a different sort, without physical bodies (like the angels). This would indicate that matter had become intrinsically evil so that it had to be banished. And then, in a sense, the Greek philosophers would have been proven right. But matter is not evil; it is part of God's good creation. Thus the goal of God's redemption is the resurrection of the physical body. Likewise, God will create a new earth on which His redeemed people can live and serve God forever with glorified bodies. Thus the universe will not be destroyed but renewed, and God will win the victory.[9]

A recent writer who has helped to clarify some of the issues is William Dumbrell in his book, *The End of the Beginning*. Dumbrell traces five topics through the Bible and relates them to Revelation 21–22: The new Jerusalem, the new temple, the new covenant, the new Israel, and the new creation. After surveying both testaments on these five topics, Dumbrell concludes that the gospel has to do with a total worldview, not merely with a personal renewal. Redemption is related to new creation, new covenant, new Jerusalem, and new heaven and new earth.[10]

Writers are divided over whether the new heaven and new earth will be recreated or renovated. Whereas Walvoord insists that it will be a new creation, not a renovation,[11] Ladd believes that John is not concerned with such details.[12] Seiss devotes five pages to the defense of renovation,[13] and Newport concurs in an excursus on the new heaven and the new earth.[14] Turner argues that annihilation and re-creation would be foreign both to the Old Testament eschatological hope and to the teaching of the New Testament. Cosmic renewal is no more an annihilation of the old world than personal regeneration is an annihilation of the old person. Ethical rather than ontological transformation is in view. Inasmuch as the physical uni-

---

8. Ibid., 122–23.

9. John D. Newport, *The Lion and the Lamb* (Nashville: Broadman, 1986), 307.

10. William J. Dumbrell, *The End of the Beginning* (Grand Rapids: Lancer Books, 1985), 196.

11. John F. Walvoord, *The Revelation of Jesus Christ* (Chicago: Moody, 1966), 311.

12. Ladd, 276.

13. J. A. Seiss, *The Apocalypse* (Grand Rapids: Zondervan, 1964), 483–87.

14. Newport, 306–9.

verse did not commit sin, we have no reason to suppose that it must cease to exist because of sin.[15] While conceding the validity of some of the arguments advanced by advocates of re-creation (especially the language of 2 Pet. 3:10–13), this writer believes that the evidence favors renovation. The new heaven and new earth are in partial continuity with the old heaven and old earth, not in radical discontinuity.

The last issue cannot be settled in a work such as this one. The chronology of the Book of Revelation and the subject of the millennium have been the subject of many volumes in the history of biblical interpretation. Newport's "Excursus on the Millennium"[16] is a concise presentation of the arguments for a premillennial view of the millennium. As a premillennialist Newport considers the millennium as a necessary phase in the subjection of the cosmos to the Lordship of Jesus Christ. But John does not call the millennium "new" and the millennium per se is not indispensable to newness. Those who subscribe to amillennialism or postmillennialism must include the new Jerusalem and the new heaven and new earth in their system as a part of newness despite their understanding of the exact form that these new entities will take. For any system, however, the new heaven and the new earth are the consummation of redemption and the goal to which all Christians should look.

For Further Study

Dumbrell, William J. *The End of the Beginning.* Grand Rapids: Lancer Books, 1985.

   Dumbrell presents a thorough biblical study of the interrelationship between the "End of Creation" and the "Beginning of Creation."

Fiorenza, Elisabeth Schüssler. *The Book of Revelation: Justice and Judgment.* Philadelphia: Fortress, 1985.

———. *The Apocalypse.* Chicago: Franciscan Herald, 1976.

   While Fiorenza is theologically liberal, her insights in these two volumes and her expertise in apocalyptic are very helpful in approaching the subject of this chapter.

---

15. David L. Turner, "The New Jerusalem in Revelation 21:1–22:15: Consummation of a Biblical Continuum," in *Israel and the Church: A Contemporary Dispensational Perspective,* ed. Craig Blaising and Darrell Bock (Grand Rapids: Zondervan, 1992), 25–26.
16. Newport, 294–97.

11

All Things New

*N*ot only is the word "all" one of the smallest words in the Bible, but it is also one of the most difficult to interpret. A popular cliché is, "All always means all and that is all that all means." To this cliché the writer has often responded somewhat sarcastically, "All does not always mean all and that is not all that all means." All can have either an inclusive or exclusive sense. It can be inclusive of all things, most things, or some things, and it can be exclusive of some things. The word in and of itself cannot determine the scope intended by the speaker or writer using it. The interpreter must allow context and common sense to determine the scope of "all" in any particular Bible passage.

Matthew 1:17, the first occurrence of "all" in the New Testament, shows the elasticity of this word when it says that "there were fourteen generations in all from Abraham to David." Almost any critical commentary on Matthew will indicate the schematic structure of Matthew's genealogy and the absence of names included in the Old Testament genealogies of the period.[1] Thus "all" simply means all the names Matthew chose to include to make the total of fourteen, a symbolical number. When Paul declares in 1 Corinthians 6:12 that "all things are lawful" to the Christian, he certainly does not include all sinful things!

The vague limits to the word πάντα, "all things," make its interpretation in Revelation 21:5 difficult. The NIV text reads, "I am making everything

---

1. A good example is W. D. Davies and Dale C. Allison, Jr., *A Critical and Exegetical Commentary on the Gospel According to Saint Matthew*, ICC, 3 vols. (Edinburgh: T. & T. Clark, 1988), 1:161–65.

[πάντα] new!" The KJV reads, "Behold, I make all things [πάντα] new." (The Greek literally reads, "Behold new things I make all things"). As Bloomfield points out, the text does not read, "I make all new things."[2] But just what is included in the "all things"? Apparently *not* Satan, demons, unbelievers, or the lake of fire, or Revelation would be teaching universalism!

Since John is not explicit, commentators offer various suggestions about the content of "all things." Ladd suggests "souls, body, and the physical environment."[3] Swete offers "all the fruits of the New Covenant."[4] Rist says it is "God's new age."[5] Walvoord invokes his favorite phrase, "the eternal state."[6] For Caird it is "the internal work of God."[7] Mounce and Hailey give the phrase a different emphasis. For Mounce it is "the totally new order,"[8] whereas for Hailey it is the "things of the old order."[9] Newport maintains that it is "the new creation to the last detail."[10] Others are more specific. Smith names the new heaven, the new earth, and the new Jerusalem.[11] And Charles lists the new name, new song, new heaven, new earth, and new city, that is, all of the things designated "new" in Revelation![12]

One can either despair or rejoice over the inability of learned students of the Bible to know exactly how extensive "all things" will be. Perhaps God never intended to spell out the specifics to allow himself the freedom to surprise those of us who will share in this new work. Sauer's short outline perhaps best captures the intent of the verse: on us—a new name; in us—a new song; around us—a new Jerusalem; under us—a new earth; over us—a new heaven; before us—always new revelations of the never-ending love of God.[13] Could anyone ask for more?

2. Arthur E. Bloomfield, *All Things New* (Minneapolis: Bethany, 1959), 314.

3. George E. Ladd, *A Commentary on the Revelation of John* (Grand Rapids: Eerdmans, 1972), 278.

4. Henry Barclay Swete, *The Apocalypse of St. John* (Grand Rapids: Eerdmans, 1908), 279.

5. Martin Rist, *The Revelation of St. John The Divine* (Nashville: Abingdon, 1957), 531.

6. John F. Walvoord, *The Revelation of Jesus Christ* (Chicago: Moody, 1966), 316.

7. G. B. Caird, *A Commentary on the Revelation of St. John The Divine*, HNTC (New York: Harper and Row, 1966), 266.

8. Robert H. Mounce, *The Book of Revelation*, NICNT (Grand Rapids: Eerdmans, 1977), 373.

9. Homer Hailey, *Revelation* (Grand Rapids: Baker, 1979), 408.

10. John D. Newport, *The Lion and the Lamb* (Nashville: Broadman, 1986), 313.

11. J. B. Smith, *A Revelation of Jesus Christ* (Scottdale, Pa.: Herald, 1961), 284.

12. R. H. Charles, *A Critical and Exegetical Commentary on the Revelation of St. John*, ICC, 2 vols. (Edinburgh: T. & T. Clark, 1920), 2:201.

13. Eric Sauer, *The Triumph of the Crucified* (Grand Rapids: Eerdmans, 1966), 200.

For Further Study

Seiss, J. A. *The Apocalypse.* Grand Rapids: Zondervan, 1964.

The only writer who provides extensive commentary on "all things new" is Seiss (see his "Lecture Forty-Eighth," 483–92).

Part 3
The Significance of Newness

12

Newness and the Individual Christian

*I*mportant consequences grow out of the theme of newness for the individual Christian. Of primary importance are three areas of the Christian life: (1) freedom in Christ, (2) life in the Spirit, and (3) warfare against the flesh. The majority of the discussion will revolve about Pauline texts since he contributes more to the theme of newness than any other New Testament writer. However, passages from other New Testament writers will be included as they are relevant to the topics.

Freedom in Christ

Three Greek words form the "freedom" word-group: ἐλευθερία (noun); ἐλεύθερος (adjective); and ἐλευθερόω (verb). Christian freedom grows out of "newness" in Christ. Paul considered freedom as one of the most significant results of Christ's redemptive work for the Christian,[1] and he was very concerned that the Christian not fall prey to some yoke of bondage imposed by people, particularly the "Judaizers." The Christian's only bondage was to God through Jesus Christ.

Unfortunately, many believers are confused over the nature of Christian freedom. An induction of New Testament passages where the above three words occur leads to the conclusion that Christian freedom is based on three things.

First, Christian freedom is based on the work of Christ on the cross. Two texts are relevant to this facet of freedom: John 8:36 and Galatians 5:1. In

---

1. See Peter Richardson, *Paul's Ethic of Freedom* (Philadelphia: Westminster, 1979).

John 8 Jesus confronts Jews who had believed what he had taught up to this point (8:31). He warned them that they must *continue* in the truth he was teaching if they were to become free from their bondage to sin (v. 34). Unless Christ set them free they would not continue in the Father's house forever (i.e., have eternal life). The Jews were insulted and retorted that they had never been in any (interior) bondage to any person (v. 33). Of course, Israel had been in military bondage to the surrounding empires since the eighth century B.C. and were still in bondage to Rome. Their point was that they were a "free" people on the inside even if they were a subjugated nation on the outside. During Jesus' extended confrontation with this group in John 8, he challenges the notion whether they were truly free on the inside. Jesus contended that they were not free on the inside either since they were murderous in their intent toward him. And this murderous intent was externalized when the Jews took up stones to kill him for blasphemy (v. 58).

Paul's development of this internal bondage to sin is found in the Books of Romans and Galatians. In Romans 6 Paul teaches that Christ has freed Christians from bondage to sin through his death. By obeying the apostolic gospel, the Roman Christians had been freed from sin and had become enslaved to righteousness (6:18). Their responsibility was to consider (λογίζομαι) the redemptive-historical freedom through Christ's atoning work a fact (6:11), and to implement in their lives the reality of their freedom by presenting their members to righteousness (6:13, 19).

Galatians 5 is another Pauline plea to the Galatians that they not return to the bondage that characterized their pre-Christian lives by getting entangled in a new yoke of Jewish bondage. The Galatians needed to choose whether they would align themselves with the line of bondage or the line of freedom. The line of bondage was represented by Hagar, Ishmael, Sinai, the old covenant, the present earthly Jerusalem, and Jews. The line of freedom was represented by Sarah, Isaac, the new covenant, the future heavenly Jerusalem, and Christians. Without question Christ had transferred Christians, especially Jewish Christians, from the line of bondage to the line of freedom. The Galatians were to hold firm their new status in Christ and not become entangled again in the yoke of bondage. Any submission to Jewish forms such as circumcision would negate the death of Christ (2:21). The death of Christ, therefore, was the means whereby the sinful orientation possessed by a person in Adam could be overcome by the new life in the Spirit (Rom. 8:1–17; Gal. 5:16–26).

Second, Christian freedom is based on the truth (John 8:32). The Johannine emphasis on truth is astounding (see John 1:14, 17; 3:21; 4:23–24; 5:33; 8:32, 40, 44, 45, 46; 14:6, 17; 15:26; 16:13; 17:17, 19; 18:37; 1 John 1:6, 8; 2:4, 21; 3:18, 19; 4:6; 5:6; 2 John 1, 2, 3, 4; 3 John 1, 3, 4, 8, 12).[2] A consideration

---

2. See Ignace de la Potterie, *La Verite Dans Saint Jean, Tome l Le Christ et la verite, L' Espirit et la verite; Tome ll Le croyant et la verite* (Rome: Biblical Institute Press, 1977).

of these passages shows that truth is a part of the new age introduced by Jesus Christ. Truth is personalized in the Son and in the Holy Spirit. These two reveal the truth to believers so that they might live in truth. The new age does not concentrate on externals but is concerned with worship in the realm of Spirit and truth (John 4:23–24).

For Paul, Christians are not to live according to the old pattern of malice and wickedness but according to the new pattern of integrity and truth (1 Cor. 5:8), and Christian love rejoices in truth (1 Cor. 13:6). Paul's ministry as a servant of the new covenant is a presentation of the truth (2 Cor. 4:2). His concern for the Galatians is that they may exchange truth for error (Gal. 2:5; 5:7). The new man has been created by God in righteousness and holiness [produced by] the truth (Eph. 4:24). The truth frees one from a bondage to asceticism (1 Tim. 4:3) and results in godliness (Tit. 1:1, 14).

Third, Christian freedom is based on the work of the Holy Spirit. The Spirit is the Spirit of Truth (John 16:13) who guides the way into all christological truth (John 16:13). The Spirit sets the Christian free from the bondage of sin to a life of fulfilling the requirements of the law (Rom. 8:2). As the greatest gift under the new covenant, the Spirit produces freedom, which transforms Christians from glory unto glory (2 Cor. 3:17–18).

Yet Christian freedom is neither unstructured nor free from all restraints and limitations. Children often believe that they will experience true freedom when they are free from parental control and can do anything they please. Actually, they fall prey to even greater bondage when they have this so-called freedom, especially when they experience drug addiction, AIDS, bankruptcy, arrest, loss of self-respect, and many other things. Total freedom, then, is actually a new form of bondage. Structure gives most people a sense of order and thus of security and purpose in their lives. True freedom is built on what Jesus Christ has done in transferring people from the bondage of sin to the freedom of righteousness. This freedom is the freedom to implement what God has revealed about the truth as it is embodied in Jesus Christ and what the Holy Spirit can do to translate the life of Christ into Christian behavior.

The first implication of the freedom brought by Christ is that Christian freedom is not legalism. Legalism is a difficult concept to define because of the ambiguity of the term and the emotional overtones associated with it. Also, the New Testament has no Greek words that are translated "legalism." Therefore, this writer will attempt to define legalism based upon his observations of the New Testament.

Legalism as an Addition to the Gospel

The first definition of legalism that can be gleaned from the New Testament, especially Paul, is that it is any addition to the gospel that is either a requirement for becoming a Christian or staying a Christian, or anything

that is a source of pride and self-righteousness before God. That Paul opposed Jewish legalism in Galatians and Romans has been well-argued by
Schreiner. According to Schreiner, Paul detected legalism in Judaism because its soteriology was synergistic (i.e., human beings could cooperate
with God in securing their salvation).[3] At the heart of legalism is the delu-
sion that human beings are good, and that their works can be the basis for
salvation.[4] When the Judaizers added requirements for the Gentiles as a
basis for salvation (see also Acts 15:1), Paul accused them not only of perverting the gospel but of changing it altogether (Gal. 1:6–8). The argument
of Galatians is that Christ's death is totally sufficient for salvation. It is unnecessary to add anything to his death for a person either to become a Christian or to stay a Christian. His death alone provides full satisfaction for sin.
The Judaizers were saying that Christ's death was important and Christ's
death on the cross certainly satisfied the wrath of God. But there were additional obligations that all Christians must meet if they were to "get in"
or "stay in" the Christian community of faith. Their strongest argument
may have possibly been that Jesus never explicitly abrogated the Old Testament law (Matt. 5:17–18). If Gentiles were to be regarded as true Christians, they needed to enter Israel and live like good Jews lived.

Paul's response to these legalists was that any additions to the gospel in
effect nullify the gospel. Thus Paul wrote in Galatians 2:21 that if righteousness was through the law, then Christ died needlessly. His redemptive work and propitiatory death would lose their value. So any additions to
the gospel that become requirements for becoming a Christian or staying a
Christian are legalism and bondage. Christ came to free Christians, not en-
slave them.

In Galatians 6:12–13 Paul argues that the reason why the Judaizers were
requiring circumcision of Gentile converts was that they might boast in the
Gentiles' adherence to their program. They were trying to make a good impression on their fellow Jews, and they were filled with pride and self-righteousness. But Paul refused to pride himself in anything but the cross of
Jesus Christ. Only those who walked by Paul's rule would experience God's
peace in salvation.

Legalism as Hypocritical Compliance

Legalism is not only making additions to the gospel for becoming a
Christian or staying a Christian, but it is also complying with requirements
without a real commitment or desire to do so. This type of legalism is more
subtle than the previous expression of it. This legalism is much more subjective, personal, and internal. The other type of legalism spells out the re-

3. Ibid., 94.
4. Ibid., 98.

quirements and everything is "up front." This second type of legalism masks itself by going through the motions of religious activity without any real commitment to the activities themselves. Compliance often involves bitterness and resentment because one has been forced into compliance by fear of punishment, group pressure, or some other type of intimidation.

Throughout both Testaments God censures people for worshiping him with their lips while their heart is far away from him. This is the essence of this second type of legalism. Jesus upbraided the Pharisees for tithing mint, anise, and cumin while neglecting the weightier matters of the law (Matt. 23:23). When the rich young ruler came to Jesus to learn what he could do to inherit eternal life, he went home sorrowful when Jesus told him to sell all his possessions. His legalistic attitude prevented him from making the heart commitment of selfless love for God. He had no desire to comply with Jesus' demand and left depressed. His outward compliance with the Mosaic directives probably caused him to have a reputation as one of the most religious men in his community. In the parable of the prodigal the so-called prodigal son usually receives the attention in popular preaching because of his departure from the father. But the elder brother is the ultimate point of Jesus' parable because he represents Jesus' accusers, the Pharisees and the Scribes (Luke 15:2). The elder brother is a legalist, which is amply displayed in his attitude toward the father. His angry response shows his real state of mind: "Look! All these years I've been slaving for you and never disobeyed your orders. Yet you never gave me even a young goat so I could celebrate with my friends" (Luke 15:29). To him service was nothing but slavery. He had no joy and his compliance was only external.

The enforcement of legalism is maintained by those in positions of power and influence: parents, teachers, police, pastors, even the "Christian community conscience." If the legalist were given another alternative without any strings attached, he would not comply because he would have no personal conviction about the demands placed on him. The legalist complies because of the fear of negative consequences or because of group pressure.

Throughout its history the church has been busy adding requirements for Christians or intimidating them into complying with man-made (church-made?) regulations. Every Christian group has its own unique set of additional requirements ranging from A to Z. For example, the anti-tobacco group has no problem with automobiles, and the anti-automoblile group grows tobacco as a major incoming-producing commodity.[5] Each group then sits in judgment of the other groups and believes that they serve

---

5. Consider, for example, the influence that Jacob Amman had on his group, the Amish. On this, see Elmer Lewis Smith, *The Amish Today* (Allentown, Pa.: Schlechters, 1961), 275–76.

God faithfully. Self-righteousness is the inevitable concomitant to giving up things beyond even that which the Bible requires.

What is legalism to one is not legalism to another. People have their own set of extrabiblical rules that seem appropriate to them. But then each person's set becomes *the* standard for other Christians. The person who has power and influence will soon gain a large following whose adherents will believe that their "set" is the true set. Those individuals in the group who do not necessarily accept that set as legitimate may still comply out of fear of punishment, ostracism, and "shunning."[6] All of these superogations become identified with Christianity and build up an unnecessary wall between the church and the world. We should not be surprised when people reject Christianity for the wrong reason, thinking that they must give up movies or some other item on someone's list in order to become a true believer. What a terrible distortion of Scripture and true Christianity! In essence another gospel has been created that leads to confusion within and without the church.

At this juncture we should state that it would be a gross misunderstanding of Paul's teachings to introduce the "weaker brother" argument to controvert the preceding comments. In the writings of Paul the weaker brother is the person who will come to spiritual ruin if he or she actually engages in activities that violate his or her conscience. The weaker brother is not like the legalist who demands extrabiblical rules. Legalists would not be caught dead doing the things on their list, and they are not intimidated by stronger Christians. On the contrary, legalists seek to impose their own life-style commitments on other Christians whether they are strong or weak.

In closing, let us illustrate the problem of legalism using four hot dogs. Two hot dogs are all-beef and two are all-pork. One beef hot dog and one pork hot dog have been offered to idols. The questions are, How many and which hot dogs could a strong Jew eat in good conscience? A strong Gentile? A weak Jew? A weak Gentile? Applying Paul's teachings in Romans 14 and 1 Corinthians 8–10, the answers are as follows: A strong Gentile could in good conscience eat all four hot dogs. A strong Jew could also eat all four. A weak Gentile could eat only two hot dogs—the all-beef and the all-pork hot dogs that had not been offered to idols. The weak Jew could eat only one hot dog—the all-beef one that had not been offered to an idol. Is there any intrinsic difference between the hot dogs other than the fact that two are beef and two are pork? According to Paul, "The earth is the Lord's, and everything in it" (1 Cor. 10:26; see also 1 Tim. 4:1–5). So why is there a problem? Because of the commitments of the consumers. *They* make the difference! The whole problem reduces to one of perspective or attitude. To the person who considers something "unclean," that thing is "unclean" (Rom. 14:14).

6. Ibid., 40–41.

Freedom Is Not License

While freedom in Christ is certainly not legalism, it also is not license. License is the removal of all limitations and living without any parameters or controls. The key passage that warns against using freedom as an excuse for license is Galatians 5:13. Paul is drawing his discussion to an end regarding the Judaizers' attempt to force legalism on the Galatians. In 5:7 Paul asks who has hindered the Galatians and kept them from the truth. Their current inclination toward the Judaizers had not come from God who called them but from a few who surreptitiously came in and stirred up the Galatians. Paul declared that he was not preaching circumcision. If he were, he would not be persecuted like he was. Had he preached circumcision, Paul would have effectively abolished the offense of the cross and avoided persecution. But he did not preach circumcision because his preaching was not for the purpose of pleasing people. Paul's indignant response to those who persecuted him for not preaching circumcision was, "Let the knife slip!"

However, Paul did not want the Galatians to interpret their freedom in Christ as a license to sin. Although freedom was not to be surrendered to the bondage introduced by the Judaizers, freedom as taught by Paul should not be distorted into a regulation-free gospel. In other words, Paul was not teaching antinomianism. Freedom should not be used as an excuse for sin to operate. Freedom should not lead to an expression of the "flesh," that is, the sinful orientation still retained by Christians even though they have been transferred from "in Adam" to "in Christ." The sinful orientation remains a powerful force that must be overcome through the power of the Holy Spirit. Paul's basic premise both in Romans and in Galatians is that there can be victory over the flesh in this life by means of the Spirit—a real, but not permanent, victory over sin. To accomplish this the Galatians must "live by the Spirit, and you will not gratify the desires of the sinful nature" (Gal. 5:16). Although the "flesh" (NIV "sinful nature") is always present as a potent enemy, it need not be dominant. The Spirit can and will be dominant if the Galatians will live their lives by means of the Spirit.

Freedom in Christ does not include license to give expression to the works of the flesh, that is, to allow sin to express itself in all its ugliness and alienation from God. What are the works of the flesh? The works of the flesh are diametrically opposed to the Spirit, and therefore are those things that Christians do not want to do, but are nevertheless drawn to do. It is important to notice that Paul describes the Christian's inability to stop sinning apart from divine assistance. This thought is paralleled in Romans 7:13–24. Thus Christians are in a constant tension between wanting to do the will of God and discovering that sin hinders them from achieving that desire. It is the Holy Spirit who provides the enablement to overcome the sin hindrance. The Spirit of life in Christ has freed Christians from the law of sin and death so that they might fulfill the will of God (Rom. 8:1–4).

If Christians use freedom for license, what deeds will they do that express the "flesh"? In Galatians 5:19–21 Paul provides a partial list:[7]

1. Sexual immorality (πορνεία)—this is the most general Greek term for illicit sexual behavior of all kinds.
2. Impurity (ἀκαθαρσία)—this literally means "uncleanness" and is a catch-all word for all kinds of sexual aberrations.
3. Debauchery (ἀσέλγεια)—this is another broad term referring to a debased style of living.
4. Idolatry (εἰδωλολατρία)—this was ubiquitous in the ancient world. The Greeks had so many idols that Paul noticed a statue at Athens dedicated to the "unknown God" (Acts 17:23). Apparently these Athenians were careful not to omit any possible gods!
5. Witchcraft (φαρμακεία)—this was widely practiced in Paul's time and has continued until now in the presence of the occult.
6. Hatred (ἔχθραι)—hostility toward other people.
7. Discord (ἔρις)—a spirit of strife toward others.
8. Jealousy (ζῆλος)—envious.
9. Fits of rage (θυμοί)—explosive anger, "losing one's cool."
10. Selfish ambition, dissensions, factions (ἐριθεῖαι, διχοστασίαι, αἱρέσεις)—these terms are difficult to distinguish from each other, but they refer to the divisions, cliques, and schisms that separate Christians from each other. Paul was deeply concerned that factions and fighting within his churches would threaten the unity of the church (see esp. 1 Cor. 1–4). Therefore, he exhorted Christians to be diligent to maintain the unity that the Holy Spirit had created in the body of Christ (Eph. 4:3).
11. Envy (φθόνος)—envy, jealousy, spite.
12. Drunkenness, orgies (μέθαι, κῶμοι)—these terms are closely related, with μέθαι referring to intoxication and κῶμοι referring to the parties that stimulate μέθαι.
13. And the like (τὰ ὅμοια τούτοις)—things that are like these things (i.e., things that are similar to the preceding vices).

Paul states flatly that those who practice the sins mentioned in this list will not inherit the kingdom of God. Freedom is not an open invitation to do anything one wants to do. Although good works cannot earn salvation, certainly they must characterize true salvation. Robert Gundry has co-

---

7. A very helpful discussion of the works of the flesh and the fruit of the Spirit can be found in William Barclay, *Flesh and Spirit* (London: SCM, 1962).

gently stated the truth that in Paul works are never *instrumental* for salvation, but they are certainly *evidential* of salvation.[8]

In other epistles Paul lists additional works of the flesh such as lying, stealing, unwholesome words, bitterness, slander, malice, coarse joking, acting foolishly, and other immoral and undesirable practices. Some exhortations are very general while others are very specific. Liberty can never excuse these sins. But if freedom in Christ is neither legalism nor license, what is it?

Freedom as Ability to Love God and to Love One's Neighbor

True freedom in Christ is the ability to love God with one's whole heart, soul, and mind, and to love one's neighbor as oneself (Rom. 13:8–10; Gal. 5:13; 6:2; see also Matt. 22:34–40). This concept of freedom casts a new light on things. Some Christians may think that God's will is something dangerous. It may involve a less than "happy" life. They are therefore not accustomed to thinking that true Christian freedom is God's enablement to do his will.

One of the main reasons for the death of Christ was to destroy the works of the devil (1 John 3:8). Salvation is not only deliverance from sin but deliverance to righteousness. It is not only release from the penalty of sin but release from the power of sin. As we discussed earlier, salvation is a transfer from "in Adam" to "in Christ" (see chapter 8, "New Man"). It is a change of masters: from bondage to sin to bondage to Christ (Rom. 6:15–23). Freedom is based on the enablement provided by the Holy Spirit who frees people to love God fully, unshackled by sin as they formerly were shackled by sin in Adam. Christians are now free to love their neighbor and produce the fruit of the Spirit: love, joy, peace, patience, kindness, goodness, faithfulness, gentleness, and self-control. Freedom is therefore predicated on obedience to the will of God and developing habits of holiness. It involves the reckoning and presenting according to Romans 6. It is based on a decision (aorist tense), but it involves an entire life process: Paul uses the verb "walk" to describe that the Christian life is not merely a "sign up" but a complete course through which to pass (Rom. 6:4; 8:4; 13:13; 14:15; 1 Cor. 3:3; 7:17; 2 Cor. 4:2; 5:7; 10:2; Gal. 5:16; Eph. 2:10; 4:1, 17; 5:2, 8, 15; Col. 1:10; 2:6; 3:7; 4:5; 1 Thess. 2:12; 4:1, 12; 2 Thess. 3:6, 11).

Perfection is not possible, if by "perfection" we mean sinlessness. Christians are never free from sin until they are with the Lord. But it is possible to live basically the way God wants Christians to live. The reason that Christians experience so much confusion and even hopelessness over this matter is probably due to two things. First, they think that a holy life is op-

8. Robert Gundry, "Grace, Works, and Staying Saved in Paul," *Biblica*, 66 (1985): 11.

tional and that they can pick and choose what they will or will not do. Second, they think the Christian life is such a great mystery or so difficult to live that only a few have found the "secret." The truth is that the Christian life is clearly described in the New Testament. It is no mystery or secret. Rather it is possible and necessary to live it, although it is not easy to live because of the "flesh." In addition, it is not impossible to live because the Holy Spirit is present as a constant helper and he will cause the growth and development that are necessary if the Christian will live by his power. The freedom that Christ has provided guarantees success.

Life in the Spirit

The second aspect of the significance of newness for the individual Christian is life in the Spirit. The Holy Spirit plays a central role in New Testament theology because, as we demonstrated earlier (see chapter 5, "New Covenant"), the Holy Spirit is one of the central attributes of the new covenant. The Greek noun πνεῦμα, which can mean "Spirit," "breath," "wind," or "spirit," occurs 379 times in the New Testament.[9] This noun occurs 146 times in Paul (40% of the total) and 106 times in Luke-Acts (30% of the total). Obviously, both Paul and Luke regard the new covenant age as the age of the Spirit. For Paul, having the Holy Spirit is the sine qua non of being a Christian (Rom. 8:9).[10]

The best way to understand Paul's concept of the Christian's life in the Spirit is to regard the references to ἐν πνεύματι as locatives of sphere.[11] Ἐν πνεύματι is parallel with ἐν Χριστῷ and ἐν σαρκί is parallel with ἐν Αδαμ, and the first pair is in contrast with the last pair. In other words, when the transfer was made from "in Adam" to "in Christ" a corresponding transfer was made from "in flesh" to "in Spirit." In Romans 8:9 Paul states flatly that Christians are not "in flesh" but "in Spirit." These locatives must be realms of relationship. The Christian is no longer related to Adam and flesh, but to Christ and the Holy Spirit. Just as a fish lives and functions in the medium or sphere of water, Christians must live and function in the new realms into which they have been transferred through Christ's death. Although the fish lives and functions oblivious to the fact that the water

9. Robert Morgenthaler, *Statistik des neutestamentlichen Wortschatzes*, 2d ed. (Zürich: Gotthelf-Verlag, 1973), 133.

10. The statistical breakdown of references to πνεῦμα in Paul is as follows: Romans, 34 times; 1 Corinthians, 40; 2 Corinthians, 17; Galatians, 18; Ephesians, 14; Philippians, 5; Colossians, 2; 1 Thessalonians, 5; 2 Thessalonians, 3; 1 Timothy, 3; 2 Timothy, 3; Titus, 1; Philemon, 1. Eighty of these 146 uses of πνεῦμα clearly refer to the Holy Spirit; 76 references may refer to the Holy Spirit, one's personal spirit, or even Satan (Eph. 2:2).

11. James D. G Dunn, *Baptism in the Holy Spirit*, Studies in Biblical Theology, Second Series, 15 (Naperville, Ill.: Allenson, 1970), 128.

surrounding it contains life-giving oxygen, removal from the water suddenly brings it into the life-threatening crisis of life outside the water. If it is not returned to the water soon, it will die. Likewise, Christians are often unaware of their immersion in the Spirit as the life-giving medium for their Christian existence. If they were "in flesh" again, they would suddenly realize their tremendous dependence on the Spirit and would die just like a fish out of water (Rom. 8:10–11).

To be "in Spirit" means that Christians now have the dynamic of the Spirit available to them that permits them to live as God wants them to live. Their new life "in Spirit" produces four new dimensions in relationships: (1) the personal; (2) the interpersonal; (3) the revelational; and (4) the motivational.

The Personal Dimension of Life in the Spirit

Not only do Christians appropriate the redemptive-historical transfer from "in flesh" to "in Spirit" when they believe the gospel, but they also place themselves under the existential obligation to begin living *according to* the Spirit. In addressing this obligation, Paul carefully distinguishes between two Greek prepositions: "in" (ἐν) and "according to" (κατά). Christians are not "in flesh" but they can certainly live "according to the flesh." Although they are "in Spirit" because of their position "in Christ," they do not automatically live "according to the Spirit." The grammatical nuance of "according to" (κατά) is "according to the standard of" or "according to the dictates." To live according to the flesh is to live according to the dictates of the flesh. To live according to the Spirit is to live according to the dictates of the Spirit. When Christians "walk" (i.e., live) according to the Spirit, they live in a vital, personal relationship with the living God. The Holy Spirit is a person and the Christian's relationship with the Holy Spirit is personal. Despite the neuter form of the word for *Spirit*, the Spirit is certainly no abstraction. More importantly, he certainly is not a doctrine to be analyzed and objectified coldly and impersonally, and then relegated to a theological encyclopedia!

The Interpersonal Dimension of Life in the Spirit

When Christians are immersed in the Spirit, they are also immersed in the body of Christ, the church. No longer do they exist in isolation, but they have a new responsibility to their fellow Christians. When Paul talks about the Spirit, he often talks about the church and vice-versa (1 Cor. 3:16; 12:4, 7, 8, 9, 10, 11, 13; Eph. 2:18, 22; 4:3, 4, 30; Phil. 1:27; 2:1; 1 Thess. 5:19). Christians must pay attention to all of the "one-another's" in Paul's directives to the church. (We will discuss these in the next chapter of this book.) Certainly the Christian cannot live by Cain's motto: "Am I my brother's keeper?" (Gen. 4:9). The church is the community of the Spirit. Christians

must recognize that the transfer from Adam and from flesh not only resolves the vertical alienation with God but also the horizontal alienation
with their fellow human beings. No Christian can live as an island to himself or herself. Christians are part of an organism and have definite responsibilities to their fellow believers in Christ, such as, "Let us consider how
we may spur one another on toward love and good deeds. . . . let us encourage one another" (Heb. 10:24–25). Although their responsibilities to fellow
Christians are primary, they also have responsibilities to their fellow
human beings outside Christ (Gal. 6:10).

The Revelational Dimension of Life in the Spirit

The so-called paranetic sections (ethical sections) of the New Testament
are all revelational of what life in the Spirit entails. (The ethical structure
of the new man has already been developed in chapter 8.) Christians do not
have to grope in the dark trying to find what is pleasing to the Lord. Life in
the Spirit is not some mysterious or elusive encounter intended to be experienced by only a few elite Christians. Nor does it consist of "secrets" that
can be shared only in special books, video tapes, or seminars. The "manual
for Christian living" is the New Testament. A major passage on the revelational work of the Spirit in terms of the life of the Christian is
1 Corinthians 2:10–16. In this passage Paul insists that the Holy Spirit has
provided Christians with the mind of Christ so that they can make the ethical decisions they need to make. The writer of the Book of Hebrews re-
bukes his readers for their failure to apply what they have been taught to
making ethical choices (Heb. 5:11–14). Probably one of the best statements
of the sufficiency of Scripture for living the Christian life is Peter's assurance that God has given Christians everything they need for life and godliness (2 Pet. 1:3).

The Motivational Dimension of Life in the Spirit

The Holy Spirit provides the motivational impetus for the Christian to
live the Christian life. The Spirit accomplishes this in two ways: (1) nega-
tively, by convicting the Christian of sin; and (2) positively, by prompting the
Christian to live righteously. The Spirit gives this motivation by pouring out
the love of God in the hearts of Christians (Rom. 5:5). Only those who are led
by the Spirit of God are the sons of God (8:14). As Christians live under the
direction of the Spirit, they gain assurance that they belong to the family of
the Spirit, and the Spirit assures them of their adoption into God's family
(8:15–16). The Spirit serves as the rule of life for Christians as they live according to the standards that the Spirit sets in the revelational dimension.

How the Spirit motivates the Christian or just how the Christian and the
Spirit interface is unclear. This writer suggests that the Spirit operates

through the three aspects of the person: intellect (mind), sensibility (emotions), and will. In regard to the intellect, the apostle Paul greatly stresses the need for the transformation of the Christian's mind (Rom. 12:2; Eph. 4:23). The unregenerate mind is characterized by darkness, ignorance, hardness, and insensitivity (Eph. 4:17–19). When a person becomes a Christian, the Holy Spirit begins a work of transformation and renewal so that the Christian's mind is enlightened concerning the truth of God, Christ, and the gospel. The Spirit also softens believers' minds so that they are sensitive, no longer resisting the Lord but learning as much as they can about the Bible, theology, and the Christian life. → *axiology*

At the same time, the emotions must also be transformed. The long lists of characteristics of the old man in Ephesians and Colossians contain many words that are emotionally related, including anger, jealousy, hatred, humility, bitterness, malice, compassion, forgiveness, and kindness. The work of the Holy Spirit is to convict Christians of emotional responses that are sinful and to motivate Christians to replace these sinful emotions with righteous emotions, such as love, joy, peace, patience, kindness, goodness, and gentleness. Only when Christians begin to display these godly emotions can they claim to be walking according to the Spirit and living according to the ethical structure of the new man.

Finally, the Spirit must transform the will of the Christian. While the unbeliever's basic stance toward God is "I won't" (John 5:40), the believer's disposition must be "I will" (Eph. 5:17). Paul begged the Roman Christians to present themselves to the Lord as a living sacrifice so that they might discern the will of the Lord and do it (Rom. 12:1–2). The Lord's will must become the Christian's will. Thus the work of the Holy Spirit is to bring the will of the Christian into greater and greater submission to the will of the Lord (Col. 1:9–12).   *motivation*

In conclusion, for Paul life in the Spirit is almost synonymous with life in Christ. To have the one is to have the other. To live in the one is to live in the other. To please the one is to please the other. If Christianity is Christ, it is also the Holy Spirit. The Spirit is the other Paraclete. He is the gift par excellence of the risen, ascended Christ to his church.

Warfare against the Flesh

Flesh is often the antithesis of Spirit in the Pauline corpus. Because of this common negative meaning for flesh, many readers of Paul conclude that all occurrences of flesh have a pejorative connotation. This is an unfortunate misunderstanding that has led to erroneous conclusions about texts in which Paul uses flesh in a good or neutral sense. According to Anthony Thiselton, flesh has at least five meanings in Paul:

    ; of people, animals, birds, or fish;
       ..ships that are transitory;
      ..at which is human, creaturely, and frail;

4. that which is "according to" (κατά), or based on, external or natural considerations;

5. a person in his opposition to God's aims—an outlook that is oriented toward the self, or that which pursues its own ends in self-sufficient independence of God.[12]

Burton lists seven meanings:

1. the soft, muscular parts of an animal body;
2. the whole material part of a living being;
3. the basis or result of natural generation;
4. a corporeally conditioned living being;
5. the external as distinguished from the internal;
6. all that comes to a person by inheritance rather than from the operation of the divine Spirit;
7. that element in man's nature that is opposed to goodness, that in him which makes for evil.[13]

It is not justifiable to saddle a word that has a good sense in four out of five or six out of seven meanings with a uniformly bad sense that is true of only one of its meanings.

Since Paul uses the term *flesh* 91 times out of a total of 147 occurrences in the New Testament, it seems legitimate to conclude that flesh is a major word in Pauline theology.[14] Out of this total number of occurrences, Paul seems to use flesh in the negative sense in perhaps as many as 41 instances.[15] These texts are the basis for developing a Pauline theology of that opposition to the Spirit that Paul calls "flesh."

It should be clear from the preceding discussion that the word *flesh* does not connote evil or something bad per se. One of the heresies of Docetism

12. A. C. Thiselton, "Flesh," in *The New International Dictionary of New Testament Theology*, ed. Colin Brown, 3 vols. (Grand Rapids: Zondervan, 1975), 1:674–76.

13. Ernest De Witt Burton, *A Critical and Exegetical Commentary on the Epistle to the Galatians*, ICC (Edinburgh: T. & T. Clark, 1921), 492–95.

14. Morgenthaler, 140. The breakdown of occurrences in Paul is as follows: Romans, 26 times; 1 Corinthians, 11; 2 Corinthians, 11; Galatians, 18; Ephesians, 9; Philippians, 5; Colossians, 9; 1 Timothy, 1; Philemon, 1. The only other New Testament writer to have double-digit occurrences is John.

15. The following is a list of thirty-six passages: Rom. 7:5, 18, 25; 8:3, 4, 5, 6, 7, 8, 9, 12, 13; 9:8; 13:14; 1 Cor. 1:26; 2 Cor. 7:1; 10:2, 3; 11:18; Gal. 3:3; 4:23, 29; 5:13, 16, 17, 19, 24; 6:8, 12; Eph. 2:3; Phil. 3:3, 4; Col. 2:11, 13, 18, 23. In addition to these texts, five more are possible: Rom. 6:19; 1 Cor. 5:5; 10:18; 2 Cor. 5:16; Gal. 6:13.

and Gnosticism has been to equate flesh with the body and then to pronounce both evil. The body is never looked upon as something bad or evil in either the Old or New Testament.[16] To read a negative connotation into texts in which flesh refers to the body is to commit an egregious theological blunder.[17] If there is something intrinsically evil about flesh, then Jesus could not have become flesh. In Romans 5 Paul is very careful to say that death entered the world because of the *sin* of a person, not because of the *flesh* of a person. When Paul speaks of Christ's incarnation, he states that Christ was made in the *likeness* of sinful flesh (Rom. 8:3). The addition of "likeness" makes all the difference in the world.

In Paul's writings the pejorative connotations of flesh occur in terms of sin; it is therefore difficult to understand exactly what Paul means by flesh. It is clear that Paul transposes "in flesh" over against "in Spirit." He seems to view these two locatives of sphere as realms of existence or relationship. The key text is Romans 8:9 where Paul insists that Christians are not "in flesh" (although they are still in the body) but "in Spirit" if Christ's Spirit dwells in them. If anyone does not have Christ's Spirit, that person is not a Christian! The flesh must be a realm or status that an unregenerate person has "in Adam" from which one must be transferred if one is to have a proper standing before God. The close relationship of "in flesh" with "in Adam" and "in Spirit" with "in Christ" shows that Paul is talking about a person's identification that can change from one alignment to another alignment.

But flesh is more than a status that a person has in Adam. It is also a sinful orientation or inclination that a person has as a part of one's deepest being that causes him or her to sin. Modern secular thinking is wrong when it assumes that a person is basically good and suffers only from a lack of knowledge, finances, or opportunity. This view assumes that if a person receives enough knowledge, money, and opportunities for advancement, then that person can gradually remove barriers and overcome limitations and antisocial behavior. Ultimately, secularists believe, that a person will move higher and higher until he or she lives at peace with other fellow human beings and the world becomes a glorious place!

In Paul's mind, however, the problem that people face is not a lack of knowledge or finances or opportunity, but alienation—people have broken

---

16. See J. A. Schep, *The Nature of the Resurrection Body* (Grand Rapids: Eerdmans, 1964), esp. chaps. 1, "Flesh and Body in the Old Testament," and 3, "Flesh and Body in the New Testament."

17. In the following texts, σάρξ, "flesh," is used without any negative connotations: Rom. 2:28; 1 Cor. 7:28; 2 Cor. 4:11; 7:5; 10:3; 12:7; Gal. 2:20; 4:14; Eph. 2:11, 14; 5:29; Phil. 1:22, 24; Col. 1:24; 2:1, 5; 1 Tim. 3:16.

the relationship between themselves and the true and living God, who is the source of all holiness, righteousness, and truth. Because people have alienated themselves from God, they have plunged themselves into an estranged state that has certain ethical ramifications and a manifestation called sin. People are exceedingly sinful because of their alienated status before God and their alignment with Adam, both of which have a negative effect on their ethical conduct.

Alienated people walk in darkness rather than light, in flesh rather than Spirit, and according to the flesh rather than the Spirit. People produce the products of their iniquity because of the status and nature they possess. There is an inescapable nexus between the relationship and the results of that relationship. The fallen status of people not only constitutes them as sinners but results in sinning as a pattern of life for them. Romans 5:12–21 is a key passage that describes the status of people in Adam as sinners and the "many trespasses" (v. 16) that result from their character as sinners.

"In flesh," therefore, is the realm in which people function. It is like a sea in which a fish swims with no hope of extricating itself. Just as the fish swims in its watery environment, fallen people, "in flesh," move about in their sinful "environment" inherited from Adam, thinking that their environment is "natural" and even excusable because all other people "swim" with them (Rom. 1:32). If it were not for God's revelation to people of the offense of their sins to God and their condemnation as sinners, people would continue to live unconscious of their need for redemption (7:7–11). God's revelation reveals sin to be "exceedingly sinful" (7:13) and convinces people of their need for Christ.

Romans 6 is the major passage in Paul that develops the need for the subjective appropriation of the objective work of Christ. The key term of appropriation is "consider" (λογίζομαι) in Romans 6:11. The key term for application to life is "present" (παρίστημι) in Romans 6:13, 16, 19, and 12:1. As the following chart demonstrates, Paul alternates the indicative and the imperative throughout Romans 6:

Indicatives	**Imperatives**
We died to sin (v. 2).	. . . count yourselves dead to sin but alive to God in Christ Jesus (v. 11).
. . . all of us who were baptized into Christ Jesus were baptized into his death (v. 3).	. . . do not let sin reign in your mortal body so that you obey its evil desires (v. 12).

We were therefore buried with him through baptism into death. . . . (v. 4).

Do not offer the parts of your body to sin, as instruments of wickedness, but rather offer yourselves to God, . . . and offer the parts of your body to him as instruments of righteousness (v. 13).

If we have been united with him like this in his death, we will certainly also be united with him in his resurrection (v. 5).

. . . offer them [the parts of your body] in slavery to righteousness leading to holiness (v. 19).

. . . our old self [person] was crucified with him so that the body of sin might be done away with (v. 6).

. . . anyone who has died has been freed from sin (v. 7).

Now if we died with Christ, . . . we will also live with him (v. 8).

. . . you have been set free from sin and have become slaves to God (v. 22).

The indicative states the objective truth that the transfer has taken place. The imperative states the need for the subjective appropriation of the truth of the transfer. This appropriation entails a true acknowledgment that the transfer is real and a presentation of one's body to God as an instrument of righteousness. The presentation is the initial—not final—step in a life lived under the direction of the Holy Spirit. As the Christian lives this life, the Holy Spirit transforms the intellect, sensibility, and will so that the Christian's orientation to sin is subjugated to the new life in the Spirit. This transformation is an ongoing process. The numerous imperatives in Paul (and other New Testament writers) show that the choice to walk according to the Spirit must be made continually because the flesh is a continual enemy and a built-in antithesis to the Spirit (Gal. 5:16–17). Christians must develop habits of holiness that will gradually replace the old habits they had when they were in Adam and in flesh.

The pastoral need is to instruct Christians in the *progressive* transformation from living according to the flesh to living according to the Spirit. Many Christians expect to walk in newness of life immediately, and when they fail (as they inevitably will), they become discouraged and think that the Christian life is impossible to live. Christians must be taught that their new life in Christ is a day-by-day enterprise with slow progress. But over time the new habits of holiness will replace the old habits of unholiness.

Christians must learn that only over time will the new habits of holiness develop. A lifetime of unholy habits takes time to reverse and transformation takes effort to succeed. Maturity in Christ develops from growth multiplied over time. Of course, if there is no growth, then forty years as a Christian does not yield much maturity! But growth alone does not yield maturity. Growth must be multiplied by the time over which growth takes place to produce true Christian maturity. Thus chronological age alone will not necessarily correlate with spiritual maturity. On the other hand, spiritual maturity should not be expected from new Christians! They must be allowed time to grow!

The focus of ministry within the body of Christ must constantly be upon Scripture, prayer, and fellowship. These are the means of grace that God has given his new covenant people to produce maturity (Eph. 4:11–16). If the level of maturity of the flock is low or if spiritual growth does not proceed as rapidly as the leaders of God's flock would like, they should not be discouraged. Instead the pastor-teacher must patiently feed and lead Christ's sheep step-by-step, equipping the saints for the work of ministry, and causing Christians to grow to maturity. The ministry must help people work out existentially what has been accomplished redemptive-historically in terms of newness. This need for ministry in the flock of Christ leads to the next topic of discussion: Newness and the Corporate Church.

For Further Study

Barclay, William. *Flesh and Spirit.* London: SCM, 1962.

His exposition of the works of the flesh and the fruit of the Spirit in Galatians 5 is the best known to this writer.

Deidun, T. J. *New Covenant Morality in Paul.* Rome: Biblical Institute Press, 1981.

This is a very stimulating study of New Testament ethics with an emphasis on love in relation to the new covenant and the law.

Gundry, Robert. "Grace, Works, and Staying Saved in Paul." *Biblica*, 66 (1985): 1–38.

Gundry's article is a very balanced discussion of the relationship between faith and works. Works are never instrumental *for* salvation, only evidential *of* salvation.

Richardson, Peter. *Paul's Ethic of Freedom.* Philadelphia: Westminster, 1979.

Richardson's book is a basic study of freedom in Paul's writings.

Schep, J. A. *The Nature of the Resurrection Body.* Grand Rapids: Eerdmans, 1964.

Schep's book is one of the best discussions of the body as it relates to "flesh" in both testaments.

So what chapter.

13

Newness and the Corporate Church

*N*ewness not only has great implications for the life of the individual Christian but also for the corporate church. This chapter will
develop the implications of newness for the corporate church in two main
areas: community and ministry.

Community

Of paramount importance to the church is the development of a functional
ecclesiology that will enable the church to function in any time and any place.
Newness has freed the church from clocks and cities. The universalism of the
gospel brought the need for new forms of approach to God. A temple building
and a central city, Jerusalem, were too restrictive for the explosion of the gospel
throughout the world. The focus of the church is on people. In fact, wherever
two or three people gather together in Jesus' name, he promises to be in their
midst (Matt. 18:20). The key phrases in the verse are, "gather together," "in my
name," and "in the midst." The risen Christ is now head of this gathered group
(Eph. 1:22), a gathered community called the body of Christ (1 Cor. 12:12–31)
to whom he has given gifts (Eph. 4:7–16). The emphasis is thus on a corporate
fellowship who bear mutual responsibilities to one another.

A survey of the New Testament reveals that very little apparatus is connected with the church. Even leadership is functional. Deacons were appointed when the need arose (Acts 6). Paul did not appoint elders in the
churches of Lystra, Iconium, and Antioch of Pisidia until his return visit to
them (Acts 14:23). Job descriptions for elders and deacons seem somewhat
broad and general: they must lead, feed, shepherd, care for, and serve. Their

qualifications as given in 1 Timothy 3 and Titus 1 are character-oriented rather than task-oriented. This was probably intentional so that the community of the redeemed would have flexibility any place they gathered together on the face of the earth. The more complex the structure, the less adaptable the church would be in various cultures and periods of history. Matthew 18:20 indicates that the size of the group is unimportant: "... where two or three come together...." Even Judaism required at least ten adult males for the formation of a synagogue.[1] In the early church people simply gathered together in the name of the Lord (Acts 4:31; 11:26; 14:17; 15:6, 30; 20:7–8; 1 Cor. 5:4) for mutual edification through the exercise of individual spiritual gifts.

The whole purpose of the gifts that the exalted Christ gave through the Holy Spirit to every Christian was the edification of the saints (1 Cor. 14:5). He gave the basic gifts of apostles, prophets, evangelists, and pastor-teachers to equip the church for the task of ministry so that the whole church might be built up into a holy temple in the Lord and made perfect in love (Eph. 4:7–16). Thus, when the church gathers, its goal is the edification of believers within the community of faith (1 Cor. 14:26). When the church scatters, its purpose is the evangelization of the world outside of the community of the redeemed.

Therefore, the church has two functions: *edification* and *extension*. Edification involves gathering together in Christ's name as a community of the redeemed to build up one another in the faith. Edification also involves teaching, the breaking of bread, fellowship, and prayer (Acts 2:42), as well as singing and thanksgiving (Eph. 5:19–20). Extension involves the scattering of the redeemed into the world to extend the gospel and win converts to Christ (Matt. 28:19–20). Extension also involves the preaching of the gospel and engaging in a host of activities designed to win converts to Christ.

A study of the Book of Acts shows the use of approximately fifty different Greek words to describe the evangelistic activities of the early church. A list of these words, their basic meaning, and Scripture references appear in Figure 13.1.

Figure 13.1

Evangelistic Activities in the Early Church According to the Book of Acts

Greek Term	Lexical Meaning	Scripture Reference(s)
ἀναγγέλλω	report, announce	Acts 14:27; 15:4; 20:20, 27
ἀναπείθω	persuade	18:13

---

1. Everett Ferguson, *Backgrounds of Early Christianity*, 2d ed. (Grand Rapids: Eerdmans, 1993), 546.

Greek Term	Lexical Meaning	Scripture Reference(s)
ἀνοίγω	open	26:18
ἀπαγγέλλω	proclaim, report	26:20
ἀποδίδωμι	give out	4:33
ἀποκρίνομαι	answer	3:12
ἀπολογέομαι	defend oneself	25:8; 26:1
ἀπολογία	defense	22:1
ἀποφθέγγομαι	declare boldly	2:14; 26:25
διακατελέγχομαι	defeat, refute	18:28
διαλέγομαι	discuss	17:2, 17; 18:4, 19; 19:8, 9; 20:7; 24:25
διαμαρτύρομαι	warn	2:40; 8:25; 10:42; 18:5; 20:21, 24; 23:11; 28:23
διανοίγω	explain	17:3
διαφέρω	spread a teaching	13:49
διδάσκω	teach	11:26; 15:35; 18:11, 25; 20:20; 21:21, 28; 28:31
διδαχή	teaching	13:12
ἐκδιηγέομαι	tell in detail	15:3
ἐκτίθημι	explain, set forth	18:26; 28:23
ἐξηγέομαι	explain, interpret	15:12
ἐπιστηρίζω	strengthen	14:22; 15:32, 41; 18:23
εὐαγγελίζω	preach the gospel	5:42; 8:4, 12, 25, 35, 40; 11:20; 13:32; 14:7, 15, 21; 15:35; 16:10; 17:18
ζήτησις	debate	15:2
καταγγελεύς	proclaimer	17:18

Greek Term	Lexical Meaning	Scripture Reference(s)
καταγγέλλω	proclaim	4:2; 13:5; 15:36; 16:17; 17:3, 13
κηρύσσω	preach, announce	8:5; 9:20; 10:42; 19:13; 20:25; 28:31
λαλέω	speak	2:11; 4:1, 20, 29, 31; 5:20, 40; 8:25; 9:29; 11:19; 16:6, 13; 17:19; 18:9, 25; 26:26
λειτουργέω	render service to God	13:2
μαρτυρέω	bear witness, testify	23:11
μαρτύρομαι	testify	20:26;26:22
μάρτυς	witness	2:32; 3:15; 5:32; 10:39; 26:16
νουθετέω	warn	20:31
ὁδηγέω	lead, guide, instruct	8:31
ὁμιλέω	talk	24:26
παρακαλέω	appeal to	2:40; 11:23; 14:22; 15:32; 16:40; 20:1
παράκλησις	exhortation	13:15
παρατίθημι	demonstrate, point out	17:3
παρρησιάζομαι	speak fearlessly	9:27, 28; 13:46; 14:3; 18:26; 19:8; 26:26
πείθω	convince	13:43; 17:4; 18:4; 19:8, 26; 28:23
προσκαρτερέω	be busily engaged in	2:42; 6:4
προσλαλέω	speak to	13:43
στάσις	dispute, argument	15:2
στερεόω	make strong, make firm	16:5
συγχέω	confound	9:22

Greek Term	Lexical Meaning	Scripture Reference(s)
συζητέω	dispute, debate, argue	6:9; 9:29
συμβάλλω	converse	17:18; 18:27
συμβιβάζω	prove, offer proof	9:22
συνέχω	absorbed in	18:5
ὑπηρέτης	servant, helper	26:16
φθέγγομαι	call out loudly	4:18

SEE NOTES 2/10/97 2/12/97

This long list indicates that the early church used an assortment of approaches in preaching the gospel and instructing converts. The list also indicates that it is impossible to make a rigid distinction between what is public and what is private teaching or what takes place inside or outside the Christian assembly. All the verbal activities were directed toward the two major goals of the church: the edification of God's people and the extension of the gospel into the world. Interestingly, only one text shows an unbeliever coming into the gathered assembly (1 Cor. 14:23–25). In this text Paul warns the Corinthians that verbal communication must be intelligible, otherwise unbelievers within their midst may surmise that the Christians are "out of their minds" (v. 23). This text is the only hint that Christian meetings might include evangelism. It seems clear, however, that the early church was concerned with edification when they gathered together and evangelism when they dispersed. They used every verbal means available to accomplish these goals. Not locked into any one particular method, they used any and every means to meet people where they were, convert them, and build them up. Dialogue, argumentation, proclamation, teaching, and many other methods were used to present the message intelligibly.

In contrast to a balanced approach in the early church to edify the community is the penchant in the contemporary church to focus on only one method, emphasizing that approach to the exclusion or minimization of all other approaches. The result is a lack of balance in which the church is well-nourished in one area but starved in another important area.

Contemporary Models of the Church

Ralph Martin has written a book in which he discusses four contemporary models of the church that can be found in almost any church of any denomination.[2] Each one of these four models has a part to play in the totality of achieving God's purposes for the church. While none of these models is intrinsically wrong, too much emphasis on any one particular model can distort and neglect the important purpose and functions of the church. Any one of the models, followed to the exclusion of the others, results in an unbalanced church and a loss of community. An unbalanced church will result in unbalanced Christians whose improper spiritual diet will lead to "spiritual scurvy." A church that loses community becomes merely an organization whose members feel like cogs in a huge machine that grinds along regardless of their needs.

The four models proposed by Martin include: (1) the lecture room model; (2) the theater model; (3) the large corporation model; and (4) the fellowship model. Without trying to be critical or overly simplistic so as to develop a caricature, the writer suggests that each of these four models is particularly identified with a denomination or a church name. The Bible church is often identified with the lecture room model, Pentecostal groups usually fit the theater model, Baptist churches follow the large corporation model, and the Plymouth Brethren tend to fit the fellowship model. While none of these groups are tied exclusively to one model, their emphasis usually manifests itself by following one model more closely than the others.

THE LECTURE ROOM MODEL

Churches that follow the lecture room model focus their ministry on Bible exposition. The Scriptures are central in the service and the person in the pulpit is expected to be skilled in Bible exposition. People usually come in order to learn the Bible. Strong emphasis is given to careful exegesis of the text, consistent inductive biblical theology, and a well-planned teaching program following a fairly strict schedule alternating between an Old Testament book and a New Testament book. Time is of no great importance; it may take ten years to work through the Gospel of John. A Sunday sermon (lecture) may be devoted to just one verse. This is not a problem since the goal is careful exposition. The role of the people is to bring notebooks in order to take extensive notes on the passage under exposition. The atmosphere approaches that of a "lay seminary" and the leaders usually have advanced academic degrees from prestigious schools. These expositors work through the text carefully, giving exegetical alternatives and arguing strenuously for their "correct" interpretation.

In this model the people receive an opportunity to acquire a high level of theological education within a church building that functions as a lecture room. Often an overhead projector is used with diagrams and charts to fa-

---

2. Ralph P. Martin, *The Family and the Fellowship* (Grand Rapids: Eerdmans, 1979), 112–21.

cilitate learning. The lecturer is the pastor and the students are the congregation, and it is not uncommon to refer to the congregation as the "class." In terms of the exercise of spiritual gifts, the overall situation is very unbalanced. It would seem that only the pastor has the gift of pastor-teacher, since all of the other members are only passively involved. The other activities listed in Acts 2:42, such as fellowship, breaking bread, and prayer, are essentially ignored. Music and any other elements in the service are usually preliminaries that move toward the whole focus of the gathering: the lecture. It is easy to get the impression that anything other than the lecture is a nuisance and must be tolerated for the sake of tradition. In other words, the service is the lecture. Everything else is really not that important.

THE THEATER MODEL

The focus in this model is on a great "show." The pageantry and music are so awesome that the production could compete with professional entertainment. In fact, the service is often televised. The "actors" on the stage are attractive people, fashionably dressed, with a great deal of charisma. People "enjoy" this service. Even when it comes time for the "message," the preacher is usually a high-profile personality who is very persuasive and captivating. After the audience has been warmed up by the pageantry and music, he "enters." With every eye fixed on him, he moves into the spotlight to begin his performance. His aim is not to exegete a passage of the Bible but to move the audience emotionally so that when he closes, the audience will do anything he asks. There is probably not a company in the world that would not like to have a person of this preacher's ability on its sales staff.

Pentecostal churches usually follow the theater model. Even though the audience is not up on the stage with the "actors," they are very much a part of the performance. Even though they are not "performing," they become very emotionally involved. Anything but passive, they may leave the service actually exhausted from all of the physical movement and expenditure of emotional energy.

In the theater model many within the church community have ample opportunity to participate in the drama. Almost nothing is ruled out. Such a model is highly attractive to musicians who would receive little or no opportunity to play or sing in the lecture room model. In the theater model the emphasis on music is a musician's dream. This model may include a twenty-five to thirty piece orchestra, including five trumpets, five trombones, five saxes, piano, organ, electronic keyboard or synthesizer, electric and acoustic guitars, drums, and violins, as well as an organ that generates a tremendous volume of sound. The production may include a choir of over 100 people as well as other groups of special singers. Usually no restrictions are placed on the style of music played, so people whose musical tastes extend beyond Bach and traditional hymns find that they can play and sing music more to their liking than they could in any other model of church. After a production like this the typical comment may be, "Wasn't that great!"

THE LARGE CORPORATION MODEL

This model focuses on organization, leadership, and "programs." If at all possible, this model includes a large staff with a well-defined chain of command running right up to the "senior pastor," who in a very real sense functions like the CEO of a corporation. He is usually a person with a very strong personality who has well-defined goals and plans for realizing them. This model tends to emphasize growth: more and/or larger facilities (buildings), greater numbers of people (bodies), and increased financial resources (bucks). The larger, the better. Programs have been designed to meet every conceivable need. These churches are into "marketing." It is often difficult to find the right room where a particular program is running. The crowds are so large that it is difficult to find a parking space, which often necessitates being shuttled in from a distant parking lot. With an atmosphere that resembles a football game, Sunday School attendance may reach 11,000 people and the membership role may be as high as 33,000![3] It is not unusual for the large corporation model to have an elementary, junior and senior high school, a four-year liberal arts college, a graduate school, and a theological seminary on site or at least run under the auspices of the church. It also may have its own press that publishes literature reflecting the particular theological viewpoint embraced by the CEO. Daily radio broadcasts and televised services, which may be as many as five or six on a Sunday, are another expected aspect of the large corporation's overall "investments."

Many Baptist churches reflect this large corporation model, a model that is widely viewed as the model of success. The more buildings, staff, and programs the church has, the more successful it is considered to be. Unfortunately, comparisons are made and many young ministers may feel that they just don't have what it takes because they are unable to develop the large corporation church. They may become disillusioned and drop out of ministry altogether. Or they may become a part of the staff of the large corporation and experience "success" overnight!

The congregation in such churches plays a minimal role in the operation of the corporation. The people seem to exist for the corporation instead of the corporation existing for the people. Decisions come from the top down (a power-based view of administration). This model leaves little room for opposition to the leaders or for alternative ways of achieving the

3. Ed Dobson, Ed Hindson, and Jerry Falwell, *The Fundamentalist Phenomenon* (Grand Rapids: Baker, 1986), 110.

goals of the church. Because of the size of the church, the people experience very little sense of community. If any community is achieved, it is accomplished only through a number of little "churches" within the corporation church. The members constantly struggle for personal identity and one cannot be sure whether the person across the aisle is a charter member or a new visitor!

As is true with any large organization, its dynamics foster depersonalization. The close, intimate dynamics of small-group interaction are lost as everything shifts toward the dynamics of the crowd. While the power of leadership increases and centralizes, the responsiveness of followers declines. Unless the large corporation model church takes drastic steps to insure individual identity and input, the individual is inevitably lost in the crowd.[4]

THE FELLOWSHIP MODEL

This model emphasizes equality and sharing. The goal is the involvement of all (male) members of the congregation in ministry. Leadership can lead to domination and reduction of the opportunity for everyone (at least males) to share and participate in ministry. Thus, leadership is regarded as a threat to the equality of the group and is de-emphasized. Seating may be in a circle to emphasize equality and to inhibit individuals from dominating the group. Structure and organization are minimal or even nonexistent. In fact it seems that no one is in charge of anything and that the group has no clearly defined goals. No single individual is responsible for regular biblical exposition since this would "fix" theology and interpretation and undermine the equality of viewpoints. The goal in Bible study is to share with other Christians "what the passage means to you" or "what the Lord has laid on your heart." Apparently no text of Scripture has a fixed meaning. Rather a text can have as many meanings as there are people to find it. By way of contrast, the expositor in the lecture room model would be scandalized by the lack of strict hermeneutical and exegetical control in the fellowship model and would be quick to expose the fallacies of all inaccurate interpretations of the Scripture text.

Although it is difficult to identify any one particular group of Christians with the fellowship model, perhaps the Plymouth Brethren come quite close. The Brethren have a christological focus in the meeting that is admirable. The emphasis on the "breaking of bread" at the earlier service is a moving experience. The opportunity to "give a word of exhortation" is available to any male present. The blend of Scripture reading, singing, and

---

4. The symptoms of "institutionalism" are listed by Gene A. Getz, *Sharpening the Focus of the Church* (Chicago: Moody, 1974), 193–94.

meditation on the cross are difficult to find in the other three models. A large number of Christians who have been deeply wounded spiritually by the lecture room, theater, and large corporation models have been drawn to the fellowship model. Fearing the loss of freedom, initiative, spontaneity, and ultimately the "leading of the Holy Spirit," Christians within a church that embraces the fellowship model have an aversion to adopting any of the characteristics of the other three models.

Conclusion

The truth of the matter is that each of the preceding four models has something essential to contribute to the people of God. Each, however, is an unbalanced approach. Also, each of these models has serious flaws and weaknesses that can destroy the very essence of church as the community of the redeemed living under the new covenant.

The contribution of the lecture room model is systematic and structured teaching, something that is essential for the growth of Christians. According to Acts 2:42, the early church continued in the teaching of the apostles. Perhaps Luke gave teaching the preeminent place on the list because of its fundamental and foundational character. Without teaching, apostolic tradition is not transmitted to the church and Christians flounder in what they should believe.

In addition to teaching, Christians also need outlets for creativity and expression, particularly in drama, art, and music. The strength of the theater model is its provision for creativity and expression. Since creativity is part of the divine image in people, they become frustrated when it is repressed. In this writer's opinion, the opportunity for creative expression from the whole church (including women!) has been one of the causes for the growth of the Pentecostal movement.

In addition to teaching and creative expression, the church also needs organization. The church certainly has a need for clearly defined goals (biblical goals, of course!) and for methods to achieve those goals. Without goals, the church lacks direction. An organization with able leaders helps to define those goals and supply the direction to achieve them.

Members within the church also have a vital need for sharing and interaction on a personal level. People are social beings and must be able to interact with other human beings. To stifle such interaction is to turn people into faceless nonentities. They need to be recognized and ministered to on a one-to-one level. The fellowship model thus supplies the dynamics for sharing and caring among Christians. Wuthnow's recent study of the explosion of small groups in the United States reveals the great need that people feel for a sense of community.[5] Icenogle's recent study on small group ministry may indicate that the foundations of the megachurch model are crumbling.[6]

So the church needs to recognize the strengths inherent in each of the various models. Then the challenge for the church is to make a conscious effort to include those strengths, keep them in balance, and eliminate their respective weaknesses. After this the question to ask is, How much emphasis should be given to each model? Only each gathering of Christ's people can determine that emphasis since needs vary from group to group and from place to place. But the Holy Spirit is present along with the New Testament as the guidebook for those who seek the will of the Lord Jesus Christ for their particular assembly. And the church must continually look to the Spirit, the Word, and the Head of the new covenant community, Jesus Christ, for guidance and direction.

Ministry

One of the changes in ministry effected by newness is the concept of the church as the body of Christ. It is clear from the New Testament that the whole church of Jesus Christ ministers. Although the church has leaders, no separate "clergy" function as priests within the church as the Aaronic and Levitical priesthood functioned under the old covenant. In the preface to his book, *Freed To Serve*, Michael Green states that the purpose of his book is to reexamine the first principles of Christian leadership.[7] According to Green, those first principles "seem very radical, because the Christian church has departed so far from the patterns of ministry to be found in the New Testament. We have got a long way away from Jesus the Servant. It is time to take stock and to reform."[8] Green discusses fourteen ways in which the church today differs from the church in the New Testament. He believes that these changes have quenched the idea of newness and in many ways have returned the church to the old covenant paradigm of ministry.

1. *In the New Testament, ministry had to be received before it was exercised.* By this Green means that only Christians exercised ministry. One had to experience the ministry of Christ and the Holy Spirit personally before one could minister to others. Green

5. Robert Wuthnow, *Sharing the Journey: Support Groups and America's New Quest for Community* (New York: The Free Press, 1994).

6. Gareth Weldon Icenogle, *Biblical Foundations for Small Group Ministry* (Downers Grove, Ill.: InterVarsity, 1994). For a defense of the megachurch approach, see Leith Anderson, *Dying for Change* (Minneapolis: Bethany, 1990), and *A Church for the 21st Century* (Minneapolis: Bethany, 1992).

7. Michael Green, *Freed to Serve* (Dallas: Word, 1988), 7.

8. Ibid.

contends that in many Western churches it is possible to become ordained without having had any vital experience of the cleansing of Christ.[9] This is, in part, due to the professionalization of ministry. Credentials replace character as the qualification for ministry.

2. *In the New Testament, all Christians were called to ministry, not some.*[10] According to Green, today the church distinguishes between clergy and laity, which has resulted in a passive, inert church. As discussed under the lecture room and large corporation models of church, the professional leaders are the individuals who minister. The rest are ministered to. Howard Hendricks, professor of Christian education at Dallas Seminary, perceptively compares the Christian church to a football game—60,000 spectators in the stands are desperately in need of exercise while 22 men down on the field are desperately in need of rest!

3. *In the New Testament, ministry was a function, not a status.*[11] The New Testament emphasizes function. The church today seems to emphasize office. This has resulted not only in hierarchicalism but a reduction in the number of gifted persons within the church who can actually preach and teach. In today's church the savior of spiritual gifts has been the Sunday School. If it were not for the Sunday School, the only Christian in most churches allowed to exercise his gift of pastor-teacher is the *one* person holding the office of "pastor." One could argue that the office of elder or overseer is the New Testament nomenclature, while pastor-teacher is a spiritual gift. In other words, a person could have the gift of pastor-teacher without holding the office of elder or overseer. Be that as it may, the New Testament clearly indicates that a one-man ministry or even a multiple-staff ministry that eliminates ministry, including the ministry of teaching and preaching, from the laity is a serious perversion.

4. *In the New Testament, ministry was something corporate and shared.*[12] According to Green, the singular ἐπίσκοπος in 1 Timothy 3:1 is a generalizing singular,[13] which does not contradict the plural πρεσβύτεροι found elsewhere in the New Testament. Leadership is always plural in the New Testament.[14]

9. Ibid., 10.
10. Ibid.
11. Ibid.
12. Ibid., 11.
13. Ibid., 47.
14. For a book-length defense of this statement, see Alexander Strauch, *Biblical Eldership* (Littleton, Colo.: Lewis and Roth, 1988).

5. *In the New Testament, authorization followed ministry rather than preceded it.*[15] Those who served had to be proven first. Today the procedure is to look to seminaries and Bible colleges for "ministers," ordain them, and then give them the full responsibilities of ministry with little or no prior experience.

6. *In the New Testament era, character, not intellect was the most important condition.*[16] First Timothy 3:1–13, Titus 1:5–9, and 1 Peter 5:1–5 list character traits rather than credentials as the qualification for ministry.[17] Today credentials are emphasized and character traits are often a matter of hope rather than a prerequisite. The recent scandals in televangelism have publicized to the non-Christian public the lack of integrity in ministry.

7. *In the New Testament, they selected their leadership from men of experience.*[18] No novice was considered. Since the church was based upon the family and met in homes, it was natural to look to the older, experienced men in the church community for leadership (1 Tim. 3:4–7). Today the church views ministry as a career structure. Education, personal charisma, and managerial skills appropriate for the business world are valued over age, character, and experience.

8. *In the New Testament, men were trained on the job as apprentices, not in a college.*[19] Admittedly, colleges and seminaries did not exist in New Testament times, but the truth remains that servants of Christ received on-the-job training, in the laboratory of life, with all of its stress and strain, and sometimes even controversy.

9. *In the New Testament, leaders were either local or circulating.*[20] Gifted leaders such as apostles, prophets, and evangelists often circulated among the churches, while local churches were led by elders, deacons, and deaconesses. Today churches go to a seminar or a crusade led by a circulating leader rather than the circulating leader coming to the churches.

10. *In New Testament days, local ministry consisted of people*

15. Green, 11.

16. Ibid.

17. In the New Testament the term "elder" was a title of honor, not of office, according to Alastair Campbell, *The Elders: Seniority Within Earliest Christianity* (Edinburgh: T. & T. Clark, 1994).

18. Green, 12.

19. Ibid.

20. Ibid., 13. See also Vincent Branick, *The House Church in the Writings of Paul* (Wilmington, Del.: Michael Glazier, 1989), 84.

called to serve and lead in their own locality.[21] Ministry used to be performed by ministers who came from within the community, rather than by those who came from the outside and who stayed for only a few years before moving on to the next church. Today the church looks to a school or agency hundreds of miles away for its "pastor." Further, the turnover rate among pastors is tremendous with many remaining in a church for less than five years.

11. *In New Testament days, leaders were normally not paid.*[22] That is, money was given more as a gift than as an income or a salary. Leaders like Paul could receive money, but Paul chose not to receive any from the Corinthians (1 Cor. 9:8–12). He wanted to serve without depending on any church for financial support. Churches had a responsibility to "reward the ox" (1 Tim. 5:17) and to share with those who taught (Gal. 6:6). But money was never to be the driving force of ministry (1 Pet. 5:2). Unfortunately, churches today will not call a man until they feel they can support him, and some men will not seriously consider a call if the financial package is "inadequate."

12. *In the New Testament, the leaders saw their ministry as one of enabling.*[23] The task of gifted men was to equip the saints for a work of ministry (Eph. 4:12). Leaders were really support people, holding up the whole building, the church (Eph. 2:20). Today, the church usually expects the paid pastor to do the work of ministry. His role is active; theirs is passive.

13. *In the New Testament, doctrine was important.*[24] Since Green is writing out of a context broader than fundamentalism, this shift is more applicable to churches of very latitudinarian theological commitments. In the light of David Wells' recent analysis, however, theology in the evangelical church is collapsing.[25]

14. *In the New Testament, ministry was seen in terms of people, not buildings.*[26] According to Green, mission is in bondage to maintenance. More time can be spent on planning a budget, which is largely devoted to paying for buildings, than on easing the burdens of people who desperately need help and care. This is especially true with benevolence, where the amount of dollars in the

---

21. Green, 13.
22. Ibid.
23. Ibid., 14.
24. Ibid.
25. David F. Wells, *No Place for Truth: Or Whatever Happened to Evangelical Theology* (Grand Rapids: Eerdmans, 1993).
26. Green, 14.

total church budget intended for benevolence is only a fraction of the amount for buildings.

The Vocabulary of Ministry

In light of these fourteen observations about ministry in the New Testament versus ministry in the contemporary church, we will now explore what was involved in ministry in the New Testament. Through a study of the basic words in the ministry word-group, διακονέω, "serve;" διακονία, "service;" and διάκονος, "servant," we will develop a clearer understanding of the New Testament conception of ministry.

"SERVE" (διακονέω) TEXTS

1. *Jesus is the model for ministry* (Matt. 20:28; Luke 22:27). Διακονέω is first used in one of the primary New Testament passages concerning ministry. The context is that of a mother who comes to Jesus to seek preeminence for her sons in Jesus' kingdom. The Gentiles were accustomed to desiring preeminence, lording it over others, but Jesus declared that this was not the pattern for his disciples. Rather, the one desiring to be great must serve. His disciples were to follow his example: "The Son of Man did not come to be served, but to serve, and to give his life as a ransom for many" (Matt. 20:26). If Jesus came to serve rather than be served, his servants must do the same (John 13:12–17). This is a tremendous statement about humility and Christian leadership. According to Philippians 2, Paul stated that it was necessary for Jesus to take upon himself the form of a servant during his first advent. The suffering preceded the glory (Luke 24:26; 1 Pet. 1:11). Thus Jesus became the model for ministry for those who would serve him in the interim period between Jesus' two advents. The follower of Jesus who would minister to God's people must continually have the mind of Christ, not thinking on his own interests but on the needs of other people. In New Testament ecclesiology leaders exist to serve and support those who are led.

2. *Ministry involves sacrifice* (Matt. 20:28; John 12:25–26). Ministry often involves great personal sacrifice. The Lord Jesus laid down his life for his sheep and gave his life as a ransom for many. Paul regarded himself as a drink-offering being poured out for the Philippians (Phil. 2:17–18). He regarded the expenditure of his energy as working death in himself but life in others (2 Cor. 4:12).

3. *Ministry to others is ultimately ministry to Christ* (Matt. 24:44). This idea comes from Paul's persecution of the church in Acts 9. When Paul was persecuting the church, the ascended Christ stated the idea when he asked Paul, "Why do you persecute Me?" (Acts 9:4). To persecute the church was to persecute Christ. Conversely, to serve the church is to serve Christ.

4. *Ministry by women to Jesus and to the disciples' physical needs was a vital service that they performed* (Matt. 27:55; Luke 8:3). Ministry has a financial dimension and meeting the financial needs of people is genuine ministry.

5. *Even after his return, the Lord Jesus will still function as a servant* (Luke 12:37). Even when he is King of Kings and Lord of Lords, he will continue to serve his people! Although a great contrast exists between the humiliated Jesus at his first advent and the exalted Jesus at his second advent, servanthood per se is not necessarily restricted to his humiliation phase. Servanthood seems to be a constant in Christ's style of leadership, not something thrust aside when his power and glory become evident to all. Jesus will still be a servant at his eschatological banquet! Can his followers be anything other than servants, too?

6. *A leader must be a servant* (Luke 22:26). This statement is an example of what many have called Jesus' "theology of reversal." In the kingdom of Jesus Christ, the last will be first and the first last; the humble exalted and the proud humiliated. What people consider great, God considers insignificant. For Jesus Christ, the best leader is the best servant.

7. *God the Father honors the one who serves Christ* (John 12:26; Rev. 2:19). Service for Jesus Christ seems to be the highest calling in life. People honor power, influence, brilliance, riches, skill, and ability, but God honors service and humility. Kingdom values are entirely different than Madison Avenue values.[27]

8. *While all ministries are important and needful, ministry has priorities and not all people devote themselves to the same ministry* (Acts 6:2). A common mistake is to view all ministries as equally important or reduce ministry to only one ministry: pastor. But the body of Christ includes a diversity of gifts and ministries—all important, but not equally important. While some ministries have a higher priority, others are supportive in nature. Those who have a high-priority ministry should not dilute their ministry by trying to do everything (see Acts 6:2). Rather other people must

27. See Donald B. Kraybill, *The Upside-Down Kingdom* (Scottdale, Pa.: Herald, 1978).

minister in these support roles to permit those with higher priority ministries to devote themselves to such.

9. *Some of the most helpful ministries are those that take place in the background rather than in the spotlight* (Acts 19:22). Timothy and Erastus served Paul in many capacities, encouraging him and serving the churches he founded, writing letters for him, and assisting him all along the way.

10. *Ministry in the financial area is a vital and indispensable ministry to the body of Christ* (Rom. 15:25, 31; Acts 6:1–4; 11:29; 2 Cor. 8:4; 9:1, 11–12). One of Paul's most pressing concerns was the collection for the poor saints in Jerusalem.[28] According to Nickle, this project had three levels of significance: (1) it was an act of Christian charity among fellow believers motivated by the love of Christ; (2) it was an act expressing the solidarity of the Christian fellowship by presenting irrefutable evidence that God was calling the Gentiles to faith; and (3) the eschatological pilgrimage of the Gentile Christians to Jerusalem would confront the Jews with the undeniable reality of the gift of God's saving grace to the Gentiles and would motivate the Jews to finally accept the gospel.[29]

11. *The task of a deacon is to serve* (1 Tim. 3:10). The church can easily lose sight of this aspect of being a deacon and view a deacon simply as one who ushers or counts money. The deacon can have a significant ministry to the needs of people within the body of Christ even when the church is dispersed. Many churches have developed a deacon-caring ministry. This ministry is a real ministry of service, and when done well, meets real needs in the lives of people.[30]

12. *Those who serve well will acquire a good standing for themselves in the Christian community as well as great assurance in their faith in Christ Jesus* (1 Tim. 3:13). Service has a great reward, both presently within the community of God's people and eschatologically when the Master rewards his faithful servants.

13. *Onesimus served Paul in prison as a surrogate for Philemon* (Philemon 13). Paul was miles away from Colossae and yet the theme of the Colossians serving him and having compassion on him was accomplished through Onesimus.

28. Keith F. Nickle, *The Collection*, Studies in Biblical Theology, 48 (Naperville, Ill.: Allenson, 1966).

29. Ibid., 142.

30. For a fine exposition on the New Testament deacon, see Alexander Strauch, *The New Testament Deacon* (Littleton, Colo.: Lewis and Roth, 1992).

14. *Serving the saints is one evidence of salvation* (Heb. 6:10). God does not forget the work of his servants who serve his saints and continue to do so. Thus, serving is one evidence of salvation because it is one of the things that accompany salvation.

15. *Everyone is to serve as a steward of God's multifaceted grace* (1 Pet. 4:11). Grace is not only preaching and teaching. God has given a variety of gifts to the church and each servant receives grace to serve the Lord in his or her place within the body of Christ.

16. *Ministry needs the strength that God supplies* (1 Pet. 4:11). It is impossible for Christians to serve only by their own abilities, relying upon their own resources, education, energy, or intelligence. Without the work of God and the power of the Holy Spirit, all service for God accomplishes very little. Ministry is a *spiritual* service.

17. *God receives glory through ministry* (1 Pet. 4:11). This is the ultimate reason for all service. Just as Jesus Christ, the model servant, cried out at the close of his ministry on the earth, "I have brought you glory on earth by completing the work you gave me to do" (John 17:4), Christians must repeat the same cry when they have finished their service here on the earth (2 Tim. 4:7–8).

"SERVICE" *(διακονία) TEXTS*

1. *The ministry of the gospel should be a lifelong commitment* (Acts 20:24). Paul said that the orientation of his entire life was to finish his course with joy and to continue preaching the gospel, which was a commitment that he kept until his death. Christians do not reach a point in life when they "retire" from ministry.

2. *Missions is a ministry* (Acts 21:19; Rom. 11:13). Ministry and missions are inseparable. To call someone a minister and another person a missionary is to create a false dichotomy. Both minister and both are missionaries.

3. *Ministry is a gift of God* (Rom. 12:7; Eph. 3:7). Two of the church's greatest errors have been to portray the ministry as a profession and to propagate the idea that one chooses ministry. Ministry is the calling of every member of the body of Christ. Christians serve because God calls them and gifts them for service.

4. *Ministry takes different forms* (1 Cor. 12:5). The church finds it difficult to discard the notion that each assembly of God's people

has only one "minister." All members have gifts and all are called to serve one another. To fail to grasp this truth and implement it in practice has been one of the greatest shortcomings of the church.

5. *New covenant ministry is a ministry of the Holy Spirit* (2 Cor. 3:8; 4:1). Much has already been written on this topic earlier in the book so that no further comment is necessary here. Please refer to the material in chapter 5 on the "New Covenant."

6. *Ministry has a primary task of reconciling men to God* (2 Cor. 5:18). Even though the church has diverse forms of ministry, one of its major tasks should never be neglected—the reconciliation of people to God through Jesus Christ.

7. *Ministry must continue despite many hindrances and attempts to stop it* (2 Cor. 6:3–10). Paul was not an ivory-tower theologian, but rather a pragmatic missionary who encountered and surmounted many hindrances to the spread of the gospel. Nonetheless, by concluding the Book of Acts with the words "without hindrance" (ἀκωλύτως, "unhindered"), Luke showed that despite obstacles to the advance of the church and the gospel, the ministry continued and was ultimately unhindered. Every apostle faced hindrances and the church today will also face them. But it is essential to reaffirm Jesus' promise that the gates of Hades will not overcome the church (Matt. 16:18).

8. *Spiritual gifts equip people for ministry* (Eph. 4:12). Two possible interpretations explain the sequence of the conjunctions in this verse. The first view maintains that the gifts are for the perfecting of the saints and that perfection leads to two separate tasks: (1) the work of the ministry; (2) the edification of the body of Christ. The second view is that the gifts are for the perfecting of the saints for the work of ministry, which in turn leads to the edification of the body of Christ. The view of most commentators is the second. In either case there is little difference concerning the task of spiritual gifts: the risen Christ gave gifts to build up his church. This building up of the church involves the intermediate step of equipping Christians for ministry. The bottom line is that ministry is an activity of the total body, not just the purview of a select few.

9. *Ministry is a legacy from the Lord and must be brought to completion* (Col. 4:17; 1 Tim. 4:5). Divine compulsion for ministry seems to be lacking in the church. Lacking the drive and endurance that Paul demonstrated, too many ministers drop out and leave ministry unfinished. Perhaps it is time to think of ministry

as mission and to make commitments based on a willingness to endure.

10. *Faithfulness is an indispensable qualification for ministry* (Eph. 6:21; Col. 1:7; 4:7; 1 Tim. 1:12; 2 Tim. 2:2; see also Matt. 24:45; 25:21, 23; Luke 16:10; 19:17; 1 Cor. 4:2). This observation dovetails nicely with the previous one. Dependability is more important than any other personal qualification. It is easy to start, but hard to finish. It is much easier to make commitments with the mouth than to follow through on them with the feet. Unfaithful servants are a real problem in the church and a terrible witness to the outside world. Paul had at least two distasteful experiences with unfaithfulness: Mark (Acts 15:38) and Demas (2 Tim. 4:10). Perhaps these experiences caused him to devote so many passages in his letters to the need for faithfulness.

11. *A person who became unprofitable for ministry became profitable for ministry later* (2 Tim. 4:11). Mark was not permanently rejected from ministry because of a lapse of faithfulness. Barnabas took Mark under his wing and developed him. Paul must have revised his assessment of Mark and directed Timothy to bring Mark with him to Rome because Mark was profitable to Paul for ministry. The church always has room for forgiveness and restoration of the unfaithful. But this fact should not serve as an excuse for unfaithfulness or a cavalier attitude toward faithfulness.

"SERVANT" (διάκονος) TEXTS

1. *Greatness in the kingdom of God is based on service during the interim* (Matt. 20:26; 23:11). This is another theology of reversal statement. Those who are servants become masters in the kingdom of God. Those who live like masters are reduced to servants. The road to the top is from the bottom.

2. *Phoebe, a woman, had a vital ministry in the church at Cenchrea* (Rom. 16:1). This is not the place to discuss the vexed issue of the role of women in the church. The literature on this subject is already enormous and increasing monthly.[31] But it should be clear from any reading of Romans 16:1 that Paul commended Phoebe for the faithful ministry she had in the church at Cenchrea.

---

31. For an introduction to and survey of the problem, see Carl B. Hoch, Jr., "The Role of Women in the Church: A Survey of Current Approaches," *Grace Theological Journal*, 8, no. 2 (Fall 1987): 241–51.

3. *Even the apostles were simply servants through whom people were evangelized and churches were planted* (1 Cor. 3:6). This passage shows the great humility on Paul's part over against the arrogance and pride of the Corinthians. Although he and Apollos had done great things, Paul is trying to show that they were nothing but servants through whom God was at work. Ministry is for the edification of the church, not for the inflation of egos.

4. *There is a Satanic ministry* (2 Cor. 11:25). This amazing verse seems to suggest that Satan is in ministry, be it a diabolical one, and is recruiting accomplices. His is a negative, destructive, deceitful ministry, but a ministry nonetheless.

5. *Warning believers against false doctrine and nourishing them in sound doctrine constitutes a good ministry* (1 Tim. 4:6). Ministry is both curative and preventative. Not only do sheep need to have their cuts bandaged, but they also need to be protected from the barbed wire that causes the wounds. The good shepherd is like a well-trained border collie who remains alert and prevents the sheep from potential dangers.

From this survey we can draw a number of conclusions about ministry in the New Testament. First and foremost, Christ is the model of ministry as the servant of the Lord. Ministry is a gift from God, and involves personal sacrifice, commitment, and faithfulness. Contrary to what many may think, character is much more important for ministry than education. Ministry is an activity that involves the entire body and seeks to edify the church. Whereas ministry is diverse, no ministry is insignificant. Satan is also active and can take away seed that is sown (Luke 8:12). Rewards for ministry ultimately come from the Lord when he commends by saying "Well done, good and faithful servant! . . . Come and share your master's happiness!" (Matt. 25:21).

The Reciprocal Nature of Ministry

"ONE ANOTHER" TEXTS

The reciprocal nature of ministry within the church is demonstrated by the biblical texts that include the phrase "one another." These texts emphasize the whole-body nature of ministry and the responsibilities that Christians have toward one another in the body of Christ. Distinct from an organization, the church is an organism in which each member needs and depends upon every other member.

The New Testament uses two Greek words to convey the mutuality of "one another": ἀλλήλων and ἑαυτῶν. The passages that use ἀλλήλων teach that Christians have numerous responsibilities toward one another (see Figure 13.2).

Figure 13.2

"One Another" (ἀλλήλων) *Commands in the New Testament*

Command	Scriptural Reference(s)
be at peace with each other	Mark 9:50, *Eph 2:11, Eph 4:1-3*
wash one another's feet	John 13:14
love one another	John 13:34–35; 15:12, 17; Rom. 13:8; 1 Thess. 3:12; 4:9; 2 Thess. 1:3; 1 Pet. 1:22; 1 John 3:11, 23; 4:7, 11, 12; 2 John 5
we belong to/are members of one another	Rom. 12:5; Eph. 4:25
be devoted to one another	Rom. 12:10
honor one another above yourselves	Rom. 12:10
live in harmony with one another	Rom. 12:16; 15:5
stop passing judgment on one another	Rom. 14:13
make every effort to do what leads to peace and mutual edification [for one another]	Rom. 14:19
accept one another	Rom. 15:7
instruct one another	Rom. 15:14
greet one another with a holy kiss	Rom. 16:16; 1 Cor. 16:20; 2 Cor. 13:12; 1 Pet. 5:14
wait for each another [when eating the agape fellowship meal]	1 Cor. 11:33

Command	Scriptural Reference(s)
have equal concern for each other	1 Cor. 12:25
serve one another	Gal. 5:13
don't bite and devour each another	Gal. 5:15
[stop] provoking/challenging each other	Gal. 5:26
[stop] envying each another	Gal. 5:26
carry each other's burdens	Gal. 6:2
be patient, bearing with one another	Eph. 4:2; Col. 3:13
be kind and compassionate to one another	Eph. 4:32
submit to one another	Eph. 5:21 ✓ good sermon
consider others better than yourselves	Phil. 2:3 Humility.
do not lie to each other	Col. 3:9 — integrity
encourage each other/one another	1 Thess. 4:18; 5:11 —
be kind to each other	1 Thess. 5:15 ⌣
spur one another on toward love and good deeds	Heb. 10:24 Bapt / preach Gospel/Lord's supper / Mutual care for one another & good deed.
do not slander one another	James 4:11
don't grumble against each other	James 5:9 — Matt 18.
confess your sins to each other	James 5:16
pray for each other	James 5:16
offer hospitality to one another	1 Pet. 4:9 ⚡
clothe yourselves with humility toward one another	1 Pet. 5:5

The texts that employ ἑαυτῶν enjoin Christians to practice additional responsibilities toward one other (see Figure 13.3).

Figure 13.3

"One Another" (ἑαυτῶν) Commands in the New Testament

↳ covers what a hinbur does not cover.

Command	Scriptural Reference(s)
be gracious to	Eph. 4:32; Col. 3:13
speak to one another in Psalms, hymns, and spiritual songs	Eph. 5:19
teach and instruct	Col. 3:16
live at peace with	1 Thess. 5:13
exhort	Heb. 3:13
do not make distinctions with	James 2:4
have fervent love toward	1 Pet. 4:8
serve	1 Pet. 4:10
build up	Jude 20
keep one another in the love of God	Jude 21

From these lists of commands we can clearly see that the New Testament teaches reciprocal Christian living, placing specific responsibilities upon each and every member in the body of Christ. Therefore, the church must practice interpersonal or relational Christianity, and Christians need to minister to one another. Due to their reconciliation to each other, they have new covenant responsibilities to each other. Now that Christ has given them newness of life and has placed them into his body, the church, they cannot live their lives independent of each other ever again.[32]

For Further Study

Banks, Robert. *Paul's Idea of Community*. Grand Rapids: Eerdmans, 1980. Revised Edition. Peabody, Mass.: Hendrickson, 1994.

Banks has written a penetrating study of New Testament commu-

32. For an excellent series on the "one-anothers," see Gene A. Getz, *Building Up One Another* (Wheaton, Ill.: Scripture Press, 1976); *Loving One Another* (Wheaton, Ill.: Scripture Press, 1979); *Encouraging One Another* (Wheaton, Ill.: Scripture Press, 1981); *Praying for One Another* (Wheaton, Ill.: Scripture Press, 1982).

nity in the Pauline writings that challenges traditional views of the church.

Branick, Vincent. *The House Church in the Writings of Paul.* Wilmington, Del.: Michael Glazier, 1989.

In a day of large buildings and the quest for the superchurch, Branick's investigation of the house church in Paul is a strong alternative to the emphasis on size. *Archeologically → 1st church 170 AD.*

Burtchaell, James Tunstead. *From Synagogue to Church.* New York: Cambridge University Press, 1992.

This is a very thorough study of ministry in the New Testament. While Burtchaell demonstrates that leadership in the church is a New Testament theme, this leadership never functions as a law unto itself or to the exclusion of ministry by the laity.

Dobson, Ed, Ed Hindson, and Jerry Falwell. *The Fundamentalist Phenomenon.* Grand Rapids: Baker, 1986.

While this book is an exploration of the larger dimensions of fundamentalism, it is an excellent study of the fundamentalist quest for the megachurch.

→ Good for Bible Studies

Getz, Gene A. *Sharpening the Focus of the Church.* Chicago: Moody, 1974.
———. *Building Up One Another.* Wheaton, Ill.: Scripture Press, 1976. *God*
———. *Loving One Another.* Wheaton, Ill.: Scripture Press, 1979. *Excess*
———. *Encouraging One Another.* Wheaton, Ill.: Scripture Press, 1981.
———. *Praying For One Another.* Wheaton, Ill.: Scripture Press, 1982. *Communication*

Getz has a great grasp of New Testament ecclesiology. All of his books are of great value in building a sound biblical view of the church.

Green, Michael. *Freed to Serve.* Dallas: Word, 1988.

This is one of the best books on the contrast between ministry in the New Testament and ministry in the contemporary church.

Hoch, Carl B., Jr. "The Role of Women in the Church: A Survey of Current Approaches." *Grace Theological Journal,* 8, no. 2 (Fall 1987): 241–51.

In this article this author surveys three contemporary approaches to the role of women in the church. He shows the reasons for the controversy and provides a bibliography of the advocates of each approach.

Icenogle, Gareth Weldon. *Biblical Foundations for Small Group Ministry.* Downers Grove, Ill.: InterVarsity, 1994.

In this author's opinion, this book is the best available book on small groups. Not only does it build an exegetical and theological base for small groups, but it provides practical advice on their implementation.

Martin, Ralph P. *The Family and the Fellowship*. Grand Rapids: Eeerdmans, 1979.

Martin shows the shortcomings of various models of the church in the light of the New Testament.

Strauch, Alexander. *Biblical Eldership*. Littleton, Colo.: Lewis and Roth, 1988.

————. *The New Testament Deacon*. Littleton, Colo.: Lewis and Roth, 1992.   *Now available with work Books*

Strauch's exegetical analysis of the ministries of elder and deacon may not be acceptable to many who are locked into unbiblical concepts of these two offices, but his two books must be refuted exegetically before any alternative paradigm is adopted or continued.

Wells, David F. *No Place for Truth: Or Whatever Happened to Evangelical Theology?* Gran
d Rapids: Eerdmans, 1993.

Wells' book has been a prophetic voice in a church that has lost theological direction. One of the symptoms of the failure of the contemporary church to do theology is the poor ecclesiology that is dominating the church, particularly in the United States.

Wuthnow, Robert. *Christianity in the 21st Century*. New York: Oxford University Press, 1993.

This book is a strong warning for the church of the twenty-first century about the consequences of the loss of community in the church and the emphasis on individualism in Christianity.

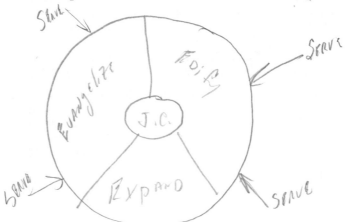

Appendix A

The Israel Problem: Is the Church the New Israel?

*T*he title of Gösta Lindeskog's article in *Svensk Exegetisk Årsbok,* "Israel in the NT—Some few remarks on a great problem,"[1] captures the difficulty in determining the precise meaning of the term *Israel* in the New Testament. The statement of Paul in Romans 9:6, "For not all who are descended from Israel are Israel," clearly demonstrates that nothing is solved by appealing to simplistic hermeneutical injunctions such as "Israel must be interpreted literally." All interpreters agree that Israel has many different senses in both the Old Testament and the New Testament, for example, the conniver, Jacob, whose name was changed to Israel; the inhabitants of the northern kingdom; the southern kingdom; both north and southern kingdoms combined; the faithful remnant within the larger ethnic group, Israel; and the land of Canaan.[2]

The controversy is not about these different semantic denotations of Israel, but whether Israel takes on a nonethnic sense, not only in the Old Testament, but much more in the New Testament where it is synonymous with the church that includes Gentiles. Construed in this sense, Israel is a name for God's people, whether they are Jew or Gentile, the ethnic group, Israel, or the transethnic group, the church. Entire systems of theology divide over this issue alone. The intensity of the debate is reflected in the enormous amount of literature addressing various aspects of the problem.[3]

1. Gösta Lindeskog, "Israel in the NT—Some few remarks on a great problem," *Svensk Exegetisk Årsbok,* 26 (1961): 57–92.
2. For a representative list, see Xavier Leon-Dufour, ed., *Dictionary of Biblical Theology,* 2d rev. ed. (New York: Seabury, 1973), 257–59.
3. See the extensive bibliographies in Henning Graf Reventlow, *Problems of Biblical Theology in the Twentieth Century* (Philadelphia: Fortress, 1986), 64–132.

In this brief survey this writer will present the four views of Israel and the church that he has read in the extant literature.

Position #1: Covenant Amillennialism—
The Church Continues Israel

This position has had a firmly entrenched place in the history of Christian interpretation.[4] While this position acknowledges the various meanings of Israel as listed above, its major contention is that the most important meaning of Israel is a theological, nonethnic one. It is simply a term for God's people. Since the continuing covenantal community, the seed of Abraham, Israel, and the church are all terms for God's one people, they can be used interchangeably without introducing theological confusion. In fact, it is necessary to give Israel this theological sense in order to maintain continuity in redemptive history and have one redeemed people of God.

The phrase found most frequently in the literature presenting this position is "true Israel." The phrase concedes that there is a larger entity, often called "Israel after the flesh," which has only a physical right to the name. Within this larger entity, however, is a smaller group who respond in faith to God and obey him. This smaller group are the "elect" who are participants in the "covenant of grace." They are the regenerate Jews under the Old Testament economy and the regenerate Jews and Gentiles under the New Testament economy. This group is the "true Israel" because they move beyond the physical plane to the spiritual plane. For this group physical requirements lose their force. The spiritual dimension is so important that Gentiles who meet the spiritual requirement can be called Israel and Jews who meet only the physical requirement no longer have any real right to the title. These Jews are Israel in name only. Thus the phrase "true Israel" refers to the elect of God in both Testaments.

It follows from this that God's promises and covenants are made with and fulfilled to this true Israel only. It matters little whether one calls this elect group "Israel" or "church," because both terms describe the seed of Abraham, the people of God, and the elect who are the heirs of God's promises.

This position does not dispute the historic acts of God with the Old Testament nation called Israel. It even allows for a greater ethnic connotation

4. A representative of this approach is William F. Cox, *Amillennialism Today* (Philadelphia: Presbyterian and Reformed, 1966). As with any system, however, some adherents have adopted somewhat of a "revisionist" position. Anthony A. Hoekema's book, *The Bible and the Future* (Grand Rapids: Eerdmans, 1979), is a good example of a revisionist viewpoint within amillennialism. Hoekema adopts the "already but not yet" language of Ladd, a premillennialist, and gives a much more prominent place to the new earth in his eschatology.

to the name during the Old Testament economy simply because few Gentiles were included in God's kingdom during the period of Old Testament history. But it argues that Israel loses any significant ethnic meaning when Gentiles believe the gospel of Jesus Christ and are added to the church.

The continuity between the Testaments can be described in terms of the redeemed: they are called different names such as those listed above, but the program of God is uniform. God has but one plan in history: to redeem a people for himself. Those whom God redeems are people of faith who trust his promises and believe in his Son. Galatians 6:16 is the favorite verse of this position: "As many as shall walk by this rule, peace be upon them, and mercy, even on the Israel of God" (author's translation).

This position minimizes the newness of the church. It makes no real qualitative distinction between the Testaments, only a *quantitative* one, namely, Gentiles are added to God's people. But their addition does not fundamentally alter the definitions of Israel and the church. Pentecost hardly seems necessary since the Holy Spirit performed all of the same works before Pentecost that he did after Pentecost. Even his advent did not produce anything radically new or different. The cross of Christ is absolutely central because it provides the basis for forgiveness of sins. But the only other strategic development after Easter will be the return of Christ in glory to consummate history, separate the sheep from the goats, and finalize God's kingdom.[5]

Position #2: Covenant Premillennialism— The Church Replaces Israel

Even though this position holds many things in common with position #1, it differs substantially from it.[6] According to position #2, the church is the "new Israel." This position places much more importance on ethnic distinc-

---

5. The very simple eschatology of amillennialism is reflected in the brief treatment of eschatology in Louis Berkhof, *Systematic Theology* (Grand Rapids: Eerdmans, 1941). Out of a 738-page volume, Berkhof devotes only seventy-seven pages to it.

6. George Eldon Ladd was the most important writer representing this viewpoint during the last fifty years (see "Bibliography" for significant titles by Ladd). Ladd remained a premillennialist until his death, but because he recognized the truth of many of the contentions of amillennialism, he was constantly under suspicion as a potential convert to amillennialism by those who felt that the only acceptable form of premillennialism is dispensational premillennialism. Actually, covenant premillennialism has a long history of advocates in church history. It did not recede into the background until the turn of this century when dispensational premillennialism captured the hearts of fundamentalists. On this, see Clarence B. Bass, *Backgrounds to Dispensationalism* (Grand Rapids: Eerdmans, 1960); C. Norman Kraus, *Dispensationalism in America* (Richmond: John Knox, 1958); and Ernest R. Sandeen, *The Roots of Fundamentalism* (Chicago: The University of Chicago Press, 1970).

tions. It considers Israel in the Old Testament period as an empirical entity, that is, physical descendants of Abraham. It usually considers the church to be a new development subsequent to the first advent of Jesus Christ. While employing phrases such as "Jesus and the new people of God" in its representative literature, it still maintains a critical role in salvation history for Pentecost. It sees Pentecost as a dynamic outpouring of the Holy Spirit which inaugurates an age of the Spirit not experienced by Old Testament Israel. It recognizes the implications of the equality of Jews and Gentiles in Christ for a definition of church and refuses to thrust that community back into the history of Israel in the Old Testament. According to this approach, it is anachronistic to use the word *church* to refer to Old Testament Israel.[7]

This position, however, presents the church as the replacement for Israel in salvation history. Israel, as an ethnic entity, has been disinherited from the promises because of apostasy and rejection of Jesus as Messiah. Israel had to be reconstituted by Jesus from the beginning of his ministry because of Israel's apostasy and because of the inclusion of Gentiles in God's people after Pentecost. Israel loses its Old Testament ethnic content and becomes a cipher for the new people of God. Somewhere in the New Testament period the church replaced Israel in God's program.

Although not a part of the church during their lifetime, believers during the Old Testament period become part of the church after Christ's death on the cross. The position is premillennial in that it does expect the return of Christ prior to the establishment of his kingdom on the earth. But it does not allow any place for ethnic Israel apart from the church. Although many ethnic Jews may turn to Christ (viz., the "all Israel" of Romans 11:26), they will be incorporated into the church. The church inherits Old Testament Israel's promises, including the earth.

Since this position follows the usual premillennial scheme of end-time events (i.e., an interim between the first and second advents, a period of tribulation, the return of Christ, the establishment of the millennial kingdom, the final judgment, and the new heavens and new earth), it is unlike position #1 but similar to position #3. But since this position considers the church as the only post-Pentecost salvific community, it advocates a post-tribulational rapture of the church at Christ's one and only second advent. A favorite text of this position is 1 Thessalonians 2:16 where Paul says that those Jews who reject Jesus and hinder Christian missions experience the wrath of God to the uttermost.

7. As done by Woudstra, who says that the great confessions from post-Reformation times regard the church in its most comprehensive scope: "The church, so they confess, has been from the beginning of the world and will be to the end thereof" (Marten H. Woudstra, "Israel and the Church: A Case for Continuity," in *Continuity and Discontinuity*, ed. John S. Feinberg [Westchester, Ill.: Crossway, 1988], 221).

This position sees both continuity and discontinuity between the Testaments. The New Testament is a step upward (forward) redemptively and is often called an "escalation." The Old Testament economy for all purposes has been replaced by the New Testament economy. There can be no reversal eschatologically to a pre-Christ arrangement. The Old Testament temple will not be rebuilt. The Mosaic law will not be reinstituted as a governing principle for a restored Israel. Old Testament sacrifices have been discontinued forever. The millennium will be a Christian millennium, not a Jewish millennium. Christ's coming drastically alters the manifested nature of the kingdom. The only surviving aspect of the Old Testament economy will be those saints who lived during that economy and participate in Christ's salvation after death. They will join all saints under the new economy as part of the one people of God.

Position #3: Classic or Revised Dispensational Premillennialism—The Church Interrupts Israel

Even though advocates of this position argue for their position having a longer history, position #3 does not seem to have been articulated prior to the last century. Those writers who regard J. N. Darby as the popularizer of the position and C. I. Scofield as the systematizer are correct.[8] Prior to these two influential figures, no one seems to have proposed a radical disjunction between Israel and the church.

A key phrase used by proponents of position #3 is "ethnic Israel." According to this position, "Israel" always refers to the physical descendants of Abraham, that is, Jews. It never refers to Gentiles. Because the church includes Gentiles, it cannot be some kind of Israel. Therefore, Israel and the church must be kept distinct. Israel is the name for the theocratic nation that received the law at Sinai and was granted all of the promises and covenants of the Old Testament. These promises and covenants must be fulfilled with this ethnic entity. Accordingly, Gentiles cannot be the recipients of promises and covenants made to Jews.

Although Charles C. Ryrie has offered a revised update of classic dispensationalism,[9] he still insists upon a clear-cut distinction between Israel and the church. His recent essay in a book, which is edited by two Dallas Seminary graduates, attempts to assess whether "progressive dispensationalism" is a change or a development of classic or revised dispensationalism.[10]

8. T. P. Weber, "Dispensationalism," in *Dictionary of Christianity in America*, ed. Daniel Reid (Downers Grove, Ill.: InterVarsity, 1990), 358.
9. Charles C. Ryrie, *Dispensationalism Today* (Chicago: Moody, 1965), 95–96.
10. Ibid., *Issues in Dispensationalism*, ed. Wesley R. Willis and John R. Master (Chicago: Moody, 1994)

He seems very nervous about the new revisionist approach within dispensationalism reflected in the book edited by two current Dallas Seminary professors.[11] Ryrie considers the new approach to be a "change" (read "bad") rather than a "development" (read "good").

Dispensationalism is certainly in transition. In recent years a "dispensational study group" has met at the national meeting of the Evangelical Theological Society. This group has struggled to identify the characteristics of a dispensationalist and has been hard-put to set forth characteristics upon which all avowed dispensationalists can agree. It will be interesting to compare the statements of C. I. Scofield and Lewis Sperry Chafer with Ryrie, and then with a writer like Robert Saucy, who has published two significant works on the subject.[12]

In classic and revised dispensationalism, two peoples of God exist: Israel and the church. These two peoples have two distinct programs. Israel is an earthly people whose inheritance will be this earth. The church is a heavenly people whose inheritance is heaven. To confuse the programs, the peoples, and the inheritances is to introduce hopeless confusion into the interpretation of Scripture. Maintaining these distinctions results in hermeneutical clarity and provides careful controls for determining which Scripture texts are for which people.[13]

Not only do two peoples exist, but one of them has priority over the other one both historically and eschatologically. Ethnic Israel has been given this priority by God and nothing can cancel or revise it. The church is an interruption or insertion into history;[14] therefore, it interrupts Israel. This interruption is a result of Israel's failure to accept Christ as Messiah and King of Israel, which has resulted in a temporary sidelining of Israel in redemptive history. To use Ironside's famous words, "The moment Messiah died on the cross, the prophetic clock stopped. There has not been a tick upon that clock for nineteen centuries."[15] In other words Israel's priority kingdom program has been postponed. It will not be reintroduced until the church has been raptured to heaven prior to the tribulation that will last seven years. During

11. Craig A. Blaising and Darrell L. Bock, *Dispensationalism, Israel and the Church* (Grand Rapids: Zondervan, 1992).

12. Robert L. Saucy, "Israel and the Church: A Case for Discontinuity," in *Continuity and Discontinuity*, ed. John S. Feinberg (Westchester, Ill.: Crossway, 1988), 239–59; and *The Case for Progressive Dispensationalism* (Grand Rapids: Zondervan, 1993).

13. Charles L. Feinberg, *Millennialism: The Two Major Views* (Chicago: Moody, 1982), 226. Feinberg represents classic dispensationalism in its purist form. He has also jettisoned covenant premillennialism as a major view. According to him, one is either an amillennialist or a dispensational premillennialist.

14. Lewis Sperry Chafer, *Chafer Systematic Theology* (Dallas: Dallas Seminary Press, 1975), 12, 41.

15. H. A. Ironside, *The Great Parenthesis* (Grand Rapids: Zondervan, 1943), 23. See also his, *Not Wrath, But Rapture* (New York: Loizeaux, n.d.), 34.

these seven years Israel will participate in a great turning to Christ. As a result, all ethnic Israel will be saved and welcome Christ as the Messiah at his second advent. The real goal of history is the inauguration of a Jewish millennium when Christ returns. The temple will be rebuilt in Jerusalem and Old Testament sacrifices will be offered again (they are usually regarded as "memorial" offerings). Christ will rule over ethnic Israel, which will be regathered from the far corners of the earth to the land of Israel. Any Gentiles who come to Christ will have to come through Israel and will have a subordinate status as they did during the Old Testament period.

Since the church and Israel are totally unrelated, a radical discontinuity exists between the Testaments. The Old Testament is law, not grace. The New Testament is grace, not law.[16] The work of the Holy Spirit during the Old Testament period is vastly different from his work during the New Testament period. While some proponents believe that some Old Testament saints were not indwelt by the Spirit,[17] others seem to suggest that they were not even regenerated.[18] The Day of Pentecost is a dispensational watershed since it marks the inception of the church. Old Testament saints are not included in the church any more than tribulation saints and millennial saints will be included in the church.

Since the covenants are for ethnic Israel, they cannot be fulfilled in the church. Mention of the new covenant in the New Testament must refer to two new covenants: one for Israel and one for the church.[19] This interpretation avoids any conclusion that the church is somehow the Israel and Judah of Jeremiah 31 quoted in Hebrews 8.

The same can be said for other Old Testament passages that are quoted in the New Testament. Either they are simply allusions, or the Old Testament passages have a double fulfillment, that is, one fulfillment for Israel and one for the church.

According to this position the understanding of the kingdom is vastly different than positions #1 and #2. Although there are variations, position #1 basically views the kingdom as the church and embraces a "realized eschatology." One of its more recent proponents has suggested the name "inaugurated eschatology."[20] Position #2 refuses to equate the kingdom and the church. It recognizes, however, that many statements in the New Testament refer to the presence of the kingdom in some sense during this

16. Feinberg, *Millennialism*, 213–14.
17. Ryrie, *The Holy Spirit* (Chicago: Moody, 1965), 41.
18. This seems to be an accurate conclusion based on the vague statements in John F. Walvoord's, *The Holy Spirit* (Findlay, Ohio: Dunham, 1958), 72.
19. Ryrie, *The Basis of the Premillennial Faith* (Neptune, N.J.: Loizeaux, 1953), 124–25. See also John R. Master, "The New Covenant," in *Issues in Dispensationalism*, ed. Wesley R. Willis and John R. Master (Chicago: Moody, 1994), 93–110.
20. Hoekema, 17.

present age. This second position refers to the kingdom in terms of the "already" and the "not yet." It likes to think in terms of eschatology in process of realization.[21] For all practical purposes position #3 equates the kingdom with the Jewish millennium that Christ will establish after the rapture of the church and the conclusion of the tribulation.[22] This position follows what many have called "consistent eschatology." According to position #3 Israel is closely related to the kingdom, but the church is totally unrelated to the kingdom. Even when adherents of position #3 talk about some aspect of kingdom in the church, they will usually still talk about *the* kingdom, meaning the millennium.

Position #4: Progressive Dispensationalism—The Church Includes and Extends Israel

The last position on the relationship between Israel and the church has been labeled "Progressive Dispensationalism." Three recent works have been published presenting this new approach within dispensationalism.[23] This position attempts to retain those emphases of the previous three positions that appear to have solid exegetical support and to discard those points that seem to lack exegetical support. It retains the emphasis of one people of God of positions #1 and #2 but adopts the distinctive nature of Pentecost of positions #2 and #3. It retains the premillennialism of positions #2 and #3, retains the non-Jewish millennium of position #2, and rejects the exclusively Jewish millennium of position #3. Also, it retains the

21. George E. Ladd, *Crucial Questions About the Kingdom of God* (Grand Rapids: Eerdmans, 1952), chapter 3. The interesting thing is that Hoekema, an amillennialist, adopts the same terminology about the kingdom. His chapter on the kingdom of God is substantially the same as Ladd's. This illustrates again how revisionist thinkers tend to move to a more centrist position rather than retaining the old polarities or distinctives of two competing theological systems.

22. That this is still the view of classic and revised dispensationalism as seen in two recent articles by Stanley D. Toussaint, "A Biblical Defense of Dispensationalism," in *Walvoord: A Tribute*, ed. Donald K. Campbell (Chicago: Moody, 1982), 81–91; and "The Kingdom and Matthew's Gospel," in *Essays in Honor of J. Dwight Pentecost*, ed. Stanley D. Toussaint and Charles H. Dyer (Chicago: Moody, 1986), 19–34. Toussaint continually speaks of the millennium as *the* kingdom and as the last dispensation preceding the "eternal state." He maintains that all aorist tenses used with the word *kingdom* are "proleptic." It is noteworthy that the very next essay in the Pentecost volume, "Dispensational Approaches to the Sermon on the Mount," is by John A. Martin, a "progressive" dispensationalist. Martin's statements are much closer to an "already but not yet" approach to the kingdom than Toussaint's rigid distinction of *the* kingdom as the millennium.

23. Craig A. Blaising and Darrell L. Bock, eds., *Dispensationalism, Israel and the Church* (Grand Rapids: Zondervan, 1992); Craig A. Blaising and Darrell L. Bock, *Progressive Dispensationalism* (Wheaton, Ill.: Victor, 1993); Robert L. Saucy, *The Case for Progressive Dispensationalism* (Grand Rapids: Zondervan, 1993).

contention of position #3 that Israel always refers to physical descendants of Abraham, but rejects its radical discontinuity between Israel and the church and its rigid definition of the kingdom. Blaising and Bock devote almost one-third of their book to "The Kingdom of God in the Old Testament" and "The Kingdom of God in the New Testament."[24]

The main contention of position #4 is that although Israel and the church are distinct in some ways, they also overlap to a significant degree. For example, the church contains within itself a remnant of Israel, which provides continuity with Old Testament Israel. At the same time this is a Jewish remnant, not a Gentile one. Therefore, the church is distinct from Israel because it includes Gentiles, but it is a continuation of Israel because it includes Jews. Terms such as "new" or "true" Israel are not biblical categories, but theological constructs imposed on the biblical text. Of course, it is necessary to refute the contention that they are *necessary* theological constructs. Appendix B will attempt to establish exegetically the truth of the reservation of the term *Israel* to physical descendants of Abraham.

Although there is one people of God, this people has not had a uniform makeup throughout salvation history. At least 2500 years preceded the formation of Israel as a theocratic nation, and some of the most important saints of the Old Testament period lived during these years. Although they were a part of God's people (see Heb. 11), they were not a part of Israel. The people of God under the Mosaic covenant simply did not have the same requirements that the people of God under the new covenant have. The critical difference in the church is the addition of the Gentiles on an equal basis with Israel so that Gentiles now share with Israel in Israel's promises and covenants.

As outlined by Paul in Romans 3:1–2, 9:4–6, and Ephesians 2:12, Israel has a priority in terms of privilege, but not a priority in terms of program. The program of God is one: to dwell in the midst of his redeemed people (Rev. 21:1–5). But this program goes through various stages in the process of realization. Further, not only must the Lord submit the ruled to himself as the Ruler, but he must also subjugate the realm. As the scene of rebellion, the earth must be brought back to submission. Therefore, the new earth cannot fulfill this objective because it is a new renovative act of God after the destruction of the old earth by fire (2 Pet. 3:7–13). The objective must be realized on the old earth: the de facto rule of God will come, and the will of God will be done on [this] earth as it is done in heaven (Matt. 6:10).

This position believes that all of God's covenants will be fulfilled eschatologically both in the church and in ethnic Israel who turn to Christ in

24. Blaising and Bock, *Progressive Dispensationalism*, 212–83.

faith.[25] We can say, however, that position #4 has a more Christocentric emphasis than position #3 with its Israel-centric emphasis. Unlike position #3, position #4 is not quite as certain how the whole process works out eschatologically. According to Saucy, one should not exaggerate the place of the millennium in eschatology. The millennium is only the final transition phase leading to the eternal state.[26] No future revelation is unrelated to Christ and his saving activity.[27]

This position contends that it can allow fulfillment of Old Testament promises and covenants (at least partially) to the church without making Israel and the church synonymous. The key is the remnant of Israel within the church. They are the immediate heirs of the Old Testament hope. But they extend this inheritance to the Gentiles so that Gentiles become fellow heirs and members of the same body in Christ through the gospel (Eph. 3:5). Thus the church includes and extends Israel, but it is not synonymous with Israel. While the church is therefore not a new or true Israel, neither is it in radical discontinuity with Israel.[28]

25. Saucy devotes seven chapters of his book to the covenants and the nation of Israel. Blaising and Bock in the *Progressive* volume devote chapters 5 and 6 to "The Structure of the Biblical Covenants: The Covenants Prior to Christ," and "The Fulfillment of the Biblical Covenants Through Jesus Christ."

26. Saucy, *Case*, 288.

27. Ibid., 317.

28. Except for a few scattered articles and the recent appearance of three books expounding position #4 (see footnote 23 above), very little has been written on this position. One such article was Terence L. Donaldson, "Israel and the Church: A Middle Position," *Crux*, 15 (Sept. 1979): 11–13. In a telephone conversation with the writer, Dr. Donaldson said that he was in process of writing a book on this theme. This writer knows that there are other scholars who embrace this view, but they have not taken pencil to paper to expound their views. It is hoped that the present volume will provoke interest and stimulate "closet" adherents to help articulate this "middle position."

Not a hermeneutical problem

Never got around to this

Appendix B

The Term Israel in the New Testament

Dr. Hock's dissertation

From the time of Justin Martyr (A.D. 160) until the present day, a very common view of the church in the New Testament is that it is some kind of Israel. Commentaries, theological works, journal articles, and even confessional statements commonly use names such as the "Israel of God," the "true Israel," or the "new Israel" to designate the church. Kelly's comment is representative: "So far as the church is concerned, Christians are the new Israel, the people of God who were once no people, strangers and sojourners in the world awaiting their heavenly inheritance."[1] On the other hand, Walvoord asks, "Are Gentile Christians ever designated Israelites?"[2]

The task of the present discussion centers around the meaning of the term *Israel* in the New Testament. Several important questions arise within such a discussion. Is it always used of the physical descendants of Jacob or does it sometimes include Gentiles? If Gentiles are entitled to the name "Israel," what is the real meaning of Israel? Are Israel and the church interchangeable terms? Or should Israel and the church be radically differentiated? Do the two overlap some without one equaling the other and without Gentiles being included in the name "Israel"? These are the questions that we will address in this appendix.

1. J. N. D. Kelly, *A Commentary on the Epistles of Peter and Jude* (New York: Harper and Row, 1969), 26.
2. John F. Walvoord, *Israel in Prophecy* (Grand Rapids: Zondervan, 1962), 58.

263

The Problem

The Problem in Terms of History

Even a casual reading of the Gospels demonstrates that Jesus Christ was closely related to the nation of Israel. The genealogies of Matthew and Luke are based on a list of Old Testament ancestors of Jesus. He was born of a Jewish maiden and was raised in a Jewish home. His disciples were Jewish. He sent his disciples out on a mission instructing them to go neither to the Gentiles nor to the Samaritans, but only to the "lost sheep of the house of Israel" (Matt. 10:5–6). Jesus worshiped in the synagogue (Luke 4:16) and stated that he had not come to destroy the law of Moses but to fulfill it (Matt. 5:17–18). In his conversation with the Samaritan woman he rebuked her by stating that "salvation is from the Jews" (John 4:22). There does not seem to be any radical breach between Jesus and Israel during his lifetime. Such observations led Herman Reimarus and later Albert Schweitzer to conclude that Jesus founded no church. He was simply a Jewish prophet who went about preaching the imminency of the kingdom of God.[3]

At the very beginning of the Book of Acts Jesus commanded his followers not to depart from Jerusalem (1:4). When the disciples asked whether he would restore the kingdom to Israel at that time, he did not elaborate on a different kingdom nor expound the concept of a new Israel to them. He merely replied that it was not for them to know the time frame decreed by the Father. According to Tannehill:

> Jesus corrects their curiosity about times, but does not reject the possibility of a restored kingdom for Israel, and Peter, after receiving the Spirit, still holds out the hope of the "restoration of all the things which God spoke through the mouth of his holy prophets from of old" (Acts 3:21), provided the people of Jerusalem repent. Both Acts 1:6 (connected to 3:21 by the theme of restoration) and Luke 1:69–70 indicate that the messianic kingdom is among the things promised by God "through the mouth of his holy prophets from of old" (a long and solemn phrase shared by Luke 1:70 and Acts 3:21).[4]

It is significant that in Acts 2 the first Christian sermon was preached to Jews (2:5, 14). Peter addressed his Jewish audience as "brothers" (2:37). No radical breach is evident at this point, either. In fact, Jesus' followers continued in the temple and had favor with all the people of Israel (2:46–47). In Acts 3 Peter does not exhort his listeners to join the "new Israel" but to repent of their sins so that the seasons of refreshing may come from the pres-

---

3. Charles H. Talbert, *Reimarus: Fragments* (Philadelphia: Fortress, 1970), 41–43; 65–67.
4. Robert Tannehill, *The Narrative Unity of Luke-Acts, Volume 1: The Gospel According to Luke* (Philadelphia: Fortress, 1986), 1:35–36.

ence of the Lord and that he may send Jesus to earth again (3:19–21). In Acts 3:26 it was to Israel first (πρῶτον) that the good news was proclaimed. Although there is an emphasis on repentance and faith, there is no hint of national rejection or separation of Christians from Israel.

Despite the persecution against the leaders in Acts 4–5, there is no change in the mission to Israel. According to 5:42, "Day after day, in the temple courts and from house to house, they never stopped teaching and proclaiming the good news that Jesus is the Christ."

Acts 8 records an extension of the church to Samaria. The close ties with the Jerusalem church and Israel are maintained through the descent of Peter and John to Samaria to lay hands on the Samaritans so that they might receive the Spirit.

Even Saul began his ministry with Jews after his conversion. Not until Acts 11 did a pure Gentile become a part of the church. Interestingly, the Gentiles were not *substituted* for Israel but became *partakers with* Israel in salvation. In Peter's report of the Cornelius episode to the Jerusalem church he used the emphatic Greek καί in Acts 11:18 to stress the addition of the Gentiles to the sphere of God's blessing rather than their substitution. The reserve with which the leaders of the Jerusalem church accepted Peter's story is seen in their careful interrogation of Peter. Acts 11:19–20 shows that only some in the church preached to others than strict Jews. Not until Antioch did any mission to Gentiles take place on a wide scale.

Even when a full-scale mission to the Gentiles begins in Acts 13, the witness is through the door of the synagogue (13:5, 14). Acts 13:46 again indicates that the witness is first (πρῶτον) to the Jews. Paul continues to call Jews "brothers" (13:26).

Not until 14:46 did the church react against the unbelief of Israel by turning to the Gentiles. Even so, the church still did not pursue an exclusive ministry to the Gentiles.

In Acts 16:3 Paul circumcised Timothy in order not to offend the Jews. Paul preached three Sabbaths in the synagogue at Thessalonica (17:1–2), and in the synagogue at Berea (17:10), Athens (17:17), and Corinth (18:4). Although Paul apparently rejected the Jews in favor of the Gentiles at Corinth (18:6), he later took a Jewish vow (18:18) and returned to the synagogue at Ephesus (18:19).

According to 19:10 and 20:21 both Jews and Greeks hear the gospel. Although 20:6 does not state so directly, the verse implies that Paul kept the Passover at Philippi. According to 20:16 Paul's aim was to celebrate Pentecost in Jerusalem.

Paul did not tell James that he did not need to demonstrate that he was a good Jew by taking on a vow because the church was the new Israel. He complied with James's request and insisted right up to the end of his life that it was for the hope of Israel that he continued to testify to the resurrection of Jesus (Acts 26:6–7). According to Acts 26:17–18 the Gentiles' inheritance was not in Israel, but among those who have been sanctified (ἐν τοῖς ἡγιασμένοις). Verse 17 still speaks of the Jews as people (λαός). The ministry of Paul was directed to both the λαός and to the ἔθνη (26:23).

Despite the fact that Acts 7, 10, 13, 14, 15, 21, and 28 contain accounts of severe hostilities between Christians and Jews, there is no evidence of a takeover by the church of the name Israel. One must look to a later date than Acts if one is to find a complete breach between church and synagogue or a substitution of the church for Israel.

According to Richardson, the first Christian to equate explicitly the church with the true Israel was Justin Martyr about A.D. 160 in his *Dialogue with Trypho*.[5] Dahl thinks that the takeover is found in the *Epistle of Barnabas*, also.[6] It is problematic whether the so-called synagogue ban against the *minim* led to this new development because recent writers like Cohen challenge the extent to which this ban pervaded the first century synagogue.[7] Richardson sees the defeat of Bar Kokhba as the decisive event because Christians consistently used this obliteration of Jerusalem as a center of Judaism as evidence of God's full judgment on Israel.[8]

From the foregoing analysis it can be observed that the breach between the church and the synagogue was a gradual one through the first century and was not decisive until the middle of the second century. Richardson stresses that any break is an inference within the New Testament, not an explicit requirement from it.[9] The church through Acts 9 was almost exclusively Jewish. The introduction of the Gentiles in Acts 10 caused problems, but there is no intimation of the rejection of Israel with all its prerogatives and a transfer of the title to the church of the Gentiles.

The Problem in Terms of Terminology

The question of terminology will be the subject of the first main section of this inquiry. That the term *Israel* is used of physical descendants of Jacob is acknowledged by people who stand on all sides of the semantic question. The point of debate arises in regard to whether Israel and Jew are emptied of their historical meanings and filled with a different theological content that allows these terms to be used of Gentiles who become spiritual "Israelites" and "Jews." Such a theological redefinition quickly leads to the in-

5. Peter Richardson, *Israel in the Apostolic Church* (Cambridge: At The University Press, 1969), 1.

6. Nils Alstrup Dahl, "The People of God," *The Ecumenical Review*, 9, no. 2 (Jan. 1957): 157.

7. Shayne J. D. Cohen, *From the Maccabees to the Mishnah* (Philadelphia: Westminster, 1987), 227–28.

8. Richardson, 203.

9. Ibid., 2.

terchange of the two terms, Israel and church.[10] The church acquires the title, "Israel of God." This last step denies any significant ethnic dimension to Israel. Israel is a theological term referring to the continuing covenantal community, the seed of Abraham, the redeemed, the people of God, the elect, Christians, or simply, the church. The argument for a theological connotation for Israel is not a lexical or even semantic one. As subsequent discussion will demonstrate, many arguments are introduced beyond the terminological one to support the theological connotation, namely, the use of honorific terms for Israel in the Old Testament for the church, the use of quotations from the Old Testament in the New Testament, key New Testament texts, and Paul's olive tree figure in Romans 11.

The Problem in Terms of Hermeneutics

The hermeneutical struggle has been brightly displayed in the recent volume edited by John Feinberg, *Continuity and Discontinuity*.[11] As Feinberg indicates in his closing summary of the issues, the problem is not the employment of grammatical-historical hermeneutics.[12] Advocates of each of the four major views of the relationship between Israel and the church all claim to use the grammatical-historical method. No one is a consistent "spiritualizer." The real culprit is theological systems that come into play and cause the exegesis of individual passages to differ. One quickly realizes that if he were to take a different path at each hermeneutical fork in the exegesis of key passages, he would end up with an entirely different conclusion than if he took the other path that another exegete took! Such a frightening thought prevents one from assuming that the task of exegesis and biblical theology is simple and that the problem would evaporate if one would only interpret literally!

An Analysis of the Use of the Term *Israel* in the New Testament

Israel occurs a total of sixty-eight times in sixty-six verses of the New Testament.[13] It occurs twice in Romans 9:6 and in Romans 9:27. Since the meaning of *Israel* is disputed in only eleven of the sixty-eight verses, the

10. Lucien Cerfaux, *The Church in the Theology of St. Paul* (New York: Herder and Herder, 1959), 20.
11. John S. Feinberg, *Continuity and Discontinuity* (Westchester, Ill.: Crossway, 1988).
12. Ibid., 312.
13. W. F. Moulton and A. S. Geden, *A Concordance to the Greek New Testament* (Edinburgh: T. & T. Clark, 1963), 500–501.

discussion will be broken down by sections of the New Testament and between undisputed and disputed passages.

Israel in the Gospel and Acts

THE UNDISPUTED PASSAGES

Matthew
The undisputed passages in Matthew are 2:6, 20, 21; 8:10, 33; 10:6, 23; 15:24, 31; 27:9, 42. The meanings of *Israel* in these passages can be classified into two categories: (1) ethnic Israel (2:6; 8:10; 9:33; 10:6, 23; 15:24, 31; 27:9, 42); and (2) the land occupied by ethnic Israel, that is, Palestine (2:20, 21).

Mark
In Mark the undisputed passages are 12:29 and 15:32. The meaning in both passages is ethnic Israel.

Luke
The undisputed passages in Luke are 1:16, 54, 68, 80; 2:25, 32, 34; 4:25, 27; 7:9; and 24:21. The term *Israel* in all these texts refers to ethnic Israel. It is worthy of notice that Israel is contrasted with Gentiles (ἐθνῶν) in 2:32.

John
The undisputed passages in John include 1:31, 49; 3:10; and 12:13. All four references are to ethnic Israel.

The Book of Acts
The undisputed passages in Acts are 1:6; 2:36; 4:10, 27; 5:21, 31; 7:23, 37, 42; 9:15; 10:36; 13:17, 23, 24; and 28:20. All references are to ethnic Israel. Israel is again contrasted with Gentiles in 4:27 and 9:15.

THE DISPUTED PASSAGES

Out of the forty-five occurrences of Israel in the Gospels and Acts, only two are disputed concerning whether the term includes Gentiles. The two texts are Matthew 19:28 and Luke 22:30. It is true that commentators refer to Israel in the other passages surveyed with designations like "people of God," "chosen people," and "spiritual Israel" in order to give the term a theological connotation that may be easily emptied of any ethnic significance; but none actually extends the term to Gentiles.

Matthew 19:28
The context for this verse is Peter's question about what Jesus would give to his followers because they had left all to follow him in contrast to the rich ruler who could not surrender his riches. The Lord replied that in the παλιγγενεσία when the Son of Man would sit upon his glorious throne,

the Twelve would sit upon twelve thrones ruling or judging (κρίνοντες) the twelve tribes of Israel.

It is immediately apparent that two words are important to determine the meaning of the Lord's statement. The first is παλιγγενεσία. The second is κρίνω. Buchsel defines παλιγγενεσία as follows: "This word derives from πάλιν and γένεσις and thus means 'new genesis' either in the sense of a. 're- turn to existence', 'coming back from death to life', or of b. 'renewal to a higher existence', 'regeneration' in the usual sense."[14] Montefiore adds that Josephus used the word for the new birth of the Jewish nation after her re- turn from the Babylonian exile and Philo used it of the new birth of the earth after the flood and after its destruction by fire.[15]

Since the word is used only once elsewhere in the New Testament (Tit. 3:5), it is difficult to determine its specific meaning in Matthew 19:28. Buchsel states that the meaning in Matthew is in full agreement with the meaning in Philo and Josephus, that is, "The Jewish faith in the resurrec- tion of the dead and the renewal of the world is clothed in this term."[16] Montefiore adds that, "The new birth here denotes the world of Israel at the time of the second advent—at the Parousia."[17]

Sherman Johnson says, "The idea is that in the age to come there will be a new heaven and a new earth (Isa. 65:17; Rev. 21:1–5), a new or renewed creation (Gal. 6:15; Rom. 8:18–22; 2 Bar. 32:6; 2 Esdras 7:75)."[18] Gundry feels that the term probably refers to Israel's renewal when God fully estab- lishes his kingdom on earth. He finds the concept amply attested in Jewish literature and expands the passages listed by Johnson.[19]

Although κρίνω basically means "to judge," it often means "to govern" in the Old Testament.[20] Kugelman points out that judging was considered an essential act of royal power in ancient civilizations.[21]

There are four views of this passage. The first view maintains that the apostles will judge the church. A second view is that although the original hearers probably understood Jesus' words in terms of Jewish apocalyptic

---

14. Friedrich Buchsel, "παλιγγενεσία," *Theological Dictionary of the New Testa- ment*, ed. Gerhard Kittel, 10 vols. (Grand Rapids: Eerdmans, 1964), 1:686.

15. C. G. Montefiore, *The Synoptic Gospels*, 2 vols. (New York: KTAV, 1968), 2:270.

16. Buchsel, 1:688. See also Robert Tannehill, *The Narrative Unity of Luke-Acts, Vol- ume 2: The Acts of the Apostles* (Minneapolis: Fortress, 1980), 2:16 n. 19.

17. Montefiore, 2:270.

18. Sherman E. Johnson, "The Gospel According to St. Matthew," in *IB*, ed. George Buttrick et al. (New York: Abingdon-Cokesbury, 1951), 7:488.

19. Robert H. Gundry, *Matthew: A Commentary on His Literary and Theological Art* (Grand Rapids: Eerdmans, 1982), 392.

20. Alan Hugh McNeile, *The Gospel According to St. Matthew* (London: Macmillan, 1961), 282.

21. Richard Kugelman, "Hebrew, Israelite, Jew in the New Testament," *The Bridge*, ed. John M. Oesterreicher, I (1955), 212 n. 18.

hopes for a millennial kingdom, Matthew and his readers understood the sense as the "new Israel," the church.[22] A third view is that the apostles will judge the entire nation of ethnic Israel from the patriarchs to the last day. This judgment will take place at the last day in heaven.[23] A fourth view is that the twelve apostles will judge and rule the twelve tribes of ethnic Israel who come to faith in Christ during the millennial kingdom on earth.

The writer believes that the fourth view is best for the following reasons: (1) it is in harmony with the basic meaning and extrabiblical use of the term παλιγγενεσία as explored above; (2) it is in harmony with the reference to Daniel 7:13–14 concerning the Son of man in this verse; (3) it is in harmony with Matthew's ethnic use of Israel elsewhere in his Gospel; (4) it does not require two meanings for one word, that is, one for the original hearers and another for Matthew's readers; (5) it does not require the Twelve to redefine Israel as the church; and (6) Allen,[24] A. B. Bruce,[25] Johnson,[26] Lenski,[27] Meyer,[28] Montefiore,[29] Plummer,[30] Carson,[31] Gundry,[32] Harrington,[33] and Schweizer[34] all support an ethnic sense to the term, even though they may reject premillennial reconstructions of the future of ethnic Israel.

Luke 22:30

The context is the Last Supper. After rebuking the disciples for their dispute over who would be the greatest in the kingdom, the Lord promised the disciples that they would have a reward for their humble service. In his kingdom they would eat and drink at his table and take their seats upon thrones, judging the twelve tribes of Israel.

22. Ibid., 212.

23. R. C. H. Lenski, *The Interpretation of St. Matthew's Gospel* (Minneapolis: Augsburg, 1943), 760.

24. Willoughby C. Allen, *A Critical and Exegetical Commentary on the Gospel According to S. Matthew*, ICC (Edinburgh: T. & T. Clark, 1912), 212.

25. Alexander Balman Bruce, "The Synoptic Gospels," in *The Expositor's Greek Testament*, ed. W. Robertson Nicoll (Grand Rapids: Eerdmans, 1961), 1:252.

26. Johnson, 488.

27. Lenski, 760.

28. Heinrich August Wilhelm Meyer, *Critical and Exegetical Handbook to the Gospel of Matthew*, ed. Frederich Crombie and William Stewart (New York: Funk & Wagnalls, 1890), 347.

29. Montefiore, 2:270.

30. Alfred Plummer, *An Exegetical Commentary on the Gospel According to S. Matthew* (London: Elliot Stock, 1910), 270.

31. D. A. Carson, "Matthew," in *The Expositor's Bible Commentary*, ed. Frank E. Gaebelein, 10 vols. (Grand Rapids: Zondervan, 1984), 8:426.

32. Gundry, 393.

33. Daniel J. Harrington, *The Gospel of Matthew* (Collegeville, Minn.: The Liturgical Press, 1991), 279.

34. Eduard Schweizer, *The Good News According to Matthew* (Atlanta: John Knox, 1975), 389.

Many commentators reject any reference to ethnic Israel for this text also. Arndt considers it "picture language."[35] But Plummer notes that the Jews commonly regarded the messianic kingdom as a banquet (see also Luke 13:29, 14:15).[36] Therefore, he interprets the verse as a reference to the role the Twelve play in judging ethnic Israel for her acceptance or rejection of the gospel.[37]

Again the writer believes that in this verse Israel refers to ethnic Israel. Such an understanding is in keeping with Luke's use of Israel elsewhere in his Gospel, the contextual references to an eschatological banquet that first century Jews interpreted as the messianic kingdom, and the same meaning in the parallel expression in Matthew 19:28.

Except for two disputed passages, then, the uniform use of Israel in the Gospels and Acts is in terms of ethnic Israel. A consideration of Matthew 19:28 and Luke 22:30 has shown that there is no compelling reason to abandon the usual meaning of the term elsewhere. In fact, good exegetical reasons were presented in favor of interpreting Israel in these problem verses as a reference to ethnic Israel. Such a meaning does not demand adherence to any particular eschatological scheme. It is therefore concluded that the meaning of Israel in the Gospels and Acts is always ethnic Israel.

Israel in the Pauline Epistles

THE UNDISPUTED PASSAGES

Of the seventeen occurrences of Israel in the Pauline Epistles, five are disputed. In fact, the controversy really centers around only three of these five passages: Romans 9:6; 1 Corinthians 10:18; and Galatians 6:16. Most exegetes now agree that Israel retains its ethnic meaning in the other two texts, Romans 11:26 and Ephesians 2:12. However, since some have extended Israel to include Gentiles in Romans 11:26 and Ephesians 2:12, these passages will be included under disputed passages.

The undisputed passages in the Pauline literature include Romans 9:27, 31; 10:19, 21; 11:2, 7, 25; 2 Corinthians 3:7, 13; and Philippians 3:5. All of these passages employ the term in the usual sense of ethnic Israel. This usual sense is underscored by Paul when he gives his pedigree: he is of the people (γένος) of Israel, of the tribe of Benjamin (Phil. 3:5).

35. William F. Arndt, *Bible Commentary: The Gospel According to St. Luke* (St. Louis: Concordia, 1956), 443.
36. Alfred Plummer, *A Critical and Exegetical Commentary on the Gospel According to S. Luke,* ICC (Edinburgh: T. & T. Clark, 1922), 505.
37. Ibid., 502–503.

THE DISPUTED PASSAGES

Romans 9:6

It is clear from Paul's employment of Israel twice in this verse that he is making some distinction between one sense of Israel and another sense. But what specific distinction he is making is not so clear. Hamilton represents many who maintain that Paul is distinguishing between true Israel and the nation of Israel. For Hamilton, this true Israel is just another name for the church.[38]

Such a sense for the second Israel seems to ignore Paul's argument in this section of Romans. As even Hamilton himself acknowledges, Paul never mentions Gentiles until verse 24.[39] Verse 6 refers to ethnic Israel. Paul has been arguing that there has always been an election of believers within ethnic Israel. The present remnant of believing Jews (of which Paul is a part) within ethnic Israel is proof that the promises of God have not failed. The examples Paul gives in verses 7–18 are all physical descendants of Jacob. With verse 24 Paul begins to show that God's elective mercy can be extended to Gentiles; but he does not call Gentiles Israel. This is clear from the δέ and the repetition of Israel in verse 27. Bourke cautions that here Paul is speaking only of a selection made among the physical descendants of the patriarchs.[40]

Paul's point in this passage, therefore, is that physical descent from Jacob alone is not sufficient for the fulfillment of God's promises to his people, Israel. This physical birth must be accompanied by a spiritual birth. But Paul is talking about Jews, not Gentiles. The real contrast Paul is making is "not between physical descent and spiritual adoption, but between the true Israel consisting of Jews who receive the promise by faith, and the old Israel consisting of Jews who do not," according to Hanson.[41]

Therefore, although the term Israel is still restricted to the physical descendants of Jacob, there is a division within this physical descent: (1) those who are merely physical descendants; and (2) those who are not only physical descendants but also believers.

Romans 11:26

Although it was customary for older commentators following Calvin to interpret "all Israel" as a reference to the church, the trend among recent

---

38. Floyd E. Hamilton, *The Epistle to the Romans* (Philadelphia: Presbyterian and Reformed, 1958), 151.

39. Ibid.

40. Myles M. Bourke, *A Study of the Metaphor of the Olive Tree in Rom. XI* (Washington, D.C.: The Catholic University of America Press, 1947), 25.

41. Anthony Tyrell Hanson, *The Pioneer Ministry* (Philadelphia: Westminster, 1961), 31.

exegetes is toward ethnic Israel. Even John Murray insists that it is impossible to give Israel in 11:26 a different sense than it had throughout the chapter.[42] There is a sustained contrast between Israel and the Gentiles throughout the chapter. Paul is speaking of ethnic Israel and this Israel cannot possibly include Gentiles because such a meaning would reduce the preceding verse to absurdity. F. F. Bruce also declares that "it is impossible to entertain an exegesis which takes 'Israel' here in a different sense from 'Israel' in verse 25."[43] Hendriksen seems to be in the small minority of interpreters when he tries to make Israel in Romans 11:26 include Gentiles.[44]

1 Corinthians 10:18

The difficulty with this verse is not the term Israel found in it, but the following phrase "according to the flesh" (κατὰ σάρκα) that is attached to it. Is there an implied "Israel according to the Spirit" in this phrase? If so, what is this Israel "according to the Spirit"? Is it the church? All interpreters concede that Israel means ethnic Israel. But most add that Paul is implying another Israel "according to the Spirit," that is, the church. Three views of this verse have arisen, therefore. The first view maintains that a corresponding "according to the Spirit" is implied by the "according to the flesh." This "Israel according to the Spirit" is the church. A second view also recognizes an implied "according to the Spirit." But those who adopt this view do not believe that it is necessary to open this Israel up to Gentiles. They restrict the meaning to Jews and present an exegesis similar to that adopted previously in the discussion of Romans 9:6. Paul is simply contrasting the wider ethnic entity, Israel, with a narrower ethnic entity, the believing remnant in Israel. The third view denies that the phrase "according to the flesh" demands a corresponding "according to the Spirit" complement.

In the preceding verses of 1 Corinthians 10, Paul has been developing the implications of his statement back in 9:27 about how he controls his appetites so that he should not be disapproved as a servant of Christ. He uses the example of the Israelites in the wilderness to show that confidence in the flesh and egregious sin against God caused the desert pilgrims to forfeit their inheritance in the land of Canaan. Like these Israelites, the Corinthians were in danger of idolatry when they participated in idol feasts. Idol feasts must be avoided. First Corinthians 10:16–22 employs two illustrations to demonstrate the thesis that participation in worship implies a sharing in that to which the worship is directed. Participation of Christians in the Lord's Supper is a sharing in the blood and body of Christ. Likewise, eat-

---

42. John Murray, *The Epistle to the Romans*, 2 vols. (Grand Rapids: Eerdmans, 1968), 2:96.

43. F. F. Bruce, *The Epistle to the Romans* (Grand Rapids: Eerdmans, 1963), 221–22.

44. William Hendriksen, *Israel and the Bible* (Grand Rapids: Baker, 1968), 49ff.

ing of the prescribed sacrifices in the historical worship of Israel was a sharing in the altar of sacrifice and ultimately in the One whose altar it was. Hence, any participation in heathen feasts is incongruous with fellowship at the Lord's table.

To introduce his second illustration, Paul employs the clause, "learn a lesson from Israel according to the flesh" (author's translation of Greek). Although it is possible to imply a corresponding "according to the Spirit" in Paul's phraseology, it is not necessary to do so. According to Schrenk, Paul is showing the invalidity of the Jewish worship in his illustration from Israel. If any complement is implied, it is to that Israel within Israel who has been freed from the old sacrifices of Israel and has come into the community of Christ.[45] Schrenk continues that there are many cases in Paul's letters where the complement "according to the Spirit" is neither possible nor required (see Rom. 4:1; 9:3, 5; 1 Cor. 1:26; 2 Cor. 1:17; and Col. 3:22). Although such an expression is implied in 2 Corinthians 5:16, 10:2, and 11:18, this does not permit one to supply a complement every time the phrase "according to the flesh" appears. He concludes, "Therefore, by all means 1 Cor. 10:18 can also present a pure negative assertion; it stands without any other known complement in the background. Paul speaks of the obsolete worship of the earthly Israel. Its invalidity is underlined through the *kata sarka* without permitting this expression to be surpassed by some higher conception."[46] Richardson supports Schrenk's argument: "The theory that *Israel kata sarka* demands a correlative *Israel kata pneuma* = *tou theou* cannot be accepted. Many things which take *kata sarka* do not have a correlative *kata pneuma.*"[47] Even if a κατὰ πνεῦμα is implied, it still needs to be demonstrated that such a phrase refers to the church that includes Gentiles. The correlative may simply distinguish between two ethnic Israels: one composed of believing Jews, and the other composed of unbelieving Jews.

Galatians 6:16

Since practically everyone who advocates an equation of the church with some kind of Israel appeals to this passage for support of the nonethnic sense of the term Israel, considerable space will be devoted to it.

Galatians 6:11–18 forms the conclusion to this epistle. Most commentators concede that Paul took up the pen at this point to write the concluding paragraph. According to Burton, Paul's motives were twofold: (1) to authenticate the letter; and (2) to emphasize the main points of the letter.[48]

45. Gottlob Schrenk, "Was bedeutet 'Israel Gottes'?" *Judaica*, 4 (1949): 89–90.

46. Ibid., 90.

47. Richardson, 122 n. 5.

48. Ernest De Witt Burton, *A Critical and Exegetical Commentary on the Epistle to the Galatians*, ICC (Edinburgh: T. & T. Clark, 1921), 347–48.

After contrasting the heretics' motives with his own motives, Paul states in verse 15 that, "Neither circumcision nor uncircumcision means anything; what counts is a new creation." Then Paul adds, "Peace and mercy to all who follow this rule, even to the Israel of God." The reference of "this rule" is to verse 15 where Paul has mentioned the new creation in Christ that lives by the Spirit. Most modern editors adopt the future for "follow" rather than the present tense contained in some witnesses to the text.

The last part of verse 16 contains the crux interpretum. To the phrase "peace and mercy to all who follow this rule," Paul adds "even to the Israel of God." What is meant by "the Israel of God"? The difficulty is increased by the fact that this is the only place in the entire Greek New Testament where this phrase is used.[49]

In 1949 and 1950 the journal *Judaica* carried a debate between Gottlob Schrenk and Nils Dahl concerning this phrase in Galatians 6:16. Schrenk took the position that Paul always reserves the term Israel for the Jews.[50] Since this use of Israel was the normal one for Paul, it follows that Paul could not have meant the Christian church by "Israel of God" because the church includes Gentiles. Schrenk insisted that "Israel of God" must mean Jewish believers in Christ.[51] Dahl admitted that it was customary for Paul to reserve the term Israel for the Jews.[52] But Paul's transfer of Israel's honorific titles such as "children of Abraham," "circumcision," and "people of God" to the church composed of Gentiles argued for the possibility of a transfer of terminology also for Israel to mean the church.[53] Schrenk immediately replied to Dahl in a long article[54] in which Schrenk again insisted that the linguistic usage of Paul was definitely against any designation of the church as Israel. Schrenk conceded that terms like "seed," "children of Abraham," "circumcision," and "people of God" were transferred from Israel to the church. But he argued that this transfer failed to prove that the most significant title for God's covenant people, Israel, was ever transferred to the church.[55]

This debate between Schrenk and Dahl raises the question being addressed in this appendix. Does the New Testament use the term Israel for

49. John Eadie, *Commentary on the Epistle of Paul to the Galatians* (Grand Rapids: Zondervan, n.d.), 469.

50. Schrenk, 81.

51. Ibid., 93.

52. Nils A. Dahl, "Zur Auslegung von Gal. 6,16," *Judaica*, 6 (1950): 162.

53. Ibid., 163.

54. Gottlob Schrenk, "Der Segenswunsch nach der Kampfepistel," *Judaica*, 6 (1950): 170–90.

55. Ibid., 187.

the church? Since Galatians 6:16 is so critical, a list of the various punctuations of the text and interpretations of the verse follows.

1. It is possible to place a comma after "mercy" and translate the following "and" (καί) as "even" or "namely." This is the so-called epexegetical sense of this conjunction. The translation of the verse would be: "As many as shall walk by this rule, peace be upon them and mercy, namely, upon the Israel of God." Construing the verse in this way, the Israel of God is the church.

2. Place a comma after "mercy" and give the conjunction the normal sense of "and." The translation would be: "As many as shall walk by this rule, peace be upon them and mercy, and upon the Israel of God." According to this arrangement, Paul is promising God's peace and mercy upon Gentile Christians who walk by the rule and upon Jewish Christians, the true Israel of God.

3. Place a comma after "them," remove the comma after "mercy," and translate the conjunction as "also." This is the adjunctive sense of καί. The translation would be, "As many as shall walk by this rule, peace be upon them, and may there be mercy also upon the Israel of God." Taken this way, Paul would be pronouncing peace upon all who walk by the rule (whether Jewish or Gentile Christians). At the same time he adds a prayer for God's mercy upon those within the nation of Israel, who, although elect, had not yet come to faith in Christ.

Since there were no punctuation marks in the original manuscripts, all three punctuations above are possible. There has been considerable controversy, however, over the legitimacy of the first translation. Ellicott argued strenuously against a "namely" translation for καί.[56] Schrenk said that although such a meaning for καί is possible (see 1 Cor. 8:12; 12:27; 14:27; 15:38; 2 Cor. 5:15), such a meaning always specializes, limits, or defines the annexed particular closer to the general.[57] Schrenk felt that if Paul had wanted to call the church Israel, he would have removed all ambiguity by simply omitting the καί and writing "upon the Israel of God" right after "mercy."[58]

Richardson has pointed out that the problem is far more than a "battle of the καί." The verse contains a double "upon," a double καί, and two attributes (peace and mercy) in a unique order. Richardson shows that there

---

56. Charles J. Ellicott, *A Critical and Grammatical Commentary on St. Paul's Epistle to the Galatians with a Revised Translation* (Andover: Warren F. Draper, 1880), 154.
57. Schrenk, "Was bedeutet," 85.
58. Ibid., 85–86.

is no instance in either the New Testament or the Septuagint where the order is peace followed by mercy. The order is always mercy followed by peace. Therefore, this strange order must have some significance or reason.[59] Burton concurs and asserts that the mercy clause is a Pauline afterthought. This clause is something that Paul added after he had finished his main sentence.[60]

Many have noticed a parallel between this wish of Paul's and the *Shemoneh Esreh* of the Jewish synagogue.[61] The *Shemoneh* was a collection of eighteen benedictions forming the second important section of the daily Jewish prayers at the morning, afternoon, and evening services, as well as the additional service on Sabbaths and holy days. At the time the benedictions became fixed, they numbered nineteen. They are grouped into three blessings of praise, thirteen petitions, and three benedictions of thanks. The first three and the last three were used at every service.[62]

The parallel to Galatians is found in the nineteenth and last benediction that reads at the beginning, "Bestow peace, happiness, and blessing, grace, loving-kindness, and mercy upon us and upon all Israel Thy people."[63] Although the passage in the *Shemoneh* and Galatians 6:16 are analogous, they are not identical. Richardson again states that the sentence in Galatians gives the impression of being an interpreted reflection on the benediction.[64] Richardson believes that Paul has in mind those Israelites who had not yet come to their senses and believed the good news of Christ. But as in Romans 11:26, Paul held out the hope that they would not continue in unbelief. Paul therefore prays that God will have mercy upon them and bring them to repentance.[65]

The conclusion, therefore, is that Paul is wishing peace upon all those believers who walk by the rule of verse 15. As an afterthought Paul wishes mercy also upon those elect within the nation of Israel who have not yet believed but nevertheless are still God's people, Israel. Although they do not yet walk by the rule, Paul prays for their salvation and assumes that

---

59. Richardson, 77–81.
60. Burton, 357–58.
61. Paul Billerbeck, "Die Briefe des Neuen Testaments und die Offenbarung Johannis," *Kommentar zum neuen Testament aus Talmud und Midrasch* von Herman L. Strack und Paul Billerbeck (München: C. H. Beck'sche Verlagsbuchhandlung, 1954), 3:579; Schrenk, "Was bedeutet," 92–93; Raymond T. Stamm, "The Epistle to the Galatians," in *IB*, ed. George A. Buttrick et al. (New York: Abingdon-Cokesbury, 1953), 10:591; Richardson, 79ff.
62. Emil G. Hirsch, "Shemoneh Esreh," in *The Jewish Encyclopedia*, ed. Cyrus Adler et al. (New York: Funk and Wagnalls, 1905), 11:270.
63. Ibid., 271.
64. Richardson, 80.
65. Ibid., 81.

they will walk by the rule when they believe. Such an interpretation explains why Paul used the future tense for "walk"—it left the door open to those who were not yet walking but would walk in the future. By adding this prayer, Paul does not play into the hands of the Judaizers. He is not conceding that Gentiles must come into Israel via circumcision. Gentiles must walk by the rule as Jews must also walk. Only in Christ can either Jew or Gentile be recipients of God's peace (Rom. 5:1; Eph. 2:14). On the other hand, Paul is not arguing some "replacement" theology. Israel has great privileges from the covenant God of Israel, which Paul lists in Romans 3:1–3; 9:4–6; and Eph. 2:12. Paul is a good Jew as well as a good Christian. While refuting the need for circumcision for Gentiles in Galatians, he still retains his great concern for Israel: that they might be saved (Rom. 10:1).

The following reasons support this interpretation of this highly contested verse:

1. Such an interpretation is in line with Paul's consistent use of the term Israel only for the physical descendants of Jacob, whether believers or unbelievers.
2. This interpretation accounts for the unusual sequence of peace and mercy, the double καί, and the double "upon" (ἐπί).
3. This interpretation does not strain the meaning of καί.
4. This interpretation is in harmony with the use of "mercy" in Paul's other letters.
5. This interpretation accounts for the origin of the last phrase in a prayer that Paul as a Jew had prayed many times.
6. This interpretation eliminates the charge that Paul would be conceding too much to the Judaizers. Paul is both a good Christian and a good Jew. He will not allow Gentiles to be circumcised, but he apparently was a Torah-practicing Jew in many ways. He never lost his hope that his own people, Israel, would see the error of their ways and come to faith in Christ. He, therefore, prays for his people in the conclusion of a letter that has been very harsh and could easily be interpreted as anti-Semitic. While Paul is an anti-Judaizer when it comes to Gentile freedom, he is not anti-Semitic. He is very much pro-Israel.
7. This interpretation (not in all details) is supported in the main not only by Richardson, but also by Burton, Duncan,[66] Bruce,[67] and Stamm in their commentaries and by S. Lewis Johnson, Jr. in a very careful study.[68]

---

66. George S. Duncan, *The Epistle of Paul to the Galatians*, MNTC (London: Hodder and Stoughton, 1938), 192–93.

67. F. F. Bruce, *Commentary on Galatians*, NIGNTC (Grand Rapids: Eerdmans, 1982), 274–75.

Ephesians 2:12

Although Ephesians 2:11–22 is an extremely complex passage and there is no unanimity among commentators in regard to its details, the main outlines of the passage are clear:

1. Gentiles before the coming of Christ were completely estranged from God. They had no position of privilege involving the covenants and the promised Messiah such as the nation of Israel had.
2. In Christ the Gentiles have been brought near to God.
3. The Mosaic law, which was done away in Christ, is no longer a barrier to fellowship between Jews and Gentiles. Instead, God has created in Christ one new entity by reconciling both Jew and Gentile to God.
4. Through Christ both Jews and Gentiles have equal access to God in the Spirit.
5. Gentiles and Jews in the church are now fellow citizens and members of the family of God.
6. Together Jews and Gentiles are being built into a new building that is a holy temple in which God dwells.

The problem for the present discussion is the implication of the phrase "estranged from the commonwealth of Israel" in verse 12. Although Israel appears to be a simple reference to the nation of Israel, many have emptied the term of this ethnic connotation and have given it a highly theological meaning of "the true people of God." According to this exegesis, Gentiles have become members of "the Israel of God."

The solution to the problem lies in noticing carefully what Paul does and does not say. Paul does not say that the Gentiles are incorporated into the old commonwealth of Israel or into the commonwealth of the new Israel. Although Paul may imply a concept without using the actual words of that concept, one should hesitate in using terms like "new Israel" and "true Israel" when Paul consistently avoids using these designations of the church. However, he does say that both Jews and Gentiles have been created into "one new man" (2:15). He does not say that the Gentiles have become proselytes to Judaism but that Gentiles are now fellow citizens with the saints. According to Schrenk, Hoffmann, B. Weiss, von Soden, Dibelius, K. L. Schmidt, Schlatter, Haupt, Ewald, and Lueken, these "saints" are the Jewish Christians.[69] Both Gentile Christians and Jewish Christians are fellow

---

68. S. Lewis Johnson, Jr. "Paul and 'The Israel of God': An Exegetical and Eschatological Case-Study," in *Essays in Honor of J. Dwight Pentecost*, ed. Stanley D. Toussaint and Charles H. Dyer (Chicago: Moody, 1986), 181–96.
69. Schrenk, "Der Segenswunsch," 189.

citizens and household members of this new entity, the church. Verse 20 clearly shows that this new entity is in the process of being built. It is not something rebuilt. It is entirely new.

Why then does Paul bring up Israel at all in Ephesians 2:12? Because Paul is endeavoring to show the absolute estrangement of Gentiles in contrast to Israel from God before the coming of Christ and the beginning of the church. Paul's emphasis is not on Israel per se, but on Israel's privileges: covenants, promise, hope of eternal life, and knowledge of the one true God (see also Rom. 9:4–6). That Paul is thinking of Israel's privileges under the old covenant is seen by the addition of "and strangers to the covenants of the promise." Paul indicates the status of Gentiles in relationship to God prior to the coming of Christ as opposed to the status of the nation of Israel. But Christ has changed the salvific, not ethnic, status of the Gentiles. They have not been incorporated into Israel as if they were merely proselytes coming into Israel under the old covenant. The Gentiles have an equal status with Israel. Both Jewish and Gentile believers can have fellowship with one another in the new organism, the church. Both Israel and Gentiles thus are raised to a new level in Christ. Therefore, Israel retains its normal meaning of ethnic Israel.[70]

Israel in Hebrews Through Revelation

THE UNDISPUTED PASSAGES

Hebrews 11:22
The reference to the time of Joseph shows that Israel means the patriarch, Jacob.

Revelation 2:14
Since the context is Balak's placing a stumbling block before the sons of Israel, ethnic Israel is certainly to be understood.

THE DISPUTED PASSAGES

Hebrews 8:8, 10
Both occurrences of Israel are found in a quotation from Jeremiah 31:31–34 with regard to the new covenant. That Israel and Judah are to be understood in their normal sense in Jeremiah 31 is generally acknowledged. What their meaning is in Hebrews 8 is another problem. The normal ethnic meaning of both terms can be retained if the new covenant of Jeremiah 31 is fulfilled initially with the twelve apostles and Jewish Christians who are

---

70. For a thorough exegetical discussion of this passage, see Carl B. Hoch, Jr., "The New Man of Ephesians Two," in *Dispensationalism, Israel and the Church*, ed. Craig A. Blaising and Darrell L. Bock (Grand Rapids: Zondervan, 1992), 98–126.

a remnant within the larger ethnic Israel. These Jewish Christians have every right to the title *Israel*. The extension to Gentiles of another of Israel's covenants so that Gentiles share with Israel (see also the discussion of Eph. 2 above) does not make Gentiles "Israel and Judah." This passage then reinforces the consistent theology found elsewhere in the New Testament that Gentiles share with Israel without becoming a part of either ethnic Israel or some "spiritual Israel [and Judah]." Israel in Hebrews 8 retains its normal reference to physical descendants of Jacob and is not equivalent to the church because the church includes Gentiles who are not Israelites.

Revelation 7:4

Without entering into a discussion of the whole program of eschatology, it is hoped that the problem with this verse can be solved simply from the context and from probability of meaning.

The context of this passage does not seem to convey a contrary to normal meaning for the term Israel. The scene is the earth. The word earth (γῆ) occurs five times in Revelation 7:1–3. The judgment of the seventh seal is not to take place until the servants of God have been sealed. A mark is placed upon their foreheads. Beckwith says that this is an allusion to Ezekiel 9:4.[71] In the context of Ezekiel those faithful believers in ethnic Israel who had the mark of God on their foreheads were to be preserved from the coming judgment upon Jerusalem by the Chaldeans. Keil points out the parallel with Exodus 12:13, 22 with regard to the placing of the blood on the doorframes in view of the coming plague.[72] In terms of historical precedent, an exegesis that posits another preservation of ethnic Israel during a time of judgment would have higher probability than one that does not, unless any future for ethnic Israel is ruled out on theological grounds.

The number sealed is stated as 144,000 specifically. This number is then broken down into 12,000 in each tribe. Although the number 12,000 may be symbolical of completeness,[73] it is difficult to assess what the naming of each tribe symbolizes unless the reference is to ethnic Israel. The tribes of Ephraim and Dan are omitted. This omission can be explained if one takes the reference to be to ethnic Israel. It is difficult to account for the omission if the twelve tribes are meant to picture the unity and completeness of the church.

Although those who interpret Israel as the church merely consider the next vision as a further description of the same truth, other interpreters see a contrast between the 144,000 out of Israel in 7:1–8 and the innumerable

---

71. Isbon T. Beckwith, *The Apocalypse of John* (Grand Rapids: Baker, 1967), 542.
72. Carl Friedrick Keil, *Biblical Commentary on the Prophecies of Ezekiel* (Grand Rapids: Eerdmans, 1950), 2:130.
73. Beckwith, 542.

multitude from all nations and tribes and peoples and tongues of 7:9. These latter groups are not on earth but around the throne in heaven.[74] Therefore, Bengel's conclusion that Israel in the strict sense is denoted by the 144,000 is adopted as the correct interpretation.[75]

Revelation 21:12

Following the approach of Swete and others to the Book of Revelation, it is possible to regard the reference to the twelve tribes of Israel as indicating the unity of the "whole Israel of God," the church. But it is just as possible, and more in harmony with the usage of Israel elsewhere in the New Testament, to retain the ethnic meaning for Israel here. The inclusion of the twelve tribes of ethnic Israel in the New Jerusalem shows the unity of God's people throughout redemptive history. Ethnic Israel and Gentiles from every nation on earth join together as the redeemed of God in the eternal city. The twelve tribes of Israel and the twelve apostles of the Lamb aptly depict the final unity of all God's people, in spite of the distinctions within that people that have been a part of the historical development of God's redemptive program.

Conclusion

This section has analyzed the sixty-eight occurrences of the term Israel in the New Testament. Eleven passages were found to be disputed (viz., Matt. 19:28; Luke 22:30; Rom. 9:6; 11:26; 1 Cor. 10:18; Gal. 6:16; Eph. 2:12; Heb. 8:8, 10; Rev. 7:4; 21:12). A discussion of these passages demonstrated that there were no exegetical considerations that demanded that one depart from the normal meaning of Israel as an ethnic entity for any of these passages. On the contrary, strong exegetical support was adduced for the proposition that Israel is not extended to Gentiles in New Testament usage but is reserved for physical descendants of Jacob. In addition, it was apparent that the numerical preponderance was in favor of an ethnic meaning. If it were not for other arguments that have been introduced to prove that Israel has a higher, nonethnic sense in the New Testament, the discussion of Israel could conclude at this point. But other arguments for Israel as a synonym for the church in the New Testament must now be examined.

---

74. J. B. Smith, *A Revelation of Jesus Christ,* ed. J. Otis Yoder (Scottdale, Pa.: Herald, 1961), 130–33.

75. John Albert Bengel, *Gnomon of the New Testament* (Edinburgh: T. & T. Clark, 1873), 4:233.

The Problem of the *Ehrentiteln* of Israel Used Also of the Church

One of the most frequently used arguments for the equation of Israel and the church is the application of many titles of honor (Ehrentiteln) or terms of privilege and other descriptions used of Israel in the Old Testament for the church in the New Testament. Cox is representative of this line of reasoning when he writes, "That the Christian church replaced Israel is obvious when one notes that the Jewish-Gentile Christian church of the New Testament is given the same titles which in the Old Testament were given to national Israel."[76] Minear lists numerous "images" of the church in the New Testament used also of Israel in the Old Testament: seed of Abraham, circumcision, diaspora, elect, firstfruits, flock, house, Jerusalem, nation, new covenant, Passover, people, pilgrims, priesthood, race, sheep, temple, Twelve, vineyard, and witnesses.[77]

It is impossible to consider all these expressions. Neither is it necessary. It can be shown by taking a few of the expressions that are mentioned most frequently in theological literature as proving the identity of Israel and the church that terms can be used of two separate things without identifying them. The reason for using the terms may be other than identification. It may be possible to demonstrate that the old mathematical axiom that "two things equal to a third thing are equal to each other" does not necessarily hold true in theology. Commonality does not demand identity any more than commonality between the thirteen original colonies and England meant the two were the same.

A better solution to the difficulty seems to lie in the fact that those titles and terms that were perverted by historic Israel have been restored to their original spiritual significance through Jesus Christ. Believers in Christ, whether Jews or Gentiles, demonstrate the original significance of these prerogatives of Israel. Some prerogatives are adapted, others are transformed, while others are completely superseded. Many are used in a typological sense because of the repetitive patterns God uses in redemptive history. But Israel does not thereby become the church, and the church does not displace Israel by becoming the "new" or "true" Israel.

The People of God

The writer has examined all the uses of the Hebrew term עַם in the Old Testament and the Greek term λαός in the New Testament. It appears that

76. William E. Cox, *Amillennialism Today* (Philadelphia: Presbyterian and Reformed, 1966), 49.
77. Paul S. Minear, *Images of the Church in the New Testament* (Philadelphia: Westminster, 1960).

when the definite article is used before either word for "people" that ethnic Israel is indicated. When the Gentiles is the referent, the article is omitted or the plural is used. This data seems to show that ethnic Israel had a certain priority as God's people. But the New Testament opens a new dimension because of Christ's work on the cross. Gentiles who were formerly not God's people have now become his people (1 Pet. 2:10). Nowhere does the addition of something, like the Gentiles, imply cancellation of that which is prior, like Israel. On the other hand, one cannot interpret the Epistle to the Hebrews with any idea of two separate peoples of God. The writer of Hebrews views the people of God as the household of God (3:6). Christians are members of the same people and household as Moses and the other Old Testament saints. However, the writer of Hebrews does distinguish between "they" and "us" in 11:39–40. "They" refers to believers under the old covenant; "us" refers to believers under the new covenant. Therefore, the writer seems to make a historical distinction between Israel and the church. Israel lived under the old economy; the church lives under the new economy. The saints under the old economy did not experience "perfection" during their lifetimes; Christians experience this "perfection" because they stand on the post-Cross side of things. Although there is one people redemptively, this one people must be carefully separated into different groups who lived during different eras of redemptive history. Gentiles were not a people under the old economy (Rom. 9:24–26; 1 Pet. 2:10). They are now God's people under the new economy. It is this critical development that makes the church the church. A reasonable conclusion is that although there is one people of God, this people has been formed throughout various segments of redemptive history: antediluvian people of God, postdiluvian people of God, patriarchal people of God, Israel as people of God, and Gentiles as people of God who share together with Israel on an equal basis. The last segment is no more equal to Israel than the pre-Israel segments are.

Seed of Abraham

The key here is to delineate carefully the various senses of the phrase, *seed of Abraham*. At the most basic level, the seed of Abraham are the physical descendants of Abraham. But even in the Old Testament it is clear that not all physical descendants of Abraham followed Abraham's faith in and obedience to God or were part of the elect line. Many were physical seed but not spiritual seed nor elect seed. This distinction is sharpened in the New Testament. The Jews claimed to be Abraham's seed in a debate with Jesus (John 8:33). Jesus conceded that they were Abraham's seed in the physical sense (8:37). But he denied that they were Abraham's spiritual seed (8:39). Paul develops the same distinction between physical and spiritual seed within ethnic Israel in Romans 9:7–8. He even calls the servants of

Satan "seed of Abraham" in 2 Corinthians 11:22! But in the ultimate sense, Christ is the seed of Abraham par excellence (Gal. 3:16, 19). In terms of the seed of Abraham, Galatians 3:29 is parallel to 1 Peter 2:10 with regard to the people of God. By virtue of being in Christ (not in Israel) who is *the* seed of Abraham, Gentiles become Abraham's seed. Christ is the key for the seed just as he is the key for the people. Gentiles are only people and seed because they are "in Christ." Gentiles do not lose their ethnic identity any more than Israel does. But Israel cannot rely on physical descent any more than Gentiles' physical descent excludes them from becoming Abraham's seed. Only the spiritual seed from both Israel and the Gentiles become heirs to the promise God made to Abraham through faith in Christ. Gentiles are part of Abraham's seed, but they are not the only seed or a spiritual Israel as Pieters contends.[78] The correct view has been stated by Wilkinson:

> All believers in Christ are thus by the authority of scripture Abraham's spiritual seed. But this does not imply that believers of Gentile origin are spiritual Israelites. One does not include the other; one excludes the other. No one but a converted natural Israelite is properly and scripturally a spiritual Israelite.[79]

The reason seed of Abraham is used of Gentiles, then, is not to teach that Gentiles become spiritual Israelites, but that believing Gentiles by exercising the same kind of faith Abraham exercised are blessed *with* Abraham (see also Gal. 3:9).

Ἐκκλησία

A common line or argument is this: קָהָל is used in the Hebrew Bible as a designation for the people of God in the Old Testament; since ἐκκλησία is used in the Septuagint to translate קָהָל, the New Testament simply took over a ready-made term from the Septuagint to designate the church as equal to Israel.[80]

J. Y. Campbell, however, has challenged this argument. He argues that קָהָל has a wider range of meaning than ἐκκλησία. Ἐκκλησία does not translate קָהָל in the first four books of the Old Testament; συναγωγή does. Even in the later books of the Old Testament where ἐκκλησία does translate קָהָל, συναγωγή also translates קָהָל sixteen times. Campbell insists that "there is no good evidence that in the Old Testament קָהָל ever means anything but an actual assembly or meeting of some kind, like ἐκκλησία in ordinary Greek."[81] Since the term קְהַל יְהוָה is found only in seven passages in the

---

78. Albertus Pieters, *The Seed of Abraham* (Grand Rapids: Eerdmans, 1950), 121.
79. John Wilkinson, *Israel My Glory* (London: Mildmay Mission to the Jew's Book Store, 1894), 17.
80. Fenton John Anthony Hort, *The Christian Ecclesia* (London: Macmillan, 1897), 3.

whole Old Testament, there is "no adequate basis for the assertion that in the Old Testament קְהַל יְהוָה is the usual term for Israel as the people of God, nor yet for the supposition that a Christian reader of the Septuagint would be led to think that ἐκκλησία κυρίου (which he would find in only five passages) had that meaning."[82] Furthermore, if ἐκκλησία involved the claim to be the true Israel of God, one would expect the word in a passage such as 1 Peter 2:4–10 where attributes of Israel are being applied to the church. Yet ἐκκλησία is not used here or anywhere else in 1 Peter.[83] Campbell's conclusion is as follows:

> We must conclude, therefore, that there is no good evidence for the generally accepted view that in using the word *ecclesia* the early Christians were borrowing an Old Testament term in order to express their claim to be the true people of God, the legitimate successor of the Israel of the Old Covenant. The probability is that at first they used it as an obvious name for those simple 'meetings' which were the most conspicuous and distinctive feature in the life of the early Church. For this use there was some precedent in the Psalms and in Ecclesiasticus. There is nothing at all surprising or unusual in the development by which the word came to mean, not only the actual meeting, but also the body of people habitually meeting together, a local 'congregation'; the word 'congregation' itself shows the same development, and so, to have some name for the Christian community as a whole it was all but inevitable that the same word should be used; to have chosen some other name would have obscured the fact that the whole Church was made up of the individual *ecclesiai* or churches.[84]

Barr agrees:

> The suggestion that the use of *ecclesia* constitutes a claim to be the 'true Israel of God' seems to presuppose that *qahal* is *the* term *par excellence* in which the nature of Israel as the people of God is expressed. Now even if this were the case it is far from clear that the use of the Greek *ecclesia* would be understood by anyone to point unambiguously to this term *par excellence*, for this latter is translated by *synagoge* and not by *ecclesia* in about one case in three in the Septuagint, and *ecclesia* predominates only in the historical books and Psalms and not in the important sections of the Pentateuch and Prophets.[85]

---

81. J. Y. Campbell, "The Origin and Meaning of the Christian Use of the Word *EKKLESIA*," *Journal of Theological Studies*, 49 (1948): 133. This article has been reprinted in J. Y. Campbell, *Three New Testament Studies* (Leiden: Brill, 1965), 41–54.
82. Ibid., 136.
83. Ibid., 140.
84. Ibid., 141–42.
85. James Barr, *The Semantics of Biblical Language* (London: Oxford University Press, 1961), 127–28.

Barr considers the argument under examination as another example of the trend in much modern biblical theology in reading the maximum possible theological content into a linguistic choice. According to Barr, it is equally possible that the church chose ἐκκλησία to distinguish itself from the συναγωγή of Israel.[86]

Although Acts 7:38 is often cited as teaching a "church" during the Old Testament period, its normal meaning of "assembly" or "congregation" is all that is required to make sense of Stephen's sentence.[87] As Dahl suggests, "the counterpart to the 'Ecclesia' in the wilderness is not the new Ecclesia, but the Jewish people at the time of Jesus."[88]

This writer concludes, therefore, that the term ἐκκλησία simply means "assembly" and that it does not imply any identification of the church with Israel.

Circumcision

The central passage adduced to prove that the church is the true circumcision over against Israel is Philippians 3:3. There is no need to deny that the church has entered into the real significance of the term circumcision. But circumcision of the heart is not unique to the New Testament. This is also an Old Testament theme (see Deut. 10:16; 30:6; Jer. 4:4; 6:10; 9:26; Ezek. 44:7). Circumcision of the flesh only was never the will of God. Circumcision of the heart was the true goal. The external sign represented an internal reality. Without the internal reality, the external sign was a sham.

Three passages are usually adduced to support the thesis that the church is the true circumcision and is therefore a replacement for Israel.

ROMANS 2:25–29

In the preceding section (Rom. 2:17–24), Paul has been censuring the Jew for failure to match practice with profession. This inconsistency of the Jew has resulted in God's name being blasphemed among the Gentiles. Beginning with verse 25, Paul takes up the "visible badge of the Jew's superiority," circumcision.[89] Paul's first point is that circumcision only has value for the Jew if he keeps covenant. If his practice does not conform with that which the outward sign was intended originally to signify, a seal of faith righteousness (4:11), then his circumcision was really no better than uncir-

86. Ibid., 129.

87. Geddes MacGregor, *Corpus Christi: The Nature of the Church According to the Reformed Tradition* (Philadelphia: Westminster, 1958), 113.

88. Nils Alstrup Dahl, *Das Volk Gottes: eine Untersuchung zum Kirchenbewusstsein des Urchristentums* (Darmstadt: Wissenschaftliche Buchgesellschaft, 1963), 196.

89. C. K. Barrett, *A Commentary on the Epistle to the Romans*, HNTC (New York: Harper and Row, 1957), 58.

cumcision. On the other hand, if the uncircumcised Gentile demonstrates in life what circumcision was intended to represent, then that Gentile's uncircumcision is actually regarded as if he were physically circumcised. The Gentile's conduct will condemn the Jew's conduct regardless of the Jew's physical circumcision. The solution for the Jew is to match his outward physical circumcision with an inner circumcision of heart that recovers God's original intention in giving circumcision. The true Jew in God's sight is the Jew who has a heart circumcision corresponding with his fleshly circumcision. In other words, Paul wants the Jew to be a Jew outwardly and inwardly. Commentators try to make Paul infer that the Gentile is a spiritual Jew. But Paul is not dealing with Gentiles at this point. He is dealing only with the Jew in verses 28 and 29. The Gentile is introduced for comparison, not definition. Romans 3:1–2 show that physical circumcision still has value for the Jew. So in verse 29 Paul is not trying to say that a Jew is anyone who has heart circumcision. He is saying that a true Jew is one whose circumcision is not only outward, but inward as well. This man's praise (a play on the meaning of Judah as "praise") is from God rather than men.[90] If Paul were writing the Jews off to the point that Gentiles were "true Jews" and the term "Jew" no longer had any ethnic content, then his argument in 3:1ff. makes no sense whatsoever when he states that the Jew has an advantage and has the great privilege of having received the "oracles of God."

PHILIPPIANS 3:3

Beginning with Philippians 3:2, Paul warns the Philippians, "Watch out for those dogs, those men who do evil, those mutilators of the flesh." Richardson identifies this group as those Jews who had been dogging Paul's footsteps and were making circumcision the requirement for Gentile salvation.[91]

The difficult question is the identity of the "we" in verse 3. Many commentators assume that the only possible reference is to all Christians and hastily remark about the church as the "true circumcision" or the "Israel of God." However, certain factors lead this writer to question whether this "we" is as all-inclusive as many make it. After all, Paul's use of "we," "us," and "you" is anything but uniform. He can leap back and forth between an inclusive and exclusive use to the point where it becomes impossible to determine in some cases what he had in mind. This writer has tried to determine Paul's use of "we" and "us" in Ephesians and found it impossible to

---

90. Samuel Hinds Wilkinson, *The Israel Promises and Their Fulfillment* (London: Mildmay Mission to the Jews, 1936), 23.
91. Richardson, 113–14.

be certain where "we" means "we Jews" and where it means "we Christians."[92]

If those in 3:2 were Jewish opponents of Paul, then it seems likely that Paul is contrasting himself as a Jewish Christian who preaches only heart circumcision for Gentiles over against these other Jews (Christians?) who demand that Gentiles be circumcised. It is interesting to note that the "we" in verse 17 refers to Paul and Timothy. Paul is not thinking in an inclusive sense when he writes "we," but in an exclusive sense. The following arguments support such a restrictive use of the "we" in verse 3:

1. The verb λατρεύω had a "very special sense to denote the service rendered to Jehovah by the Israelite race, as his peculiar people."[93] In every instance where Paul uses this verb to describe service to God, he uses it of his own personal ministry (see also Acts 24:14; 26:7; 27:23; Rom. 1:9; 2 Tim. 1:3).

2. When Paul refers to possible confidence in the flesh in Philippians 3:5–6, he mentions, "circumcised on the eighth day, of the people of Israel, of the tribe of Benjamin, a Hebrew of Hebrews; in regard to the law, a Pharisee; as for zeal, persecuting the church; as for legalistic righteousness, faultless." Paul is definitely contrasting his pre-Christian experience with his present Christian Jewish experience. Saying "we" are the circumcision may have been his way of anticipating the list of his pre-Christian credentials versus his new position in Christ.

3. According to Hanson, the Philippian Gentile Christians would have no reason to boast in the flesh anyway. To call Gentiles the true circumcision at this point reads ideas into the text that are more characteristic of the Reformation than Paul's thought.[94]

It is this writer's conclusion, therefore, that Paul is not claiming that the Christian church composed of both Jews and Gentiles is the "true circumcision" over against Israel. Paul does not supply the word "true" before circumcision. Translators and commentators have supplied it. The contrast in Philippians 3:3 is between Paul's (and possibly Timothy's) valid circumcision as a Jewish Christian over against either Christ-rejecting Jews or over against Jewish Christians who are preaching another gospel and deserve the castigation "anathema" (see also Gal. 1:6–9).

92. Carl B. Hoch, Jr., "The New Man of Ephesians," 101.
93. J. B. Lightfoot, Saint Paul's Epistle to the Philippians (Grand Rapids: Zondervan, 1953), 145.
94. Hanson, 35.

COLOSSIANS 2:11

Although all Christians have an inner circumcision of heart according to this text, Paul does not call Gentiles "the circumcision." Circumcision has nothing to do with the body. It is a metaphor for the cutting away of the heart of stone (new covenant terminology) and implanting a heart of flesh. Paul's emphasis is not on circumcision, but upon the believer's identification with Christ. That baptism has not replaced circumcision can be easily seen from the fact that Paul did not attempt to refute the Judaizers' demand that Gentiles be circumcised with the statement, "They have no need of circumcision; they have been baptized! You all know that baptism has replaced circumcision as the sign of the covenant!" Apparently Paul regarded physical circumcision as still valid for Jews and Jewish Christians (he circumcised Timothy!). But physical circumcision was not valid for Gentile Christians (Paul wrote the entire letter to the Galatians to refute that premise!). "True circumcision" only makes sense in a Jewish debate. Since Gentiles are not Jews and yet they are Christians, they cannot be called "true circumcision" over against Jews. Since the church is composed of both Jews and Gentiles, the church cannot be set over against Israel with the word circumcision. The issue is much too complex. There are Jews who are circumcised in flesh but not in heart. There are Jewish Christians who are circumcised in both flesh and heart. There are Gentile Christians who are circumcised in heart but not in flesh. What then is "true circumcision"?

Διασπορά

This term is especially problematical in James 1:1 and 1 Peter 1:1. James is probably writing to Jews (mainly Christian Jews, but possibly some non-Christian Jews in light of 5:1–6). If this is so, there is no take-over in the term διασπορά in James. These readers were dispersed geographically.

The problem is more acute in 1 Peter. Beare's arguments for a Jewish and Gentile Christian readership are convincing to this writer.[95] So διασπορά is a term for Christians dispersed throughout the earth awaiting their homeland, heaven.[96] But the key to the use of a term for Israel in 1 Peter may be Peter's extensive use of typology throughout the epistle. Peter uses Noah as

95. Francis Wright Beare, *The First Epistle of Peter* (Oxford: Basil Blackwell, 1961), 48.
96. See Charles H. Talbert, "Once Again: The Plan of I Peter," in *Perspectives on First Peter*, ed. Charles H. Talbert (Macon, Ga.: Mercer University Press, 1986), 144. Talbert, along with this writer, believes that John H. Elliott's restriction of the "pilgrims" and "sojourners" in 1 Peter to socioeconomical categories with no idea of estrangement from their heavenly homeland does not suit the text of 1 Peter, esp. 1 Pet. 2:11. See John H. Elliott, *A Home for the Homeless: A Sociological Exegesis of I Peter, Its Situation and Strategy* (Philadelphia: Fortress, 1981), 43.

a type of preservation from judgment through identification with God's or-dained means of salvation. It would not be logical to assume that since the experiences of Noah were used in a typical application to the church that the church is therefore a "new Noah," or "true Noah." The conclusion fol-lows that although Peter uses numerous typological parallels between Is-rael and the church, these parallels do not imply that the one is the other.

The Twelve

Many have looked upon Jesus' selection of twelve disciples and twelve apostles as proof positive that the church is the new or true Israel that re-places ethnic Israel in God's program.[97] But it is possible that the reason Jesus selected twelve is that the Twelve represented the faithful remnant of Israel within Israel. Their inclusion in the church does not make the church a "new Israel." It merely illustrates the truth of Paul's statement in Romans 11:5 that at the present time there is a remnant of Israel in the church according to God's gracious election. Instead of teaching the rejec-tion of Israel, the Twelve actually look backward to the mercy of God to Is-rael before the church was founded and forward to his future mercy to Israel when "all Israel will be saved" (Rom. 11:26). The Twelve, therefore, do not take the place of Israel; they are true Israelites within Israel.[98]

The Temple

Writers like Fraeyman[99] and Wenschkewitz[100] view the "spiritualiza-tion" of the concepts of worship in the New Testament as implying the "spiritualization" of the term Israel.

This writer concedes that the Christian church is a temple, a habitation of God through the Spirit, a body of priests, living stones built upon the chief cornerstone, Jesus Christ, and a worshiping community that offers spiritual sacrifices to God (1 Cor. 3:16–17; 2 Cor. 6:16–7:1; 1 Pet. 2:4–10). Even a casual reading of the New Testament would convince anyone of these truths.

But the point at issue is the logical fallacy of assuming that the setting aside of Israel's temple in Jerusalem with its animal sacrifices and the re-placement by the one permanent sacrifice of Jesus Christ along with the liv-ing temple composed of redeemed saints necessitates the rejection of Israel and the "spiritualization" of the name Israel, also. The temple was a part of

97. R. Newton Flew, *Jesus and His Church* (London: Epworth, 1943), 38.
98. Richardson, 61.
99. M. Fraeyman, "La Spiritualisation de L'Idee du Temple dans les Epitres Paulini-ennes," *Ephemerides Theologicae Lovanienses*, 23 (1947): 378–412.
100. Hans Wenschkewitz, *Die Spiritualisierung der Kultusbegriffe: Temple, Priester, und Opfer im Neuen Testament* (Leipzig: Verlag von Eduard Pfeiffer, 1932), 166.

Israel's worship system. On the other hand, the church is God's temple. In other words, the temple is the church but the temple was not synonymous with Israel. While one of Israel's institutions was replaced, Israel herself has not been replaced. The form has been superseded (see also the parable of the garments and wineskins), but the people have not been superseded. At most the people have been reconstituted. McKelvey states that, "Christianity supersedes Judaism and Samaritanism, not because Christianity is spiritual and the other two are material, but because Christianity is centered in a person rather than in a place."[101] Jesus Christ replaces the stone temple of Israel with the people temple, the church. But the fact remains that it is the temple that is replaced, not Israel!

Summary

This section has investigated the problem of Israel's titles of honor that are also used of the church. Although all such Ehrentiteln could not be studied because of space limitation, the major ones were discussed, including people of God, seed of Abraham, ekklesia, circumcision, diaspora, Twelve, and temple. It was demonstrated that none of these terms that have applied to the church in the New Testament demands the replacement of Israel or the "spiritualization" of the term Israel. The term "seed of Abraham" was seen to be used of Abraham's physical seed, his spiritual seed within the physical, and his spiritual seed apart from the physical. Gentiles become spiritual seed of Abraham by virtue of their faith in Christ who is the ultimate seed of Abraham. The term ἐκκλησία simply means "assembly" and was probably a term used by Christians to distinguish themselves from the synagogue rather than a theological term meaning the "people of God" corresponding to קָהָל in the Old Testament. Circumcision through the coming of Christ was restored to its original significance for the Jewish believer. The Gentile believer in Christ experiences the same spiritual circumcision of heart that God had originally intended for the physically circumcised Jew in the Old Testament. The church as such is not the true circumcision over against Israel; they are the heart circumcision over against every form of rejection of Christ, whether Jew or Gentile. Christians are in a spiritual diaspora because, like Israel, God has ordained Christians to be pilgrims and sojourners upon the earth. This parallel in character between Israel and the church no more demands that the church equal Israel than do parallels between a horse and a giraffe demand that either is the other. The number twelve is significant for the selection of the disciples because they served as a nucleus of that faithful remnant within Israel at the time of Christ's ministry. In the church the Twelve are a part of the remnant of Israel. As such they furnish evidence that "God has not

101. R. J. McKelvey, *The New Temple* (London: Oxford University Press, 1969), 80.

rejected his people." He will bring the nation of Israel back to a place of salvation and blessing when the "Deliverer comes out of Zion." The New Testament teaching that the church is a temple is not a basis for some doctrine of the rejection of Israel. Instead, one of the institutions of Israel had to be replaced because Israel's Messiah offered the permanent sacrifice that made the sacrifices and the building in which they were offered obsolete. Although Jesus Christ replaced the temple, the church does not replace Israel.

It can be concluded that none of the foregoing expressions used of both Israel and the church proves or necessitates an identification of the two or substantiates the teaching that the Christian church is a new Israel.

The Problem of the New Testament Use of the Old Testament

The importance of the use of the Old Testament in the New Testament for New Testament theology has become increasingly recognized during recent years. The explosion of literature devoted to this subject during the last forty years shows that exegesis can no longer ignore or superficially examine the many Old Testament quotations and allusions used by the writers of the New Testament.

After all of the intensive work on this subject, one would expect some degree of unanimity among scholars. But there seems to be more disagreement than agreement on how one should approach the use of the Old Testament in the New Testament. For example, the recent debate in evangelical circles over the use of midrash by Matthew reflects the emotional intensity that can be generated among competent scholars and the consequences that can result from their disagreement over the use of midrash.[102]

One area of disagreement is the kind of inference one can draw from a New Testament writer's hermeneutical use of the Old Testament. If the New Testament writer seems to argue for direct fulfillment, does this prove that the New Testament writers interpret the Old Testament literally as some have argued? What inferences can be drawn if the usage is typological, rhetorical adaptation, gezerah shewa, pesher, or midrash? It is also very easy to jump to conclusions about the use of certain texts based upon certain theological presuppositions held by the interpreter. The amillennialist draws completely different inferences for his system than the dispensationalist does for his system. The writer has selected five passages for examination that are consistently quoted as key texts in the debate over Israel and the church. While these

---

102. See, e.g., Robert H. Gundry, *Matthew: A Commentary on His Literary and Theological Art* (Grand Rapids: Eerdmans, 1982). Gundry's defense of the use of midrash in the Gospel of Matthew led to his eventual expulsion from the Evangelical Theological Society.

texts are only representative of the larger problem, they do illustrate the problem of the use of the Old Testament in the New Testament.

Acts 2:16–21

THE NEW TESTAMENT CONTEXT

After his resurrection, Jesus Christ remained on earth for forty days speaking of the things pertaining to the kingdom of God. He told his disciples that they should not depart from Jerusalem but should wait for the fulfillment of the promise of the Father that Jesus told them they would receive (see also John 14:16–17; 16:7–15). This was the promise of the baptism in the Spirit (Acts 1:5). Upon reception of the Holy Spirit they would receive power to inaugurate the program of worldwide evangelization. After this forty-day period, Jesus was received up into heaven.

The disciples obeyed Jesus' command and returned to Jerusalem from Mt. Olivet to await the fulfillment of the promise. Ten days later, the Feast of Pentecost began. While they were all gathered together, they were filled with the Holy Spirit and began to speak in foreign languages. As a result, those who had gathered together from many nations into Jerusalem heard those who had been filled with the Spirit speaking the magnificent things of God in each one's own language, although the speakers were all Galileans. This caused great amazement and perplexity among those who beheld the phenomena as to an explanation. Some suggested that the speakers were drunken. In response to this accusation Peter stood up and boldly declared to the crowd that such an accusation was ridiculous because it was only nine o'clock in the morning. Peter's explanation was, "This is what was spoken by the prophet Joel."

THE OLD TESTAMENT CONTEXT

Peter quoted from Joel 2:28–32 (MT 3:1–5) to explain what had just occurred. Evidently there had been a plague of locusts in Joel's day that was part of the divine chastening upon Israel. Joel asked the old men whether they had ever seen or heard of such an invasion. The story of this invasion should be passed on to future generations. Four different stages of development of the locusts had completely desolated the land. The desolation had destroyed crops, starved cattle, cut off the source of the drunkards' wine, and caused a shortage of food in the temple. The people should lament over the terrible devastation. The priests were to mourn, repent, set apart a fast, and call an assembly of all the people to the house of the Lord.

Joel used this plague to foreshadow the day of the Lord. The locusts became a type of an invasion of heathen armies that the Lord would bring against Israel to execute judgment upon her and bring her to repentance.

The Lord promised that if Israel would turn in true repentance to him, deliverance would come, and the invading armies would be driven away and destroyed. The prosperity of the land and the rich blessing upon their crops would be restored, and the former and latter rains would be restored. Israel would know that the Lord was in the midst of Israel and that he alone was Israel's God. After this God would pour out his Spirit upon all flesh, signs would appear upon earth and in the heavens, and the day of the Lord would come. A remnant would call upon the name of the Lord and be delivered.

COMPARISON OF TEXTS

There are a number of textual differences between the New Testament, Septuagint, and the Masoretic text. The details of these differences have been discussed by Blanc.[103] The most important difference is Peter's substitution of "in the last days" for "after these things" of the Septuagint and "after thus" of the Masoretic text. This substitution was intended to make the time more definite, that is, the last days were the days in which Peter and the other Christians were living. Other important changes are the addition of "and they shall prophesy," "above," "signs," and "below" to the Septuagint text. These glosses show a "pesherizing" technique on the part of Peter.

THE HERMENEUTICAL USAGE

The problem is complicated by the meaning of "this is that" as an introductory formula. Since this is a very rare introductory formula in the New Testament, three different views have been proposed to explain it. One view sees a complete historical fulfillment of Joel on the day of Pentecost. Another view regards the events of Pentecost as simply an analogy to what will occur in the tribulation period and millennial age in relationship to Israel. A third view maintains that what occurred at Pentecost was a complete fulfillment of the pouring out of the Spirit and a partial fulfillment of the eschatological details.

This writer subscribes to the third view. The introductory formula is used in the Qumran scrolls as a pesher formula showing fulfillment of Old Testament texts in the community.[104] The additions to the Septuagint show that Peter is glossing the text to show fulfillment in the apostolic community where every level of the community was engaged in prophetic activity. Age, gender, and socioeconomic distinctions were no longer observed as the poured-out Spirit created the equality of the redeemed within the church.

On the other hand, there is no evidence in Acts 2 that the sun was transformed into darkness or the moon into blood on the day of Pentecost. Such

103. Ronald Lee Blanc, "An Exegesis of Peter's Quotation of the Joel Passage," (Th.M. thesis, Dallas Theological Seminary, 1964), 3–14.
104. Joseph A. Fitzmyer, *Essays on the Semitic Background of the New Testament* (Missoula, Mont.: Scholars, 1974), 12.

phenomena awaited the coming of the day of the Lord. Peter apparently quoted them in order to get to the last line of the prophecy: "And everyone who calls on the name of the Lord will be saved." This line from Joel provided a transition from the emphasis on Pneumatology to an emphasis on Christology that culminated in the invitation from Peter to his listeners to "invoke the name of the Lord [Jesus]."

THE THEOLOGICAL IMPLICATIONS

This partial fulfillment of Joel's prophecy does not equate the church with Israel or exhaust the content of the prophecy. Once again the faithful remnant of Jewish Christians are the recipients of the promise. The fact that Gentiles later share in the poured out Spirit does not make the church a new Israel. It proves again the contention of this writer that Gentiles share with Israel when they believe on Christ without becoming Israel. Even though these Gentiles partake of the "fatness" of the olive tree, from Romans 11:26 and many Old Testament passages it is clear that the then unbelieving portion of Israel will turn to the Lord at his second advent and enter into the blessings that believing Jews and Gentiles now share during this interim period. Partial fulfillment of Joel 2 on the day of Pentecost does not mean that Israel's promises are fulfilled completely in the church or that the church is some sort of Israel.

Acts 15:14–17

THE NEW TESTAMENT CONTEXT

The ministry of Paul and Barnabas to Gentiles on their first missionary journey had provoked a reaction on the part of legalistic Jewish Christians concerning the relationship of circumcision to the salvation of Gentiles. The burning issue resulted in the church at Antioch's sending Paul, Barnabas, and others up to Jerusalem to meet with the apostles and elders. Consequently the first Apostolic Council was held about A.D. 49 to decide the question.

Peter spoke first. He declared that it was through his mouth that the Gentiles had heard the message of the gospel and had believed. Then Barnabas and Paul related how God had done signs and wonders among the Gentiles through them. James stood up and called for a hearing. Peter, Barnabas, and Paul had just stated a truth that the Old Testament prophets had expounded: through the testimony of Israel Gentiles would hear God's message and come to the Lord. There was no need for a movement of Gentiles *into* Israel because the movement was *outward* to them. Circumcision was not needed because no incorporation into Israel was involved. Then James quoted Amos 9:11–12 to prove the point.

THE OLD TESTAMENT CONTEXT

In Amos 7:1–9:10 the prophet was given five visions concerning judgment upon Israel, including a vision of locusts, fire, plumb line, summer fruit, and smitten lintel. Through Amos's intercession judgment by locusts had been averted and judgment by fire had been delayed. However, because of Israel's continued wickedness, judgment could not be postponed any longer. This was indicated by the plumb line. Just as summer fruit is of short duration, Israel's judgment was imminent. Despite judgment, Israel would not be utterly destroyed since a remnant would be preserved. In a future day God would raise up the fallen tabernacle of David and Israel would possess the remnant of Edom and all the nations upon whom the Lord's name was invoked. Israel would be restored to the land to be plucked up no more.

COMPARISON OF TEXTS

The variations between the New Testament, Septuagint, and Masoretic texts are many and significant. The main changes are the substitution of "after these things" by James for the "in that day" of the Septuagint and the Masoretic text; the omission of "as the days of old" from James' text; the change of subject in the New Testament and Septuagint from "they" (Israel) in the Masoretic text to "the remnant of men;" the reading "men" in the Septuagint and the New Testament for "Edom" in the Masoretic text; the reading "seek" in the New Testament and Septuagint for "possess" in the Masoretic text; and the addition of "the Lord" and "known from of old" in the New Testament text.[105]

The writer believes that James deliberately altered the phrase, "in that day" to "after these things" to generalize the time period. James regarded his "day" as subsequent to Amos but not yet the day of the Lord. Therefore, he could not use the phrase, "in that day."

The phrase "hut of David" has received numerous interpretations.[106] The best interpretation in keeping with the lexicography and usage is the Davidic house in Amos's prophecy. The question is, What did this phrase indicate to James? A recent find at Qumran is the catena of messianic texts contained in the document 4Q Florilegium. This very phrase from Amos 9 is included in the catena of texts and receives the astonishing interpretation, "this is he who will arise and save Israel."[107] The Qumran community

---

105. See Michael A. Braun, "James' Use of Amos at the Jerusalem Council: Steps Toward a Possible Solution of the Textual and Theological Problems," *Journal of the Evangelical Theological Society*, 20, no. 2 (June 1977): 113–21.

106. See Walter C. Kaiser, Jr., "The Davidic Promise and the Inclusion of the Gentiles (Amos 9:9–15 and Acts 15:13–18): A Test Passage for Theological Systems," *Journal of the Evangelical Theological Society*, 20, no. 2 (June 1977): 101–102.

107. A. Dupont-Sommer, *The Essene Writings from Qumran* (Gloucester, Mass.: Peter Smith, 1973), 313.

interpreted the restored "hut of David" as the Messiah! Did James follow this same interpretation? One cannot be sure. It is possible that James interpreted the restored Davidic house as those Jewish Christians who had come to faith in Christ.

The omission of the phrase "as in the days of old" is critical at this point. James omitted this phrase because during his time this restoration to the state of "the days of old" had not yet taken place. Such a restoration awaited the return of Christ and the conversion of Israel (see also Acts 3:19–20). Then the kingdom would be restored to Israel and things would be as "in the days of old." But at this time in history only a remnant had believed and only part of the house had been restored. Consequently the restoration could only be partial until the whole nation turned to the Lord.

A grammatical point ignored in the discussion of this passage is the presence of ὅπως ἄν in Acts 15:17. This conjunction shows purpose. It also involves sequence; that is, event A must occur so that event B can take place. This grammatical point is, in the writer's opinion, indispensable to a proper exegesis of the passage. The "hut of David" had to be partially restored in either the resurrected Christ or the remnant of Jewish Christians in the church (or possibly both). The restored portion of Israel was the "A" in the sequence so that the purpose could be achieved in "B," the Gentiles who sought the Lord [Jesus] and had his name invoked upon them. It is crucial to note that the tabernacle of David is not equated with Gentiles. The tabernacle of David is rebuilt so that Gentiles. . . . Hence the tabernacle of David cannot be the Christian church composed of Jews *and* Gentiles. It should be also insisted that James was really not perverting the sense of the Masoretic text even if he was following a different Hebrew Vorlage behind the Septuagint text form.[108] The Masoretic text said that Israel would possess the remnant of Edom. Edom was generally recognized as representative of a wider circle of people. Even though Edom was not included in the church at present, the circle beyond Israel that Edom represented was coming to believe on the Lord Jesus *through* Israel. Cornelius had believed *through* Peter, and a large number of Gentiles had believed *through* Barnabas and Paul. Prophecy was in process of fulfillment!

THE HERMENEUTICAL USAGE

James's use of Amos 9 is another partial fulfillment of the Old Testament. James was trying to show that the present taking of some from the Gentiles to form a people for God's name was in harmony with the words of the prophets. According to Isaiah 43:10, 12; 44:8, Gentiles would find the

108. Braun, 117.

Lord through the testimony of Israel. Even though Old Testament Israel had largely failed in this divine mission, through the coming of Christ and his acquisition of a believing remnant within Israel, God was fulfilling his original purpose. On the day of Pentecost 3000 Jews were added to the church (Acts 2:41). The tabernacle of David was being restored and rebuilt. Through the ministry of the Palestinian and Antiochian Jewish Christians, Gentiles began to be saved. This salvation of the Gentiles through Israel's ministry (even though it was only a remnant of Israel) was in perfect harmony with the Old Testament, as James pointed out. But the tabernacle of Israel was only partially rebuilt since the majority of the nation had not yet believed. The completion of the building process awaited the return of Christ and the establishment of the millennial kingdom. In the meantime Gentile salvation did not preempt this process because salvation of Gentiles through the witness of Israel was an Old Testament theme. In fact, Paul would later use a similar line of reasoning when he stated that the salvation of Gentiles was intended to provoke the unbelieving portion of Israel to jealousy (Rom. 11:11).

This writer believes that the preceding exposition deals adequately with the quotation from Amos, explains the textual changes made by James, does not accuse James of perverting the Masoretic text, does not equate the tabernacle of David with the whole church, since the tabernacle is not Gentiles, and deals adequately with both the soteriological and eschatological questions in the minds of James's listeners.[109]

Romans 9:25–26

THE NEW TESTAMENT CONTEXT

After expressing his deep concern for the salvation of Israel, Paul sought to answer the objection that God's word had failed because Israel for the most part had not believed. He went on to demonstrate that God's promises involve election. This fact has been true throughout Israel's history. It can be seen in the choice of Isaac and Jacob as the seed through whom the promises would be fulfilled. It is evident in the choice of Pharaoh to demonstrate God's power and name. As the Creator and Redeemer, God is free to determine the destiny of his creatures. The created thing cannot accuse its Creator of malpractice. In all things God's choice is according to his will, not man's. The fact that God has called Gentiles as well as Jews is not proof of his fickleness, but of his mercy. The church is made up of both Jews and

---

109. For further support, see Lloyd Gaston, *No Stone on Another, Studies in the Significance of the Fall of Jerusalem in the Synoptic Gospels*, Supplement to Novum Testamentum, 23 (Leiden: Brill, 1970), 309; and Nils A. Dahl, " A People For His Name," *New Testament Studies*, 4 (1957–58): 324.

Gentiles. This inclusion of Gentiles is in keeping with a principle of God's dealings with people as found in Hosea.

THE OLD TESTAMENT CONTEXT

Paul's quotation is a composite of two texts: Hosea 1:10 and 2:23. Hosea 1–3 contains a personal illustration of Israel's covenant relationship with Yahweh. The command to Hosea to marry a woman who would become a harlot was given to portray vividly both to Hosea and to Israel the breach of covenant on the part of Israel due to Israel's idolatry. The three children born to Hosea were given symbolical names to portray the punishment that would come on Israel due to Israel's adulterous behavior. The reference to Genesis 22:17 in 1:10 (MT 2:1) shows that the promises concerning Abraham's seed demand that no cutting off of Israel can be final. Although Israel has broken the covenant at Sinai and the curses of the broken covenant will be executed if there is no repentance, yet both Israel and Judah will be gathered back to the covenanted land under one head, the Lord Jesus Christ. A promise of future restoration for Israel is also given (2:14–23; MT 2:16–25). Although Israel has forgotten Yahweh, he has not forgotten Israel. He will woo Israel again in the place of bondage. The valley of tribulation will become a door of hope. Yahweh will renew his covenant with his people. When the new relationship is established, Israel will know Yahweh in a close personal relationship and will acknowledge him for who he is: the faithful One. The covenantal blessings will again be poured out.[110]

COMPARISON OF TEXTS

Paul's quotation of Hosea 1:10 is in verbal agreement with the Septuagint and the Masoretic text with the exception of the addition of "there" in the New Testament and in the Septuagint. The Septuagint and the Masoretic texts of Hosea 2:23 are in verbal agreement, but Paul introduces a few minor changes. He substitutes "I will call" for "I will say"; he uses the accusative rather than the dative for "people"; and he transposes the clauses and substitutes "beloved" for "having received mercy." The only important variation seems to be the transposition of the clauses. The primary position of "not my people" emphasizes the mercy extended to the Gentiles.

THE HERMENEUTICAL USAGE

Once one grasps Paul's theology of salvation in Romans and Galatians, the hermeneutical usage in this passage is not difficult. Paul is applying a

---

110. Carl B. Hoch, Jr., "The Relation of Hosea's Prophecy to the Sinaitic Covenant" (Th.M. thesis, Dallas Theological Seminary, 1966), 33–34.

principle of divine action in these verses: God shows mercy and love to all those who turn to him in faith.[111] This is true for both Jews and Gentiles.[112] Paul's quote from Isaiah 28:16 in Romans 9:33 confirms this interpretation and applies the principle again: whoever believes on Jesus Christ, receives God's mercy and love. He will not be ashamed.

THE THEOLOGICAL IMPLICATIONS

Paul's theology is not one of substitution, but of extension. God's grace is extended to Gentiles through their faith in Christ. Jewish Christians enter into what belonged to Israel by covenant promise. They have never lost their status as people and they have never forfeited God's mercy. Only those within the nation who reject Christ are cut off from the olive tree of covenantal promise. They do not receive God's mercy, but his wrath (see also 1 Thess. 2:16). Gentiles were never people before Christ and were outside mercy. It is only because of faith that Gentiles become God's people and receive his mercy. Gentiles are a wild olive tree grafted into the olive tree because of faith. They do not replace Israel. They replace the unbelieving portion of Israel. This aspect of Paul's theology will be developed later when the olive tree of Romans 11 is discussed.

Hebrews 8:7–13

THE NEW TESTAMENT CONTEXT

Hebrews 8 is found in a section of the epistle where the writer is developing Christ as the High Priest according to the order of Melchizedek. After showing the superiority of Jesus Christ's priesthood after the order of Melchizedek to that of the order of Aaron (7:1–28), the writer of Hebrews then demonstrates Jesus' superiority to Aaron by virtue of the fact that Jesus is the mediator of a better covenant than the Mosaic covenant because the new covenant has been established upon better promises (8:6). The fact that the first covenant was imperfect necessitated the institution of the second covenant (8:7). The writer of Hebrews then quotes Jeremiah 31:31–34 because it contains the prophecy of the new covenant. After quoting Jeremiah, the writer concludes that the very adjective *new* has antiquated the *old* Mosaic covenant. This first covenant that is becoming obsolete and growing old is close to disappearing.

111. Bruce, *The Epistle of Paul to the Romans*, 196.
112. Gregory Baum, *Is The New Testament Anti-Semitic? A Re-Examination of the New Testament* (Glen Rock, N.J.: Paulist, 1965), 311–12.

THE OLD TESTAMENT CONTEXT

Jeremiah 31 falls in the section of the book containing prophetic messages concerning the captivity (Jer. 21:1–39:18). After the messages concerning the captivity (21:1–29:32), the prophet delivers messages announcing rest and deliverance (30:1–33:26). Jeremiah is instructed by the Lord to write in a book all the words the Lord has spoken to him. The Abrahamic covenant will be fulfilled in a future day when God restores his people to the land. This restoration will be preceded by the time of Jacob's trouble in which Israel will suffer as a woman in labor. Israel, however, will be saved out of this time. Although she will be punished, God will preserve her and judge the nations. Israel will be punished for its unconfessed sin and the nations for their treatment of Israel. Jerusalem will be rebuilt and the nation's captivity turned. All of this will take place in the latter days. Israel will be restored because of Yahweh's love for her. A remnant will be recovered from universal dispersion. All nations will acknowledge that Yahweh is a shepherd to Israel. The land will prosper and Israel will attach herself to her Messiah in worship and in loyalty. God will make a new covenant with Israel and Judah. This covenant will not be like the Mosaic covenant, but will be one in which God's law is written on men's hearts. All of God's people will know him and he will forgive their sins. This covenant will continue as long as the sun and the moon shine. Jerusalem will be rebuilt, be holy, and will never be thrown down again.

COMPARISON OF TEXTS

There are a few minor variations between the text of Hebrews and the Septuagint, but both texts are essentially in verbatim agreement with the Masoretic text.

THE HERMENEUTICAL USAGE

The standard amillennial position is that since the new covenant was to be made with Israel and Judah and the new covenant was made with the church, then the logical conclusion must be that the church is Israel and Judah.[113] In reaction to this amillennial contention, classic dispensationalism has posited two new covenants: one with Israel and Judah, first and primary; a second with the church, secondary and hardly as significant as the one with Israel and Judah.[114]

---

113. Oswald T. Allis, *Prophecy and the Church* (Philadelphia: Presbyterian and Reformed, 1964), 154–56.
114. Charles C. Ryrie, *The Basis of the Premillennial Faith* (Neptune, N.J.: Loizeaux, 1953), 118.

Bell has presented a third interpretation that does not require two new covenants and that does not at the same time equate the church with Israel. Bell set forth seven propositions at the beginning of his thesis:

1. The Bible speaks of a new covenant to be instituted with Israel and Judah subsequent to the days of Jeremiah, a covenant that will essentially be in contrast with the old Mosaic covenant.
2. The New Testament speaks of a new covenant that was operative then and now, of which Christ is said to be the Mediator and of which Christians are said to be the ministers.
3. The new covenant that the New Testament declares to be presently operative was announced by Jesus Christ in the upper room on the eve of his death and became operative the next day when he died on the cross.
4. The new covenant instituted by Jesus Christ is the same new covenant spoken of in the Old Testament, particularly in Jeremiah 31, and it was instituted with Israel and Judah as prophesied. The New Testament gives evidence of no other new covenant.
5. The Israelites with whom the new covenant was instituted did not forfeit their covenantal status when they were baptized into the body of Christ on the day of Pentecost. Rather they constitute a part of the remnant spoken of in Romans 11:5.
6. Gentile believers today share in the provisions of the new covenant as a result of their admission to the body of Christ as "fellow citizens with the saints" no longer "strangers from the covenants of promise."
7. Some aspects of the new covenant are yet unfulfilled and await the second advent of Jesus Christ, at which time "all Israel shall be saved" and shall participate in the blessings of the new covenant in the millennial age and in the eternal state.[115]

If Bell's seven theses are correct, then the usage of the Old Testament here in Hebrews is parallel with Peter's use of Joel in Acts 2. The soteriological details of Old Testament prophecy are being fulfilled during the present age to believing Jews within the church and extended to Gentiles within the church on an equal basis with believing Jews. The eschatological fulfillment of other details such as the land awaits the future turning of the unbelieving portion of Israel to the Messiah at his second advent.

115. William Everett Bell, Jr., "The New Covenant" (Th.M. thesis, Dallas Theological Seminary, 1963), 10–11.

1 Peter 2:9–10

This passage is used with almost as much regularity as Galatians 6:16 to prove that the church is Israel.

THE NEW TESTAMENT CONTEXT

After outlining the hope and inheritance that believers have in Jesus Christ (1 Pet. 1:3–12), Peter then exhorts his readers to set their hope on the coming of Christ, to holiness of life, and love for the brethren (1:13–25). This love for one another will be achieved through laying aside the things of the former life and growth in the Christian life (2:1–2). The growth is to be collective because of the nature of the community: it is a building composed of living stones who are being built into a spiritual house, a holy priesthood that offers acceptable spiritual sacrifices to God through Jesus Christ. Peter uses a catena of Old Testament texts (Isa. 28:16; Ps. 118:12; and Isa. 8:14) to show that the foundation of the building laid in Zion, rejected by some, was chosen by God and brings honor to those who believe on him (1 Pet. 2:3–8). In contrast to those who stumble at the word of prophecy that makes Jesus the chief cornerstone are those who believe and thus are an elect race, a royal house, a body of priests, a holy nation, and a people for God's possession. Although they were not a people formerly, now they are God's people; formerly they did not receive God's mercy, but now they do (2:9–10). The character of those who believe on Christ is derived from three Old Testament passages: Isaiah 43:20; Exodus 19:5–6, and Hosea 2:23.

THE OLD TESTAMENT CONTEXTS

Isaiah 43 contains the fourth sermon of the section 40:1–66:24 and promises Israel "blessed restoration, issuing from his love and operating by redemption." God will crush the Chaldeans and restore Israel, his chosen people. Exodus 19 is an account of God's words to Moses before instituting the old covenant. Moses was to tell Israel that if they would keep Yahweh's covenant, then they would be a peculiar treasure from all the peoples, a kingdom of priests, and a holy nation to him. After Moses delivered this message, Israel responded that they would do all that the Lord had spoken. The context of Hosea 2:23 has already been outlined under Romans 9:25–26 and will not be repeated here.

All three of these passages have a very interesting connection. All deal with the Mosaic covenant: Exodus with its institution; Isaiah and Hosea with its breach and renewal. Isaiah 42:10 speaks of the work of the Servant in terms of a light to the Gentiles. This ministry is closely connected with Israel's function as a kingdom of priests and holy nation (Exod. 19:6). Israel was to be Yahweh's witnesses and chosen servant (Isa. 43:10). She was to offer sacrifice as part of the covenant (Exod. 20:24). Yet Israel had sacrificed to idols (Hos. 4:13; Isa. 43:23–28). Because of this debased worship, Israel had broken covenant. As a result they would remain many days without sacrifice (Hos. 3:4). And yet Israel will repent and be restored to a place of blessing (Hos. 3:5; 14:4–9).

COMPARISON OF TEXTS

The composite nature of the quote makes comparison difficult. Peter is extracting, combining, adding, and subtracting. One omission seems to be the "my" from "race" in Isaiah 43 and from "people" in Hosea 2:23. The "my" is retained by Paul in Romans 9:26, so Peter's omission may not have been intentional. The substitution of "declare" for "relate" was probably made because the former word was more appropriate to the proclamation of the gospel.[116] The participle "have received mercy" is not found in Hosea, but it still is a part of the sense. The phrase "people belonging to God" is actually not present in any of the texts but is implied in "my people."

THE HERMENEUTICAL USAGE

It is generally recognized that Peter is "steeped in the Old Testament."[117] This truth is immediately apparent from the manner in which Peter has extracted and combined phrases and words in these verses. A glance at the boldface type of the Nestle text of the Petrine Epistles will readily convince anyone of Peter's debt to the Old Testament. A passage such as 3:10–12 (a quote from Ps. 34:12–16) indicates that Peter used the Old Testament in a rhetorical and typological sense. The word ἀντίτυπος in 3:21 again shows that he can use the Old Testament typically. One should therefore exercise caution before jumping to conclusions about the manner in which Peter is using these Old Testament texts here.

It is this writer's view that Peter is using typology between Israel and the church in this passage. Cranfield notes that the word "elect" is used in the Old Testament of Israel, the Servant of the Lord, the faithful remnant, David, Solomon, Zerubbabel, and others.[118] Does it follow that the church is a "new or "true" David, Solomon, or Zerubbabel simply because the same word is used of these Old Testament saints as is used of the church?

If the kingdom was taken away from the portion of Israel who rejected Christ and given to those who believe on him (Matt. 21:43), it follows that the church will do what Israel was called to do if it is to "bring forth the fruits" of this kingdom. Since Israel failed in its missionary vocation, this

116. Beare, 105.
117. William Barclay, *The Letters of James and Peter* (Philadelphia: Westminster, 1960), 234.
118. C. E. B. Cranfield, *I & II Peter and Jude* (London: SCM, 1960), 63–64.

vocation has become the church's responsibility. To maintain such a witness, the church functions as a body of priests to all of humankind just as Israel was supposed to function. The church is like Israel without being Israel. In other words, the pattern (τύπος) that God established in Israel is recapitulated in the church who is the ἀντίτυπος.

This writer concludes, therefore, that Peter is not calling the church a "new Israel," a term he could have easily used, when he combined Isaiah 43, Exodus 19, and Hosea 2:23 in 1 Peter 2:9–10. Peter's purpose was to show that the church is called to exercise those spiritual functions that it was equipped to do as the dwelling place of the Spirit. As a community indwelt by the Spirit, elect of God, the church was to preach the gospel of the One who called it out of darkness into his marvelous light. Thus the hermeneutical usage of the Old Testament is typological.

SUMMARY

The argument that the New Testament use of the Old Testament demonstrates that the Christian church has become the "new Israel" taking over all the titles and privileges of the old Israel has been examined. The five main passages adduced to prove the equation of the church with Israel have been investigated in terms of the New Testament context, the Old Testament context, the comparison of texts, and the hermeneutical usage. It was discovered that the New Testament writers used the Old Testament in a variety of ways.

A study of Acts 2:16–21 showed that the events of Pentecost were a partial fulfillment of Joel's prophecy concerning the pouring out of the Spirit. The future eschatological fulfillment of the astronomical upheaval and the day of the Lord awaits the return of Christ when the unbelieving portion of ethnic Israel will enter into the blessing that believing Jews and Gentiles now share during the interim.

James's use of Amos 9 in Acts 15:14–17 was classified as a partial fulfillment of the rebuilding of the tabernacle of David through those from ethnic Israel and the resurrected Christ that were the nucleus of the church. This remnant of Israel within the church was beginning to fulfill the Old Testament prophecies that promised that the nations of the earth would find the true God through the witness of Israel. The complete restoration of the tabernacle of David awaits the return of the unbelieving portion of Israel to the Lord Jesus at his second advent.

When Paul used Hosea 1:10 and 2:23 in Romans 9:25–26 in describing Gentiles, he was using a principle he saw inherent in God's dealings with men, namely, those who walk before him in faith are regarded as his people and experience his mercy and love despite their ethnic origin. Gentiles who believe on Jesus Christ as a result of this principle become God's people. The new covenant of Jeremiah 31 quoted in Hebrews 8:7–13 was instituted with those Jewish disciples of Jesus Christ in the upper room on the eve of his death and became operative the next day when he died on the cross. Gentiles believers share along with believing Jews in the blessings of Israel's new covenant. These blessings are primarily soteriological during this present age. The eschatological blessings await the time when "all Israel will be saved" through faith in Jesus as Messiah at his second advent.

The typological use of Isaiah 43, Exodus 19, and Hosea 2 in 1 Peter 2:9–10 shows that the church has been called to fulfill a mission for God similar to Israel's mission. This mission can be described with words formerly used of Israel. The fact that the same pattern is used of Israel and the church shows their typological relationship, not their generic relationship.

This writer concludes, therefore, that the use of the Old Testament in the New Testament does not create a wide gulf between Israel and the church, as classic dispensational writers have advocated, but neither does it permit the equation of the Christian church, composed of believing Jews and Gentiles, with a new or true Israel.

Miscellaneous Issues

This section will investigate the remaining matters that have a bearing on the question whether the name Israel is ever emptied of its ethnic sense in the New Testament.

The Remnant

In the writer's opinion, a biblical theme that has received scant notice in biblical studies outside of the monograph on the theme in the Old Testament, primarily in Isaiah, by Gerhard Hasel[119] is the term *remnant*. The idea of a remnant is important because of its introduction by Paul into his discussion of Israel in Romans 11:5. This is the only New Testament occurrence of λεῖμμα. A compound, ὑπόλειμμα, is found in Romans 9:27. The thought of the remnant as a theological concept stems from the prophets, particularly Isaiah. This remnant in the Old Testament is that remainder of faithful believers within Israel after the sifting and separating process of judgment has taken place. The establishment and preservation of the remnant are based upon the zeal, righteousness, grace, mercy, help, and forgiveness of God. The remnant is commonly linked with Jerusalem or Zion. It is eschatologically related to the Messiah. According to Schrenk, "Paul makes use of only a small part of the great prophetic heritage."[120]

---

119. Gerhard Hasel, *The Remnant* (Berrien Springs, Mich.: Andrews University Press, 1974).
120. Gottlob Schrenk, and Volkmar Herntrich, "λεῖμμα," in *Theological Dictionary of the New Testament*, ed. Gerhard Kittel, 10 vols. (Grand Rapids: Eerdmans, 1967), 4:209.

Although the idea of a remnant is a major theme of the prophets, Paul states that the concept of a remnant was present in Elijah's day (Rom. 11:2–4). Further, in the light of Paul's discussion and summary in Romans 9:27–29, Israel has always had a remnant who were true Israelites.

According to Hasel, there has been a remnant throughout the Old Testament. This remnant began in Genesis with people like Abel who obeyed God in contrast to Cain who murdered Abel. This remnant continued throughout history as God preserved a few in times of apostasy or many as in the times of prosperity under Joshua who sought to do God's will. This remnant continued on into the New Testament period with godly Jews like Zecharias and Elizabeth who were blameless because they lived according to the commandments and requirements of the Lord (Luke 1:6). It expanded through the many followers of Jesus who believed that he was the Messiah. It continued in the church first through the Twelve and then through all those Jews in the first nine chapters of Acts who believed the gospel and were added to the church. This Jewish remnant was proof that God had not rejected his people (Rom. 11:1). The remnant will be enlarged to include the majority of the nation of Israel at the second advent of Christ (Rom. 11:26). This enlargement will be in fulfillment of Old Testament prophecy (Isa. 10:20–24; Jer. 23:3–6; Ezek. 34:11–16; 37:21–28; Zech. 8:1–8; 12; 14). This remnant forms a part of the church during this age, but it is not the whole church because Gentiles do not form a part of this remnant. According to Schrenk and Herntrich, this remnant will give way to "all Israel" after the "fullness" of the Gentiles has come in (Rom. 11:25).[121]

The doctrine of the remnant thus teaches that the church composed of both believing Jews and Gentiles is not a new or other kind of Israel, although a remnant of Israel composed of Jewish Christians is present in the church. At the same time, it provides substance to the view that ethnic believing Israel has a future, unless the ability of God to accomplish such a goal is denied. According to Richardson, the remnant shows that "the rest of Israel, far from being totally rejected, is only temporarily put to one side (Rom. 11:11ff.)."[122]

The Σύν-*Compounds*

One of the most neglected areas, in the writer's opinion, that has a significant contribution to make to the problem under discussion are the σύν-compounds in the New Testament.[123] These σύν-compounds clearly indi-

121. Ibid., 4:211–12.
122. Richardson, 135 n. 5.
123. Carl B. Hoch, Jr., "The Significance of the 'Syn'-Compounds for Jew-Gentile Relationships in the Body of Christ," *Journal of the Evangelical Theological Society*, 25, (June 1982): 175–83.

cate the position of the Gentile in relation to the Jew in the church. That position is one of equality and sharing. There is no hint of substitution or replacement of Israel en toto by Gentiles or a neutralizing of Israel in the church. The Gentiles are only substituted in place of the unbelieving part of Israel (Rom. 11:17–24). But they share with the believing portion of Israel in the church in Israel's covenants and blessings.

The σύν-compounds are most frequent in Ephesians. According to Ephesians 2:19 Gentiles are fellow citizens (συμπολῖται) with Jewish Christians. Verse 21 speaks of all the building composed of Jews and Gentiles as being joined together (συναρμολογουμένη) and growing into a holy temple in the Lord. The inclusion of the Gentiles in this building is stressed by the σύν-compound, συνοικοδομεῖσθε, in verse 22. Paul does not stop here; he goes on in chapter three to continue his discourse on the place of the Gentiles. He uses three compounds in 3:6 to underscore the equality of Gentiles with believing Jews in the body of Christ: "fellow heirs" (συγκληρονόμα), "of the same body" (σύσσωμα), and "fellow sharers" (συμμέτοχα). Paul employed rare words to express this new relationship that was a mystery in former generations. Συναρμολογέομαι in 2:21 is not found again apart from Paul.[124] Συγκληρονόμος, σύσσωμος, and συμμέτοχος are rare words. Robinson suggests that σύσσωμος was perhaps formed by Paul for this occasion.[125] Barth states that "Ephesians is outstanding among the Pauline epistles because of the number of daring combinations of the Greek preposition *syn* ('with', 'together with', 'same') with nouns and verbs (2:19–22; 3:6; 4:3, 16)."[126]

Another important passage where this sharing with believing Jews is found is Romans 11:17. There the Gentiles are said to be a fellow sharer (συγκοινωνός) of the root of fatness of Israel's olive tree.

A third important, but neglected passage, is Romans 15:7–13. The details of this section have been developed by this writer in a separate paper.[127] The key verse is verse 10, where Paul exhorts the Gentiles to rejoice "together with" (μετά) his people, Israel, by citing Deuteronomy 32:43.

The reason why Gentiles can be spoken of as sharing with believing Israel is that the Gentiles, like believing Jews are in Christ. The numerous uses of the preposition σύν demonstrate this truth beyond dispute. Christians have died with Christ (Rom. 6:8; Gal. 2:20; Col. 2:20), shall rise and have risen with Christ (2 Cor. 4:14; Col. 2:12–13), have their life hidden with Christ in

124. J. Armitage Robinson, *St. Paul's Epistle to the Ephesians* (London: James Clarke, n.d.), 166.

125. Ibid., 169.

126. Markus Barth, *Israel and the Church* (Richmond: John Knox, 1969), 92. Barth has been very helpful in determining the relationship between Israel and the church.

127. Carl B. Hoch, Jr., "Romans 15:7–13: A Neglected Passage in Discussions Concerning the Relationship Between Israel and the Church" (unpublished paper read at the meeting of the Midwest Section of the Evangelical Theological Society, March, 1989).

God (Col. 3:3), shall be manifested in glory with Christ (Col. 3:4), and those who have fallen asleep will return with Christ (1 Thess. 4:14).

Rather than teaching a replacement of Israel by Gentiles, the uses of σύν separately and in compound in the New Testament, particularly Ephesians, indicate a *sharing with* the believing portion from Israel in all that Christ accomplished and inaugurated. According to Ephesians 3, this equality between Jew and Gentile was not revealed in former times but is a distinct New Testament revelation concerning the body of Christ, the church. Although the Jew has no claim on God's favor in a soteriological sense, it is still true that the Jew and Israel stood in a covenant relationship with God and had certain privileges not enjoyed by the Gentile (Eph. 2:11–22). To deny this truth is to ignore Romans 3:1–3; 9:4–6, and to make Paul's list of Israel's privileges in Ephesians 2:12 completely superfluous. Israel's privileges were not discontinued when the church was inaugurated. On the contrary, Jewish Christians enter the fulfillment of these privileges as true Israelites, and Gentile Christians through faith in Israel's Messiah *share with* them. The unbelieving portion of the nation Israel will also enter into these covenantal privileges when they turn in faith to Jesus Christ at his second advent (Acts 3:19–20; Rom. 11:26).

Problem Passages

MATTHEW 21:43

A common interpretation of this verse as part of the parable of the wicked husbandmen is that the nation of Israel has been rejected forever in favor of a new people of God, the new Israel or the Christian church.[128] While common, this interpretation is not universally accepted. According to Lovsky, the parable does not teach the rejection of the vineyard, that is, Israel as a people, but rather of the religious rulers of Israel, the vinedressers.[129]

A survey of various works reveals that there are three views of the "nation" (ἔθνος; NIV "people") in verse 43. The first view holds that the nation is the disciples.[130] This interpretation has received little support because of the absence of any designation of the disciples as a nation elsewhere in the New Testament. A second view has suggested that the nation is the faithful Jewish remnant living at the second advent of Christ.[131] The

---

128. James Calvin DeYoung, *Jerusalem in the New Testament* (Kampen: Kok, 1960), 77ff.

129. F. Lovsky, "Remarques sur la nation de rejet par rapport au mystere d'Israel et a l'unite de l'Eglise," *Revue d'histoire et de philosophie religieuses*, 43 (1963): 39.

130. Martin Kiddle, "The Conflict Between the Disciples, the Jews, and the Gentiles in St. Matthew's Gospel," *Journal of Theological Studies*, 36 (Jan. 1935): 34.

131. A. C. Gaebelein, *The Gospel of Matthew, An Exposition* (New York: Our Hope Publications Office, 1910), 2:138.

weakness of this view is found in the fact that Matthew elsewhere in his Gospel uses nation of Gentiles, not Israel. The claim that nation is used of Israel in John 11:48, 50, 51, and 52 is offset by the fact that the church (including Gentiles) is called a nation in 1 Peter 2:9 and in Romans 10:19. The third view, that the nation is any body of people on the face of the earth who brings forth the righteous fruits of the kingdom seems to be the best view. Either Jewish or Gentile Christians qualify for the nation who are given the kingdom.

Is it to be concluded, then, that the church has received the kingdom so that it has replaced Israel forever? A negative answer can be supported from the following considerations. Matthew 23:39 indicates that Israel has not been rejected forever. The vineyard will be rented (Matt. 21:43, ἐκδώσεται) to other farmers who will repay the Lord of the vineyard with the required fruits in their seasons. The vineyard is not an exclusive possession of the farmers. It belongs to its owner. The possession of the vineyard will depend on the faithfulness of the farmers. The "nation" will possess the kingdom only as long as it produces the fruits of it. This responsibility is also taught in Romans 11:19–21. The passages in the rest of the New Testament that teach the apostasy of many in the church (1 Tim. 4:1–3; 2 Tim. 3:1–5; 4:3–4; 2 Pet. 2:1–22; 3:3–6; Jude 1–25) show that care of the vineyard is not unconditional but conditional only on faithfulness to the owner. Luke 18:8 seems to teach that faith will be a precious commodity when the Son of man returns.

It is concluded that this verse teaches that the kingdom of God belongs to those who bring forth its fruits. During the interim a faithful remnant within Israel and believing Gentiles bring forth those fruits. Therefore the kingdom belongs to them. But the verse allows for a future exclusion of any who stop producing the fruits and a future inclusion of those who repent and begin to produce fruit. When unbelieving Israel once more brings forth the fruit of the kingdom, then the kingdom will be given back to her. Paul's teaching in Romans 11 clearly supports this understanding.

JOHN 10:16

This verse has been employed to support the view that the church is a "new Israel." The statement, "I have other sheep which are not of this fold" is interpreted to imply that Gentiles are incorporated into Israel. The one flock with one Shepherd is therefore the new Israel. But Bligh proposes another interpretation. Since John does not use the Greek verb εἰσάγω for the relationship of the other sheep to the flock, the Gentiles are not brought into Israel. On the contrary, the sheep are to be combined into one flock under one shepherd, outside the fold of Israel. The Gentiles are not gathered into the fold of Israel. Jews out of Israel and Gentiles out of heathendom are gathered into one flock, the church.[132]

Instead of teaching a doctrine of the church as some sort of Israel, this verse teaches the same truth that this writer has proposed throughout this entire discussion: a remnant from Israel join Gentiles who believe on Jesus Christ to share a common salvation on an equal basis in the church, not in Israel (see also Eph. 2:14–17).

GALATIANS 3:28

Those who assert that the terms Israel and church are interchangeable in the New Testament often appeal to Galatians 3:28 to support the view that all distinctions on every level are completely eliminated since the advent of Jesus Christ. Pentecost denies the existence of a remnant of the nation of Israel within the church because "in the body of Christ all national distinctions disappear."[133] The conclusion of this understanding of Galatians 3:28 is that Israel and Gentiles are emptied of their historic significance and Israel especially becomes a purely theological term.

If this exegesis is correct, it is strange that Paul can still say, "I am an Israelite myself, a descendant of Abraham, from the tribe of Benjamin" (Rom. 11:1). If all distinctions on every level are obliterated in Christ, then why should Paul even bother about his membership in the tribe of Benjamin?

That Galatians 3:28 is speaking of distinctions in terms of soteriology is clear not only exegetically, but logically. Even though slaves and freedmen, male and female are included along with Jew and Gentile in the body of Christ, Paul continues to address slaves and masters, children and parents, men and women as distinct groups within the church, even using the generic article with each group to set them off as a class (Col. 3:18–4:1 et passim). These groups do not lose their positions within society nor cease playing their roles within society. [134]

In Galatians 3:28 Paul is saying that no one, neither Jew, Gentile, slave, freedman, male, or female can claim his or her nationality, station in life, or gender before God as a basis for special consideration in terms of salvation.

---

132. John Bligh, "The Church and Israel According to St. John and St. Paul," *Studiorum Paulinorum Congressus International Catholicus*, Analecta Biblica, 17–18, Vol. 1 (Rome: E Pontifico Instituto Biblico, 1963), 152.

133. J. Dwight Pentecost, *Things to Come, A Study in Biblical Eschatology* (Findlay, Ohio: Dunham, 1958), 293.

134. Markus Barth, "Conversion and Conversation—Israel and the Church in Paul's Epistle to the Ephesians," *Interpretation*, 17 (1963): 6.

1 THESSALONIANS 2:16

Amillennialists appeal to this verse continually to prove that ethnic Israel is set aside forever in the program of God and that the church has replaced Israel as the "Israel of God."

The two exegetical problems present in the verse are the classification of the aorist ἔφθασεν and the meaning of the phrase εἰς τέλος. There is disagreement over whether the aorist is proleptic or consummative. Τέλος is difficult to assess semantically because it can mean "completely," "continually," "forever," and "at last."[135]

It is not necessary to make a clear-cut decision about the above two problems. Paul is not talking about all Jews. He is distressed by the opposition that unbelieving Jews have caused to the preaching of the gospel. God's wrath will come (proleptic aorist) or has come (consummative aorist) completely, at last, or to the end upon this resistant group. This verse does not suggest that *all* Israel has been rejected or that the church has become the new or true Israel. The objects of Paul's heated remarks are identical with the branches who have been cut off in the olive tree figure of Romans 11. Some branches have been cut off, but the tree has not been cut down!

It can be concluded that none of the matters discussed in this appendix requires the equation of the term Israel with the church. On the contrary, the concept of a remnant argues for a future for ethnic Israel and the σύν-compounds show that Gentiles share with believing Jews in the fulfillment of Israel's covenants and privileges through faith in Jesus Christ.

Paul's Teaching in Romans 11   ↑ *True Redemptively*

The Argument of Romans 11:1–14

There is a general agreement among commentators concerning Paul's argument in the first 14 verses of Romans 11 with disagreement over the details. The essential thrust of Paul's argument is as follows. After asking the rhetorical question, "Did God reject his people?" Paul continues to outline the reasons why Israel's rejection is only partial in verses 1–10 and only temporary in verses 11–32. The first reason Paul advances for God not having rejected his people is that Paul himself as a Jewish Christian is still a member of the covenant people. A second reason is that Israel is God's elect, covenant people whom God had promised in his Word that he would not cast off (1 Sam. 12:22; Ps. 94:14; see also Jer. 31:37). A third reason for the nonrejection of Israel is the grace of God displayed in the preservation of a remnant throughout the times of national apostasy. In Elijah's day 7000 within Israel

---

135. James Everett Frame, *A Critical and Exegetical Commentary on the Epistles of St. Paul to the Thessalonians,* ICC (Edinburgh: T. & T. Clark, 1912), 114.

had not bowed the knee to Baal (1 Kings 19:10, 14, 18). Thus at the present time the apparent repudiation of Israel is not necessarily more absolute or final than it was in Elijah's time. The proof of this is that there is a remnant of Israel within the church composed of Jewish believers in Christ. This present remnant shows that God continues his faithfulness to his people.

This election, however, is entirely of grace, not of works. Since works could not avail, that portion within the nation who exercised faith attained righteousness, while the rest of the nation were hardened. Unbelief and hardening within Israel are nothing new. God's hardening of Israel in Paul's day is simply parallel to that in the days of Moses and Isaiah (Deut. 29:4; Isa. 29:10). As David said in Psalm 69:22–24, the wrath of God is against those who have made themselves enemies of his will. Those who in David's day were the enemies of God's people are typical of those Jews in Paul's day who have shut their ears to the gospel and have made their ritualistic worship the basis for their confidence.

Lest anyone suggest that the hardening of the majority of the nation Israel results in a frustration of God's purposes and covenant with his people, Paul asks, "Did they stumble so as to fall beyond recovery?" (Rom. 11:11). Paul replies, "Not at all!" God turned tragedy into blessing. As a result of Israel's transgression, salvation was extended to the Gentiles (see also Acts 13:45–49; 28:28). Moreover, the salvation of Gentiles was intended to provoke the unbelieving portion of Israel to jealousy. If the transgression of Israel resulted in worldwide blessing and their diminishing to a small number of believers brought spiritual riches to the Gentiles, what blessing and riches to the world will their restoration to the complete state of a people mean?

Paul continues by reminding the Gentiles that his ministry among them has an ulterior motive: the salvation of Israel. The more Paul makes of his ministry among the Gentiles, the more jealous will the Jews become and this will ultimately lead to their salvation. The conversion of Israel will in turn lead to a worldwide spiritual resurrection (ζωὴ ἐκ νεκρῶν). Such a view of Israel's relationship to the world is in perfect harmony with the Old Testament portrayal of Israel in the millennial age (Isa. 61:6; Jer. 16:19–21; Zeph. 3:20; Zech. 8:20–23; 14:16–21).

The Olive Tree

The further one progresses in Romans 11, the less unanimity one finds among commentators and writers in terms of Paul's teaching. A case in point is the interpretation of the olive tree. One of the difficulties facing any interpretation of the olive tree is a delineation of the symbolism. The tree is said to represent Israel,[136] true Israel,[137] the Israel of God,[138] true people

136. Anders Nygren, *Commentary on Romans* (Philadelphia: Fortress , 1949), 399.
137. Allis, 109.
138. George Johnston, *The Doctrine of the Church in the New Testament* (Cambridge: At the University Press, 1943), 78.

of God,[139] God's chosen people,[140] the continuing permanent covenant community,[141] the body of those in whom the grace of Christ has been truly operative,[142] the church in history,[143] the mystical body of Christ,[144] the place of privilege,[145] the kingdom of God,[146] and the Abrahamic covenant.[147]

Younce has attempted to cut a swath through this interpretive jungle. He demonstrates that the tree cannot represent the church for the following reasons:

1. Gentile Christians could not be threatened with the possibility of severance from the church;
2. the word "church" is not mentioned in the passage;
3. the argument of the passage is to show the future of Israel as a nation and to allay Gentile pride;
4. such a view obliterates all distinction between Israel and the church.

Younce shows that the tree cannot be Israel since Israel cannot be both the tree, the branches, and distinguished from itself (Rom. 11:26). If Israel is intended by the figure, then the Gentiles would become Jews. Yet Gentiles are distinguished from Israel and Jews in the passage. Further, fatness (v. 17, πιότης, "fatness, richness"; NIV "nourishing sap") does not refer to salvation but to blessing. Younce also maintains that the tree cannot be the place of privilege because this definition is too broad. It would apply to anyone related favorably to God. On the other hand, the context shows that the olive tree is something specifically Jewish (see also 11:24, "their own olive tree"). Younce's conclusion is that the tree is the Abrahamic covenant, the root is Abraham (11:28), the natural branches are the nation of Israel, and the wild branches are the Gentiles. Therefore, the "fat root" denotes the opportunity of spiritual relationship to Abraham.[148]

139. Flew, 151.
140. Kugelman, 218.
141. Pieters, 89.
142. H. L. Ellison, *The Mystery of Israel* (London: Paternoster, 1966), 89.
143. James I. Packer, "The Nature of the Church," in *Basic Christian Doctrines*, ed. Carl F. H. Henry (New York: Holt, Reinhart and Winston, 1962), 242.
144. Bourke, viii.
145. Charles C. Ryrie, *Biblical Theology of the New Testament* (Chicago: Moody, 1959), 214.
146. Bourke, 77.
147. Dale Richard Younce, "An Exegetical Interpretation of the Figure of the Olive Tree of Romans Eleven" (Th.M. thesis, Dallas Theological Seminary, 1963), 53. See also Carl B. Hoch, Jr., "The Significance of the 'Syn'-Compounds," 182.
148. Younce, 40–53.

That the olive tree figure teaches only the rejection of the unbelieving portion of Israel rather than the nation itself is made clear by Nygren. He notes that if Israel were cut off, "we might have expected a different illustration, that God had the unfruitful tree cut down, and in its place planted a new one by the hand of Christ." [149]

The Place of the Gentiles

It is this writer's conviction that Romans 11 is as important in understanding the place of the Gentiles in God's program as it is for Israel's place. The themes presented here regarding the Gentiles are echoed and enlarged upon elsewhere in the New Testament. These parallels will be taken up later, but the teaching in Romans 11 must be examined first.

The first point to be noticed is that only some of the branches of Israel have been broken off (Rom. 11:27). The Gentiles as a wild olive tree have been grafted in among the believing Israelites in place of the unbelieving portion. That the apostle is talking about the Gentiles as a group rather than as individuals is seen by the contrast between Gentiles as a group and Jews as a group. The believing Gentiles as a group replace the unbelieving Jews as a group. From this statement it may be deduced that the Gentiles were made partakers in something of which they were not partakers previously, while a part of Israel was estranged from something of which they were formerly possessors.

The next point is the position of believing Gentiles as a result of this engrafting process. They become a fellow sharer of the root of fatness of the olive tree. The question that is immediately raised is, A sharer with whom? The most natural and consistent Pauline answer is that believing Gentiles become fellow sharers with believing Jews in the fatness of the tree, that is, in the blessings of the Abrahamic covenant. There is no hint of Gentiles replacing Israel en toto or the church replacing Israel. The facts are that believing Gentiles fill up the place left by unbelieving Jews, while the remnant of Jews within the church share with Gentiles what always belonged to the Jews.

A third point is that Gentiles share with believing Israel simply by faith alone, while believing Israel enters into the blessing both by faith and by covenant privilege. That Israel retains her place of privilege is clear from Romans 3:1–3 and 9:4–6. Therefore, believing Jews enter into the fulfillment of their covenant privileges and promises by faith while believing Gentiles share with them by faith.

In the light of the preceding discussion, it should be evident that the church does not replace or interrupt Israel but includes and extends Israel. Gentiles replace only unbelieving Israel. Israel's privileges are extended to

149. Nygren, 399.

Gentiles. The close affinity with Ephesians 2 can be seen in the same themes in both passages: Gentiles who were afar off have been made near to Israel's covenants in Christ to share with Israel. The key factors are "in Christ" and "by faith." Jews who believe in Christ enter into their messianic inheritance, while Gentiles purely through faith in Israel's Messiah share with Israel in the same messianic blessings.

The Future of Israel

That Israel has a future is acknowledged by most modern commentators.[150] But they do not agree on what that future entails. The debated verse is Romans 11:26.

It is instructive to observe that Paul designates the temporal hardening of part of the nation Israel as a mystery. The usual understanding of mystery is that it means something unknown in the Old Testament that has now been revealed in the New Testament. But Saucy has shown that mystery also includes bringing something into reality or existence that was not previously a reality.[151] The mystery must be the hardening of Israel against the gospel in Paul's day and the incorporation of Gentiles into God's people through faith in Christ in place of these hardened Jews.

First Kings 12:1, 2 Chronicles 12:1, and Daniel 9:11 show that "all Israel" does not include every Jew. The rabbinic tractate Sanhedrin 10:1 has a long list of exclusions from the age to come. This exclusion is from "all Israel." "All Israel" must, therefore, mean *all elect* Israel.

The majority of modern commentators agree that here Paul is speaking of the future conversion of unbelieving ethnic Israel at the second coming of Christ on the basis of the future "shall come" and the eschatological character of the quotation from Isaiah 59. That this coming is to the earth is clear from many passages.[152] The teaching of these passages is that Jesus Christ will personally return to the present earth, execute judgment, be received by Israel, reward believing Israel and Gentiles, establish and restore the kingdom of God, fulfill his promise to his twelve apostles, destroy the man of sin, and rule over the earth as King of Kings and Lord of Lords.

Just exactly how "all Israel" will be saved is not spelled out by Paul or any other New Testament writer. It has been the contention throughout this discussion that salvation is only in Christ. So this eschatological group must believe the gospel of Jesus Christ. They will also enjoy all the bless-

150. One of the most provocative treatments of this theme to appear recently is Franz Mussner, *Tractate on the Jews* (Philadelphia: Fortress, 1984).

151. Robert L. Saucy, *The Case for Progressive Dispensationalism* (Grand Rapids: Zondervan, 1993), 150ff.

152. See, e.g., Matt. 19:28; 23:39; 24:30; 25:31–34; Luke 19:12; 21:24; 22:30; Acts 1:6–7; 3:19–21; 7:13, 35; 15:16; 1 Thess. 5:1–11; 2 Thess. 2:1–10; Rev. 5:10; 11:15–19; and 20:4–6.

ings that Christ has secured through his death, burial, and resurrection. And they will receive those promises God made to Israel in the Old Testament that they have not yet enjoyed, such as possession of the land of Palestine. Their position in terms of Jews and Gentiles within the church at present is not clear. The pre- or posttribulational rapture of the prior group creates problems with terminology for "all Israel." Should they be called church? Saints? People of God? Or some other title? What should believers prior to the Exodus be called? This is a problem for any system, not only premillennialism. But it is an acute problem for premillennialism because the millennial kingdom will include believers who were not raptured and resurrected when the church was raptured and resurrected (whether pre-, mid-, or posttribulationism is adopted does not ease the problem). What label can a premillennialist give to this group of redeemed? This writer does not believe that biblical revelation to this point offers enough clear information to come to a conclusive decision on the problem. (Of course, theological systems can always provide "clarity" where none exists in the text!) One can only follow Paul in his exclamation, "Oh, the depth of the riches of the wisdom and knowledge of God! How unsearchable his judgments, and his paths beyond tracing out!" (Rom. 11:33).

Hoek discusses what is meant by Israel in the N.T. Is it the nation? The new church?

Israel is almost always referred to as "Ethnic Israel" not the "New Church."

Gentiles share with Israel w/o becoming a part of Ethnic Israel or some "spiritual Israel"

Pg 309, Top, key to all of Hoek's argument On the relationship of Israel & Gentiles

Says true to Abrahamic covenant. Abraham is root, while other trees/gentiles are grafted in. Israel must believe to be grafted in. — Only cut off by unbelief

Bibliography

Albright, William F., and C. S. Mann. *Matthew*. AB. Garden City, N.Y.: Doubleday, 1971.

Alder, Cyrus, et al., eds. *The Jewish Encyclopedia*. New York: Funk and Wagnalls, 1905.

Allen, Leslie C. *Ezekiel 20–48*. WBC. Dallas: Word, 1990.

Allen, Willoughby C. *A Critical and Exegetical Commentary on the Gospel According to S. Matthew*. ICC. 3d ed. Edinburgh: T. & T. Clark, 1912.

Allis, Oswald T. *Prophecy and the Church*. Philadelphia: Presbyterian and Reformed, 1964.

Anderson, Bernhard W. "The New Covenant and the Old." In *The Old Testament and Christian Faith*, edited by Bernhard W. Anderson. New York: Harper & Row, 1963.

Anderson, Leith. *A Church for the 21st Century*. Minneapolis: Bethany, 1992.

————. *Dying For Change*. Minneapolis: Bethany, 1990.

Arndt, William F. *The Gospel According to St. Luke*. St. Louis: Concordia, 1956.

Arp, William E. "An Interpretation of 'Be Filled in Spirit' in Ephesians 5:18." Th.D. diss., Grace Theological Seminary, 1983.

Aune, David E. *Prophecy in Early Christianity and the Ancient Mediterranean World*. Grand Rapids: Eerdmans, 1983.

Badenas, Robert. *Christ the End of the Law*. Journal for the Study of the New Testament Supplement Series. Sheffield: JSOT, 1985.

Bahnsen, Greg L. *Theonomy in Christian Ethics*. Nutley, N.J.: Craig, 1977.

Baker, D. L. *Two Testaments: One Bible*. Rev. ed. Downers Grove, Ill.: InterVarsity, 1991.

Banks, Robert. *Paul's Idea of Community*. Grand Rapids: Eerdmans, 1980.

Barclay, John. *Obeying the Truth*. Studies of the New Testament and Its World. Edinburgh: T. & T. Clark, 1988.

Barclay, William. *Flesh and Spirit*. London: SCM, 1962.

————. *The Letters of James and Peter*. 2d ed. Philadelphia: Westminster, 1960.

————. *The Lord's Supper*. Nashville: Abingdon, 1967.

Barker, Kenneth L. "The Scope and Center of Old and New Testament Theology and Hope." In *Dispensationalism, Israel and the Church*, edited by Craig A. Blaising and Darrell L. Bock. Grand Rapids: Zondervan, 1992.

Barker, William S., and W. Robert Godfrey, eds. *Theonomy: A Reformed Critique*. Grand Rapids: Zondervan, 1990.

Barnes, Albert. *Isaiah*. Vol. 2. *Notes on the Old Testament*. Enl. ed. Grand Rapids: Baker, 1971.

Barr, James. *The Semantics of Biblical Language*. London: Oxford University Press, 1961.

Barrett, Charles K. *A Commentary on the Epistle to the Romans*. New York: Harper and Row, 1957.

————. *From First Adam to Last*. London: Adam & Charles Black, 1962.

————. "The Imperatival Participle." *The Expository Times* 59 (April 1948): 165–66.

————. *Paul: An Introduction to His Thought*. Louisville: Westminster/ John Knox, 1994.

Barrs, Jerram. *Shepherds and Sheep*. Downers Grove, Ill.: InterVarsity, 1983.

Barth, Markus. "Conversion and Conversation—Israel and the Church in Paul's Epistle to the Ephesians." *Interpretation* 17 (1963): 3–24.

————. *Israel and the Church*. Richmond: John Knox, 1969.

Bartlett, David L. *Ministry in the New Testament*. Overtures to Biblical Theology. Minneapolis: Fortress, 1993.

Bass, Clarence B. *Backgrounds to Dispensationalism*. Grand Rapids: Baker, 1977.

Bauer, David R. *The Structure of Matthew's Gospel*. Journal for the Study of the New Testament Supplement Series. Sheffield: Almond, 1988.

Bauer, Walter. *A Greek-English Lexicon of the New Testament and Other Early Christian Literature*. 2d ed. Translated and Edited by William F. Arndt, F. Wilbur Gingrich, and Frederick Danker. Chicago: University of Chicago Press, 1979.

Baum, Gregory. *Is the New Testament Anti-Semitic? A reexamination of the New Testament*. Rev. ed. Glen Rock, N.J.: Paulist, 1965.

Bauman, Clarence. *The Sermon on the Mount: The Modern Quest for Its Meaning*. Macon, Ga.: Mercer University Press, 1985.

Baxter, J. Sidlow. *A New Call to Holiness*. Grand Rapids: Zondervan, 1973.

Bear, James E. "The People of God." *Union Seminary Review* 52, no. 1 (October 1940): 33–63.

————. "The People of God According to the Fathers of the Early Church." 52, no. 4 (July 1941): 351–74.

————. "The People of God in Light of the Teaching of the New Testament." *Union Seminary Review* 52, no. 2 (January 1941): 128–58.

Beare, Francis Wright. *The First Epistle of Peter*. 2d. rev. ed. Oxford: Basil Blackwell, 1961.

————. *The Gospel According to Matthew*. San Francisco: Harper & Row, 1981.

Beasley-Murray, George R. *The Book of Revelation*. New Century Bible. Greenwood, S.C.: Attic, 1974.

————. *John*. Word Biblical Commentary. Waco: Word, 1987.

Beasley-Murray, George R., Herschel Hobbs, and Ray Robbins. *Revelation: Three Viewpoints*. Nashville: Broadman, 1977.

Beckwith, Isbon T. *The Apocalypse of John*. Grand Rapids: Baker, 1967.

Beckwith, Roger T. "The Daily and Weekly Worship of the Primitive Church in Relation to its Jewish Antecedents." *The Evangelical Quarterly* 56, no. 2 (1986): 65–80.

———. "The Daily and Weekly Worship of the Primitive Church: Part II." *The Evangelical Quarterly* 56, no. 3 (1986): 139–58.

Beker, J. Christian. *Paul's Apocalyptic Gospel.* Philadelphia: Fortress, 1982.

Bell, William Everett. "The New Covenant." Th.M. thesis, Dallas Theological Seminary, 1963.

Bengel, John Albert. *Gnomon of the New Testament.* Vol. 4. Translated by James Bryce. Edinburgh: T. & T. Clark, 1873.

Berkhof, L. *Systematic Theology.* 2d ed., rev. and enl. Grand Rapids: Eerdmans, 1941.

Bernstein, Alan E. *The Formation of Hell.* Ithaca, N.Y.: Cornell University Press, 1993.

Betz, Hans Dieter. *Essays on the Sermon on the Mount.* Translated by L. L. Welborn. Philadelphia: Fortress, 1985.

———. *Galatians.* Hermeneia. Philadelphia: Fortress, 1979.

Billerbeck, Paul. *Die Briefe des Neuen Testaments und die Offenbarung Johannis.* Vol. 3. *Kommentar zum neuen Testament aus Talmud und Midrasch.* Munchen: C. H. Beck'sche Verlagsbuchhandlung, 1954.

Birkey, Del. *The House Church.* Scottdale, Pa.: Herald, 1988.

Blackman, Philip, ed. *Mishnayoth.* Vol. 4. *Order Nezekin.* 2d ed. rev., corr., and expand. New York: Judaica, 1963.

Blaiklock, Edward M. "Dura Europos." In *The New International Dictionary of Biblical Archaeology,* edited by Edward M. Blaiklock and R. K. Harrison. Grand Rapids: Zondervan, 1983.

Blaising, Craig A., and Darrell Bock, eds. *Dispensationalism, Israel and the Church.* Grand Rapids: Zondervan, 1992.

———. *Progressive Dispensationalism.* Wheaton, Ill.: Victor, 1993.

Blanc, Ronald Lee. "An Exegesis of Peter's Quotation of the Joel Passage." Th.M. thesis, Dallas Theological Seminary, 1964.

Bligh, John. "The Church and Israel According to St. John and St. Paul." *Studiorum Paulinorum Congressus International Catholicus.* Analecta Biblica, vol. 17–18. Rome: Pontifico Instituto Biblico, 1963.

Blomberg, Craig L. *Interpreting the Parables.* Downers Grove, Ill.: InterVarsity, 1990.

Bloomfield, Arthur E. *All Things New.* Minneapolis: Bethany, 1959.

Boa, Kenneth, and William Proctor. *The Return of the Star of Bethlehem.* Garden City, N.Y.: Doubleday, 1980.

Boring, M. Eugene. *Revelation.* Interpretation. Louisville: John Knox, 1989.

Bornkamm, Gunther. *Paul.* New York: Harper & Row, 1971.

Bornkamm, Gunther, Gerhard Barth, and Heinz Joachim. *Tradition and Interpretation in Matthew.* The New Testament Library. Philadelphia: Westminster, 1963.

Bourke, Myles M. *A Study of the Metaphor of the Olive Tree in Rom. XI.* Washington: The Catholic University of America Press, 1947.

Bozak, Barbara A. *Life 'Anew': A Literary-Theological Study of Jer. 30–31*. Analecta Biblica, vol. 122. Rome: Biblical Institute, 1991.

Branick, Vincent. *The House Church in the Writings of Paul*. Zacchaeus Studies: New Testament. Wilmington, Del.: Michael Glazier, 1989.

Bratcher, Robert G. *A Translator's Guide to the Gospel of Matthew*. Helps for Translators. New York: United Bible Societies, 1981.

Braun, Michael A. "James' Use of Amos at the Jerusalem Council: Steps Toward a Possible Solution of the Textual and Theological Problems." *Journal of the Evangelical Theological Society* 20 (June 1977): 113–21.

Briggs, Charles Augustus. *The Messiah of the Gospels*. Edinburgh: T. & T. Clark, 1894.

Bright, John. *The Kingdom of God*. Nashville: Abingdon-Cokesbury, 1953.

Broadus, John A. *Commentary on the Gospel of Matthew*. Vol. 1. An American Commentary on the New Testament. Valley Forge, Pa.: Judson, 1886.

Bromiley, Geoffrey W., Everett F. Harrison, and Roland K. Harrison, eds. *The International Standard Bible Encyclopedia*. Rev. ed. 4 vols. Grand Rapids: Eerdmans, 1979–1988.

Brooks, Oscar Stephen. *The Sermon on the Mount*. Lanham, Md.: University Press of America, 1985.

Brooks, Roger. *The Spirit of the Ten Commandments*. San Francisco: Harper & Row, 1990.

Brown, Colin, ed. *The New International Dictionary of New Testament Theology*. 3 vols. Grand Rapids: Zondervan, 1975–78.

Brown, Raymond E. *The Birth of the Messiah: A Commentary on the Infancy Narratives in Matthew and Luke*. Garden City, N.Y.: Doubleday, 1979.

———. *The Gospel According to John I–XII*. AB Garden City, N.Y.: Doubleday, 1966.

———. *The Gospel According to John XIII–XXI*. AB. Garden City, N.Y.: Doubleday, 1966.

Bruce, Alexander B. "The Synoptic Gospels." In *The Expositor's Greek Testament*. Vol. 1. Edited by W. Robertson Nicoll. Grand Rapids: Eerdmans, 1961.

Bruce, F. F. *The Book of the Acts*. NICNT Rev. ed. Edited by F. F. Bruce. Grand Rapids: Eerdmans, 1988.

———. "The Church of Jerusalem in the Acts of the Apostles." *Bulletin of the John Rylands Library* 67 (Spring 1985): 641–61.

———. *The Epistle of Paul to the Romans*. Grand Rapids: Eerdmans, 1963.

———. *The Epistle to the Galatians*. NIGNTC. Edited by I. Howard Marshall and W. Ward Gasque. Grand Rapids: Eerdmans, 1982.

———. *1 and 2 Corinthians*. NCB. Edited by Ronald E. Clements and Matthew Black. Greenwood, S.C.: Attic, 1971.

———. *Paul: Apostle of the Heart Set Free*. Grand Rapids: Eerdmans, 1977.

———. *Tradition: Old and New*. Grand Rapids: Zondervan, 1970.

Bruner, Frederick D. *The Christbook*. Waco: Word, 1987.

———. *The Churchbook*. Dallas: Word, 1990.

Bryan, Mike. *Chapter and Verse: A Skeptic Revisits Christianity*. New York: Random House, 1991.

Bullinger, E. W. *The Apocalypse*. Greenwood, S.C.: Attic, 1972.

Bultmann, Rudolf. *Theology of the New Testament.* Vols. 1 and 2. New York: Charles Scribner's Sons, 1951.

Burnett, Fred W. *The Testament of Jesus-Sophia: A Redaction Critical Study of the Eschatological Discourse in Matthew.* Lanham, Md.: University Press of America, 1981.

Burns, J. Lanier. "The Future of Ethnic Israel in Romans 11." In *Dispensationalism, Israel and the Church,* edited by Craig A. Blaising and Darrell L. Bock. Grand Rapids: Zondervan, 1992.

Burtchaell, James T. *From Synagogue to Church: Public Services and Offices in the Earliest Christian Communities.* New York: Cambridge University Press, 1992.

Burton, Ernest DeWitt. *A Critical and Exegetical Commentary on the Epistle to the Galatians.* ICC. Edinburgh: T. & T. Clark, 1923.

———. *A Source Book for the Study of the Teaching of Jesus.* Chicago: The University of Chicago Press, 1923.

Caird, G. B. *A Commentary on the Revelation of St. John the Divine.* HNTC. Edited by Henry Chadwick. New York: Harper and Row, 1966.

Campbell, Alastair. *The Elders: Seniority Within Earliest Christianity.* Studies of the New Testament and Its World. Edited by John Riches. Edinburgh: T. & T. Clark, 1994.

Campbell, Donald K. *Walvoord: A Tribute.* Chicago: Moody, 1982.

Campbell, J. Y. "The Origin and Meaning of the Christian Use of the Word EKKLESIA." *Journal of Theological Studies* 49 (1948): 130–42.

———. *Three New Testament Studies.* Leiden: Brill, 1965.

Campbell, Roderick. *Israel and the New Covenant.* Philadelphia: Presbyterian and Reformed, 1954.

Carson, D. A. *From Sabbath to Lord's Day.* Grand Rapids: Zondervan, 1982.

———. "The Function of the Paraclete in John 16:7–11." *Journal of Biblical Literature* 98 (1982): 547–66.

———. *The Gospel According to John.* Grand Rapids: Eerdmans, 1991.

———. *Matthew.* In The Expositor's Bible Commentary. Vol. 8. Edited by Frank E. Gaebelein. Grand Rapids: Zondervan, 1984.

———. *The Sermon on the Mount.* Grand Rapids: Baker, 1978.

———. *Teach Us to Pray.* Grand Rapids: Baker, 1990.

———. *When Jesus Confronts the World.* Grand Rapids: Baker, 1987.

Carson, D. A., and H. G. M. Williamson, eds. *It Is Written: Scripture Citing Scripture.* New Rochelle: Cambridge University Press, 1988.

Cerfaux, Lucian. *The Christian in the Theology of St. Paul.* Translated by Lilian Soiron. New York: Herder and Herder, 1967.

———. *Christ in the Theology of St. Paul.* New York: Herder and Herder, 1962.

———. *The Church in the Theology of St. Paul.* New York: Herder and Herder, 1959.

———. "Le Privilege D'Israel Selon Saint Paul." *Ephemerides Theologicae Lovaniences* 17 (1940): 5–26.

Chafer, Lewis Sperry. *Chafer Systematic Theology.* Vol. 2: *Angelology, Anthropology, Hamartiology.* Dallas: Dallas Seminary Press, 1947.

————. *Chafer Systematic Theology.* Vol. 4: *Ecclesiology and Eschatology.* Dallas: Dallas Seminary Press, 1975.

————. *He That Is Spiritual.* Findlay, Ohio: Dunham, n.d.

Chance, J. Bradley. *Jerusalem, the Temple, and the New Age in Luke-Acts.* Macon, Ga.: Mercer University Press, 1988.

Charles, R. H. *A Critical and Exegetical Commentary on the Revelation of St. John.* ICC. Vols. 1 and 2. Edited by S. R. Driver, A. Plummer, and C. A. Briggs. Edinburgh: T. & T. Clark, 1920.

Charlesworth, James H., ed. *The Old Testament Pseudepigrapha:* Vol. 1. *Apocalyptic Literature and Testaments.* Garden City, N.Y.: Doubleday, 1983.

————. *The Old Testament Pseudepigrapha:* Vol. 2. *Expansions of the "Old Testament" and Legends, Wisdom and Philosophical Literature, Prayers, Psalms, and Odes, Fragments of Lost Judeo-Hellenistic Works.* Garden City, N.Y.: Doubleday, 1985.

Chenderlin, Fritz. "Do This As My Memorial." Analecta Biblica, vol. 99. Rome: Biblical Institute, 1982.

Cochrane, Arthur C. *Eating and Drinking with Jesus.* Philadelphia: Westminster, 1974.

Cohen, Gary. *Understanding Revelation.* Chicago: Moody, 1978.

Cohen, Shaye J. D. *From the Maccabees to the Mishnah.* Library of Early Christianity, edited by Wayne A. Meeks. Philadelphia: Westminster, 1987.

Collins, Raymond F. "'A New Commandment I Give to You, That You Love One Another. . . .'" Chap. 5. In *Christian Morality.* Notre Dame: University of Notre Dame Press, 1986.

————. "'A New Commandment I Give to You, That You Love One Another . . .'" Chap. 12. In *These Things Have Been Written.* Louvain Theological & Pastoral Monographs, edited by Raymond F. Collins and Thomas P. Ivory, vol. 2. Grand Rapids: Eerdmans, 1991.

Conzelmann, Hans. *An Outline of the Theology of the New Testament.* New York: Harper & Row, 1969.

Cornfeld, Gaalya, ed. *Josephus: The Jewish War.* Grand Rapids: Zondervan, 1982.

Court, John M. *Myth and History in the Book of Revelation.* Atlanta: John Knox, 1979.

Cox, William F. *Amillennialism Today.* Philadelphia: Presbyterian and Reformed, 1966.

Cranfield, C. E. B. *The Epistle to the Romans.* ICC. Vols. 1 and 2. Edited by J. A. Emerton and C. E. B. Cranfield. Edinburgh: T. & T. Clark, 1975.

————. *I & II Peter and Jude.* London: SCM, 1960.

Crater, Timothy D. "The Filling of the Spirit in the Greek New Testament." Th.M. thesis, Dallas Theological Seminary, 1971.

Crosby, Michael H. *House of Disciples: Church, Economics, and Justice in Matthew.* Maryknoll, N.Y.: Orbis, 1988.

————. *Spirituality of the Beatitudes.* Maryknoll, N.Y.: Orbis, 1981.

Cullmann, Oscar. *Christ and Time.* Rev. ed. Translated by Floyd V. Filson. Philadelphia: Westminster, 1964.

———. *Early Christian Worship.* Vol. 10. Studies in Biblical Theology, edited by C. F. D. Moule. London: SCM, 1966.

———. *The Early Church.* Abridged ed. Philadelphia: Westminster, 1966.

———. *Salvation in History.* New York: Harper & Row, 1967.

Cullmann, Oscar, and F. J. Leenhardt. *Essays on the Lord's Supper.* Atlanta: John Knox, 1958.

Dahl, Nils A. "A People for His Name." *New Testament Studies* 4 (1957–58): 319–27.

———. *Das Volk Gottes.* 2d ed. Darmstadt: Wissenschaftliche Buchgesellschaft, 1963.

———. "The People of God." *The Ecumenical Review* 9 (January 1957): 154–61.

———. "Zur Auslegung von Gal 6, 16." *Judaica* 6 (1950): 161–70.

Dana, H. E., and Julius R. Mantey. *A Manual Grammar of the Greek New Testament.* New York: Macmillan, 1927.

Danell, Gustaf A. *Studies in the Name Israel in the Old Testament.* Uppsala: Appelbergs Boktryckeri, 1946.

Danker, Frederick W. *Jesus and the New Age: A Commentary on St. Luke's Gospel.* Completely rev. and exp. ed. Philadelphia: Fortress, 1988.

Davenport, Gene L. *Into the Darkness: Discipleship in the Sermon on the Mount.* Nashville: Abingdon, 1988.

Davidson, Richard M. *Typology in Scripture.* Vol. 2. Andrews University Seminary Doctoral Dissertation Series. Berrien Springs, Mich.: Andrews University Press, 1981.

Davies, J. G. "Architectural Setting." In *The Westminster Dictionary of Worship,* edited by J. G. Davies. Philadelphia: Westminster, 1972.

Davies, W. D. *The Sermon on the Mount.* New Rochelle, N.Y.: Cambridge University Press, 1966.

———. *The Setting of the Sermon on the Mount.* New Rochelle, N.Y.: Cambridge University Press, 1966.

Davies, W. D., and Dale C. Allison Jr. *A Critical and Exegetical Commentary on the Gospel According to Saint Matthew.* ICC. Vol. 1. Edited by J. A. Emerton, C. E. B. Cranfield, and G. N. Stanton. Edinburgh: T. & T. Clark, 1988.

Deidun, T. J. *New Covenant Morality in Paul.* Analecta Biblica, edited by Albert VanHoye and Stanislas Lyonnet, vol. 89. Rome: Biblical Institute, 1981.

Denney, James. "St. Paul's Epistle to the Romans." Vol. 2. In *The Expositor's Greek Testament,* edited by W. Nicoll Robertson. Grand Rapids: Eerdmans, 1967.

DeRidder, Richard R. *Discipling the Nations.* Grand Rapids: Baker, 1975.

DeYoung, James Calvin. *Jerusalem in the New Testament: The Significance of the City in the History of Redemption and in Eschatology.* Kampen: Kok, 1960.

Dobson, Ed, Ed Hindson, and Jerry Falwell. *The Fundamentalist Phenomenon.* 2d ed. Grand Rapids: Baker, 1986.

Dodd, Charles H. *According to the Scriptures.* Digswell Place, England: James Nisbet, 1961.

———. *The Apostolic Preaching and Its Developments.* New York: Harper & Row, 1964.

Donaldson, Terence L. "Jesus on the Mountain." *Journal for the Study of the New Testament: Supplement* 30, edited by Bruce D. Chilton and David J. A. Clines. Sheffield: JSOT, 1985.

Donaldson, Terry L. "Israel and the Church: A Middle Position." *Crux* 15 (September 1979): 11–13.

Drane, John W. *Paul: Libertine or Legalist?* London: SPCK, 1975.

Duhon, Duane A. "The Referent for the Pauline Phrase 'Not Under Law.'" Th.M. thesis, Grand Rapids Baptist Seminary, 1990.

Dumbrell, William J. *The End of the Beginning.* Grand Rapids: Lancer, 1985.

Duncan, George S. *The Epistle of Paul to the Galatians.* London: Hodder and Stoughton, 1938.

Dunn, James D. G. *Baptism in the Holy Spirit.* Studies in Biblical Theology. Vol. 15. 2d ser. Edited by C. F. D. Moule. Naperville, Ill./Philadelphia: Alec R. Allenson/Westminster, 1970.

———. *The Epistle to the Galatians.* Black's New Testament Commentary. Edited by Henry Chadwick. Peabody, Mass.: Hendrickson, 1993.

———. *Jesus and the Spirit.* Philadelphia: Westminster, 1975.

———. *Jesus, Paul and the Law.* Louisville: Westminster, 1990.

———. "Messianic Ideas and Their Influence on the Jesus of History." In *The Messiah,* edited by James H. Charlesworth. The First Princeton Symposium on Judaism and Christian Origins. Philadelphia: Fortress, 1992.

———. *The Partings of the Ways.* Philadelphia: Trinity Press International, 1991.

———. *Romans 1–8.* WBC. Dallas: Word, 1988.

Dupont-Sommer, A., ed. *The Essene Writings from Qumran.* 2d ed. rev. and enl. Translated by G. Vermes. Gloucester, Mass.: Peter Smith, 1973.

Eadie, John. *Commentary on the Epistle of Paul to the Galatians.* Grand Rapids: Zondervan, n.d.

Eakin, Frank E., Jr. *The Religion and Culture of Israel.* Boston: Allyn and Bacon, 1971.

Easley, Kendall H. "The Pauline Usage of Pneumati as a Reference to the Spirit of God." *Journal of the Evangelical Theological Society* 27 (September 1984): 299–313.

Edwards, Richard A. *Matthew's Story of Jesus.* Philadelphia: Fortress, 1985.

Elert, Werner. *Eucharist and Church Fellowship in the First Four Centuries.* St. Louis: Concordia, 1966.

Ellicott, Charles J. *A Critical and Grammatical Commentary on St. Paul's Epistle to the Galatians with a Revised Translation.* Andover: Draper, 1880.

Elliott, John H. *A Home for the Homeless.* Philadelphia: Fortress, 1981.

Ellison, H. L. *The Mystery of Israel.* London: Paternoster, 1966.

Fee, Gordon D. *1 and 2 Timothy, Titus.* New International Biblical Commentary. Peabody, Mass.: Hendrickson, 1988.

———. *God's Empowering Presence: The Holy Spirit in the Letters of Paul.* Peabody, Mass.: Hendrickson, 1994.

Feeley-Harnik, Gillian. *The Lord's Table*. Philadelphia: University of Pennsylvania Press, 1981.

Feinberg, Charles L. *Millennialism: The Two Major Views*. 3d ed. enl. Chicago: Moody, 1982.

Feinberg, John S., ed. *Continuity and Discontinuity*. Westchester, Ill.: Crossway, 1988.

Fenton, J. C. *Saint Matthew*. Westminster Pelican Commentaries. Edited by D. E. Nineham. Philadelphia: Westminster, 1977.

Ferguson, Everett. *Backgrounds of Early Christianity*. 2d ed. Grand Rapids: Eerdmans, 1993.

Filson, Floyd V. *The Gospel According to Matthew*. 2d ed. HNTC. New York: Harper & Row, 1971.

Fiorenza, Elisabeth Schuessler. *The Apocalypse*. Chicago: Franciscan Herald, 1976.

————. *The Book of Revelation Justice and Judgment*. Philadelphia: Fortress, 1985.

Fitzmyer, Joseph A. *Essays on the Semitic Background of The New Testament*. Missoula, Mont.: Scholars, 1974.

————. *The Gospel According to Luke I–IX*. AB. Edited by William Foxwell Albright and David Noel Freedman. Garden City, N.Y.: Doubleday, 1981.

————. 1985. *The Gospel According to Luke X–XXIV*. AB. Edited by William Foxwell Albright and David Noel Freedman. Garden City, N.Y.: Doubleday, 1985.

————. *Pauline Theology*. Englewood Cliffs, N.J.: Prentice-Hall, 1967.

Flew, R. Newton. *Jesus and His Church*. 2d ed. London: Epworth, 1943.

Ford, J. Massyngberde. *Revelation*. AB. Edited by William Foxwell Albright and David Noel Freedman. Garden City, N.Y.: Doubleday, 1975.

Fowler, Harold. *The Gospel of Matthew*. 4 vols. Bible Study Textbooks Series. Joplin, Mo.: College, 1985.

Fraeyman, M. "La Spiritualisation De L'Idee Du Temple Dans Les Epitres Pauliniennes." *Ephemerides Theologicae Lovanienses* 23 (1947): 378–412.

Frame, James Everett. *A Critical and Exegetical Commentary on the Epistles of St. Paul to the Thessalonians*. ICC. Edinburgh: T. & T. Clark, 1912.

France, Richard T. *The Gospel According to Matthew*. TNTC. Edited by Leon Morris. Grand Rapids: Eerdmans, 1985.

————. *Matthew: Evangelist and Teacher*. Grand Rapids: Zondervan, 1989.

Fuller, Daniel P. *Gospel and Law: Contrast or Continuum?* Grand Rapids: Eerdmans, 1980

Fung, Ronald Y. K. *The Epistle to the Galatians*. NICNT. Edited by F. F. Bruce. Grand Rapids: Eerdmans, 1988.

Furnish, Victor Paul. *II Corinthians*. AB. Edited by William Foxwell Albright and David Noel Freedman. Garden City, N.Y.: Doubleday, 1984.

Gaebelein, A. C. *The Gospel of Matthew, An Exposition*. New York: Our Hope Publications Office, 1910.

Gaede, S. D. *Belonging*. Grand Rapids: Zondervan, 1985.

Gage, Warren Austin. *The Gospel of Genesis*. Winona Lake, Ind.: Carpenter Books, 1984.

Garland, David E. "The Intention of Matthew 23." *Supplements to Novum Testamentum: Supplement* 52. Edited by W. C. Van Unnik. London: E. J. Brill, 1979.

Gaster, Theodor H. *The Dead Sea Scriptures.* 3d ed. rev. and enl. Garden City, N.Y.: Doubleday, 1976.

Gaston, Lloyd. "No Stone on Another, Studies in the Significance of the Fall of Jerusalem in the Synoptic Gospels." *Supplement to Novum Testamentum: Supplement* 23. Leiden: E. J. Brill, 1970.

————. *Paul and the Torah.* Vancouver: University of British Columbia Press, 1987.

Gerhardsson, Birger. *The Ethos of the Bible.* Philadelphia: Fortress, 1981.

Getz, Gene A. *Building Up One Another.* Wheaton, Ill.: Scripture Press, 1976.

————. *Encouraging One Another.* Wheaton, Ill.: Scripture Press, 1981.

————. *Loving One Another.* Wheaton, Ill.: Scripture Press, 1979.

————. *The Measure of a Church.* Glendale, Calif.: Gospel Light, 1975.

————. *Praying for One Another.* Wheaton, Ill.: Scripture Press, 1982.

————. *Sharpening the Focus of the Church.* Chicago: Moody, 1974.

Glenny, W. Edward. "The Israelite Imagery of I Peter 2." In *Dispensationalism, Israel and the Church,* edited by Craig A. Blaising and Darrell L. Bock. Grand Rapids: Zondervan, 1992.

Gnilka, Joachim. *Die Verstockung Israels: Isaias 6, 9–10 in der Theologie der Synoptiker.* München: Kosel-Verlag, 1961.

Goodspeed, Edgar J. *Matthew: Apostle and Evangelist.* Philadelphia: John C. Winston, 1959.

Goppelt, Leonhard. *Typos.* Grand Rapids: Eerdmans, 1982.

Goulder, Michael D. *Midrash and Lection in Matthew.* London: SPCK, 1974.

Green, H. Benedict. *The Gospel According to Matthew.* The New Clarendon Bible. Edited by H. F. D. Sparks. London: Oxford University Press, 264.

Green, Michael. *Evangelism in the Early Church.* Grand Rapids: Eerdmans, 1974.

————. *Freed to Serve.* 2d ed. Dallas: Word, 1988.

————. *Matthew for Today.* Dallas: Word, 1989.

Grogan, Geoffrey W. *Isaiah.* The Expositor's Bible Commentary. Edited by Frank E. Gaebelein. Grand Rapids: Zondervan, 1986.

Grudem, Wayne. *The Gift of Prophecy in the New Testament and Today.* Westchester, Ill.: Crossway, 1982.

————. *The Gift of Prophecy in 1 Corinthians.* Washington, D.C.: University Press of America, Inc., 1982.

Guelich, Robert A. *The Sermon on the Mount.* Waco: Word, 1982.

Gundry, Robert. "Grace, Works, and Staying Saved in Paul." *Biblica* 66 (1985): 1–38.

————. *Matthew: A Commentary on His Literary and Theological Art.* Grand Rapids: Eerdmans, 1982.

————. "The New Jerusalem: People as Place, Not Place for People." *Novum Testamentum* 29 (1987): 254–64.

———. "The Use of the Old Testament in St. Matthew's Gospel." *Supplements to Novum Testamentum: Supplement* 18. Edited by W. C. Van Unnik. Leiden: E. J. Brill.

Guthrie, Donald. *Galatians*. NCB. Edited by H. H. Rowley and Matthew Black. Greenwood, S.C.: Attic, 1974.

Hadaway, C. Kirk, Stuart A. Wright, and Francis M. Dubose. *Home Cell Groups and House Churches*. Nashville: Broadman, 1987.

Hailey, Homer. *Revelation*. Grand Rapids: Baker, 1979.

Hamilton, Floyd E. *The Epistle to the Romans*. Philadelphia: Presbyterian and Reformed, 1958.

Hanson, Anthony Tyrell. *The Pioneer Ministry*. Philadelphia: Westminster, 1961.

Harner, Philip B. *The 'I Am' of the Fourth Gospel*. Philadelphia: Fortress, 1970.

Harrington, Daniel J. *The Gospel of Matthew*. SP. Vol. 1. Edited by Daniel J. Harrington. Collegeville, Minn.: Liturgical, 1991.

Harris, Murray J. *2 Corinthians*. The Expositor's Bible Commentary: Romans–Galatians. 10 vols. Edited by Frank E. Gaebelein. Grand Rapids: Zondervan, 1978.

———. *Jesus As God*. Grand Rapids: Baker, 1992.

———. *Raised Immortal*. Grand Rapids: Eerdmans, 1983.

Harris, W. S. *A Complete Index to the Thought and Teachings of Christ*. Nashville: Cokesbury, 1939.

Harrisville, R. A. "The Concept of Newness in the New Testament." *Journal of Biblical Literature* 74 (June 1955): 69–79.

———. *The Concept of Newness in the New Testament*. Minneapolis: Augsburg, 1960.

Harvey, Julien. "Le 'Rib-Pattern', requistoire prophetique sur la rupture de l'alliance." *Biblica* 43 (1962): 172–96.

Hasel, Gerhard. *The Remnant*. 2d ed. Andrews University Monographs Studies in Religion, vol. 5. Berrien Springs, Mich.: Andrews University Press, 1974.

Hawthorne, Gerald F., and Otto Betz, eds. *Tradition and Interpretation in the New Testament*. Grand Rapids: Eerdmans, 1987.

Hawthorne, Gerald F., Ralph P. Martin, and Daniel G. Reid, eds. *Dictionary of Paul and His Letters*. Downers Grove, Ill.: InterVarsity, 1993.

Hays, Richard B. *The Faith of Jesus Christ*. Vol. 56. SBL Dissertation Series. Edited by William Baird. Chico: Scholars, 1983.

Hendriksen, William. *Exposition of the Gospel According to Matthew*. NTC. Grand Rapids: Baker, 1973.

———. *Israel and the Bible*. Grand Rapids: Baker, 1968.

Hengel, Martin. *Crucifixion*. Philadelphia: Fortress, 1977.

———. *The Zealots*. 2d ed. Translated by David Smith. Edinburgh: T. & T. Clark, 1989.

Higgins, A. J. B. *The Lord's Supper in the New Testament*. Vol. 6. Studies in Biblical Theology First Series. Edited by C. F. D. Moule. London: SCM, 1972.

Hill, David. *The Gospel of Matthew*. NCB. Edited by Ronald E. Clements and Matthew Black. Grand Rapids: Eerdmans, 1972.

————. *Greek Words and Hebrew Meanings.* Society for New Testament Studies Monograph Series, edited by Robert Wilson and Margaret Thrall, vol. 5. Cambridge: Cambridge University Press, 1967.

————. *New Testament Prophecy.* New Foundations Theological Library. Edited by Peter Toon and Ralph A. Martin. Atlanta: John Knox, 1979.

Hillers, Delbert R. *Treaty Curses and the Old Testament Prophets.* Rome: Pontifical Biblical Institute, 1964.

Hinnebusch, Paul. *St. Matthew's Earthquake.* Ann Arbor, Mich.: Servant Books, 1980.

Hoch, Carl B., Jr. "The New Man of Ephesians Two." In *Dispensationalism, Israel and the Church,* edited by Craig Blaising and Darrell Bock. Grand Rapids: Zondervan, 1992.

————. "The Relation of Hosea's Prophecy to the Sinaitic Covenant." Th.M. thesis, Dallas Theological Seminary, 1966.

————. "The Role of Women in the Church: A Survey of Current Approaches." *Grace Theological Journal* 8 (Fall 1987): 241–51.

————. "Romans 15:7–13: A Neglected Passage in Discussions Concerning the Relationship Between Israel and the Church." Unpublished paper read at the meeting of the Midwest Section of the Evangelical Theological Society, March, 1989.

————. "The Significance of the 'Syn'-Compounds for Jew–Gentile Relationships in the Body of Christ." *Journal of the Evangelical Theological Society* 25 (June 1982): 175–83.

————. "The Term 'Israel' in the New Testament." Th.D. diss., Dallas Theological Seminary, 1971.

Hoehner, Harold W. *Chronological Aspects of the Life of Christ.* Grand Rapids: Zondervan, 1977.

Hoekema, Anthony A. *The Bible and the Future.* Grand Rapids: Eerdmans, 1979.

Hort, F. J. A. *The Christian Ecclesia.* London: MacMillan, 1897.

House, H. Wayne, and Thomas Ice. *Dominion Theology: Blessing or Curse?* Portland, Ore.: Multnomah, 1988.

Hübner, Hans. *Law in Paul's Thought.* Studies of the New Testament and Its World. Edited by John Riches. Edinburgh: T. & T. Clark, 1984.

Huffmon, Herbert B. "The Covenant Lawsuit in the Prophets." *Journal of Biblical Literature* 78 (1959): 285–95.

Hughes, Philip Edgcumbe. *Paul's Second Epistle to the Corinthians.* NICNT. Edited by F. F. Bruce. Grand Rapids: Eerdmans, 1962.

Hulbert, Terry C. "The Eschatological Significance of Israel's Annual Feasts." Th.D. diss., Dallas Theological Seminary, 1965.

Hull, Bill. *Can We Save the Evangelical Church?* Grand Rapids: Revell, 1993.

Hull, J. H. E. *The Holy Spirit in the Acts of the Apostles.* Cleveland, Ohio: World, 1968.

Hunt, Boyd. *Redeemed!: Eschatological Redemption and the Kingdom of God.* Nashville: Broadman & Holman, 1993.

Hunter, Archibald M. *A Pattern for Life: An Exposition of the Sermon on the Mount.* Rev. ed. Philadelphia: Westminster, 1965.

Hutton, W. R. "Considerations for the Translation of Greek en." *The Bible Translator* 9:4 (October 1958): 163–70.

Icenogle, Gareth Weldon. *Biblical Foundations for Small Group Ministry.* Downers Grove, Ill.: InterVarsity, 1994.

Ironside, H. A. *The Great Parenthesis.* 2d ed. Grand Rapids: Zondervan, 1943.

———. *Not Wrath, But Rapture.* New York: Loizeaux Brothers, n.d.

Jeremias, Joachim. *The Eucharistic Words of Jesus.* 3d ed. New York: Charles Scribner's Sons, 1966.

———. *New Testament Theology.* New York: Charles Scribner's, 1971.

———. *The Prayers of Jesus.* Philadelphia: Fortress, 1978.

Johnson, Alan F. *Revelation.* In The Expositor's Bible Commentary, edited by Frank E. Gaebelein and J. D. Douglas. 10 vols. Grand Rapids: Zondervan, 1981.

———. *The Sermon on the Mount.* Vol. 2. Facet Books Biblical Series. Edited by John Reumann. Translated by Norman Perrin. Philadelphia: Fortress, 1963.

Johnson, S. Lewis, Jr. "Paul and 'The Israel of God': An Exegetical and Eschatological Case-Study." In *Essays in Honor of J. Dwight Pentecost,* edited by Stanley D. Toussaint and Charles H. Dyer. Chicago: Moody, 1986.

———. "Romans 5:12—An Exercise in Exegesis and Theology." In *New Directions of New Testament Study,* edited by Richard Longenecker and Merrill Tenney. Grand Rapids: Zondervan, 1974.

Johnson, Sherman E. "The Gospel According to St. Matthew." IB. Edited by George Buttrick. Nashville: Abingdon, 1951.

Johnston, George. *The Doctrine of the Church in the New Testament.* Cambridge: Cambridge University Press, 1943.

Kaiser, Walter C., Jr. "The Davidic Promise and the Inclusion of the Gentiles (Amos 9:9–15 and Acts 15:13–18): A Test Passage for Theological Systems." *Journal of the Evangelical Theological Society* 20 (June 1977): 97–111.

———. "How Can Christians Derive Principles from the Specific Commands of the Law?" In *Readings in Christian Ethics:* Vol. 1. *Theory and Method,* edited by David K. Clark and Robert V. Rakestraw. Grand Rapids: Baker, 1994.

———. "Israel as the People of God." In *The People of God: Essays on the Believers' Church,* edited by Paul Basden, David S. Dockery. Nashville: Broadman, 1991.

———. "The Old Promise and the New Covenant: Jer. 31:31–34." *Journal of the Evangelical Theological Society* 15 (1972): 11–23.

———. *Toward an Old Testament Theology.* Grand Rapids: Zondervan, 1978.

Karleen, Paul S. *The Handbook to Bible Study.* New York: Oxford University Press, 1987.

Kasemann, Ernst. *Perspectives on Paul.* Philadelphia: Fortress, 1971.

Kaye, Bruce, and Gordon Wenham, eds. *Law, Morality, and the Bible.* Downers Grove, Ill.: InterVarsity, 1978.

Kee, Howard Clark. *Good News to the Ends of the Earth: The Theology of Acts.* Philadelphia: Trinity Press International, 1990.

Keil, Carl Friedrich. *Biblical Commentary on the Prophecies of Ezekiel.* Translated by James Martin. Grand Rapids: Eerdmans, 1950.

Kelly, J. N. D. *A Commentary on the Epistles of Peter and Jude.* New York: Harper and Row, 1969.

Kelly, Joan. "A Taxonomy of New Testament Stipulations In Acts and Paul." Unpublished Project. Grand Rapids Baptist Seminary, 1987.

Kevan, Ernest F. *The Grace of Law.* Grand Rapids: Baker, 1976.

Kiddle, Martin. "The Conflict Between the Disciples, the Jews, and the Gentiles in St. Matthew's Gospel." *Journal of Theological Studies* 36 (January 1935): 33–44.

————. *The Revelation of St. John.* MNTC. Edited by James Moffatt. New York: Harper and Brothers, 1940.

Kilgallen, John. *The Stephen Speech.* Analecta Biblica, vol. 67. Rome: Biblical Institute, 1976.

Kim, Seyoon. *The Origin of Paul's Gospel.* Grand Rapids: Eerdmans, 1982.

Kingsbury, Jack Dean. *Matthew as Story.* Philadelphia: Fortress, 1986.

————. *Matthew.* Proclamation Commentaries. 2d ed. rev. and enl. Edited by Gerhard Krodel. Philadelphia: Fortress, 1986.

————. *Matthew: Structure, Christology, Kingdom.* Philadelphia: Fortress, 1989.

Kissinger, Warren S. *The Sermon on the Mount: A History of Interpretation and Bibliography.* Metuchen, N.J.: Scarecrow, 1975.

Kitchen, K. A. *The Bible in Its World.* Downers Grove, Ill.: InterVarsity, 1978.

Kittel, Gerhard, and Gerhard Friedrich, eds. *Theological Dictionary of the New Testament.* Translated by Geoffrey W. Bromiley. 10 vols. Grand Rapids: Eerdmans, 1964–76.

Kline, Meredith G. *By Oath Consigned.* Grand Rapids: Eerdmans, 1968.

————. *Treaty of the Great King.* Grand Rapids: Eerdmans, 1963.

Kraus, C. Norman. *The Community of the Spirit.* Grand Rapids: Eerdmans, 1974.

————. *Dispensationalism in America.* Richmond: John Knox, 1958.

Kraybill, Donald B. *The Upside-Down Kingdom.* Scottdale, Pa.: Herald, 1978.

Krodel, Gerhard A. *Revelation.* Augsburg Commentary on the New Testament. Edited by Roy A. Harrisville, Jack Kingsbury, and Gerhard Krodel. Minneapolis: Augsburg, 1989.

Kruse, Colin. *New Testament Models for Ministry: Jesus and Paul.* Nashville: Thomas Nelson, 1982.

Kuen, Alfred F. *I Will Build My Church.* Translated by Ruby Lindblad. Chicago: Moody, 1971.

Kugelman, Richard. "Hebrew, Israelite, Jew in the New Testament." In *The Bridge,* edited by John M. Oesterreicher, New York: Pantheon, 1955.

Kummel, Werner George. *The Theology of the New Testament.* Nashville: Abingdon, 1973.

Kuyper, Abraham. *The Revelation of St. John.* Grand Rapids: Eerdmans, 1963.

Ladd, George E. *A Commentary on the Revelation of John.* Grand Rapids: Eerdmans, 1972.

————. *Crucial Questions about the Kingdom of God.* Grand Rapids: Eerdmans, 1952.

————. *A Theology of the New Testament.* Grand Rapids: Eerdmans, 1974.

Lambrecht, Jan. *The Sermon on the Mount.* Vol. 14, *Good News Studies*, edited by Robert J. Karris. Wilmington, Del.: Michael Glazier, 1985.

Lehne, Susanne. "The New Covenant in Hebrews." *Journal for the Study of the New Testament: Supplement* 44, edited by David Hill and David E. Orton. Sheffield: JSOT, 1990.

Lenski, R. C. H. *The Interpretation of St. Matthew's Gospel.* Minneapolis: Augsburg, 1943.

Leon-Dufour, Xavier. *Dictionary of Biblical Theology.* 2d ed., rev. and enl. New York: Seabury, 1973.

———. *Sharing the Eucharistic Bread.* New York: Paulist, 1987.

Lietzmann, Hans. *Mass and Lord's Supper.* Leiden: Brill, 1979.

Lightfoot, J. B. *Saint Paul's Epistle to the Philippians.* Grand Rapids: Zondervan, 1953.

Lindars, Barnabas. *The Gospel of John.* NCB. Edited by Ronald E. Clements and Matthew Black. Greenwood, S.C.: Attic, 1972.

Lindeskog, Gosta. "Israel in the NT—Some few remarks on a great problem." *Svensk Exegetisk Årsbok* 26 (1961): 57–92.

Longenecker, Richard N. *Galatians.* WBC. Edited by David A. Hubbard and Glenn W. Barker. Dallas: Word, 1990.

Lovsky, F. "Remarques sur la notion de rejet par rapport au mystere d'Israel et a l'unite de l'Eglise." *Revue d'histoire et de philosophie religieuses* 43 (1963): 32–47.

Luhrmann, Dieter. *Galatians.* A Continental Commentary. Translated by O. C. Dean, Jr. Minneapolis: Fortress, 1992.

Luz, Ulrich. *Matthew 1–7: A Commentary.* Translated by Wilhelm C. Linss. Minneapolis: Augsburg, 1989.

MacArthur, John. *Kingdom Living Here and Now.* Chicago: Moody, 1980.

MacGregor, Geddes. *Corpus Christi: The Nature of the Church According to the Reformed Tradition.* Philadelphia: Westminster, 1958.

Machen, J. Gresham. *The Origin of Paul's Religion.* Grand Rapids: Eerdmans, 1947.

Malatesta, Edward. *Interiority and Covenant.* Analecta Biblica, vol. 69. Rome: Biblical Institute, 1978.

Malina, Bruce J., and Jerome H. Neyrey. *Calling Jesus Names: The Social Value of Labels in Matthew.* Foundations and Facets: Social Facets. Edited by Adela Yarbro Collins and John Dominic. Sonoma, Calif.: Polebridge, 1988.

Marriott, Horace. *The Sermon on the Mount.* London: SPCK, 1925.

Marshall, I. Howard. *The Acts of the Apostles.* TNTC. Edited by R. V. G. Tasker. Grand Rapids: Eerdmans, 1980.

———. *Kept by the Power of God.* Minneapolis: Bethany Fellowship, 1969.

———. *Last Supper and Lord's Supper.* Grand Rapids: Eerdmans, 1981.

———. *Luke: Historian and Theologian.* Contemporary Evangelical Perspectives. Grand Rapids: Zondervan, 1970.

Martin, Brice L. "Christ and the Law in Paul." *Novum Testamentum Supplement*, 62. Leiden: Brill, 1989.

Martin, Ralph P. *2 Corinthians.* WBC. Edited by David A. Hubbard and Glenn W. Barker. Waco: Word, 1986.

————. *The Family and the Fellowship*. Grand Rapids: Eerdmans, 1979.

Master, John R. "The New Covenant." In *Issues in Dispensationalism*, edited by Wesley R. Willis and John R. Wesley. Chicago: Moody, 1994.

Matera, Frank J. *Galatians*. Vol. 9. SP. Edited by Daniel J. Harrington. Collegeville, Minn.: Liturgical, 1992.

Matthews, A. G. "The Puritans." In *Christian Worship*, edited by Nathaniel Micklem. New York: Oxford, 1936.

Mattison, Robin D. "God/Father: Tradition and Interpretation." *Reformed Review* 42 (Spring 1989): 189–206.

Mauro, Philip. *The Hope of Israel What Is It?* Indianapolis: Pastors Library Foundation, n.d.

Mauser, Ulrich W. *Christ in the Wilderness*. Vol. 39. Studies in Biblical Theology, edited by C. F. D. Moule and James Barr. London: SCM, 1963.

McComiskey, Thomas E. *The Covenants of Promise*. Grand Rapids: Baker, 1985.

McCormick, Scott, Jr. *The Lord's Supper*. Philadelphia: Westminster, 1966.

McDonald, James I. H. *Kerygma and Didache*. Society for New Testament Studies Monograph Series, edited by Robert Wilson and Margaret Thrall, vol. 37. Cambridge: Cambridge University Press, 1980.

McDonnell, Kilian, and George T. Montague. *Christian Initiation and Baptism in the Holy Spirit*. Collegeville, Minn.: Liturgical, 1991.

McDowell, Edward A. *The Meaning and Message of the Book of Revelation*. Nashville: Broadman, 1951.

McDowell, Josh. *Evidence That Demands a Verdict*. Arrowhead Springs, Calif.: Campus Crusade for Christ, 1972.

McKelvey, R. J. *The New Temple*. London: Oxford University Press, 1969.

McNeile, Alan Hugh. *The Gospel According to St. Matthew*. London: Macmillan, 1961.

Meechum, H. G. "The Use of the Participle for the Imperative in the New Testament." *The Expository Times* 58 (May 1947): 207–8.

Meier, John P. *Law and History in Matthew's Gospel*. Analecta Biblica, edited by James Swetnam, vol. 71. Rome: Biblical Institute, 1976.

————. *Matthew*. New Testament Message. Vol. 3. Rev. ed. Edited by Wilfrid Harrington and Donald Senior. Wilmington, Del.: Michael Glazier, 1981.

————. *The Vision of Matthew*. Theological Inquiries. Edited by Lawrence Boadt. Ramsey, N.J.: Paulist, 1979.

Mell, Ulrich. *Neue Schopfung*. Beiheft zur Zeitschrift für die neutestamentliche Wissenschaft und die Kunde der alteren Kirche, edited by Erich Grasser, vol. 56. Berlin: Walter de Gruyter, 1989.

Mendenhall, George E. "Ancient Oriental and Biblical Law." *The Biblical Archaeologist* 17 (1954): 26–46.

————. "Covenant Forms in Israelite Tradition." *The Biblical Archaeologist* 17 (1954): 50–76.

————. "Covenant." In *IDB*, edited by George Arthur Buttrick. Nashville: Abingdon, 1962.

Metzger, Bruce M., ed. *A Textual Commentary on the Greek New Testament*. New York: United Bible Societies, 1971.

Meyer, Heinrich August Wilhelm. *Critical and Exegetical Handbook to the Gospel of Matthew.* Meyer's Commentary on the New Testament. Edited by Frederich and William Stewart. Vol. 1. Rev. ed. New York: Funk & Wagnalls, 1980.

Micklem, Nathaniel, ed. *Christian Worship.* London: Oxford University Press, 1936.

Miller, Chris A. "The Relationship of Jewish and Gentile Believers to the Law Between A.D. 30 and 70 in the Scripture." Ph.D. diss., Dallas Theological Seminary, 1994.

Minear, Paul S. *Christians and the New Creation: Genesis Motifs in the New Testament.* Louisville: Westminster/John Knox, 1994.

————. *Images of the Church in the New Testament.* Philadelphia: Westminster, 1960.

Mlakuzhyil, George. *The Christological Literary Structure of the Fourth Gospel.* Analecta Biblica, vol. 117. Rome: Pontifico Instituto Biblico, 1987.

Moessner, David. *Lord of the Banquet.* Philadelphia: Fortress, 1989.

Mohrlang, Roger. *Matthew and Paul: A Comparison of Ethical Perspectives.* Society for New Testament Studies Monograph Series, edited by Robert Mcleish Wilson and Margaret E. Thrall, vol. 48. New Rochelle: Cambridge University Press, 1984.

Montague, George T. *The Holy Spirit: Growth of a Biblical Tradition.* New York: Paulist, 1976.

Montefiore, C. G. *The Synoptic Gospels.* 2 vols. 2d rev. ed. New York: KTAV, 1968.

Moo, Douglas J. "The Law of Moses or the Law of Christ." In *Continuity and Discontinuity,* edited by John S. Feinberg. Westchester, Ill.: Crossway, 1988.

Moran, W. L. "The Ancient Near Eastern Background of the Love of God in Deuteronomy." *Catholic Biblical Quarterly* 25 (1963): 77–87.

Morgenthaler, Robert. *Statistik des Neutestamentlichen Wortschatzes.* Zurich: Gotthelf-Verlag, 1973.

Morris, Leon. *The Gospel According to John.* NICNT. Edited by F. F. Bruce. Grand Rapids: Eerdmans, 1971.

Moule, C. F. D. "'Fullness' and 'Full' in the New Testament." *Scottish Theological Journal* 14 (April 1968): 293–320.

————. *Idiom Book of New Testament Greek.* Cambridge: Cambridge University Press, 1953.

Moulton, W. F., and A. S. Geden. *A Concordance to the Greek Testament.* Edinburgh: T. & T. Clark, 1963.

Mounce, Robert H. *The Book of Revelation.* NICNT. Edited by F. F. Bruce. Grand Rapids: Eerdmans, 1977.

————. *The Essential Nature of New Testament Preaching.* Grand Rapids: Eerdmans, 1960.

————. *Matthew.* Good News Commentaries. Edited by W. Ward Gasque. Peabody, Mass.: Hendrickson, 1985.

Mounce, Robert H., and Carl B. Hoch, Jr. "New; Newness." In *The International Standard Bible Encyclopedia.* 3d ed. Vol. 3. Edited by Geoffrey Bromiley. Grand Rapids: Eerdmans, 1986.

Munck, Johannes. *The Acts of the Apostles*. AB. Edited by William Foxwell Albright and David Noel Freedman. Garden City, N.Y.: Doubleday, 1967.

———. *Christ and Israel: An Interpretation of Romans 9–11*. Philadelphia: Fortress, 1967.

Murphy-O'Connor, Jerome. *St. Paul's Corinth*. Good News Studies, edited by Robert J. Karris, vol. 6. Wilmington, Del.: Michael Glazier, 1983.

Murray, John. *The Epistle to the Romans*. NICNT. Edited by F. F. Bruce. Grand Rapids: Eerdmans, 1968.

———. *The Imputation of Adam's Sin*. Nutley, N.J.: Presbyterian and Reformed, 1977.

Mussner, Franz. *Tractate on the Jews*. Translated by Leonard Swidler. Philadelphia: Fortress, 1984.

Navone, John. *Themes of St. Luke*. Rome: Gregorian University Press, 1970.

Neighbour, Ralph W., Jr. *Seven Last Words of the Church*. Nashville: Broadman, 1979.

Neubauer, A., and S. R. Driver, eds. *The Fifty-Third Chapter of Isaiah According to the Jewish Interpreters*. New York: KTAV, 1969.

Newman, Barclay C., and Philip C. Stine. *A Translator's Handbook on The Gospel of Matthew*. Helps for Translators. New York: United Bible Societies, 1988.

Newport, John D. *The Lion and the Lamb*. Nashville: Broadman, 1986.

Newsome, James D. *Greeks, Romans, Jews*. Philadelphia: Trinity Press International, 1982.

Nicholson, Ernest W. *God and His People: Covenant and Theology in the Old Testament*. Oxford: Clarendon, 1986.

Nickelsburg, George W. E., Jr. *Resurrection, Immortality, and Eternal Life in Intertestamental Judaism*. Harvard Theological Studies. Vol. 26. Cambridge, Mass.: Harvard University Press, 1972.

Nickle, Keith F. *The Collection*. Studies in Biblical Theology, edited by C. F. D. Moule, J. Barr, Peter Ackroyd, Floyd Filson, and G. Ernest Wright, vol. 48. Naperville, Ill.: Alec R. Allenson, 1966.

Nolland, John. *Luke 1–9:20*. WBC. Edited by David A. Hubbard, John D. W. Watts, and Ralph P. Martin. Dallas: Word, 1989.

Nygren, Anders. *Commentary on Romans*. Translated by Carl C. Rasmussen. Philadelphia: Fortress, 1949.

Oesterley, W. O. E. *The Jewish Background of the Christian Liturgy*. Gloucester, Mass.: Peter Smith, 1965.

Pache, Rene. *The Future Life*. Translated by Helen I. Needham. Chicago: Moody, 1962.

———. *The Person and Work of the Holy Spirit*. Chicago: Moody, 1954.

Packer, J. I., and Paul Fromer, eds. *The Best in Theology*. Vol. 1. Carol Stream, Ill.: Christianity Today, n.d.

———. "The Nature of the Church." In *Basic Christian Doctrines*, edited by Carl F. H. Henry. Winston, N.Y.: Holt, Reinhart and Winston, 1962.

Panikulam, George. *Koinonia in the New Testament*. Analecta Biblica, vol. 85. Rome: Biblical Institute, 1979.

Parker, James I. *The Concept of Apokatastasis in Acts.* Austin, Tex.: Schola, 1978.

Parkes, James. *The Conflict of the Church and the Synagogue.* Cleveland: World, 1961.

Patte, Daniel. *The Gospel According to Matthew.* Philadelphia: Fortress, 1987.

Pentecost, J. Dwight. *The Divine Comforter.* Chicago: Moody, 1965.

———. *Things to Come, a Study in Biblical Eschatology.* Findlay, Ohio: Dunham, 1958.

———. *Thy Kingdom Come.* Wheaton, Ill.: Scripture Press, 1990.

Peterson, David. *Hebrews and Perfection.* Society of New Testament Studies Monograph Series, edited by Robert Wilson and Margaret Thrall, vol. 47. New Rochelle: Cambridge University Press, 1982.

Pettegrew, Larry D. *The New Covenant Ministry of the Holy Spirit.* Lanham, Md.: University Press of America, 1993.

Pieters, Albertus. *The Seed of Abraham.* Grand Rapids: Eerdmans, 1950.

Piper, John. *'Love Your Enemies.'* Society of New Testament Studies Monograph Series, edited by Robert Wilson and Margaret Thrall, vol. 38. Cambridge: Cambridge University Press, 1979.

Plummer, Alfred. *A Critical and Exegetical Commentary on the Gospel According to S. Luke.* ICC. 5th ed. Edinburgh: T. & T. Clark, 1922.

———. *A Critical and Exegetical Commentary On The Second Epistle of St. Paul to the Corinthians.* ICC. Edited by S. R. Driver, A. Plummer, and C. A. Briggs. Edinburgh: T.& T. Clark, 1915.

———. *An Exegetical Commentary on the Gospel According to S. Matthew.* 2d ed. London: Elliot Stock, 1910.

Potterie, Ignace de la. *La Verite Dans Saint Jean.* Analecta Biblica, vols. 1 and 2. Rome: Biblical Institute, 1977.

Poythress, Vern. *The Shadow of Christ in the Law of Moses.* Brentwood, Tenn.: Wolgemuth & Hyatt, 1991.

Prabhu, George M. *The Formula Quotations in the Infancy Narrative of Matthew.* Analecta Biblica, edited by James Swetnam, vol. 63. Rome: Biblical Institute, 1976.

Prat, Fernand. *The Theology of Saint Paul.* Westminster, Md.: The Newman Bookshop, 1952.

Przybylski, Benno. *Righteousness in Matthew and His World of Thought.* Society of New Testament Studies Monograph Series, edited by Robert Wilson and Margaret Thrall, vol. 41. New Rochelle: Cambridge University Press, 1980.

Quebedeaux, Richard. *The Worldly Evangelicals.* New York: Harper & Row, 1978.

Rackham, Richard Belward. *The Acts of the Apostles.* Westminster Commentaries. Edited by Walter Lock. 14th ed. London: Methuen, 1951.

Raisanen, Heikki. *Paul and the Law.* Wissenschaftliche Untersuchungen zum Neuen Testament, edited by Joachim Jeremias and Otto Michel. Vol. 29. Tubingen and Philadelphia: J. C. B. Mohr (Paul Siebeck) and Fortress, 1983, 1986.

Raitt, Thomas M. *A Theology of Exile.* Philadelphia: Fortress, 1977.

Rapa, Robert Keith. "The Works of Law *erga nomou* in Galatians and Romans." Th.M. thesis, Grand Rapids Baptist Seminary, 1989.

Reumann, John. *Ministries Examined.* Minneapolis: Augsburg, 1987.

————. *Righteousness in the New Testament.* Philadelphia: Fortress, 1982.

————. *The Supper of the Lord.* Philadelphia: Fortress, 1985.

Reventlow, Henning Graf. *Problems of Biblical Theology in the Twentieth Century.* Philadelphia: Fortress, 1986.

Rhyne, C. Thomas. *Faith Establishes the Law.* Society of Biblical Literature Dissertation Series, edited by Howard C. Kee, vol. 55. Chico, Calif.: Scholars, 1981.

Richard, Earl. *Acts 6:1–8:4 The Author's Method of Composition.* Society of Biblical Literature Dissertation Series, edited by Howard C. Kee and Douglas A. Knight, vol. 41. Missoula, Mont.: Scholars, 1978.

————. "Pentecost as a Recurrent Theme in Luke-Acts." In *New Views on Luke-Acts,* edited by Earl Richard. Collegeville, Minn.: Liturgical, 1990.

Richardson, Peter. *Israel in the Apostolic Church.* Society of New Testament Studies Monograph Series, edited by Robert Wilson and Margaret Thrall. Cambridge: Cambridge University Press, 1969.

————. *Paul's Ethic of Freedom.* Philadelphia: Westminster, 1979.

Ridderbos, H. N. *Matthew.* The Bible Student's Commentary. Translated by Ray Togtman. Grand Rapids: Zondervan, 1987.

————. *Paul: An Outline of His Theology.* Grand Rapids: Eerdmans, 1975.

Ringer, Robert J. *Winning Through Intimidation.* 2d ed. New York: Funk & Wagnalls, 1974.

Rissi, Mathias. *The Future of the World.* Studies in Biblical Theology, edited by Peter Ackroyd, James Barr, C. F. Evans, Floyd Filson, and C. F. D. Moule, vol. 23. Naperville, Ill.: Alec R. Allenson, 1966.

Rist, Martin. *The Revelation of St. John the Divine.* Edited by George Buttrick. Vol. 12. Nashville: Abingdon, 1957.

Robertson, A. T. *A Grammar of the Greek New Testament in the Light of Historical Research.* Nashville: Broadman, 1934.

Robertson, A. T., and W. Hersey Davis. *A New Short Grammar of the Greek Testament.* 10th ed. Grand Rapids: Baker, 1977.

Robertson, O. Palmer. *The Christ of the Covenants.* Grand Rapids: Baker, 1980.

Robinson, J. Armitage. *St. Paul's Epistle to the Ephesians.* London: James Clarke, n.d.

Rushdoony, Rousas John. *The Institutes of Biblical Law.* Nutley, N. J.: Craig, 1973.

Ryrie, Charles C. *The Basis of the Premillennial Faith.* Neptune, N.J.: Loizeaux, 1953.

————. *Biblical Theology of the New Testament.* Chicago: Moody 1959.

————. *Dispensationalism Today.* Chicago: Moody, 1965.

————. *The Holy Spirit.* Chicago: Moody, 1965.

Sampley, J. Paul. *Pauline Partnership in Christ.* Philadelphia: Fortress, 1980.

————. *Walking Between the Times: Paul's Moral Reasoning.* Minneapolis: Fortress, 1991.

Sandeen, Ernest R. *The Roots of Fundamentalism.* Chicago: The University of Chicago Press, 1970.

Sanders, E. P. *Jesus and Judaism.* Philadelphia: Fortress, 1985.

———. *Jewish Law from Jesus to the Mishnah.* Philadelphia: Trinity Press International, 1990.

———. *Paul and Palestinian Judaism.* Philadelphia: Fortress, 1977.

———. *Paul, The Law, and the Jewish People.* Philadelphia: Fortress, 1983.

Sanders, J. N. *The Gospel According to St. John.* HNTC. Edited by Henry Chadwick. New York: Harper & Row, 1968.

Saucy, Robert. *The Case for Progressive Dispensationalism.* Grand Rapids: Zondervan, 1993.

———. "The Church as the Mystery of God". In *Dispensationalism, Israel and the Church,* edited by Craig A. Blaising and Darrell L. Bock. Grand Rapids: Zondervan, 1992.

Sauer, Erich. *The Triumph of the Crucified.* Grand Rapids: Eerdmans, 1966.

Scharlemann, Martin H. *Stephen: A Singular Saint.* Analecta Biblica, vol. 34. Rome: Pontifical Biblical Institute, 1968.

Schep, J. A. *The Nature of the Resurrection Body.* Grand Rapids: Eerdmans, 1964.

Schlatter, Adolf. *The Church in the New Testament Period.* Translated by Paul P. Levertoff. London: SPCK, 1955.

Schmitt, Harley H. *Many Gifts One Lord.* Minneapolis: Augsburg, 1993.

Schoeps, Hans J. *Paul.* Rev. ed. Translated by Harold Knight. Philadelphia: Westminster, 1991.

Schrage, Wolfgang. *The Ethics of the New Testament.* Translated by David Green. Philadelphia: Fortress, 1988.

Schreiner, Thomas R. *The Law and Its Fulfillment.* Grand Rapids: Baker, 1993.

Schrenk, Gottlob. "Der Segenswunsch nach der Kampfepistel." *Judaica* 6 (1950): 170–90.

———. "Was bedeutet 'Israel Gottes.'" *Judaica* 5 (1949): 81–94.

Schweizer, Eduard. *The Good News According to Matthew.* Translated by David E. Green. Atlanta: John Knox, 1975.

———. *The Lord's Supper According to the New Testament.* 3d ed. Philadelphia: Fortress, 1967.

Scobie, Charles H. H. *John the Baptist.* London: SCM, 1964.

Scofield, C. I., ed. *The Scofield Reference Bible.* New York: Oxford University Press, 1909.

Seiss, J. A. *The Apocalypse.* 5th ed. Grand Rapids: Zondervan, 1964.

Senior, Donald. *The Passion of Jesus in the Gospel of Matthew.* The Passion Series. Vol. 1. Wilmington, Del.: Michael Glazier, 1985.

———. *What Are They Saying About Matthew?* Ramsey, N.J.: Paulist, 1983.

Sevenster, J. N. "Do You Know Greek? How Much Greek Could the First Jewish Christians Have Known?" *Supplements to Novum Testamentum: Supplement 19,* edited by W. C. van Unnik. Leiden: Brill, 1968.

Shedd, Russell Phillip. *Man in Community.* Grand Rapids: Eerdmans, 1964.

Shedd, William G. T. *Commentary on the Epistle of St. Paul to the Romans.* Grand Rapids: Zondervan, 1967.

Shelton, James B. *Mighty in Word and Deed: The Role of the Holy Spirit in Luke-Acts.* Peabody, Mass.: Hendrickson, 1991.

Sigal, Phillip. *The Halakah of Jesus of Nazareth According to the Gospel of Matthew.* Lanham, Md.: University Press of America, 1986.

Simon, Marcel. *St. Stephen and the Hellenists in the Primitive Church.* New York: Longmans, Green and Co., 1958.

Simpson, Robert L. *The Interpretation of Prayer in the Early Church.* The Library of History and Doctrine, edited by S. L. Greenslade. Philadelphia: Westminster, 1965.

Skibbe, Eugene M. *Protestant Agreement on the Lord's Supper.* Minneapolis: Augsburg, 1968.

Smedes, Lewis B. *All Things Made New.* Grand Rapids: Eerdmans, 1970.

Smith, Dennis E., and Hal E. Taussig. *Many Tables.* Philadelphia: Trinity Press International, 1990.

Smith, Elmer Lewis. *The Amish Today.* The Pennsylvania German Folklore Society. Vol. 24. Allentown, Pa.: Schlechters, 1961.

Smith, J. B. *A Revelation of Jesus Christ.* Scottdale, Pa.: Herald, 1961.

Smith, Ralph L. *Old Testament Theology.* Nashville: Broadman and Holman, 1993.

Squires, John T. *The Plan of God in Luke-Acts.* Society of New Testament Studies Monograph Series, edited by Robert Wilson and Margaret Thrall, vol. 76. New York: Cambridge University Press, 1993.

Stamm, Raymond T. "The Epistle to the Galatians." In *The Interpreter's Bible,* edited by George Buttrick. Vol. 10. Nashville: Abingdon, 1953.

Stanton, Graham, ed. *The Interpretation of Matthew.* Issues in Religion and Theology, edited by Douglas Knight and Robert Morgan, vol. 3. Philadelphia: Fortress, 1983.

Stevens, George. *The Theology of the New Testament.* 2d rev. ed. Edinburgh: T. & T. Clark, 1918.

Stevens, R. Paul. *Liberating the Laity.* Downers Grove, Ill.: InterVarsity, 1985.

Stockhausen, Carol Kern. *Moses' Veil and the Glory of the New Covenant.* Analecta Biblica, vol. 116. Rome: Biblical Institute, 1989.

Stonehouse, Ned B. "The Elders and the Living-Beings in the Apocalypse." In *Paul Before the Areopagus.* Grand Rapids: Eerdmans, 1957.

Stott, John. *Baptism and Fullness.* Downers Grove, Ill.: InterVarsity, 1976.

————. *Christian Counter-Culture: The Message of the Sermon on the Mount.* The Bible Speaks Today, edited by J. A. Motyer and John R. W. Stott. Downers Grove, Ill.: InterVarsity, 1978.

————. *The Spirit, the Church, and the World.* Downers Grove, Ill.: InterVarsity, 1990.

Strachan, R. H. *The Second Epistle of Paul To The Corinthians.* MNTC. Edited by James Moffatt. London: Hodder and Stoughton, 1935.

Strauch, Alexander. *Biblical Eldership.* 2d ed. Littleton, Co.: Lewis and Roth, 1988.

————. *The New Testament Deacon.* Littleton, Co.: Lewis and Roth, 1992.

Strauss, David Friedrich. *The Life of Jesus Critically Examined.* Lives of Jesus, edited by Leander E. Keck. 4th ed. Philadelphia: Fortress, 1972.

Strauss, James. *The Seer, the Saviour, and the Saved.* Bible Study Textbook. Rev. ed. Joplin: College Press, 1972.

Strawson, William. *Jesus and the Future Life.* Philadelphia: Westminster, 1959.

Strecker, Georg. *The Sermon on the Mount.* 2d ed. Translated by O. C. Dean, Jr. Nashville: Abingdon, 1988.

Stronstad, Roger. *The Charismatic Theology of St. Luke.* Peabody, Mass.: Hendrickson, 1984.

Suggs, M. Jack. *Wisdom, Christology, and Law in Matthew's Gospel.* Cambridge, Mass.: Harvard University Press, 1970.

Swete, Henry Barclay. *The Apocalypse of St. John.* 3d ed. Grand Rapids: Eerdmans, 1988.

Talbert, Charles. "Once Again: The Plan of 1 Peter." In *Perspectives on First Peter,* edited by Charles H. Talbert, Macon, Ga.: Mercer University Press, 1970.

———. *Reimarus: Fragments.* Lives of Jesus, edited by Leander E. Keck. Philadelphia: Fortress, 1970.

Tannehill, Robert. *The Narrative Unity of Luke-Acts.* Vol. 1. *Foundations and Facets.* Edited by Robert W. Funk and Burton L. Mack. Philadelphia: Fortress, 1986.

———. *The Narrative Unity of Luke-Acts.* Vol. 2: *The Acts of the Apostles.* Minneapolis: Fortress, 1990.

Tenney, Merrill C., and Steven Barabas, eds. *The Zondervan Pictorial Encyclopedia of the Bible.* Vol. 4. Grand Rapids: Zondervan, 1975.

Theissen, Gerd. *The Social Setting of Pauline Christianity.* Philadelphia: Fortress, 1982.

Thielman, Frank. "From Plight to Solution." *Supplements to Novum Testamentum, Supplement* 61, edited by C. K. Barrett, A. F. J. Klijn, and J. Smit Sibinga. Leiden: Brill, 1989.

Thompson, J. A. *Handbook of Life in Bible Times.* Downers Grove, Ill.: InterVarsity, 1986.

Thompson, William G. *Matthew's Advice to a Divided Community.* Analecta Biblica, edited by James Swetnam, vol. 44. Rome: Biblical Institute, 1970.

———. *Matthew's Story: Good News for Uncertain Times.* Mahwah, N.J.: Paulist, 1989.

Thornton, L. S. *The Common Life in the Body of Christ.* Westminster: Dacre Press, 1941.

Tidball, Derek. *Skillful Shepherds.* Grand Rapids: Zondervan, 1986.

Tillapaugh, Frank R. *Unleashing the Church.* Ventura, Calif.: Regal, 1982.

Tomson, Peter J. *Paul and the Jewish Law: Halakha in the Letters of the Apostle to the Gentiles.* Vol. 1. *Compendia Rerum Iudaicarum ad Novum Testamentum.* Edited by Y. Aschkenasy, T. Baarda, W. J. Burgers, D. Flusser, and P. W. van der Horst. Minneapolis: Fortress, 1990.

Toussaint, Stanley D., and Charles H. Dyer, eds. *Essays in Honor of J. Dwight Pentecost.* Chicago: Moody, 1986.

Trench, Richard. *Commentary on the Epistles to the Seven Churches in Asia.* Minneapolis: Klock & Klock, 1978.

Trilling, Wolfgang. *Das wahre Israel.* Vol. 10. *Studien zum Alte und Neuen Testament.* Munchen: Kosel-Verlag, 1964.

Turner, David L. "The New Jerusalem in Revelation 21:1–22:15: Consummation of a Biblical Continuum." In *Dispensationalism, Israel and the Church,* edited by Craig Blaising and Darrell Bock. Grand Rapids: Zondervan, 1992.

———. "Paul and the Ministry of Reconciliation in 2 Cor. 5:11–6:2." *Criswell Theological Journal* 4 (Fall 1989): 77–95.

Turner, Max M. B. "The Concept of Receiving the Spirit in John's Gospel." *Vox Evangelica* 10 (1977): 24–42.

———. "The Significance of Spirit Endowment for Paul." *Vox Evangelica* 9 (1975): 56–69.

———. "Spirit Endowment in Luke/Acts: Some Linguistic Considerations." *Vox Evangelica* 12 (1981): 45–63.

Turner, Nigel. "The Preposition *en* in the New Testament." *The Bible Translator* 10 (1959): 113–20.

———. *Syntax.* Vol. 3. *A Grammar of New Testament Greek,* edited by James Hope Moulton. Edinburgh: T. & T. Clark, 1963.

VanGemeren, Willem. *The Progress of Redemption.* Grand Rapids: Zondervan, 1988.

Van Unnik, W. C. "La Conception Paulinienne De La Nouvelle Alliance." In *Litterature et theologie pauliniennes.* Vol. V. Brussels: Desclee DeBrouwer, 1960.

Vaught, Carl G. *The Sermon on the Mount: A Theological Interpretation.* Albany, N.Y.: State University of New York Press, 1986.

Volf, Judith Gundry. *Paul and Perseverance: Staying in and Falling Away.* Louisville: Westminster/John Knox, 1990.

Von Allmen, Jean-Jacques. *The Lord's Supper.* Vol. 19. Ecumenical Studies in Worship, edited by J. G. Davies and A. Raymond George. Richmond: John Knox, 1969.

Walker, Thomas. *The Teaching of Jesus and the Jewish Teaching of His Age.* New York: George H. Doran, 1923.

Walton, John H. *Covenant: God's Purpose, God's Plan.* Grand Rapids: Zondervan, 1994.

Walvoord, John F. *The Holy Spirit.* Findlay, Ohio: Dunham, 1954.

———. *Israel in Prophecy.* Grand Rapids: Zondervan, 1962.

———. *The Revelation of Jesus Christ.* Chicago: Moody, 1966.

Ware, Bruce A. "The New Covenant and the People(s) of God." In *Dispensationalism, Israel and the Church,* edited by Craig A. Blaising and Darrell L. Bock. Grand Rapids: Zondervan, 1992.

Weber, T. P. "Dispensationalism." In *Dictionary of Christianity in America,* edited by Daniel Reid. Downers Grove, Ill.: InterVarsity, 1990.

Weiss, Bernhard. *Biblical Theology of the New Testament.* Vols. 1 and 2. Edinburgh: T. & T. Clark, 1885.

Wells, David F. *No Place for Truth: Or Whatever Happened to Evangelical Theology?* Grand Rapids: Eerdmans, 1993.

Wenschkewitz, Hans. *Die Spiritualisierung der Kultusbegriffe: Tempel, Priester, und Opfer im Neuen Testament.* Leipzig: Edward Pfeiffer Verlag, 1932.

West, Nathaniel. *The Thousand Years in Both Testaments.* New York and Grand Rapids: Revell and Kregel, 1880, 1993.

Westerholm, Stephen. *Israel's Law and the Church's Faith.* Grand Rapids: Eerdmans, 1988.

Westermann, Claus. *Isaiah 40–66.* OTL. Edited by G. Ernest Wright, John Bright, James Barr, and Peter Ackroyd. Philadelphia: Westminster, 1977.

Wevers, John W. *Ezekiel.* NCB. Edited by Ronald E. Clements and Matthew Black. Grand Rapids: Eerdmans, 1982.

Wiles, Gordon P. *Paul's Intercessory Prayers.* Society for New Testament Studies Monograph Series, edited by Matthew Black and T. Mcl. Wilson, vol. 24. New Rochelle: Cambridge University Press, 1974.

Wilkinson, John. *Israel My Glory.* London: Mildmay Mission to the Jew's Bookstore, 1894.

Wilkinson, Samuel Hinds. *The Israel Promises and Their Fulfillment.* London: Mildmay Mission to the Jews, 1936.

Williams, Sam K. 'Promise in Galatians': A Reading of Paul's Reading of Scripture." *Journal of Biblical Literature* 107 (December 1988): 709–20.

Willis, John T. *Isaiah.* The Living Word Commentary on the Old Testament, edited by John T. Willis and David G. Jones. Austin, Tex.: Sweet , 1980.

Willis, Wesley R., and John R. Master, eds. *Issues in Dispensationalism.* Chicago: Moody, 1994.

Willmington, H. L. *Willmington's Guide to the Bible.* Wheaton, Ill.: Tyndale, 1987.

Windisch, Hans. *The Meaning of the Sermon on the Mount.* Rev. ed. Translated by S. Maclean Gilmour. Philadelphia: Westminster, 1951.

Wood, Leon J. *The Holy Spirit in the Old Testament.* Grand Rapids: Zondervan, 1976.

Worley, Robert C. *Preaching and Teaching in the Earliest Church.* Philadelphia: Westminster, 1967.

Wuthnow, Robert. *Christianity in the 21st Century.* New York: Oxford University Press, 1994.

———. *Sharing the Journey: Support Groups and America's New Quest for Community.* New York: The Free Press, 1994.

Younce, Dale Richard. "An Exegetical Interpretation of the Figure of the Olive Tree of Romans Eleven." Th.M. thesis, Dallas Theological Seminary, 1963.

Young, Edward J. *The Book of Isaiah.* Vol. 3. Grand Rapids: Eerdmans, 1972.

Zimmerli, Walter. *Ezekiel 1.* Hermeneia, edited by Frank Moore Cross and Klaus Baltzer. Translated by Ronald E. Clements. Philadelphia: Fortress, 1979.

———. *Ezekiel 2.* Hermeneia, edited by Paul D. Hanson and Leonard Jay Greenspoon. Translated by James D. Martin. Philadelphia: Fortress, 1983.

love/41